F MUSIC

uccess!

TRAGEDIAN

NCE

ETT

MPANY!

Y 25th, 1873

Play, in 5 Acts, entitled

THE VIII

RENCE BARRETT

LOVELL...............................N. HARLOCK
THE DUKE OF BUCKINGHAM...R. J. BROWNE
Ambassador to Charles V. of Spain, W. MARSTON
....H. SHEPPARD
....J. CONNOR
QUEEN OF ENGLAND...MISS E. J. PHILLIPS
....MISS IONE BURKE
....MRS. L. R. SEYMOUR
....MISS MAY ROBERTS

Y,

ORGIE REIGNOLD

t and Fair."

S.

Buckingham.
eeting of King Henry

ke of Buckingham, and
atharine.
of Cardinal Wolsey.
th of Queen Katharine.

DAY, FEB'Y 26,
uest,)
TRAGEDY OF

LET

BR'Y 27th,

APPEARANCE OF

ARRETT.

BILL!

..... WILLIAM SEYMOUR.

RICES.

.......GALLERY, 50 CENTS

OPEN.

BAY, CHARLESTON, S. C.

ARCADE HALL!

Tuesday Evening, March 19, 1861

METROPOLITAN THEATRE

Lessee, . . . Mr. J. B. TOZER. | Stage Director & Manager, Mr. NICKINSON

Continued Success!

2d WEEK OF THE SEASON!

No Falling Off in Attraction!

A NIGHT WITH BULWER

SIXTH NIGHT

Of the Engagement of Mr. J.

NICKINSON

Who will appear this Evening, March 19, supported by all the POPULAR ARTISTES, in

Sir Edward Lytton Bulwer's Great

5 ACT PLAY

OF THE

Lady of Lyons

—OR—

LOVE AND PRIDE!

Produced with due regard to appropriate Scenery, Dresses and Appointments, and with the following

Excellent Cast of Characters:

Claude Melnotte.......................Mr. Simcoe Lee
Colonel Damas.........................Mr. John Nickinson
Glavis.......................................Mr. W. H. Briggs
Beauseant,.................................Mr. Davis
Mons. Deschappelles.................Mr. Ashley
Landlord,...................................Mr. Hudson
Gaspar,......................................Mr. Ward
Pauline......................................Miss E. J. Phillips
Mad. Deschappelles..................Mrs. Bradshaw
Widow Melnotte........................Miss Emily J. Miles
Marian.......................................Mrs. Ward

In accordance with the requirements of the day as to early closing, and in consequence of the length and importance of this beautiful Play, no other piece will be produced this evening

---

MADISON SQUARE THEATRE

MR. A. M. PALMER, SOLE MANAGER.

EVENINGS AT 8:30. SATURDAY MATINEES AT 2 P. M.

TUESDAY, DECEMBER 4, 1888,

AND UNTIL FURTHER NOTICE.

SECOND PRESENTATION DURING MR. PALMER'S FIFTH SEASON AT THIS THEATRE, AND FIRST PRODUCTION IN AMERICA OF

CAPTAIN SWIFT,

AN ORIGINAL DRAMA IN FOUR ACTS BY R. HADDON CHAMBERS, ESQ.

CHARACTERS;

MR. WILDING, FROM QUEENSLAND, . . . MR. MAURICE BARRYMORE
MR. SEABROOK, A COUNTRY GENTLEMAN, . . . MR. FREDERIC ROBINSON
HARRY SEABROOK, HIS SON, . . . MR. HENRY WOODRUFF
MR. GARDINER, A QUEENSLAND SQUATTER, . . . MR. E. M. HOLLAND
MARSHALL, MRS. SEABROOK'S BUTLER, . . . MR. J. H. STODDART
RYAN, A QUEENSLAND DETECTIVE, . . . MR. WALDEN RAMSAY
BATES, . . . MR. REUB FAX
MRS. SEABROOK, . . . AGNES BOOTH
STELLA DARBISHER, MRS. SEABROOK'S NIECE AND WARD, . . . MISS MARIE BURROUGHS
MABEL SEABROOK, MRS. SEABROOK'S DAUGHTER, . . . MISS ANNIE RUSSELL
LADY STAUNTON, MRS. SEABROOK'S SISTER, . . . MRS. E. J. PHILLIPS

PLACE, ENGLAND. PERIOD, THE PRESENT.

Gr...

Acting Manager, F. Nelson Drew | Treasurer, ...
Stage Director, - W. H. Reed | Musical Director, M. Rheinhart.

Second Night

OF THE

STAR COMPANY

FROM WHEATLEY & DREW'S ARCH ST. THEATRE, PHILAD'A.

MRS. D. P. BOWERS

AS PAULINE!

Tuesday Evening, July 11, 1854,

WILL BE PERFORMED, FOR THIS NIGHT ONLY, BULWER'S PLAY OF THE

LADY OF LYONS

With the following unapproachable Cast:

Claude Melnotte, : : : : : : : Mr. J. Dolman
Beauseant, : : : : : : : : D. P. Bowers
Glavis, : : : : : : : : : L. R. Shewell
Mons. Deschappelles, : : : : : : : A. Fisher
Col. Damas, : : : : : : : : : H. Bland
Major Desmoulins, : : : : : : : T. A. Hall
Captain Dupont, : : : : : : : : W. H. Reed
Servant, : Mr. Reilly Landlord, : Nunans
Pauline Deschappelles, - - - - - Mrs. D. P. Bowers
Madame Deschappelles, - - - - - Mrs. Brelsford
Widow Melnotte, - - - - - Mrs. Chippendale

Overture, - by the Orchestra.

GRAND TAMBOURINE DANCE, - Miss C. LUDLAM

To conclude with an entirely New Farce, never played in this City, called

I'VE EATEN MY FRIEND!

Hezekiah Jellytop ....Mr. F. N. DREW | Peter Stubs...........Mr. J. F. NUNAN
Christopher Cockles.........A. FISHER | Boy ....WALSH
John Wigsby...................T. A. HALL | Angelina Cockles.......Miss CAPPELL

In Rehearsal, and will shortly be produced, the Thrilling Drama of

MADELAINE!

Scale of Prices.

Dress Circle and Parquette, 50 cents	Seats in Private Boxes and Orchestra Chairs, 75 cts
Family Circle and Gallery 25 cents	Private Boxes .... $3 and $6

Doors Open at quarter past 7; Performance to commence at a quarter to 8.

Box Office open from 9 A. M. to 2 P. M.

HOYT'S THEATRE.

HOYT & McKEE, Proprietors.

WEEK COMMENCING MONDAY, DECEMBER 2, 1895.

Evenings at 8.30. Matinees Saturdays at 2.15.

The first time here of the new Farce, from the French, in Three Acts, entitled

THE GAY PARISIANS.

By GEORGE FEYDEAU and MAURICE DESVALLIERE.

Management CHARLES FROHMAN.

CAST OF CHARACTERS.

JOSEPH PINGLET, a master builder......................W. J. FERGUSON
ANGELIQUE, his wife.......................................Mrs. E. J. PHILLIPS
PAILLARD, an architect....................................CHARLES WELLS
MARCELLA, his wife..ODETTE TYLER
MATHIEU...JAMES BARROWS
HYACINTHE.......... } daughters of { ....MARGARET GORDON
VIOLET................ } Mathieu, { ....CLARA NORTON
DAISY.................. } { ....VERGIE GRAVES
ROSE .... } { ....WINONA SHANNON
MAXIME, nephew of Paillard..............................W. R. SHIRLEY
BOULOT.............. } waiters at { ....TULLY MARSHALL
BASTIEN .... } restaurant, { ....GEORGE BACKUS
EARNEST...FRANK A. CONNOR
BOTTICELLI, an Italian teacher ....VAUGHAN GLASER
BROCHARD, Police Captain................................LOUIS HENDRICKS
VICTORINE, maid at Pinglet's.............................JOSEPHINE HALL
MISS CONNELL ....MOLLIE SHERWOOD

Expressmen, Policemen, etc.

THE ART OF
Acting

The Art of
ACTING

BY

JOHN DOLMAN, Jr.

University of Pennsylvania

HARPER & BROTHERS, PUBLISHERS

NEW YORK

To the Memory of My Grandmother
ELIZABETH JANE PHILLIPS
(MRS. JOHN NICKINSON)
1830–1904
Who in Her Forty-Five Years on the Stage
Played Many Parts and Played Them Well

Contents

List of Illustrations

(The illustrations in this book, grouped in 32 plates, are, with some exceptions, only indirectly related to the text. They are chosen partly to give the young student of acting a lively consciousness that his art is an old one and did not begin with the Hollywood picture industry or with his home-town high-school plays, and partly to suggest something of the atmosphere in which the book was written, since many of the pictures hang on the walls of the author's home or repose in his albums and scrapbooks.)

Preface

LIKE its predecessor, *The Art of Play Production*, this book is for the beginner, but not the dabbler. It presupposes no stage experience or previous instruction in acting, but it does presuppose an inquiring mind, some degree of literacy, and some such maturity of attitude as might reasonably be expected of students in college, or of those more numerous students who, lacking the opportunity for academic study, are trying to arrive at equally good results by reading and thinking for themselves. It is for the reader who is not fooled by the glamour of the footlights into supposing that good acting is easy, or that the actor with talent has nothing to learn. In other words, it is for the actor who really means business, whether his ultimate objective is a professional career, an avocation in community theatre work, a richer appreciation of the arts in general, or simply the fun that an ardent hobby-rider gets out of really mastering his hobby.

I should be the last person to suggest that the art of acting can be learned entirely, or even mainly, from books—much less from one book. The student actor should seize every opportunity to get up on a stage and act. There is no substitute for such experience. But there is a difference between the elementary attempt to learn what to do and how to do it, and the more thoughtful attempt to learn why; and a book which seeks to analyze problems, formulate principles, and give reasons for them can be of some help to the actor making the latter attempt. *The Art of Acting* is intended to be that kind of book. The what and the how are by no means excluded, but the emphasis, as distinguished from that in many elementary handbooks and primers, is on the why.

The Art of Play Production was addressed to the student learning to direct plays, regardless of his own ambitions as an actor, or lack of them. *The Art of Acting* is addressed to the student actor, whether or not he has any ambition to direct. Inevitably, there are some overlapping areas between the two fields, but I have tried to avoid unnecessary repetition as far as that was possible without omitting matters essential to the student unacquainted with the other book. Some things, of course, have to be said many times, from many angles, for both groups of students, and are not likely to bore the good student or the interested reader in either group.

There must always be more actors than directors, and certainly more young people are fired with the yearning to appear on "the boards" than

xvii

to undertake the more thankless work of directing. Among them, of course, are some who mistake a kind of glamour-chasing infatuation with acting for real artistic fervor; who suppose that acting is easy because it looks easy; and who think only of the applause and adulation given at public performances to famous stars, and never of the years of study and preparation, the long weeks of grueling rehearsal, or the disappointments of the far more numerous actors who do not become stars. It would be neither honest nor kind to encourage this sort of false enthusiasm, and those who are deceived by it will not find their illusions supported in this book. The problem is not new. Four generations ago the great English actor, William Charles Macready, wrote in his *Reminiscences* (1875):

> One of the disadvantages incident to the pursuit of the theatrical art is the supposed facility of its attainment, nor is it less cheapened in public estimation by the general assumption of the ability to criticize it. . . . It surely needs something like an education for such an art, and yet that appearance of mere volition and perfect ease which costs the accomplished actor so much time and toil to acquire evidently leads to a different conclusion with many, or amateur acting would be less in vogue. Among those I have seen, the only amateurs with any pretension to theatrical talent were Charles Dickens . . . . and Miss MacTavish.

Fortunately, amateur acting and non-commercial acting are better organized in many parts of present-day America than in the England of Macready's time, and amateur actors have far more opportunity for good training, and even education, in the art. But the art itself is even more exacting now than it was then, if only because it involves more kinds of theatre and a wider range of dramatic material; and it is still true that the novice attracted to it ought to be warned against those same illusions.

This book is concerned only with acting in the theatre, by live actors— "round actors" as they were called in the war camps to distinguish them from the more familiar shadows on a screen. To be sure, much that can be said about acting is universal, and applies equally well to acting for the screen and for television; and that which is in terms of voice and sound may apply to radio acting as well. But each of these arts has its own advantages and limitations, and its own techniques, adequate treatment of which would require a full volume. All three differ from stage acting in the absence of one vital element which, in my opinion, is the chief reason for the survival of the older art in a world now largely committed to the greater economic efficiency of "piped" and "canned" entertainment. That element, of course, is direct audience response, felt and enjoyed by the actor both as appreciation and as creative participation. Two of the three—

radio and television—though still free arts in Britain, are in this country so completely and (it appears) irrevocably entangled with the more offensive aspects of commercialism that their technique is far more a matter of salesmanship than of art. As one who knew and loved the theatre before the theatrical profession got to be known as "show business," before the motion-picture "industry" so labeled itself, and before the advertizing agencies discovered the gold mine in capturing and monopolizing public entertainment as an instrument for controlling public wants, I could not write with integrity or enthusiasm about any form of acting that had wholly or partly abandoned artistic principles for commercial ones. So I leave the other forms to writers who know them better and believe in them more honestly than I could. In the Bibliography will be found a selected list of books and articles relating to those subjects, chosen on the basis of their probable usefulness to the student actor. Happily, there are still many people interested in the art of acting in the living theatre, especially in that part of it—amateur, semi-professional, or professional—which has managed to keep clear of excessive commercialism. This book is definitely for them, and not for the "hucksters."

It is well for the young actor to realize that acting is not only a complex and difficult art but a ruthlessly competitive profession, and that the chance of winning fame and fortune on the legitimate stage is constantly shrinking. At the end of 1948 something like 90 percent of American professional actors were unemployed in the theatre—though many were working in other fields, from television to dishwashing. Stage acting, as distinguished from screen and radio acting, is a rewarding avocation, but a miserable way to earn a living nowadays. Moderate talent means little, for it is very plentiful. Talent plus luck may bring success to a few. But only talent plus profound and tireless study will make an actor worthy or likely to succeed in so tough a struggle. That is another reason why I have not attempted to make the art of acting seem elementary, simple, or easy.

If I have drawn a good many ideas and illustrative examples from my own limited experience or the experiences of my family and friends, it is because they were available to me and not so well known to others; and if I have been frank about labeling them it is to be sure that they are taken at face value and no more. I am grateful for the vicarious experiences that have come down to me from my grandparents (three of whom were professional actors of some prominence in their time), and for their voluminous collections of old programs, photographs, engravings, press notices, criticisms, correspondence, keepsakes, and theatre lore, which have helped me to see the modern theatre in wider perspective. But I am

not so stupid as to imagine that their achievements in the art of acting reflect any credit upon me, or give my opinions any more authority than they would merit on their own logic. I have been fortunate in the opportunity to study theatre arts from more different angles and with more facilities in research than they enjoyed, and that is my sole reason for offering my opinions at all.

It is a pleasure to acknowledge the assistance of Miss Lousene Rousseau, whose helpful criticisms of the manuscript and whose aid in locating illustrations have been invaluable; of Mr. Benjamin Rothberg, who has kindly read and checked my references to Stanislavsky and his teaching; and of Miss May Davenport Seymour, who has been most gracious in helping me to find the more elusive illustrations. Specific credits and releases will be found in the list of illustrations.

University of Pennsylvania
March, 1949

JOHN DOLMAN, JR.

THE ART OF
Acting

. . . for the truth is, that in order to
be a good player, there is required a
greater share of genius, knowledge,
and accomplishments, than for any
one profession whatever; for this
reason, that the profession of player
comprehends the whole system of
human life. . . .

JAMES BOSWELL

CHAPTER I

The Genesis of Acting

IT MUST be obvious to anyone who has thought about the matter at all that most human beings like to act. There are many, of course, who have no ambition to go on the professional stage, or even to take part in serious community theatre production, but there is hardly anyone who does not at some time in his life feel the impulse to project himself imaginatively into another character; to mimic some other person, real or imaginary, or to masquerade as somebody or something that he is not.

There is nothing new or transitory about this impulse. It is as old as the human race, and is even more obvious in children and savages than in civilized adults. It does not make everybody a good actor in the artistic sense; yet it must have some significance in relation to the nature of good acting, and to the nature of that universal appeal which good acting and good drama are known to have.

It would be easy to explain the play-acting impulse by saying that it is merely the instinct to imitate—that we are all educated monkeys, and that "monkey sees, monkey does." Actually the matter is far more complex, for many motives and impulses enter into the history of acting, even in its primitive stages. Doubtless they can never be fully explained, since the facts are buried in the mists of antiquity; but we can reconstruct at least a part of the story by comparing what we know of ancient dramatic ceremonial with the corresponding ceremonial of those few primitive tribes which still survive in remote corners of the world, and also with the dramatic behavior of children. It is said that the child repeats in his own development the history of the race, and that in the behavior of our children we can discern to some extent the probable behavior of our remote ancestors.

But why waste time, one may ask, considering the behavior of our ancestors and our children? Why indulge in idle speculation on the motives of primitive acting when there is so much to learn about the practical problems of the modern theatre and of modern acting technique?

The answer is that our modern civilization and culture are after all relatively new in human history, and decidedly external and objective; that

subjectively and emotionally we are much the same as our ancestors; and that the soundest art today is that which, beneath its apparent refinement, makes the most honest and most basic appeal to the real human being. The late Professor Brander Matthews, speaking of playwriting, said, "The true dramatist is like the true statesman in recognizing that nothing survives which is not a development of institutions already existing." He could have said the same of acting. The modern actor feels, consciously or unconsciously, the same impulses which his ancestors felt when they mimicked their gods and totems, or danced their ceremonial dances about the campfire; and he acts for an audience of human beings who respond subjectively very much as their ancestors responded. Styles change, novelties come and go, refinements increase, but the best acting remains that which is most fundamentally true to the inner nature of man.

The difficulty of studying human nature and institutions in their present state is that the very complexity and sophistication of civilization obscure them. The most important characteristic of civilization is restraint, which often results in reticence or concealment; to understand our own real natures we must go back and study the frankness of more primitive times, or of childhood.

It will do the student actor no harm, therefore, to consider briefly a few of the motives that enter into the more primitive forms of acting, and as much of their interrelation as can be established.

The Mimetic Instinct

There can be no doubt that instinctive imitation, while not the complete explanation of acting, is at least one of its motives, and perhaps the most fundamental one. Certainly it is ancient and universal, for it is observable not only in the youngest children and the most primitive men, but in other animals as well—in the young bird learning to fly or dig worms, or the kitten learning to keep itself clean. Biologically, imitation is an extremely important element in selective evolution, for individuals possessing an imitative instinct naturally imitate their surviving elders—whose traits are presumably conducive to survival, else they would not have survived—and so increase their own chances of survival. In this way the trait of imitation is itself perpetuated.

The exact place of imitation in the learning process is a matter of dispute. Some psychologists maintain that learning in infancy does not begin with imitation, but with random activity, which gradually becomes "conditioned" by association and experience. The imitation, they say, comes

later, after the infant has performed a random action a number of times and has come to notice its resemblance to the action of another. However that may be, no individual gets very far in the learning process before the element of imitation becomes a part of it; and no race or species that consistently neglects to imitate is likely to survive very long in the process of natural selection. It seems reasonable, therefore, to regard the mimetic impulse as basic and instinctive.

To understand its significance as a motive in primitive acting, however, we must think of it not alone but in association with other motives. Among the most primitive tribes we find it tied up with such things as religious observance, magic, social custom, war, terrorization, self-excitation, communication, and entertainment. At least two of these associations, those with education and entertainment, we find among other animals as well as man. The mother bird teaching its young to fly, for example, tries to induce imitation as a means of education; and the cat chasing a ball and pretending that it is a mouse quite evidently draws entertainment from the mimic action. Perhaps the dog barking himself into a frenzy to keep his courage up can be considered an example of self-excitation. In the course of time and developing civilization these associated motives have changed so greatly in their nature and their relative emphasis that they now seem to have disappeared in a general fusion; yet it is quite possible to discover some interesting things about them which may be very helpful to an understanding of modern acting.

The Religious Motive

It is commonly accepted that the origins of drama are to be found in religious observance. Modern drama is said to have begun in the ritual of the medieval church, whence it developed through the successive stages of litany, miracle, morality, and interlude into the secular play. The tragic drama of the Greeks is known to have developed from the ceremonial dances and songs of the religious festivals in honor of Dionysus, the strictly mimetic element represented by the actors having been added at a relatively late period. The most ancient oriental drama had religious motives; so had the ceremonial drama of the Aztecs, the Incas, the African tribes, and the primitive Australians; and so have the ceremonial dances still to be seen among the Navaho and Hopi Indians. The Book of Job incorporates a drama in the Hebrew Bible.

The nature and origin of the religious impulse itself is far too abstruse a problem for consideration here. It is possible to discern in primitive re-

ligions a certain indebtedness to biological phenomena, such as the perpetual mysteries of birth and death; to dreams and hallucinations; to the forces of nature, such as fire, wind, and water; to the sun, moon, stars, and planets; to strange and terrifying animal life; and to the still more terrifying behavior of human enemies and enemy gods. Many different human emotions are involved, such as fear, wonder, curiosity, pride, loyalty, love, ambition—all these and more, woven together in endless confusion and variety.

But from the standpoint of its significance in drama and in the art of acting, the essential element in the religious motive is the supernatural, the transcendent, the otherworldly—in short, the magic. For countless generations man has felt his own weakness, has feared what he could not understand, has sought to escape the pains and limitations of reality through imaginative release. As a child clings to the superior strength and knowledge of its parents, so collective man has clung to some concept of a being or beings bigger and wiser than himself, stronger than his enemies, and superior to his material environment. In other words, the religious craving is a craving not for something smaller, weaker, or meaner, but for something larger, stronger, and nobler. It is not content with this world's values, with the real, the commonplace; it demands values above and beyond reality: mystic, imaginative, exalted.

The function of acting in its religious associations has always been, therefore, to inspire, to elevate, to point a way to the gods; and it seems likely that really great acting will always be that which points up, not down; which elevates, not degrades; which satisfies the craving for spirituality rather than reality. Not that great acting must always be religious in subject matter or purpose; but even when most secular and most realistic it must arouse in the æsthetic imagination something of the same exaltation it once aroused in the religious imagination.

To say that drama grew out of religion is not to say that the mimetic impulse grew out of the religious. In all probability neither grew out of the other. The mimetic impulse, having a biological implication, is doubtless the older; it already existed when religion first found a use for it. Because the mimic way is the most vivid way of expressing thought or feeling it was inevitably the way chosen to express primitive man's most vivid thoughts and feelings, including his religious ones. And because the vivid expression of the most vivid thoughts and feelings is the essence of drama, it is not surprising that drama has again and again grown out of religious mimetics, in many ages and many parts of the world.

The Motive of Communication

Students of speech know that bodily action and gesture are as much a part of the communicative process as words, probably antedating articulate language for that purpose. Many of the more primitive languages, in fact, consist of rather meagre word vocabularies supplemented by copious and elaborate gestures. Anthropologists have devoted considerable study to the sign languages of primitive peoples, and have not failed to point out that they are largely based on imitation or mimicry, just as written languages are based originally on pictorial symbolism. Long before man could tell his fellows in articulate speech that game was at hand he could convey that idea by imitating the movements of the bird or animal and pointing in its direction. Long before he could recite the story of his conquest of an enemy he could act it out descriptively. Articulate language may have developed very largely from the grunts and cries that accompanied such mimicry.

In other words, the mimetic impulse was very early and very fundamentally associated with the impulse to inform, to convey messages and ideas, report facts, and perpetuate memories. This association has never been lost, and ought not to be lost, even in the realistic acting of the modern theatre. In the declamatory acting of earlier days, with its preponderance of what the elocution teachers called "objective gesture," there was little danger of its being lost, since the actor strove to communicate ideas to his audience much more directly than would be acceptable today. Present-day audiences have such a keen sense of æsthetic detachment and of consistency in illusion that direct objective communication between actor and audience is generally taboo, except in occasional experimental theatre. This has led some actors to dissociate their acting so completely from the communicative impulse that they fail to project the author's message to the audience. It might help such actors to realize that this association is too fundamental to be shaken off lightly, and that what has changed is not the association itself but the technique of conveying it.

The Didactic Motive

The impulse to instruct or educate grows naturally out of the impulse to communicate or inform, and the line of distinction between them is very shadowy. Both are involved in the most primitive forms of acting. I have already mentioned the mother cat teaching her kittens to keep themselves clean. There is mimicry here, not only in the action of the young imitating

the mother, but also in the action of the mother, since she is repeating for demonstrative purposes actions not necessary for her at the moment, and thus in a sense mimicking herself.

One of the most highly developed forms of mimicry among primitive peoples is that which has for its purpose the instruction of the young initiate in the religion, traditions, and social customs of his tribe. The candidate is taken to some sacred and mysterious place known only to the adult men of the tribe. There he sees individuals, usually members of the priesthood, dressed up to impersonate tribal heroes, gods, or totems. He sees them enact dramatically the traditional incidents connected with those heroes, gods, or totems. Sometimes the effort is made to deceive him into believing that the gods themselves are before him; but more often he understands that it is all a show. In any case he is expected to take it seriously, as part of his initiation, and his elders choose this method of instruction in preference to simple language because they know that it is much more vivid and impressive. The initiation ceremonies of lodges and secret societies today are not so very different in principle; nor is the activity of the schoolteacher who employs dramatization as a classroom method.

I hope I shall not be understood as advocating a didactic style of acting or a didactic purpose in all drama, much less a propagandist purpose, when I suggest that those critics are not on very solid ground who regard didacticism in drama as a modern perversion, attributable to Ibsen, or Shaw, or the Soviet theatre, or the late American Federal Theatre. Every so often we hear some such critic declaim against the enormity of an artist turned preacher, prostituting his art to new usages of instruction. The only trouble with this notion is that it reverses history. The drama was religious and didactic long before it was æsthetic, and even the impulse to act served as an instrument of education and indoctrination before it served as an instrument of art—perhaps before it served as entertainment. It is the artist, not the preacher or teacher, who came last on the scene. One may —as I for one do—approve the æsthetic purpose as a later and higher and finer development in the evolution of art, without getting confused about the order of the evolution.

It is a fact that the greatest drama has generally been written in periods when the religious and didactic elements have been subordinated to the element of æsthetic entertainment; but not in the periods when they have been subordinated to crass commercialism or discarded altogether, to the confusion of all moral and cultural standards. Great art of all kinds usually follows a period of high religious and moral culture, when thought

is growing more liberal and the ideals of goodness and beauty are seen in harmony; but it begins to decline when religious and moral standards begin to disintegrate in a welter of extravagance, loose living, confusion and decadence.

While it is generally true that people today go to the theatre to be entertained, they still like to come away with a sense of having got something worth while to take home. A neighbor of mine, for example, insists that he goes to the theatre only "for a good belly laugh," and he refuses to go at all to see anything that he fears may be a "highbrow" play; but on leaving the theatre after seeing a comedy of more than the usual substance he was heard to remark, "That's a damn good play; it gives you something to think about!"

It will give substance to the actor's work if he will note this peculiar trait of human nature. The best actor never fails to entertain, but he does not forget the ethical and educational potentialities of his art, its peculiar power over human minds and hearts.

THE MOTIVE OF TERRORIZATION

Just how early in his mimetic history man learned to use masks and other fantastic disguises is hard to say. Doubtless it was very early. All clothing is said to have originated in the idea of adornment rather than that of shelter or concealment; and adornment may have been fantastic before it was imitative. Masks are closely associated with totemic ritual, however, and no doubt became imitative, or at least symbolic, at an early date. Fantastic adornment involving totemic imitation, and especially in the form of masks, could hardly have existed very long before the idea of terrorization became involved, to play a most important part in the development of the drama.

Primitive man had many uses for terrorization. For one thing it served very effectively to solemnize the initiation ritual, and one of the earliest uses of grotesque adornment was to frighten the young men, and sometimes the women and children, into a respect for the gods—and incidentally, of course, for the priesthood. Such uses of terrorization are not entirely unknown in more modern and supposedly less primitive religions, and they are quite common in the initiation proceedings of lodges and fraternities, and in all sorts of hazing. The association of terrorization with religious, racial, and social loyalties has been an important element in the evolution of the theatre, and has been strikingly influential in the theatre of Soviet Russia.

A second use of terrorization appeared in savage warfare. By wearing

hideous masks, or painting themselves in grotesque manner, or decorating their shields with fearful images, the warriors sought to frighten their enemies into surrender or flight. Anthropologists point out, however, that this motive was seldom as simple and direct as many people suppose. Much of the masquerading of savage warriors was in the nature of magic symbolism intended to invoke the aid of the gods rather than to frighten the enemy; and when the latter purpose existed it was usually associated with the former in the sense that the enemy was expected to be frightened at the supernatural implications of the masks and symbols rather than at their ugliness.

But there was still another aspect of terrorization in primitive ceremonial, not so generally understood by the layman, though emphasized by the anthropologist; that was terrorization directed, not against the enemy warriors themselves, but against enemy gods and evil spirits, who might be supporting human enemies or threatening in their own right. Primitive man was even more afraid of evil spirits than of human enemies. He could see the latter and understand them, and fight them by physical means. But the unseen enemies which his imagination conjured up to explain such things as thunder, lightning, famine, flood, fire, and pestilence terrified him greatly. These enemies struck suddenly and mysteriously, and he had no physical weapons against them; therefore he tried to frighten them off by magic and terrorization—by dressing up and pretending to be a god himself. The history of such defensive magic with its charms, incantations, and mimetic ceremonials is extremely complex and fascinating, and there can be no doubt that it is a very significant element in the history of acting.

Without making too insistent or too literal an application of all this to modern acting, I may suggest that the element of terrorization is by no means absent in modern theatre. Just so long as audiences can feel a proper degree of artistic detachment they actually like to be terrorized; it tickles their sense of vicarious adventure. In tragedy the most popular actor may be the one who can make his audience weep; but in melodrama it is likely to be the one who can scare the customers half out of their wits. And those who have acted in melodrama know that there is keen pleasure for the actor in scaring people effectively—all in the spirit of good clean fun, just as the child likes to scare his neighbors, and even his parents, on Halloween.

The Motive of Self-Excitation

An interesting, but quite different, lesson may be drawn from another motive in primitive ceremonial, also well known to the anthropologist: the motive of self-excitation, or self-exhortation.

The war-dance type of ceremonial was often highly mimetic, the warriors going through the motions of combat and acting out the killing and torturing of their enemies in vivid detail; but since the enemies were seldom near enough at the time to see all this the principal motive could hardly have been direct terrorization. That of appeal to the gods was doubtless present in many cases, but the chief motive here was plainly self-excitation through emotional intoxication—sometimes assisted, perhaps, by intoxication of another sort. By dressing in his war harness and mimicking the actions of fighting, dancing, shouting, and boasting, the savage got himself into such a state of emotional fervor that he felt much braver and stronger than he really was; and in that state of illusion he went into battle.

I shall resist the obvious temptation to stop and draw analogies to modern warfare. The analogy that concerns us here is to the psychology of acting—on and off the stage. We are all familiar with the phenomenon of self-dramatization by which a person works himself up into a state of fear, anger, or hysterics, as a child works himself up into a tantrum. By pretending to be abused he persuades himself emotionally that he really is abused; or by affecting hilarity he becomes hilarious. A possible explanation for this may be found in the theory that emotion is the realization, rather than the cause, of its corresponding bodily action, so that one who goes through the actions pertaining to an emotion begins to feel that emotion. For the actor the implications of this theory—often called the "James-Lange Theory," in reference to the two noted psychologists who first popularized it—are so important as to require discussion at some length in a later chapter. The only points that need be made at the moment are that the principle was understood and applied by primitive man long before the psychologists discovered and stated it, and that it operates even more readily and effectively on the group than on the individual.

The Motive of Entertainment

The last motive to be considered here is that of entertainment, which, in its primitive form of a simple play impulse, is undoubtedly very ancient. Possibly more human beings, past and present, have employed mimicry for the fun of it than for any other reason. Just before the modern craze for "social significance" struck them, the modern fine arts, including that of acting, were understood to be dedicated to the purposes of entertainment, and the worthiest art was conceived to be that which gave the highest form of æsthetic pleasure. Yet it is a curious fact that entertainment

seems always to have been a secondary rather than a primary motive, arrived at more or less by accident.

The play impulse arose from two things: leisure time and freedom from the pressure of fear and necessity. Activities performed as part of the struggle for existence are not play; but the same activities repeated accidentally or by habit in moments of leisure and freedom from anxiety often turn out to be pleasurable in themselves, and so become established as forms of play. The acting element creeps in through the repetition, in the sense that when one repeats an action without its original motive he is really mimicking himself and his kind.

I have mentioned the cat pretending to chase a mouse. What happens, no doubt, is that she first chases a real mouse for food as part of her instinct for self-preservation; later she sees another, and chases it by instinct and habit even though she does not happen to be hungry at the time; or she chases it to show her kittens how. She finds the chase itself exhilarating, and so when no mouse is at hand she chases a ball, or a leaf, or a shadow, pretending that it is a mouse, and enjoying the game. The real chase may have been pleasurable as gratifying the appetite of hunger, but the mimic chase is pleasurable in quite another way: it is voluntary, carefree, exciting, with the thrill of the real chase but without its accompaniment of hunger and concern. It is in the spirit of play.

When primitive man first devised his mimetic symbols and ceremonials it was probably not for pleasure in the play sense; it was for the serious business of communication, or instruction, or religious worship, or war. But he soon found out that the mimicry itself was entertaining, and that it grew more so when repeated, with elaborations, for pleasure alone. In this way tribal drama of various kinds came to be perpetuated in a festive spirit long after the original motives had ceased to be urgent. Religious ceremonials gradually lost their sacred character and turned into secular drama—as they unmistakably did in medieval Europe. War dances for self-excitation turned into war plays for entertainment, almost as exciting to the imagination but vastly more pleasant, because detached from the danger of real bloodshed and suffering. The old Greek religious festivals of Dionysus turned into the annual dramatic tournament, and the "goat-songs" and dithyrambs that accompanied the earlier dances passed through a gradual evolution to become the great choral dramas of the Golden Age. In the same way the liturgical drama of many races in many countries and periods of history, first conceived as an instrument of religion, has gradually become more and more popular as entertainment, more and more secular in character, and has ultimately separated itself

from religion to become a popular festival and ultimately an independent art.

In the course of this evolution the practice of mimicry has given many kinds of entertainment, some serious, some frivolous, but all more or less explainable in terms of combined motives. To discuss them exhaustively would require volumes, and involve us in endless complexity. Two elements, however, deserve special mention because they seem peculiarly significant in modern acting and modern drama.

The first of these is the element of release, already noted in connection with religion and with the play impulse. It is this element which is at the root of the festive or holiday spirit everywhere. The very word "holiday"— which once meant "holy day"—has come to mean release from the ordinary labors and cares of life. So ancient and intimate is the association between dramatic mimicry and the festive spirit, that I do not think it is an exaggeration to say that this element is a vital one in the art of acting. People still go to the theatre in a festive spirit, even when the drama itself is serious, and the most tragic acting will fail to please if it does not provide, somewhere beneath the pain and the tears, a joyous sense of imaginative and emotional release.

It should be understood that release, in the sense here intended, is a very different thing from what is commonly called escapism. Escapism is a refusal to face reality, an attempt to dodge it by the methods of the ostrich. It is extremely popular today, but is bitterly deplored by many modernists in art and criticism, and is almost hysterically attacked by those who sneer at art for art's sake because they want to use art for propaganda's sake. With the merits and faults of escapism we are not here concerned. The point is that while escapism inhibits true emotions by means of evasive tactics, release brings them out into the open by suspending inhibitions. It is release, not escapism, that is back of the long tradition of holiday festivities.

The second element is that of vicarious experience. Man is imaginative, and therefore curious. He wants to know what it feels like to be someone other than himself; to have experiences he has not had; even to undergo hardships and dangers he has been fortunate enough to escape. In the latter case his curiosity is often restrained by his better judgment, and he avoids the steeps of life when he can; yet in his imagination he plays with the idea of doing those things which in real life he cannot or dare not do. In acting or watching others act he finds a vivid opportunity for such indulgence, and enjoys all the excitement of romantic or tragic experience without its dangers and obligations. This is the very essence of his pleasure

in all the arts of fiction, and no art gives it to him in more concentrated form than the art of acting.

A TECHNIQUE OF SELF-CRITICISM

It would be most unfortunate if any part of this chapter were interpreted as implying that the modern actor should consciously imitate the ways of primitive man, or revert to the standards of another age, or, worst of all, attempt to synthesize his art consciously out of all the elements here discussed. But in the attempt to master any art one naturally seeks the aid of criticism, including self-criticism; and the most helpful criticism is that which is intelligently analytical.

The idea is not that these ancient motives are to be arbitrarily adopted by the actor; it is rather that they are already in him, and in his audience, and that a recognition on his part of their basic naturalness may give him a greater sense of freedom, a greater confidence in his right to do thus or so. Bad acting is more apt to result from false objectives and false restraints growing out of self-conscious artificiality and sophistication than from natural freedom in the expression of fundamental human motives.

Thus, if the actor discovers that he is being too subjective, or too remote from his audience, it may help him if he can diagnose this as an over-suppression of the communicative impulse. If he is too tame, or too cold, it may well be that he can afford to give more play to the motive of self-excitation, or that of terrorization. If his acting seems to be too commonplace, or too real, or too depressing, it may be that he has lost touch with the element of magic or exaltation. And if his acting impresses others as hyperæsthetic, it may be that in the effort to avoid teaching or preaching he has become too "arty."

More often, of course, no particular pattern of criticism will fit exactly. Nevertheless, the actor who has given some thought to the reasons why all sorts of men everywhere have acted is more likely to give himself intelligent self-help when in difficulty than the one whose notion of acting is confined to his own age and home town.

CHAPTER II

The Actor's Relation to His Audience

NO PROBLEM is more fundamental in the art of acting than that of the actor's relationship with his audience; yet no phase of his art has changed so often or so much. In the course of history he has been priest, public servant, vagabond, slave, mountebank, journeyman, professional gentleman, and union laborer; he has acted for the gods, for himself, for a coterie, for a patron, for his neighbors, and for the mob; he has acted in disguise and without it; he has acted rhetorically to the multitude or murmured intimately to the few; he has acted broadly and artificially to stir up emotion or naturally and realistically to create illusion; he has addressed his audience directly, serving as the mouthpiece of the author, or has exhibited himself objectively as the image of a character.

Generally speaking, each age has established its own convention in this matter, and the prevailing relationship of that age has been almost the only one. Conventions grow out of conditions and customs, and each age is normally loyal to its own, even to the point of resenting any attempt to change them. When David Garrick, more than a century and a half after Shakespeare, tried to break up the Elizabethan custom of allowing favored members of the audience to sit on the stage almost under the elbows of the actors, and tried to keep his actors in character throughout the play, even when not speaking lines, he met with a great deal of opposition, and might well have failed but for his tremendous popularity and prestige. When, a century later, the rant and bombast of Edwin Forrest and his contemporaries began to give way to the quieter and more intellectual acting of Edwin Booth, many people thought that the drama was dying. When Antoine in Paris and Belasco in this country, about 1887, started a movement towards convincing naturalism and pictorial realism, they met the same sort of inertia, and it took their methods nearly forty years to gain general acceptance.

Since about 1911, however, a very different thing has been happening in the theatre. An age of experimentation has come upon us, in which all current standards are being challenged, new ones invented, and older ones

revived and tried out in competition. Instead of one prevailing mode we now have many. The phenomenon is not confined to the relationship of actor and audience, or even to the problems of the theatre; it pervades all the arts, and all phases of life. It is part of the universal unrest and self-questioning. For the first time in history, perhaps, we have an age that is actively conscious of other ages, anxious to compare and criticize, to reject and select. To be sure it is only the liveliest thinkers who are affected; the inertia of the masses is always great, and popular institutions, including the commercial theatre, still change more slowly than experimental arts. But the lively thinkers—if not the profound thinkers—are growing more numerous, and the inertia of the masses is lessening. All life has grown more rapid, complex, and changeable; the automobile, the airplane, the motion picture, and the radio—not to mention two world wars and the fear of atomic destruction—have jolted humanity out of its leisurely rate of social evolution, and brought about a kind of cosmic restlessness. Much of this may have to be repressed or to go underground if the left-wing style of thinking prevails and individual liberty of thought and expression give way to regimented "democracy" under a police state on the Russian model. But at the moment of this writing the artistic world west of the "iron curtain" is in a ferment, and despite certain hidden censorships is fairly free to experiment—if not in what it says, at least in the way it says it.

In the theatre this means a good deal of instability, an almost hysterical search for variety and novelty, and a lack of standards. A half-century ago there was one right way of acting a play; now there are nine-and-sixty, and (to paraphrase Kipling) "every single one of them is right." In one sample week you may see on Broadway two or three classic revivals from Shakespeare and the Greeks, done in a variety of styles; a repertory of Gilbert and Sullivan; three or four smart, sophisticated comedies of ultramodern manners and Restoration morals; three or four problem plays of abnormal psychology or sex neuroses, done variously with stark realism or poetic fantasy; a spectacular revival of some children's classic; four or five propaganda plays ranging from "a little left of center" to outright Communism, some of them attacking (and of course stirring up) race prejudice, some of them highly experimental in design and method; one or two musicals dealing biographically with famous composers as an excuse for distorting their music into the "modern idiom"; and four or five stylized musicals exploiting the modern ballet. Almost the only thing you will not see is a propagandist play of right-wing tendency; the hidden censorship maintained through closed-shop unionism effectively prevents anything right of center. With all this range, however, the variety of Broadway is nothing in com-

parison with the variety to be found in the college and community theatres of the country at large.

In the midst of such variety there is naturally a good deal of dispute as to the proper relationship between actor and audience. The realists demand that the actor shall be a perfect objective image, completely aloof from his audience. "Be natural," they say; "stay in the picture, preserve the illusion." Others demand intimacy, or artificiality, or creative interpretation. "Be frankly theatrical," they say; "be direct; be impressive; be an actor facing an audience, not a photographic copy of a character in real life." The propagandists say, "Be dynamic; be a voice of protest; be a social force." The hucksters merely say, "Be funny—no matter how!" To the young actor seeking to develop his own technique all this must be very confusing.

The soundest way to approach a problem of this kind is to look beneath the surface for those principles which are sufficiently permanent to be helpful in the face of change; and the best way to do that is to consider the behavior of our primitive ancestors, and their modern counterpart, our children. There is much valuable inspiration for the theatre worker in the study of children at play. The child's game of "Let's pretend!" is play-acting in its simplest and most natural form, and therefore, in a sense, its best form. It is crude, to be sure, and naïve; but in an imaginative way it is wholly sincere, and full of the zest of life. The best adult acting is just that—duly refined for the more mature audience, but fundamentally the same.

ACTING WITHOUT AN AUDIENCE

If we return, for a moment, to the drama of primitive peoples, we see that the audience was at first relatively unimportant. It is not quite true that the primitive actor acted only for himself. The motives of communication, education, and terrorization imply an observer of some kind; and even the religious motive implies in some cases an address to the gods. For the most part, however, primitive man indulged in mimetics for his own satisfaction and that of his fellow participants, rather than to entertain or impress outsiders. In the earliest ceremonials all the members of the tribe took part; or all except the women and children. If the latter were excluded it was not to make an audience, but to dispense with the nuisance of having them about; and often they were not even permitted to witness the ceremonies.

Dancing and mimicry for self-excitation, as in the war dance, were especially free from the actor-audience relationship. The participants sought

only to arouse themselves and each other. All members of the tribe might be included, but the emotional attitude was subjective, not objective. At the present day some religious sects, even in modern America, practice emotional excitation as wild as any war dance; but when they are sincere they generally prefer to do so without an audience.

When the pleasure motive began to creep into primitive ceremonial there was probably no thought at first of entertaining outsiders. It was the participants who found themselves entertained; and they kept up their mimicry to amuse themselves and each other. It was only at a later stage, when the casual spectators had manifested their growing interest in the proceedings, that the participants discovered the additional pleasure, and sometimes the pecuniary profit, in astonishing and impressing an audience. Not until then did anyone think of building a "theatre"—that is a place for the spectators.

If this more or less accidental relationship between actor and audience is not sufficiently clear in the history of primitive peoples it is surely clear in the behavior of children. Anyone who has watched the mimetic play of children at all closely, will have observed that there is little or no consideration of an audience at first. The younger children "pretend" together for hours at a time, playing "house," or "soldiers," or acting out stories they have heard. All the children take part (except when one fails to play the game properly and gets himself ostracized) and no adult listeners are wanted. If adults happen to be in the room their presence may be tolerated, provided they appear to be minding their own business; but let them show too much interest as audience and the game disintegrates in self-consciousness.

THE IMPULSE TO SHARE EXPERIENCE

Although an individual child will sometimes play by himself, becoming oblivious to his surroundings and conjuring up a whole world of make-believe, only the introvert type of child actually prefers this solitary play. The more normal child may fall back upon it when circumstances require, but otherwise he craves some form of group play. This may be partly because of the greater stimulus to the imagination, two heads being better than one, but it is largely because of the instinct to share experience with others. Man is not by nature a solitary animal but a gregarious one, and he not only likes company, but likes to share with it his joys and miseries.

So strong is this feeling that it often induces the child, especially the child who is solitary for lack of companions and not from choice, to call

for adult sympathy and participation. "Mamma! See! Dolly's asleep!" cries the little mimic mother, after putting her child to bed. "Look, Daddy, I'm Napoleon!" her brother shouts, wearing his soldier hat sidewise. At a later period these children may do the same sort of thing in a spirit of exhibition, to enjoy the amazement or admiration of their observers; but at first, I think, they do it because they have discovered the joy of mimetic action, and it is too good to keep to themselves; they just have to share it with somebody—preferably the most sympathetic person handy.

This instinct to share imaginative and emotional experience seems to me extremely vital in the history of the theatre, not only as accounting for the origin of the audience but as suggesting the true and proper relationship between actor and audience today. The technique of the sharing process varies greatly, of course. Sometimes, as in vaudeville or musical comedy, it is very frank and outright; at other times, as in realistic drama, it is almost concealed in the subtleties of illusion. But unless the relationship itself is there—unless you have an actor and an audience eagerly, actively, sharing an imaginative experience—you do not have true theatre. That is one reason why the motion picture or the television play can never fully replace the theatre, or perform its true function.

The Motive of Exhibition

To say all this is not to say that there should never be any element of exhibition in the acting relationship. To exclude exhibition entirely would be to exclude not only the most extreme realism but all imaginative and æsthetic appeal based on objective truth and beauty.

The element of exhibition (as distinct from exhibitionism) is a perfectly natural one, observable in the later stages of primitive drama and in the play of older children. But it is secondary rather than primary, and accidental rather than instinctive, and therefore less vital than the sharing motive. It comes about through the exclusion rather than the inclusion of the observer. The nonparticipants in primitive ritual or child's play are either banished from the scene altogether or required to stand at a distance, outside the prescribed playing space. But exclusion whets curiosity, and sooner or later the excluded ones manifest interest in the ceremonies, expressing wonder, awe, and admiration, and begging to be allowed to come closer. In time this audience response becomes pleasing to the actors, stirs their pride and perhaps their profit motive, and leads them to play consciously for the audience.

It may be said, therefore, that the whole modern conception of the

theatre as a place where actors exhibit their talents for the pleasure of an audience is founded on accident. An activity once dedicated to the entertainment of the participants has been diverted—some say perverted—to the entertainment of outsiders. Of late years, some of our more restless critics have discovered this fact, and have set up loud lamentations. Confusing exhibition with realism, and both with commercialism, they condemn them all. They demand the abolition of the proscenium, the footlights, and all barriers between audience and actor, in the hope that audience participation may be achieved through intimacy, and acting again made a communal activity.

As a critical counterbalance to excessive objectivity, this outcry is a healthy influence; but it has no more chance of complete success than a movement to restore bows and arrows as weapons of war. We cannot turn history backwards. It may be unfortunate that actor and audience are separated, and that the actor is now concerned with the entertainment of the audience rather than of himself. But the accident that separated them was natural, perhaps inevitable, and took place a long time ago. The result is firmly established and generally accepted; and at that it is not altogether bad.

There are, after all, degrees and kinds of exhibition, and some of them are much less offensive than others. There is comfort here for those of us who detest virtuosity as such, and prefer feeling, humanity, and zest. We all know the type of musician, for example, whose sole objective is the display of his own skill, and who has no real feeling for music. He may have the skill, and may command admiration and applause from an undiscriminating audience, just as the savage medicine man or the medieval juggler commanded the wonder of the uninitiated; but his performance is no more true music than theirs was true drama. He represents the worst kind of exhibitionism; and there are actors, even in the best theatres, who do likewise. In contrast, there is the type of musician who, having supreme talent, is never concerned with its display; but rather with his own joy in the music, his desire to share the joy with others and to do his best for their sake. There are actors of that type also, and it seems to me that they are the best actors. Their only exhibitionism lies in a certain consciousness of obligation to the audience, and a determination, for the pleasure of that audience, to preserve the integrity of their characterizations, and to project them effectively. But it does not lie in vanity or virtuosity; and if they maintain the convention of separation between actor and audience it is solely for the preservation of the illusion they wish to share.

INTIMACY VERSUS DETACHMENT

The most troublesome problem in actor-audience relationship is that of the proper degree and kind of intimacy. Since the beginning of the modern reaction against "peephole realism" with its objective aloofness, there has been a great deal of agitation for more intimacy between actor and audience; and almost everyone feels that something of the kind is desirable. The question is, what sort of intimacy?

There are at least two reasons why the relationship should not be so directly intimate as to break down all sense of detachment.

The first is the antiquity and naturalness of the separation between player and observer. It is characteristic of primitive ceremonial that a definite playing space is marked off on the ground—a kind of magic circle, like the "orchestra" of the Greeks—within which the dancer or performer is understood to take on the glamour of otherworldliness. Inside is religion, magic, unreality, fiction, and ultimately poetry; outside is the prose of commonplace existence. The women and children, not being participants, are, as we have seen, excluded from the playing space; perhaps some of the men are excluded also and participation limited to the specialists who constitute the priesthood—the first and oldest guild of actors. The motive of the separation is not, at first, so much to impress the excluded ones, as to make the sacredness of the playing space felt by the participants, and so to inspire their performance. But when, at a later stage, the entertainment or edification of the audience begins to be a motive, the separation is maintained or made even more rigid for the sake of greater impressiveness. Rarely, in primitive ceremonials, are non-participants permitted to mingle with participants, lest illusion be shattered; and the modern manager who forbids his actor to stroll on Broadway, or objects to the publication of technical information about the theatre, or the admission of visitors back stage, is sticking pretty close to the same tradition.

The second reason is the fact that a certain sense of detachment is necessary to the highest order of æsthetic enjoyment. Writers on the philosophy of beauty have long recognized this principle, and under the name of "æsthetic distance" it has come to be well known to all studious workers in the arts. In a discussion of acting it is inescapable, and there will be considerable reference to it in other chapters of this book. Any reader who is not familiar with the principle will find it explained at length in H. S. Langfeld's excellent work on *The Æsthetic Attitude*, and with special reference to the theatre in my own book on *The Art of Play Production*. For

the present I shall merely remind the reader that æsthetic enjoyment, like other forms of pleasure, grows out of leisure time and freedom from the pressure of necessity, and is basically dependent upon the resulting sense of release or detachment. Therefore, in order to appreciate fully the artistic values of any object—including the performance of a play—the observer must be able to feel that he is not himself physically involved, however strong may be the appeal to his imagination.

Against these two reasons for detachment are two equally good reasons for intimacy. The first is the sharing instinct already described, which is just as ancient and venerable as the separation of actor and audience. The second is the fact that audience enjoyment is to some extent dependent upon crowd psychology—that is, upon the release from restraint which we all feel as members of a group. This, too, is probably the expression of our gregarious nature. We laugh with more freedom and enjoyment when others laugh with us than when we are alone or aloof; and we weep or sigh with a similar freedom, and even with a similar enjoyment. And there is no doubt that an atmosphere of intimacy helps to warm an audience up, to make it more mellow and more susceptible to this group response.

How, then, can we reconcile the reasons for and against intimacy? Really, it is not as difficult as it seems. The intimacy that is needed in the theatre is a subjective intimacy, a kind of hidden community of understanding between actor and audience. The detachment that is needed is an objective detachment, a material separation between actor and audience through which the actor may preserve the integrity of the illusion he is trying to create and at the same time keep it separate in the listener's imagination from the immediate realities of life. A good actor can manage both. He can be externally convincing, even realistic, in his acting, avoiding the sort of intimacy that breaks down æsthetic distance; while at the same time he can share with us, through some mysterious undercurrent of sympathy, his own inner appreciation and enjoyment of the play.

And that brings us to the curious phenomenon often spoken of as the dual function of the actor. It is so important that I shall reserve it for detailed discussion in a later chapter, which will be better understood if certain more general matters are disposed of first.

ACTOR AND AUDIENCE TODAY

To summarize briefly the evolution of the actor-audience relationship, we have first a mimetic element in connection with the fundamental motives and behaviors of life; then a repetition of the mimetic action in time of leisure as a source of pleasure; then a desire to share the pleasure with

others; and finally a growing consciousness of the admiration and interest of outsiders. Not until a comparatively late period is the latter element capitalized into the organization of an audience, and the preparation of drama especially for its entertainment.

What this means to the modern actor is that his acting will gain in vitality if he can preserve as far as possible some of the elemental appeal of the earlier motives; some of the joy of participation felt by his ancestors, some of the impulse to share his imaginative experiences with others, and some of the pleasure of discovering audience response.

At the same time he must remember that as a result of this evolution we have arrived at a highly developed present state, in which the whole institution of drama and theatre exists for the pleasure and satisfaction of the audience. Just as the decorative elements of primitive handicraft developed into the purely æsthetic arts of painting and sculpture, so the mimetic elements of primitive ceremonial developed into the fine art of the theatre, in which the dominant objective must always be to give æsthetic pleasure—that is, pleasure based on the æsthetic sense. The crude, physical play of primitive man and other animals, founded on leisure time and freedom from fear, has developed into the intellectual and emotional play of the fine arts, founded upon imaginative detachment.

It is not an exaggeration, therefore, to say that the real play is not the play in the author's mind, or the text he has written, or the director's visualization of it, or the actor's interpretation of it. All of these things are important, and contribute to the ultimate objective. But the real play is the play as it lives in the active imaginations of players and audience during actual performance; and the final test of the actor's attitude—as of every other element in the production—is its effect upon this unseen play of imagination. We may theorize and criticize as we choose, and suggest all sorts of reforms or reactions in the theatre, but in the last analysis the only thing that counts is the effect upon the audience; even the actor's pleasure in participation now depends largely on that. Our evolution has gone too far for us to ignore it, or turn it backwards.

CHAPTER III

The Attitude of the Audience

BEFORE proceeding to a more detailed consideration of the actor's attitude and technique, it will be well to give some attention to the attitude of the audience itself. If we agree that the actor's objective is the creation of certain images in the minds of his listeners it will be clear that his success or failure will depend upon his ability to adapt his acting to the state of those minds. It is a well-known principle of human behavior that the reaction of an individual to any stimulus depends not only on the nature of the stimulus but also on his previous experience and attitude. The reaction of an audience to what it sees and hears on the stage will depend therefore upon the experience of the individuals composing it, and also, of course, on their collective experience as an audience group.

As we have already seen, the attitude of the audience has changed greatly in the course of history. At times it has been characterized chiefly by open-mouthed wonder; at other times by religious zeal or exaltation; at others by a spirit of revelry; and at still others by æsthetic appreciation. All of these elements and many more are to be found in the attitudes of modern audiences, sometimes separately, and sometimes in combination. Their persistence and variety account for the fact that so many kinds of theatrical fare are popular at the same time—circus, vaudeville, minstrels, burlesque, opera, ballet, musical comedy, review, farce, melodrama, comedy, and tragedy, and several kinds of each. To understand the attitude of any audience toward any sort of theatre, we need to know a little about the attitudes of all audiences toward all sorts of theatre, and about the inherited or traditional elements out of which those attitudes are built.

Without making too deep an excursion into the field of æsthetics, or repeating too much of what is set down in *The Art of Play Production*, I shall try to point out the more significant of these elements, and to suggest very briefly the part they play in the attitude of the modern audience.

OPEN-MOUTHED WONDER

Doubtless the earliest and most primitive element is that of open-mouthed wonder, or curiosity. We may laugh at the spectacle of the un-

sophisticated—the yokels of the world—gazing in astonishment and admiration at the strange antics of their priests or jugglers or medicine men;
but we must not forget that their attitude is an important element in
human progress. Without wonder and curiosity human intelligence would
never have progressed. Without wonder and curiosity there would never
have been any theatre; for the very word theatre, in its Greek original,
meant "a spectators' place" or "a place for seeing shows," and it came into
use because the curious multitude crowded around to watch the priestly
ceremonies. This capacity of the audience to wonder and admire has served
the theatre as a beneficial stimulus. From it has grown a wider and livelier
play of imagination, a desire to understand and appreciate, a sense of
transcendent experience. It is perhaps the crudest, most childlike element
in audience attitude; but it is also the most vigorous, the most animating.
It is far more honestly in the direct line of æsthetic evolution than the
attitude of smug indifference affected by many modern sophisticates.

There is danger, as already suggested, that the excited wonder of the
audience will tempt the actor into conceit, virtuosity, or exhibitionism—
what the critic calls "playing to the gallery." But if he can distinguish
between their wonder at the magic or emotion of the play and their wonder
at his skill, and will work only for the former, he may draw a great deal of
legitimate inspiration from this type of audience response.

The open-mouthed attitude must have exerted a major influence not
only on ancient drama, but on many forms of drama in more recent times.
The spectacular but tawdry exploits of "ten-twenty-thirty" melodrama in
the latter half of the nineteenth century seem to have been largely inspired by it. Certainly it has been, and still is, the chief attitude appealed
to in the circus, in many types of vaudeville entertainment, in the more
spectacular phases of extravaganza, review, and even opera, and in some
manifestations of stage realism. In the more refined and artistic theatres
today, however, especially in the great cultural centers, it does not seem
so evident. The more restrained and more critical attitude of the cultivated
audience does not admit of the frank and open wonderment of childhood.
Exploits of realism or virtuosity, instead of provoking admiration in such
an audience, now challenge criticism. Audiences are no longer satisfied
with stunts, but demand imaginative consistency.

It must not be supposed, however, that we have outgrown, or ever will
outgrow, the impulse to wonder; or that it has ceased, or will cease, to be a
significant element in audience attitude. What has changed is not the impulse itself, but the terms of life and experience in which it is felt and expressed. The most refined and æsthetic audience today is really quite as

eager to be thrilled or astonished as the audiences of twenty, or two hundred, or two thousand years ago. But it is not thrilled or astonished by the same things. It has too much knowledge and too much judgment to gasp in admiration at mere physical exploits or feats of skill which it knows are not great expressions of fine thought or feeling. On the other hand, it is entirely capable of being thrilled when it does find itself in the presence of fine thought or feeling, or of a really transcendent dramatic experience.

EMOTIONAL FERVOR

Another element in audience attitude inherited from remote origins is that of emotional fervor. It derives largely, as we have seen, from the religious motive in early drama, and from the war-dance type of self-excitation.

Most people appear to have a very limited and distorted idea of what is meant by emotion. The associations of the word suggest something extreme and intense, like abject fear, or violent anger, or hysterical mirth, or sentimental pathos. People of restraint are a little ashamed of being caught in a display of such emotions. To some extent this is a reaction from the outright and sometimes false parade of emotions so popular in the oratory and drama of the romantic period. But it is also a natural outgrowth of our increasing self-consciousness, which in turn is a product of mass education. As we grow more worldly-wise, introspective, and skeptical, we become more and more afraid of entertaining false beliefs, or sentiments, or conventions; and in our anxiety to escape the false we become suspicious of the true. Expression of any emotion comes to be thought of as a sign of weakness, or unsophistication, if not of hypocrisy.

But emotion thrives on suppression; the more we restrain it the more intense it grows. There is a popular belief that grieving persons are much relieved by "a good cry," and that those who conceal their grief suffer longer and more deeply. If this is true, it seems natural to suppose that our age of emotional restraint is really an age of strong emotion. Such a conclusion is supported by the panorama of life since World War I, with its spectacle of flaming youth, jazz, gin, and tin-horn revelry. Twentieth-century women do not faint with emotion, and twentieth-century men do not shed tears; yet sophisticated, skeptical people who would lose caste with their kind if they displayed real sentiments or genuine feelings, may now, with the aid of highballs and crooners, become loud and disorderly, and cynically open in the display of physical appetites, without losing

caste at all—except of course with the doddering old fogies born before 1910. The raucous, maudlin spirit of our age is largely camouflage for emotionalism diverted from sincere and natural outlets to artificial and insincere ones.

Emotionalism must have its outlets; and the most satisfying outlets for deep, sincere, and exalted emotion have always been found in religion, and in those arts which derive most directly from it and retain some of its exaltation. In these days of declining faith, the churches fail to hold the more cynically minded against the juke box and the gin. The arts of painting and music have been somewhat overintellectualized, and have lost much ground to those forms of atonality, distortion, primitivism, or surrealism which are the highbrow expressions of the jazz spirit. The motion pictures are more frankly and honestly emotional, and so provide an outlet for the sentimentality of the masses; but they too are badly infected with juke-box standards of taste. Poetry holds its ground with the superior group, but tempts the lunatic fringe into excesses of preciosity. Only the theatre at its best seems capable of satisfying the emotional fervor of the middle group—that is, of those who are too sincere in their emotions to accept the cheap and tawdry, yet too rational to find release in religious worship as conducted in many churches today.

As I see it, the reason why such people can still find emotional satisfaction in the theatre, and why emotional fervor is still an important element of audience attitude, is that the theatre, even more effectively than the church, utilizes crowd psychology. Individually we are afraid to give way to sincere emotion, and especially to be seen doing so; but collectively we are not so much afraid. People who would not laugh aloud at a funny line in a book, will laugh with heartiness at the same line in a theatre—provided others laugh at the same time. People who would not shed tears when reading a pathetic story will shed them freely at a pathetic play. The strength of the visual appeal has something to do with this, of course; so has the sense of magic or otherworldliness. But the sense of being one of a crowd, all sharing the same emotion, is the chief reason for it. In the theatre this feeling is greatly intensified by the darkened auditorium. Just as children cling to each other in the dark for mutual protection, so we all cling together emotionally in a darkened theatre. At the same time we feel individually less conspicuous, and less ashamed of our laughter or tears. The result is a release of the feelings, enabling us to share the emotional experiences of the play without self-consciousness or cynicism as our ancestors shared those of religion or war.

Imaginative Release

Closely associated with emotional release is the release of the imagination. Undoubtedly the visual stimulus plays a large part here. It is not—as some disciples of realism seem to believe—that we must see everything in actuality before we can imagine it, but merely that the sense of sight is a bit livelier and more stimulating than the other senses. Most people find it easier, for instance, to give undivided attention to a stage play or photoplay than to a radio play. Even the radio play, however, is more vivid than a printed book, and many people to whom reading is an effort can listen easily to radio plays if the surroundings are reasonably quiet. This, of course, is because all sense stimuli are more immediate than word symbols, more directly suggestive of images. In the theatre we have both auditory and visual images presented to us very directly; the imagination has much to seize upon and work with, and is likely, in consequence, to be very active.

The actor should remember, therefore, that in playing to an audience he is playing to a group of people who are more imaginative, as well as more emotional, than the same people would be as individuals. This is not an invitation to overact; if anything it is the opposite. To appeal to the emotions of the audience it is not necessary to rant; and to stimulate the play of imagination it is not necessary to provide a surplus of ready-made images. The very fact that people in a theatre experience imaginative release means that the actor can depend upon more assistance from the imagination of his audience than almost any other artist, and that he need only supply a few well-chosen suggestions in order to keep that imagination working with him. If the reader does not believe this, let him study again the imaginative behavior of children; then let him compare the elaborateness of poor acting with the simplicity of good acting, and he will see that the latter depends in much greater degree upon the activity of audience imagination. This is one of the most important points to be learned about audience attitude.

Empathy

In the first chapter considerable attention was given to the imitative impulse as the basis of acting. In quite another way this impulse is also the basis of audience attitude; it is, in fact, the basis of appreciation in all the fine arts.

Students of psychology have long been aware that the instinct of imitation plays a much larger part in our behavior than appears on the surface.

As children we imitate, or try to imitate, much of what we see; as we grow older we are subjected to a constant process of restraint, until many of our most natural impulses, including the imitative, are thoroughly suppressed, and apparently obliterated. But every stimulus experienced by the human organism, whether real or imagined, produces some sort of bodily response; and when a bodily response is inhibited or suppressed it takes the form of a motor attitude or muscular pattern—unseen, but none the less real. This is true of all sorts of impulses, imitative or otherwise; but in the case of the imitative impulse it results in the phenomenon which the Germans call *"Einfühlung,"* and which has been called in English "inner mimicry," or "empathy."

Empathy may be defined as the tendency to respond to any object by assuming an imitative motor attitude towards it—by feeling ourselves into it, consciously or unconsciously. When we watch a tightrope walker striving to keep his balance, or a football player crashing and tearing his way through a line, or a fancy skater doing graceful figures on the ice, we unconsciously assume the corresponding muscle patterns, even though we do not express them in overt action. Somewhat less accurately, but no less imitatively, we respond to inanimate objects, endeavoring to feel like them in a physical sense. Observing the Washington Monument or the Empire State Building we instinctively stand up straighter, stretching to our full height; looking at the Pyramids we feel heavy and flat-footed; watching the stormy ocean breaking on a rocky shore we feel vigorous, active, exhilarated. Whatever the object, when we feel it in ourselves in an imitative physical way we are said to be empathizing; and when the empathic experience is pleasant we have one of the essential conditions of æsthetic appreciation.

The word "empathy" is, of course, unfortunate. It is too much like the word "sympathy"; and the verb "empathize" is too much like the verb "emphasize." An even more serious confusion develops between the adjectives "empathic" and "emphatic"; and it is almost impossible to convince a printer that the newer words exist. An English reviewer discussing an American book commented sarcastically on the "blessed word empathy," attributing it to American laboratory cant; as a matter of fact it was coined by an Oxford professor in an attempt to translate the German word *"Einfühlung."* Many people wish he had never thought of it; but as it is now in common usage, not only among psychologists but among all serious students of the fine arts, there does not appear to be much that can be done about it.

Whatever the word we use, the thing itself is very real and very im-

portant. It is by no means the same thing as sympathy, though a feeling of sympathy may involve certain empathies and derive partly from them. Empathy is a purely physical imitative response, often entirely unconscious, resulting from any sort of stimulus, animate or inanimate, and not necessarily dependent upon personal or emotional connotations. Sympathy, on the other hand, is a conscious emotional state; not a "feeling into" some objective thing, but a "feeling with" some person or personal cause. It often implies an understanding of a social or moral issue and a choice of sides thereon. Sympathy may play a part in drama, as in our choice of a hero or heroine to "root" for, or in our appreciation of a theme. But empathy, as a physical reaction, underlies all our appreciation of beauty, in the drama or elsewhere; and no real student of acting or any other art can afford not to understand it.

ÆSTHETIC DISTANCE

As stated in H. S. Langfeld's *The Æsthetic Attitude*, and again in my own book, *The Art of Play Production*, the attitude of a modern theatre audience involves a balance between strong empathic responses and the feeling of detachment which has come to be known as "æsthetic distance." This term is a little less troublesome than the term "empathy," and is fairly descriptive of the principle it stands for, though the word "detachment" would seem to me more accurate than "distance."

The idea is that for the full appreciation of an object of beauty, the full maintenance of an æsthetic attitude, one must feel somewhat detached— not aloof, not indifferent, not altogether impartial, but still not involved in an actual or personal sense. If, for example, one could assume such an attitude toward a burning house, he might see great beauty in the spectacle; but he could hardly assume it if the house were his own. In the theatre he might see poetic beauty in a death scene feelingly portrayed; but if the scene resembled too closely the death of his own wife or mother his sense of detachment would be lost, and the pleasure would be spoiled for him. Soldiers who have fought in a great war often cannot endure war stories or war plays or war pictures for years after their return, because they can not contemplate these things without losing æsthetic distance. Extreme realism, in the theatre or any other art, always involves the danger of such loss of distance; and many of the conventions and technical devices of the arts have been developed in a more or less conscious attempt to guard against it.

Thus the painter hangs his picture in a frame, to define the limits of the composition and set it apart from the reality of its surroundings. The

sculptor mounts his statue on a pedestal for the same reason. And for the same reason all artists conventionalize their work to some degree, eliminating superfluous realism of detail, and simplifying essential ideas in terms of artistic symbols. In the theatre the devices which help to maintain æsthetic distance include the proscenium frame; the raised stage; the bright lights of the stage in contrast to the darkness of the house; the non-realistic elements in the setting or lighting; and, most important of all, the impersonative, non-communicative attitude of the actor.

Students of the theatre sometimes make the mistake of supposing that the degree of empathy and the degree of æsthetic distance should be absolute and the balance between them constant. Actually both elements are highly variable and relative, and the balance between them subject to many fluctuations.

Roughly speaking, the degree of detachment necessary to an attitude of enjoyment is proportionate to the mentality and cultivation of the audience. Audiences of children or unsophisticated adults, with their less critical imaginations and less restrained empathies, can enjoy a more intimate relationship with the actor and a greater sense of imaginative participation, without loss of æsthetic distance, than an audience of theatre-wise sophisticates. There are still audiences in the small-town and neighborhood theatres that hiss the villain, applaud the hero, and shout warnings to the heroine, as did the "ten-twenty-thirty" audiences three generations ago—not in the spoofing manner in which this has been done in some modern revivals of old melodramas, but in real imaginative enthusiasm. Audiences of children still shout "Yes!" to Peter Pan's question: "Do you believe in fairies?" At a puppet show they raise pandemonium, shouting encouragement and advice to Peter Rabbit or Little Black Sambo; and they shriek with delight when the puppet hero addresses them in a confidential aside. Adult audiences which resent a soliloquy or aside speech in a modern realistic play have little difficulty in accepting the franker and more artificial asides of eighteenth-century comedy, for the very reason that they can assume a more imaginative and playful attitude toward the latter.

It is extremely important to understand that these more robust and intimate audience attitudes do not imply a surrender of æsthetic distance, nor an exception to the principle of balance between æsthetic distance and empathy. They simply mean that under different conditions the distance is differently measured; that the more naïve, frank, open and imaginative the attitude of the audience, the stronger may be its empathic responses without loss of æsthetic distance.

THE FESTIVAL SPIRIT

Before we leave the subject of audience attitude there is one other point which requires attention, and which seems to me of supreme importance; and that is the traditional association (mentioned briefly in Chapter I) of all forms of dramatic ceremonial with a spirit of festivity.

People with a serious turn of mind and a taste for what is called serious drama not infrequently lose sight of this association, or suppose that we have outgrown it and can ignore it. Because festivity is sometimes associated with frivolity they assume that it is necessarily a vain and shallow thing, inconsistent with a serious purpose or with the finer æsthetic feelings. They somehow develop the notion that serious things must be solemn; that nothing can be fine, or important, or artistic, unless it is also depressing, painful—even dull.

I should like to point out that the very words "festive," "festal," "festivity," and "festival"—like the word "holiday"—have a religious origin. All great religions recognize feast days as well as fast days; and most of them have more feast days than fast days. Feasting and merriment have from the earliest times, in all parts of the world, been associated with the celebration of important religious, or racial, or national events. Primitive man celebrated the success of a hunt or a harvest or the culmination of an initiation ceremony with ritualistic feasting; the Greeks celebrated the festival of Dionysus as a national holiday, with eating, drinking, dancing, singing, and finally drama; we celebrate the birth of Christ, the birth of our country, and our national Thanksgiving in similar ebullitions of joyous giving, fireworks, and gluttony. The human being loves an Occasion, and the more important and significant it is the more unrestrainedly he feels called upon to celebrate it.

It is true, of course, that the festive side of the celebration often runs wild, and carries us far from the original religious or national significance of the occasion. But this is merely a consequence of our essential craving for joy and merriment, and does not alter the fact that the festive spirit is normally associated with our most important social experiences. One may choose to regard this association as evidence of man's essential depravity, but one can hardly ignore it and still expect to understand the behavior of audiences in the theatre. Whether we like it or not, the tradition of the theatre—even that of the most vital and permanent theatre—is the festival tradition; and audiences instinctively feel this, if they do not know it.

A superficial thinker might suppose that a return to the festive spirit in

the theatre would necessarily mean the elimination of serious drama and the substitution of comedy, farce, or other light entertainment. It would mean nothing of the sort. The festive spirit is entirely consistent with the most earnest and artistic drama—even with tragedy. It was tragedy, more than comedy, that grew out of the Greek festival of Dionysus—the god of wine and fertility. It was tragedy, rather than comedy, that best satisfied and typified the festive spirit of the Elizabethan age.

To say, therefore, that a festive spirit is a vital part of audience attitude is not to say that audiences demand frivolous entertainment all the time. But they do demand a certain sense of exaltation, a kind of holiday sensation, a feeling that something big and important is doing, and that they are in on the celebration. The more serious the play the more important this attitude and the more difficult to maintain.

It is my personal feeling that the weakness of much modern tragedy is its failure to meet just this demand as it was met by the heroic tragedies of other days. Pity, terror, excitement, and exaltation are consistent with the festive spirit; but depression and disgust are not. Music is enormously helpful in maintaining the festive attitude, and its widespread elimination in connection with legitimate plays has come nearer to killing the theatre than anything else in history. On the other hand grand opera, which combines the liveliest and most stirring music with the most horrific tragedy, is still very much alive. These are thoughts that tempt me to elaboration, but for the present we must get back to the more personal problems of the actor.

CHAPTER IV

The Dual Function of the Actor

MODERN acting is generally looked upon as an interpretative art subservient to the creative art of the dramatist, or of the director or of both. There is a tendency to regard the director as the supreme artist of the theatre, and the actors as what Gordon Craig called "übermarionettes," sensitive to his manipulation, effacing themselves in their characters and in the totality of effect as conceived by him.

The advantage of this arrangement in respect to artistic unity is so obvious that it has gained wide acceptance—especially among directors. As a musician enjoys the sensation of playing upon a flexible and responsive instrument, or conducting a responsive orchestra, so a director enjoys working with actors who are sensitive tools in his hands, who respond to every shade of his creative feeling and are not diverted by wills and personalities of their own. If, however, their subservience is carried to its ultimate extreme, they cease to function as interpretative artists; they become nothing but instruments.

I hardly think most of us are ready to go so far. We still prefer to watch the actor who seems to us to be an artist, expressing something of himself as well as of the author and director. In spite of pictorial realism and consistent illusion we still like the feeling that the actor is somehow sharing with us his own keen, joyous appreciation of the character he is portraying, and the situation in which the character finds himself. Without that feeling we should be in danger of confusing art with reality; and we might very well prefer to go and look at reality instead of watching its imitation in the theatre.

ARTIST AND INSTRUMENT

That brings us again to the curious fact that an actor, unlike most artists, is two things at once: artist and instrument. A sculptor works with chisels on marble, or with fingers on clay. A painter works with colors and brushes on canvas. A violinist plays upon a thing of wood and strings. But the actor plays upon himself; upon the whole of himself; upon his body, his voice, his movements, his facial expression, even his emotions and imagi-

nation. Subjectively he is the artist. Objectively he is the instrument.

This is easy to say, and, in principle, easy to understand. But when one tries to explain how the trick is done he finds it not so easy, for the two functions are really quite different, and in some respects seem almost irreconcilably inconsistent.

As instrument, the actor is theoretically identified with the character he represents. Modern acting, especially realistic acting, aims at a high degree of convincingness and consistency of illusion. A character in a realistic play must be consistent with himself, and with the action of the play; and he must be convincing to the imaginations of his audience. The modern audience has a keen sense of æsthetic distance, which is easily disturbed if the character fails to remain a part of the illusion, or if the actor fails to remain in character. Nothing more completely destroys our confidence in an actor and our pleasure in the illusion than the discovery that he is looking or talking directly at us in a palpably communicative way. We demand that he shall look, speak, and behave like the character we conceive him to be, and shall remain within the magic fiction of that other world which is the play.

As artist, on the other hand, we think of him as independent of the character—as an interpreter, studying the character and making him intelligible and interesting to us. We do not ask that he be at odds with the director or the other actors in his interpretation, or that he give us an interpretation different from that intended by the author. But we do ask that he enrich and illuminate our experience by sharing with us his own wise appreciation and understanding of the author's intention.

The question is, how can he convey such an attitude to us without at the same time breaking the illusion and destroying his effectiveness as an instrument? Suppose, for example, that the character is intended to be amusingly stupid, and is to do or say funny things without himself realizing that they are funny. As instrument the actor must preserve the illusion by looking stupid and uncomprehending. As artist he must somehow let the audience know that he, in harmony with the author, does comprehend the humor of the situation and desires the audience to comprehend it; that the humor is intentional on the author's part and the actor's, though unintentional on the character's.

At first thought this seems impossible; and it might be impossible if art were not conventionalized, and acting had to be completely realistic. That it is not impossible is proved by the fact that all good actors succeed in doing it. Doubtless few of them could explain how, but we must try to find out.

Objective Realism and Subjective Appreciation

In the first place, as already stated, the instrumental function of the actor is objective, while his artistic function is subjective. This is only a rough distinction, and can easily be overemphasized; but it does afford a useful basis for an analytical study of the dual function.

What it means is that in conveying to the audience the illusion of the character the actor will employ chiefly objective means, and especially the boldest and most obvious of them. He will choose such postures, gestures, and facial expressions as belong to a realistic conception of the character and his state of mind. He will speak the lines with at least the broader inflections appropriate to the character's meaning and emotion. To preserve illusion and æsthetic distance he will refrain from looking into the eyes of his audience, or otherwise establishing overt communication with them. In short, he will be the character in every obvious external particular—every element that appeals directly to the eyes and ears of the audience and can be readily identified as belonging to the character. More important still, he will avoid any objective expression which can be readily identified as *not* belonging to the character.

On the other hand, in conveying to the audience his artistic appreciation and interpretation of the part he will contrive to use means that will seem to us more subjective than objective. I say "seem to us" because of course there are no truly subjective means of communication, short of mental telepathy. Possibly the great actor does establish his inner understanding with an audience by telepathic means; but I prefer to say that he establishes it by means that *seem* telepathic. These may include subtle modulations of voice, sly, restrained gestures or half-concealed facial expressions that are really objective, but so inconspicuous by contrast with the bolder strokes of his characterization that they seem to us to be wholly subjective. We have the feeling that they are intended to be concealed, rather than exhibited, and have escaped by accident without disrupting the illusion; or, better, that we have detected them, in spite of the actor's skill, through our own superior discernment, our telepathic second sight. We feel, in other words, an objective detachment from the actor as instrument, but a close, almost confidential, sympathy with his subjective reactions as artist.

Since it is mainly by the most intricate and delicate of subconscious coördinations that these effects are conveyed, it would be both futile and undesirable to attempt a complete analysis of them. It is possible, however, by way of illustration, to point out a few of the more common devices

employed by the best actors to establish this hidden rapport with the audience. I shall choose three: Exaggeration, signaling, and projection.

Exaggeration

It has often been pointed out that drama, to be effective, must be heightened by exaggeration. It is usually assumed, I think, that this is because of the great spaces and distances of the theatre, the potential distractions, and the fact that the audience is a group, not an individual.

But there is a certain degree of exaggeration in any art. It is a form of emphasis. The artist, having selected a significant line, or color, or word, or thought, intensifies it slightly in order to draw attention to it and emphasize its significance. In so doing, he not only tells the observer that the thing is important, but also that he, the artist, understands its importance, and is purposely pointing it out.

In precisely this way the actor can convey the humor of a character's stupidity by exaggerating it—by making the character seem just a little more stupid than the audience can believe the actor himself to be. If a vacant expression is called for he makes it just a little more vacant than it would be in real life, and thereby informs the audience that the effect is intentional. If a comic awkwardness is called for, he contrives to be almost unbelievably awkward in an amusingly appropriate way, and the audience sees at once that it is no accident on the actor's part, though seemingly so on the character's. Conversely, if poetic elevation is called for in a tragic situation, the actor contrives to make the character rise a little above his natural mood, and the audience senses the artistic feeling behind the interpretation, without losing confidence in the illusion. In short, the actor achieves the dual function, not by making the character seem less than convincing, but by making him seem more than convincing.

It is true, of course, that the taste of the present generation is for a comparatively restrained style of acting, and that the degree of exaggeration common in the acting of a century or half-century ago is no longer popular, especially in serious or tragic drama. But the difference is one of degree, not principle, and some exaggeration of the kind described will always be necessary. It is an essential part of the convention by which the art of the theatre is distinguished from the commonplace reality of life. And incidentally the actor should realize that where restraint is called for, even the restraint can be exaggerated.

Signaling

Signaling is communication by means of symbols, and there are certain symbols by which actors have learned to convey subjective attitudes

to their audiences, and which audiences have learned to recognize. Humorous attitudes—especially dry or cynical ones, are most often conveyed in this way.

Some of these signals are highly individual with particular actors or actresses, and closely associated with their mannerisms. Many elderly theatre-goers will remember the little trick of fingering his moustache by which the younger John Drew used to let his audience in on his appreciation of certain humors. Old timers will recall that Mrs. Fiske accomplished a similar purpose with a characteristic shrug of the shoulders or turn of the wrist; and that when the lines permitted it without falsifying the character, she also employed a peculiar little choking gurgle, which interrupted the flow of her speech at an unexpected place, and made the audience instantly aware of a humorous intent. George Cohan usually established a special understanding with his audience through funny little circular gestures with the hands, and graceful but peculiar movements of the feet. Lynne Fontanne signals humorous intent by a peculiar vocal inflection—usually a prolongation of the final vowel way back in the throat. Very few of these specialized signals, however, can be safely imitated by others; they are too much a part of the actor's personal trademark.

Quite apart from such individual mannerisms are certain signals which have become more or less universally accepted as established conventions in the theatre. People are not ordinarily conscious of them, but respond to them easily through force of habit, just as they respond to the tricks of motion-picture technique—the fade-out, the cutback, and so on.

One of the commonest of these conventional signals is the pretendedly innocent lift of the eyes on a humorous line. If the actor speaks such a line with eyes averted or half-closed the audience may hear it clearly and yet fail to laugh through distrust of the humorous intent. But if, just as he reaches the humorous point, he turns full face to the audience and raises ingenuous wide open eyes towards the balcony, people will laugh. They know it is all right to do so, for they have unconsciously recognized a familiar "go ahead" signal.

Another common signal is the artful pause just before the key word or phrase of an important or dramatic or humorous line. By upsetting the rhythm for an instant, it creates a quick sense of expectation, just as a significant pause in music points up the following chord. It may be managed naturally and seem entirely in character, yet the listener knows instantly that it is intentional, and signifies the artist's appreciation of the point. It is equally effective for humor or for impressiveness.

Still another signal is conveyed through the timing of illustrative "busi-

ness." An action which accompanies a significant line is speeded up a little so that it slightly anticipates the line, sharpening the attention of the audience just in time to bring out the meaning. This is done so skillfully and so consistently by experienced actors that audiences grow accustomed to it without realizing that there is any departure from natural expression.

A similar type of signal is to be found in the symbolic gesture, so familiar and well established that we recognize its significance at once—such, for example, as scratching the head to indicate perplexity, stroking the chin to indicate thoughtfulness, or rubbing the nose with the side of the finger to indicate casual indifference or comic surliness.

All of these are things that might conceivably be done by the characters themselves, yet when we see them we always seem to sense their subjective intention. Many other devices, less common and conventional, are also easy to recognize as subjective signals, and the actor who has a genuine impulse to share appreciation with his audience will be able to invent suitable ones whenever he needs them. Some of those mentioned will be analyzed in more detail in connection with specific problems of acting in later chapters.

Projection

A third device which helps to keep the actor in subjective rapport with his audience is that of projection.

No actor in his right mind, even in a realistic play, carries the objective truth of his characterization to the point of behaving on the stage exactly as the character would in real life. If he did so he would move about the stage aimlessly, with no regard to stage pictures; his face would be turned away at most inopportune times; his voice would often be muffled and inaudible; and his listeners would feel so completely left out of consideration that they would lose interest and go home.

Even the most natural actor—if he is a good actor—employs a certain amount of projection. For example, he faces, or partly faces, the audience a good part of the time, especially for important lines; he controls his voice so that it will carry effectively to all parts of the house. In short, he projects his characterization to the eyes, ears, and imaginations of his audience, making it seem objectively real to them, whereas if it actually were objectively real it would not reach them at all.

Such projection—like exaggeration—is seldom as frank or extreme in modern acting as in that of an earlier day; the outright declamation of old-style acting is gone, perhaps forever. But this only means that the methods of projection must be more subtle, better concealed, less obtrusive.

It does not mean that successful projection is any less important than it used to be; if anything it is more important because of its greater difficulty. It must be managed in such a way that it does not seem inconsistent with the objective characterization, and does not demand conscious attention. But modern audiences are just as insistent upon it as their ancestors were, and just as delicately sensitive to the precise degree and type of projection to which they are accustomed.

It is this sensitivity—usually subconscious—that enables the audience to draw subjective understanding from the projective quality of the acting. Without exactly knowing it they expect the actor to act for them, and to them, while seeming, objectively, to be the character. If his methods of projection are too obvious they will condemn him as artificial and unconvincing; but if he does not project his acting sufficiently they will resent his aloofness, no matter how truthful his impersonation.

Fortunately the means whereby projection is accomplished in the modern theatre are so familiar to us that we accept them without thought, as we accept all familiar conventions; and they do not seem to us at all inconsistent with objective truth. If we stop to think of it, we know, for instance, that the actor is speaking in a louder tone than the character would use in real life in a room the size of the stage. But we do not stop to think of it; and thus the louder tone does not strike us as in any way inconsistent with the characterization. So, when the actor, making use of familiar means, does succeed in projecting his characterization to us, we accept it at its objective value, at the same time appreciating his subjective artistry.

Mental Attitude

In the final analysis, however, it is not the mastery of any technical principle or device that preserves the dual function of the actor, so much as his mental attitude.

He himself must *feel* the dual attitude; objectively he must feel like the character, and subjectively he must feel like the artist. He must be a kind of dual personality, living on a double plane of existence. At the same time neither phase of this existence must be allowed to become independent of the other. The character, as instrument, must always be under the control of the artist; yet while functioning as artist the actor must never be out of character.

There is nothing new or revolutionary about this phenomenon, puzzling as it seems. More than a century and a half ago James Boswell wrote:

If I may be allowed to conjecture what is the nature of that mysterious power by which a player really is the character which he represents, my notion is, that

he must have a kind of double feeling. He must assume in a strong degree the character which he represents, while he at the same time retains the consciousness of his own character. The feelings and passions of the character which he represents must take full possession as it were of the antichamber of his mind, while his own character remains in the innermost recess.

And in the attempt to explain away the mystery he drew an amusing parallel from real life:

The double feeling . . . is experienced by many men in the common intercourse of life. Were nothing but the real character to appear, society would not be half so safe and agreeable as we find it. Did we discover to our companions what we really think of them, frequent quarrels would ensue.

Whether we accept the parallel or not, there can be no doubt about the truth of the principle as applied to acting. The actor who realizes the vital importance of the dual attitude, and successfully cultivates it, will have little difficulty with its technique, and will eventually develop a personal technique of his own to express it.

CHAPTER V

Emotion in Acting

ONE of the commonest platitudes about the theatre is the assertion that its appeal is largely to the emotions rather than the intellect. Discussions of emotional acting frequently end—and sometimes begin—with the declaration that all good acting is emotional; and one eminent critic has condemned the phrase "emotional actress" as tautological. "If she isn't emotional," he says, "she isn't an actress."

It does not do to lose sight of a truth because somebody loosely over-states it. There are, of course, many plays, or episodes in plays, that make an intellectual rather than an emotional appeal; and there are many actors and actresses, as well as directors, whose methods are comparatively intellectual—"cerebral," the critics are apt to say. But it is still true that the appeal of the theatre in general, to audiences in general, is emotional; and that many, if not most, of the great moments in the theatre are moments of strong emotional response.

For that reason it would seem wise for the actor to give some attention to the study of emotion. Most actors talk glibly enough about it, but very few give serious thought to the nature of emotion; to its technical aspects, its causes, effects, and limitations.

THE NATURE OF EMOTION

One difficulty, of course, is the fact that the psychologists, who are supposed to know about such things, have not been able to agree upon a definition of emotion. Some of them define it as the realization in consciousness of certain motor states; others deny, or ignore, the importance of consciousness, and describe emotion as the motor activity itself; others define it as a mental state more or less associated with visceral symptoms. There is talk of measuring emotion in terms of muscle tensions, or of gland secretions. Laboratory experiments have been made in great numbers to prove and to disprove each theory, and they seem to have succeeded about equally well in doing both. The net result is that anybody can have a try at it and his guess is likely to be as good as the other fellow's.

An exact scientific definition of emotion might be helpful if we had it; lacking it, we can still consider certain facts about the emotional behavior

of human beings that have been fairly evident to careful observers for many centuries. It is possible, for example, to draw certain contrasts between emotional and intellectual behavior, despite the fact that some psychologists insist that both are matters of muscle tensions and scientifically indistinguishable. It is certainly possible to describe those states which everybody agrees are emotional, such as fear, hatred, anger, grief, love, and mirth.

The most helpful thing which the actor can learn about emotion is that it is relatively total and inclusive, and closely associated with the instincts.

Most of our instinctive impulses are broad ones, involving the whole bodily mechanism. In responding instinctively we react all over, not just with the voice, or the hand, or the brain. Children and savages, being largely governed by instincts, rather than inhibitions, show this totality in the human mechanism more clearly than civilized adults. When they are pleased they dance all over; when they are afraid they cringe all over; when they speak they express themselves in bodily action and attitude as well as in words and tones. There are, to be sure, some instinctive reflexes that are local, such as the impulse to brush off a fly with the hand, or to blink the eye in warding off a speck of dust; but these are local only because they are trifling and habitual, and they are less local in children than in adults. The more vital the instinct—the more essential, that is, to the main business of survival—the more total the reaction.

On the other hand we have acquired, through education and civilization, the ability to do some things in a more limited and partial way. We can sit in a chair and think, with most of the body passive; and can record our thoughts with a pen or pencil by a slight movement of one hand. Extremely civilized people can take part in a controversial discussion, maintaining a composed and judicial attitude, and reacting largely with mind and voice rather than with muscles, nerves, and glands. Instead of instinctive and total activity we have controlled and partial activity.

Does this suggest a useful distinction between intellectual and emotional states? I think it does. The intellectual state is above all a limited state, involving certain portions of the mechanism more than others; while the emotional state is a total or inclusive one, involving the whole mechanism. The intellectual is controlled; the emotional is released. The intellectual is acquired, the emotional is instinctive. The intellectual is somewhat remote from physical necessity, while the emotional is closely associated with those instincts most vital in the biological struggle for existence. When we think of a thing we do so chiefly with our brains; when we feel it emotionally we feel it all over.

I am aware that this is a relative distinction only, and that it breaks down under certain laboratory tests. I think we may even concede a measure of truth to the theory that we actually think with our muscles and glands as well as our nerves and brains. Nevertheless, for all practical purposes the distinction is a useful one, and holds good in the art of acting. It helps us to understand what is meant when an actor is said to have done an especially powerful piece of emotional acting, and elicited a deep emotional response from his audience.

To do a fine piece of emotional acting the actor must discover in his imaginative concept of the dramatic situation something that relates to the vital elements of life, arouses instinctive reactions, and is felt all over, involving the total mechanism of body and mind; and he must be able to project that something to his audience and share it with them in such a way that they too will feel it all over, empathically.

Should the Actor Feel His Part?

This brings us face to face with the question which has agitated the theatrical world on and off for a century and a half: Should the actor feel his part emotionally, or should he remain emotionally insensible, the better to move others?

The question was raised, of course, by the French philosopher, Diderot, in his *Paradoxe sur le comédien*, published in 1770, and was revived a hundred and ten years later to become the subject of a heated controversy that has not yet entirely died out. I should hesitate to give it space but for the fact that the one adequate book on the subject—William Archer's *Masks or Faces*—is out of print and difficult to obtain. In *The Art of Play Production* I summarized Mr. Archer's discussion at some length, and for the benefit of the reader who is not familiar with either book I quote here the more essential portions of that summary:

In contending that the actor should be completely insensible to emotion Diderot so far overstated his case that he cannot be taken quite seriously. His theory is remembered today chiefly because Constant Coquelin revived and defended it in a widely read essay, *L'Art et le comédien*, published in 1880–81. Without quoting Diderot, Coquelin endorsed the *Paradoxe* as "literal truth," but a study of his whole essay reveals a general attitude so much more temperate than Diderot's that one is inclined to wonder whether he had read the *Paradoxe* before endorsing it. "Extreme sensibility," says Diderot, "makes middling actors; middling sensibility makes the ruck of bad actors; in complete absence of sensibility is the possibility of a sublime actor." What Coquelin says, in effect, is that acting is an art with certain natural limitations and conventions to dis-

Plate 1. David Garrick (1717–1779). Probably the most famous actor in history. Above, studying the text of *Macbeth.* Upper right: As master of ceremonies at the celebrated Stratford Jubilee in honor of Shakespeare in 1769. Right: The mug from which he pledged the memory of Shakespeare on that occasion (now owned by the author's next-door neighbor). Below: With Mrs. Pritchard in *Macbeth* (showing his rather small stature).

Richard Burbage
(1567?–1619)

John Lowin
(1576–1658?)

Thomas Betterton
(1635–1710)

Plate 2. Stars of long ago. Burbage was the leading actor of the company for which Shakespeare wrote. Lowin is reputed to have been the first Hamlet. Betterton has been called the first great English actor. Peg Woffington was Garrick's leading lady in his early years. Mrs. Siddons was the most popular of the Kembles, and Kean was one of the most famous tragedians after Garrick.

Peg Woffington
(1718–1760)

Sarah Kemble Siddons
(1755–1831)

Edmund Kean
(1787–1833)

Plate 3. A leading theatre of stock-company days. The old "stock" companies were really repertory companies—strong organizations of first-class actors with occasional visiting stars. The "Arch" was in its heyday in the fifties and early sixties, when Philadelphia was the theatrical capital of the country. The music-publishing center or tin-pan alley of the time was right around the corner in the same city, and the polka was in fashion. The illustration above is from the cover of a piece of sheet music dedicated to Mrs. John Drew, who became sole lessee of the theatre in 1861.

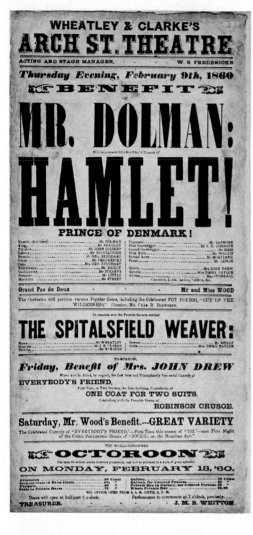

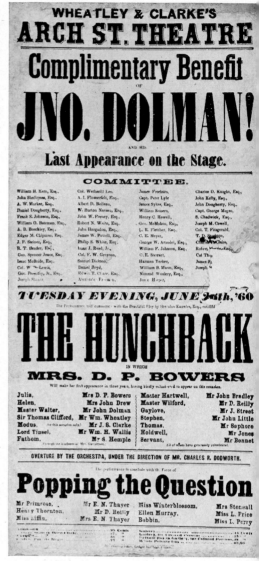

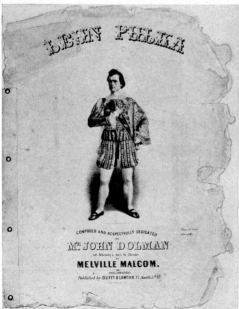

Plate 4. Arch Street Theatre handbills. In those days one could buy a full evening's entertainment for 25, 50, or 75 cents—a five-act tragedy, a short comedy, and a dance interlude, with an overture by a full orchestra. The curtain rose at seven and fell at midnight. Actors worked hard; a leading player might be called upon to act twelve or fourteen parts in two weeks, four or five of them new to him. The bill was changed nightly, though some plays were done a good many times each season. Left: Another example of sheet music dedicated to a player.

John Drew (Senior)
(1827–1862)

John Sleeper Clarke
(1833–1899)

William Wheatley
(1816–1876)

Mrs. John Drew
(1820–1897)

Mrs. D. P. Bowers
(1830–1895)

John Dolman
(1830–1895)

John Gilbert
(1820–1887)

John McCullough
(1837–1885)

E. L. Davenport (1815–1877)
as Othello

Plate 5. Arch Street Theatre players. Mrs. Drew, Davenport, and others remained active and prominent for many years; McCullough, then a young beginner, became a very popular tragedian in the Forrest tradition, and Gilbert a favorite comedian. Wheatley later gained fame as producer of *The Black Crook*, which shocked and delighted New York in 1866. From time to time such traveling stars as Charlotte Cushman and Edwin Booth also played with this company.

Metamora

Sparta[c]

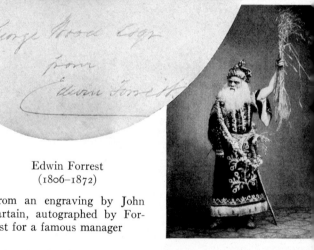

Othello

King Le[

Edwin Forrest
(1806–1872)

From an engraving by John
Sartain, autographed by Forrest for a famous manager

Plate 6. *The king of robust actors*. Most dominant figure in the art of acting since Garrick, Edwin Forrest was called by some the greatest actor of all time, and by others the worst ranter on the stage. He was also the humanitarian who endowed the Edwin Forrest Home for aged actors and actresses, to "see the players well bestowed."

William Charles Macready
(1793–1873)

great English actor whose rivalry with
rest led to the bloody Astor Place riots.

Charles Dickens
(1812–1870)

Called by Macready and others the greatest
amateur actor of his day, he really had professional
experience under an assumed name. He is here
shown as a reader.

James Edward Murdoch
(1811–1893)

. Drew called him "a delightful actor" and
ost the only one of his time who "hadn't
one of Edwin Forrest." His fine voice is
eatre tradition.

Plate 7. Some contemporaries of Forrest.

Charlotte Cushman
(1816–1876)

Lawrence Barrett
(1838–1891)

Edwin Thomas Booth
(1833–1893)

A generation younger than Forrest, he succeeded him as the foremost American tragedian. Many people considered him the greatest actor of his century and the greatest Hamlet of them all.

Plate 8. Stage pioneers. Booth profoundly influenced the history of acting by substituting a more restrained intellectual style for the noisy violence of Forrest. Barrett did much to popularize traveling repertory, taking his company with him when other stars were still traveling alone. Seymour, youthful stage manager for Barrett in 1873, helped to raise stage directing to its present dignity as an art, and was known in his old age as the dean of American directors.

Booth as Iago

Barrett as King Lear

William Seymour
(1855–1933)
as the Fool in *King Lear*

tinguish it from reality; and that for effective creative work in that art the actor must "remain master of himself throughout the most impassioned and violent action on the part of the character which he represents; in a word, remain unmoved himself, the more surely to move others. . ." He does not say, as Diderot does, that the actor should be insensible to emotion—merely that he should neither give way to it, nor depend upon it. "I am convinced," he says, "that one can only be a great actor on condition of a complete self-mastery and ability to express feelings which are not experienced, which may never be experienced, which from the very nature of things never can be experienced."

Coquelin's essay aroused a great deal of protest, and led to a spirited controversy in which Henry Irving became the leader of the opposition. The controversy interested William Archer, who, with the coöperation of Longman's Magazine, undertook to assemble and analyze all the available opinions on both sides. He distributed an elaborate questionnaire, asking several hundred actors and actresses whether they were in the habit of giving way to genuine tears, blushes or laughter on the stage; whether their acting of emotional scenes was affected by their memory of personal sorrows or other experiences; whether they found it necessary to prepare for exacting parts by working up their emotions beforehand; whether they experienced a kind of "double consciousness" in acting, and whether they believed in making use of sudden inspirations. The results of his study were published first in the magazine and later (1888) in the form of a book entitled *Masks or Faces*.

I shall not attempt to detail all of Mr. Archer's conclusions; every actor and every stage director should read *Masks or Faces* for himself. It is sufficient to say that although he is by no means unbiased in his attitude and starts out with the evident purpose to prove Diderot in the wrong, he ends by accepting a compromise position. He brings overwhelming evidence against the notion that a temperamentally insensitive person makes the best actor, but he finally agrees that a measure of self-control is essential to good acting, even in highly emotional scenes. This, after all, was Coquelin's main point, if not Diderot's, and it is admitted by Irving, Booth, Barrett, Clara Morris, and many other players quoted by Mr. Archer as supporters of the emotional theory. Clara Morris—who shed tears profusely on the stage and "felt" her parts with exquisite agony—states the compromise view clearly. "As to really losing oneself in a part," she says, "that will not do; it is worse to be too sympathetic than to have too much art. I must cry in my emotional rôles and feel enough to cry, but I must not allow myself to become so affected as to mumble my words, to redden my nose, or to become hysterical." Lambert's famous phrase, *Le coeur chaud, la tête froide* ("a warm heart but a cool head") expresses the same idea in epigrammatic form, and offers perhaps the best statement of the true paradox of acting.

. . . .

From the standpoint of the modern director William Archer's book has, I think, one or two limitations for which the student must make due allowance.

The most serious is that he appears to consider acting as an individual matter, ignoring the problem of teamwork. When an actor under stress of emotion produces an effect which not only electrifies his audience but startles his fellow actors out of their composure, one may properly ask if he is not achieving a personal triumph at the expense of the teamwork. Mr. Archer cites incidents of the kind with implied praise, and in accordance with the prevailing taste in 1888 he appears to measure excellence in acting largely by intensity of emotional effect upon the audience. The good actor, to him, is the one who "stops the show." He admits that a complete loss of self-control is bad, but he appears to think of it in terms of the individual actor and the effect upon his acting. The modern director must think in terms of the whole play, and to him the great danger in excessively emotional acting is that it will throw the actor out of his stride, disrupt the teamwork, disconcert the other actors, and unbalance the production.

A second limitation in Mr. Archer's discussion is the fact that he conducts it without definition of terms, and without knowledge of the psychological principles involved—or at any rate without reference to them. Had he believed, as most psychologists now believe, that emotion is the effect rather than the cause, of bodily activity, he would doubtless have attacked the problem in a different way. Diderot's conception of a great actor simulating perfectly the bodily manifestations of emotion and yet feeling no emotion himself is clearly improbable under the James-Lange theory. But equally improbable is Mr. Archer's conception of emotion as an inner urge, an actuating cause, moving the actor to outward expression.

Emotion, according to the James-Lange theory, is but the realization in consciousness of certain bodily activities—laughter, tears, trembling, dryness of the throat and so on—the activities themselves being induced by sensory stimuli. The emotion aroused by one set of motor activities may, of course, play a part in shaping the next set, since the motor activities are governed by past experience as well as by immediate stimuli; but that means a procession of horse-drawn carts rather than a cart before its own horse. Every emotion felt by the actor will undoubtedly affect his *subsequent* motor activities; but it cannot affect the motor activities out of which that particular emotion is built, since they precede it. From the fact that many great actors weep and suffer in sympathy with the characters they portray, William Archer seems to infer that they are great actors because they are able to weep and suffer. William James would doubtless have said that they weep and suffer because they are great actors— because they simulate the bodily activities of suffering so completely that they cannot help feeling the corresponding emotion.

The more often one rereads *Masks or Faces* the more apparent it becomes that the controversy is largely one of terminology. In essence, most actors are of the same opinion. They agree that a warm, sympathetic,

imaginative appreciation of emotional values and experiences is necessary if the actor is to get beneath the surface of his part and arouse lively empathic responses in his audience; but they also agree that he must be sufficiently in control of himself to preserve æsthetic distance.

In effect, this is just what was said in the previous chapter in terms of the dual function. As instrument the actor must be in character, and that means that he must be imaginatively true to the emotions of the character. At the same time he must not give way to those emotions to the point of losing his self-control and his interpretative function as artist. He must be two things at once: a character experiencing certain emotions, and a commentator appreciating them æsthetically.

THE JAMES-LANGE THEORY

In *The Art of Play Production* I gave a good deal of space to the so-called James-Lange theory of emotion in relation to acting. Since the publication of that book the James-Lange theory has been under fire, and some psychologists are asserting that it has been definitely disproved.

The essential part of the theory as stated by William James himself, in his *Principles of Psychology* (1890), is that "emotion follows upon the bodily expression, in the coarser emotions at least"; and he explains it as follows:

Our natural way of thinking about these coarser emotions is that the mental perception of some fact excites the mental affection called the emotion, and that this latter state of mind gives rise to the bodily expression. My theory, on the contrary, is that *the bodily changes follow directly the perception of the exciting fact, and that our feeling of the same changes as they occur* IS *the emotion*. Commonsense says, we lose our fortune, are sorry and weep; we meet a bear, are frightened and run; we are insulted by a rival, are angry and strike. The hypothesis here to be defended says that this order of sequence is incorrect, that the one mental state is not immediately induced by the other, that the bodily manifestations must first be interposed between and that the more rational statement is that we feel sorry because we cry, angry because we strike, afraid because we tremble, and not that we cry, strike, or tremble because we are sorry, angry, or fearful, as the case may be.

A somewhat similar statement was published in 1885 by Professor C. G. Lange, of Copenhagen; Lange, however, put more emphasis than James upon the idea of visceral reactions—reactions of the heart, lungs, stomach glands, etc.—as the cause of emotional sensation, and it is this phase of the theory which has been most vigorously attacked. Many psychologists and many philosophical writers on æsthetics have endorsed the James-

Lange theory in general, without in any way analyzing its detailed technical aspects; and in some instances, perhaps, without understanding it very clearly. On the other hand some of the critics of the theory do not seem to understand it any more clearly, especially the portions contributed by William James. James, though a leading psychologist, was more of a philosopher than a technician, and approached the problem of behavior from a broadly human point of view almost incomprehensible to a certain type of laboratory scientist.

One form of attack on the James-Lange theory has grown out of experiments designed to prove that certain visceral sensations commonly associated with emotion may be prevented by spinal transection without obliterating the emotion; also that widely different emotions seem to involve the same visceral changes.

Another form of attack is based upon evidence that the production of visceral symptoms by artificial means (such as drugs), in the absence of an emotional idea, does not produce the emotion.

Another is based upon experiments alleged to indicate that mental emotion takes place more quickly after the stimulus than bodily reaction. I have not seen these experiments, and cannot judge their soundness, or the soundness of the controlling conditions under which they have been performed. My own experience leads me to believe with William James that bodily reaction time is far quicker than the mental realization of emotional states.

Still another attack, backed by some very eminent psychologists, is postulated on the assertion that emotion can be distinguished introspectively from the sensations that accompany it. This is an objection that seems to me to have been effectively refuted by William James himself, in a passage too long to quote, which may be found on pages 451–452 of the *Principles of Psychology* (Vol. II). When it comes to introspective psychology I have found James the most reliable of observers.

The trouble with most of these attacks is that they are based upon limited conceptions of the James-Lange theory; they fail utterly to take into consideration the totality of response which James certainly believed in, and which many observers regard as the key to emotion. James emphasizes repeatedly the multiplicity of bodily reactions involved in the emotions, and the variation of these reactions in different people for the same emotion, and even in the same people at different times. He does not claim that the reactions for any given emotion can be catalogued; in fact, he states the opposite. Consequently, when his opponents show that certain specific reactions may be present and a given emotion absent, or vice

versa, they do not disprove his theory; they merely disprove something he does not say.

What he does say, and I think proves, is that emotion is the realization in consciousness of the sum total of bodily reactions called forth by certain types of stimuli. The stimuli which produce what he calls the coarser emotions are clearly those which have the closest associations with our vital instincts, or with past emotional experiences. As I see it, such stimuli arouse the whole sympathetic nervous system, involving body and brain in a totality of response; and when some portion of the body is cut off or anesthetized, the remaining portions take over the load, just as the sense organs of touch and hearing take over when the sense of sight is destroyed. To prevent emotion entirely when the stimulus is right the experimenter would have to anesthetize the whole mechanism; and to create it when a true stimulus is lacking he would have to produce artificially the full totality of bodily symptoms—a perfection of synthesis manifestly impossible.

Whatever may be true of the details of the theory, I still firmly believe that the conscious realization of an emotion is the effect, rather than the cause, of the physical reactions which accompany it. And this, if true, is of great significance to the actor.

THE JAMES-LANGE THEORY IN RELATION TO ACTING

The old notion of emotional acting was that you imagine a moving situation, feel the emotion, and then express it in voice and action. Most of the actors and actresses who answered William Archer's questions in 1887 obviously thought of the process in this way, and regarded emotional sensibility as a cause, rather than a result of expression. If this idea were correct, it would follow inevitably that the most accurate expression and portrayal of emotion would come from those actors who were feeling the emotion most deeply. To express suffering, one would really have to suffer; to express love, one would have to feel love as his own emotion. And he would have to feel these emotions *at every performance and in advance of their expression.*

If, on the contrary, the James-Lange theory is sound, acting becomes a somewhat different process. You first imagine the moving situation, then respond with certain motor activities which are the natural or conditioned reaction to that situation; and then—if the reactions are true—you experience the emotion.

If your reactions were completely true, involving the whole bodily, nervous, and mental mechanism in a perfect totality of response, you would

feel the emotion at its full value as an absolutely genuine thing. This, of course, never quite happens. Since acting is not real life, but an art, there is always in it some element of convention, or artistry, or conscious pretense, however slight. This interferes with the totality of reactions in some way, keeping it somewhat below one hundred percent; and the greater the element of artificiality the less the chance of the actor's feeling the emotion. Conversely, the more nearly complete his bodily response, the greater the likelihood of his feeling at least some trace of the emotion.

Just what can the actor learn from the James-Lange theory that is of practical value?

In the first place he can learn a lesson that is always useful: the lesson of moderation. If he permits himself to enter too unreservedly into the imaginative situation, his bodily response will be too complete, too instinctive, too real. As a result he will feel too much emotion, be overcome by it, and lose his self-control; and with it his æsthetic distance and that of his audience.

In the second place he can learn the opposite lesson, that too little imagination means too little bodily response, and too little bodily response means too little emotion, both on his own part and that of his audience. When his bodily response is too partial or too sketchy to engender in him any suggestion of emotion, he should take warning, for it is a sign that his imaginative concept is too limited to arouse the necessary empathic responses in the audience. The best actors "act all over"; and when you see an actor who does not, you may be sure either that he is badly inhibited, or that his imagination is incomplete, stimulating only a partial response instead of a total one.

In the third place he can learn the futility of waiting for inspiration, or depending upon it. There are moments, of course, when actors do experience those flashes of impulse which we loosely call inspiration; but they are sporadic and untrustworthy, and the more emotional they are, the less trustworthy. David Garrick, one of the greatest actors of all time, said, "I do not depend upon that inspiration which idle mediocrity awaits." If the actor would be certain of his effects, especially in repeated performances, he must depend rather upon properly chosen and well-coördinated bodily activities, well learned and accurately repeated at each performance. An understanding of the James-Lange theory will help him here in two ways. In rehearsal it will help him to select the right activities; for at the moment when his imagination is most active and his bodily responses most instinctively true, the surge of real emotion will tell him that he has, so to speak, hit the target. In performance, it will help him to

recreate the same mood by repeating as accurately as possible the same actions. It is surprising how much of the imaginative situation, if not the actual emotion, can be recalled in this way, even when the actor feels out of sorts before the performance begins.

Finally, the actor can learn from the James-Lange theory the importance of coördinating bodily movements with lines as early as possible, and of acting—really acting—at rehearsals.

Unfortunately the latter is a lesson many actors refuse to learn. There is some excuse perhaps for the oldsters, for they naturally dislike to violate the hallowed tradition learned in their youth. The tradition in question originated, of course, in the days of classic repertory, when rehearsals were held primarily to refresh the memories of actors already familiar with the play, and to give them any changes of business dictated by the visiting star. It is not strange that under those conditions experienced actors forebore to extend themselves at rehearsal in what would have seemed an unnecessary display of emotionalism or virtuosity. Even so, one may suspect that they were partly actuated by a kind of false pride, a self-conscious fear of being thought unprofessional or uncertain of their powers. But when a modern company is learning a new play—especially a modern play which does not depend upon poetry and declamation—there is no excuse for postponing all acting until the first public performance. To do so is to reduce the so-called rehearsals to the status of memory drills, and to make the first few performances the real rehearsals. This is not only a stupid waste of time, but is unsound in principle and practice; and for amateurs who are to give but one or two performances it is absurd. The most important function of rehearsals is to give opportunity for imaginative experiment, for developing those totalities of action out of which emotions arise, and for coördinating word and action, mind and body, into more or less habitual and reliable forms of expression.

CUMULATIVE EXCITATION

Neither emotions nor the actions which engender them are single, isolated experiences. They are links in a chain of experiences, and each plays its part in shaping the chain as a whole. When the actor, either by instinct or accident, responds to a situation with a totality of activities that results in a conscious emotion, that emotion affects his subsequent behavior. If not so extreme as to weaken his self-control it serves as a kind of reinspiration, stimulating his imagination, enlarging his conception of the character, and shutting out distractions. Emotions and moods are thus cumulative; they can be built up through exercise. Each emotion is the

result of certain motor activities, which in turn result from certain stimuli; but it may also serve as the cause of heightened imaginative sensibilities, which in turn produce fresh stimuli, leading to fresh responses and more emotional realization.

It was this principle, in effect, that was so early discovered by our savage ancestors, and put into practice in their war-dance ceremonials and other activities for self-excitation; and it is still understood—or at any rate practiced—by the child working himself up into a tantrum. The war dance is nothing in the world but a method of creating certain desired emotions by going through the actions associated with them. To insure his behaving properly in the real battle, despite the stress of fear or distraction, the savage acts out his part experimentally in the ceremonial which serves as a rehearsal. Subject to certain established conventions, he does this realistically and with imaginative conviction, undeterred by self-consciousness over the resulting emotion. He knows perfectly well that this is a more effective and reliable preparation than he could get by walking calmly through the positions dictated by custom or strategy, and reciting in mechanical undertones the war cries with which he is expected later to terrorize the enemy.

Why, then, should a modern actor suppose that walking through the business of a play and reciting in mechanical undertones will prepare him to act with conviction or fire, or even with reliability? A sublime egotist, superbly confident of his own genius, might suppose so; but as such a person is very unlikely to be reading a book on acting I need not address my observations to him. When a normal, reasonably well-balanced young actor persuades himself that he cannot act at rehearsals, it is usually because he has yielded to laziness, or false pride, or to that self-conscious fear of display that we sometimes miscall modesty.

It is true, of course, that there is some stimulus to the imagination in the presence of an audience, and that some very good actors find it difficult to act without one. They should remember Garrick's famous statement: "If you cannot give a speech, or make love, to a table, chair or marble as well as to the finest woman in the world, you are not, nor ever will be, a great actor!" And if an audience still seems needed at rehearsal, why not invite a few good listeners to a rehearsal, and call it a rehearsal? Why sell tickets for a rehearsal and call it a performance? Since the material success of a production is often determined by the reaction of the first two or three paying audiences, this practice is not even good business. It is certainly not good art.

The unwillingness to act at rehearsals is a characteristic of third-rate

actors; the great ones, like Garrick, have generally been less temperamental about it, though some have pretended to be more casual than they really were. Charlotte Cushman, for example, is quoted by her chief biographer, Emma Stebbins, as saying that she was content to get the general sense of her part at rehearsals; but my own grandmother, who was on the stage for forty-five years, used to say that the most stirring piece of acting she ever saw was a portrayal of Lady Macbeth, in the banquet scene, done at rehearsal, in street dress, by that same Charlotte Cushman. The great English actor, Macready, was outspoken on the subject. "Frequently," he says in his *Reminiscences*, "when I have given certain directions to actors rehearsing, the answer has been, 'Sir, I never can act at rehearsal, but I will do it at night.' To which I had only one reply: 'Sir, if you cannot do it in the morning, you cannot do it at night!' "

On the whole, we can well afford to take a lesson from our war-dancing forefathers on the cumulative effect of emotional response. As built up through whole-hearted and repeated acting at rehearsals it can be one of the most important means of controlling artistically the emotional experiences of the audience.

EMOTION AND THE ÆSTHETIC BALANCE

It is not, as we have seen, a matter of ultimate importance whether the actor feels emotion or not; his object is to induce emotion empathically in his audience. But to do so he must induce in them physical reactions which will be felt as emotions; and to do that he must suggest those reactions by his own physical behavior. When he does so correctly they will feel the emotions; and so, in all probability, will he.

On the other hand, as we have seen, the emotions of the audience must not be allowed to run away with them, destroying the balance between empathy and æsthetic distance. When the actor himself begins to feel his emotional responses overcoming him, he may well consider whether the audience is not having the same experience empathically. If so, it is his business to regain self-control and reëstablish his own æsthetic balance, to the end that that of the audience may be preserved.

"But," says the young actor, "if my acting is true to life, according to the James-Lange theory I will feel the emotions; and if I do not feel the emotions it is a sign that my acting is not true. How then can I restrain my own emotions except by restricting or falsifying my actions? And if I do that, how can I escape restricting or falsifying the empathies of my audience?"

The answer is that some limitation of audience response is implied in the

whole idea of æsthetic distance; and there can be no objection to such a degree of restriction as corresponds to the actor's own sense of detachment, provided his detachment is really that of æsthetic distance and not that of indifference or incompetence. Actually the listeners will feel a little more empathy and a little less restraint than the actor; for having no technical responsibilities they can sit back in the darkness, forget their surroundings, and yield themselves up to the story imaginatively, while the actor has to remember his lines, actions, and positions on the stage, and his technique of projection. This does not necessarily mean that the listeners are perpetually on the verge of losing their distance and being overcome by emotion; after all, they are merely feeling as empathic motor patterns what the actor is actually doing on the stage, and they are separated from him by light, space, and elevation. But it does mean that the actor can afford to keep his activities under reasonable control without danger of failing to stir up adequate emotions in his audience—provided he has imaginative sincerity and conviction.

In the study of emotion in acting one should beware of the constant temptation to forget the dual function of the actor, and to assume that we are dealing only with a single set of emotions. The actor should remind himself frequently that the character's emotions may be different from his own, and differently expressed. Emotionally, the character may be utterly unlike himself; yet the actor must contrive to understand the character's emotions imaginatively, and make them empathically evident to the audience. This does not necessarily exclude the actor's own emotions; but they should be his emotions *as artist*, and should not be confused with the emotions of the character. A great deal of the popular nonsense about emotional acting would disappear through its own absurdity if we kept reminding ourselves that the actor's emotions and the character's emotions are two different things—sometimes alike, sometimes different, and sometimes utterly opposite.

SELECTION

In acting, as in every other art, the thing which makes possible the æsthetic balance is the principle of selection.

The artist does not falsify. Sometimes he exaggerates, or distorts, for fun, or emphasis. But always he selects. He presents what is fundamentally or essentially true, but he does not present all of it. He picks out those elements which will best convey the truth, or his interpretation of the truth; and he leaves out unessential or confusing details. By doing so he creates the essential empathies that give æsthetic pleasure, and avoids

creating the unnecessary, distracting ones that would destroy æsthetic distance.

In rehearsing an emotional scene the imaginative actor finds himself in a totality of bodily response which brings with it a surge of emotional sensation. The emotional sensation, if correct, tells him that he has the right response; but if he is a good actor he does not stop there. Rather he considers what parts of his total response can best be seen or heard by the audience or successfully projected to them; and how these elements can be captured and learned, and successfully repeated at every performance. The born actor makes this selection instinctively, almost subconsciously, and never analyzes his reasons; but it is better to do it consciously than not at all. When it is done well, there is little sacrifice of essential empathies or of emotional appeal, but there is a much better maintenance of æsthetic distance.

Emotion, then, is neither a means nor an end so far as the actor himself is concerned. It is rather an incidental effect which sometimes serves as a guide to selection. What really does function as a means to good acting is imagination.

CHAPTER VI

Imagination in Acting

TO SOME people the word "imagination" implies a kind of mystic ability to conjure up something out of nothing, to invent fictitious things through sheer power of inspiration.

Such an ability is, of course, scientifically impossible. Ideas are like matter and energy. They cannot be created; they can only be transformed from one state to another. Groups of ideas can be pulled apart and re-assembled in different combinations; newly acquired ideas can be combined with old or familiar ones; old ideas can be restated in new terms. But no new idea can be conceived except in terms of elements already experienced, either directly or vicariously. Imagination is simply the power of an active, associative mind to grasp and appreciate ideas in concrete terms— that is, in terms of sights, sounds, and other sensory images. Anybody not blind can see; anybody not deaf can hear; but only the imaginative person can see in his mind's eye or hear in his mind's ear. Even he cannot do so without some stimulus, new or remembered, to suggest the image. The difference between the highly imaginative person and the relatively un-imaginative one is that the latter requires much more help from his sensory stimuli before his imagination will function, while the former seems able to seize upon the remotest and most abstract suggestion and draw from it a pageant of imaginary sights and sounds.

That a keen imagination is one of the requisites of good acting hardly needs to be said. Without imagination no actor could visualize a fictitious character and bring that character to life on the stage. One of the first concerns of the young actor, therefore, is to train and develop his imagi-native powers to the utmost. To that end, there are at least two things he can do. He can cultivate the habit of observation, and he can increase the associative powers of his mind.

The much-discussed "Stanislavsky system," as set forth in his book *An Actor Prepares*, is concerned very largely with the cultivation of the actor's imagination through observation and association. For the American reader the system is made to seem extraordinarily complex and difficult—partly because the translation into English of Russian thought processes is always

difficult; partly because the author uses a fictional method of presentation in which the student telling the story is made to scramble every scene with convenient stupidity, so that the all-wise director "Tortsov" can brilliantly unscramble it; and partly because he surrounds the whole art of acting with an awesome atmosphere of mystic elaboration. Like the baseball player who would rather make an easy catch look difficult than make a hard one look easy, he does not analyze in order to simplify; he analyzes in order to complicate. He labels many phases of imagination with special names, such as "emotion memory," "communion," "the unbroken line," the "super-objective," the "threshold of the subconscious," and so on; and he suggests many well-known and practical exercises for developing the powers of observation, association, and imaginative control in a manner to imply that they are new discoveries in occult science. He emphasizes the value of practice in improvisation as a means of stimulating imagination, and nobody who knows the tradition of the *Commedia dell' Arte*, or who ever saw James Watt Raine and his Berea Players work up a folk play through improvisation would fail to concur. But he does not let us see, as clearly as he might, that his whole book is about the development of imagination—not about a "system" of acting. Stanislavsky himself was one of the best actors I ever saw in his own special line of work, and it was mainly because he was so simply and sincerely imaginative.

Stanislavsky's method (or any other thorough method) of developing imagination through constant practice in observation, association, characterization, improvisation, and acting in rehearsal, is highly to be recommended. Stanislavsky, of course, concentrates on the particular type of restrained inner realism for which the Moscow Art Theatre is famous; and very different methods might be needed to train the imaginative attitudes required for more projective, or stylized, or abstract types of acting. But whatever the variation in emphasis, the first steps in developing imaginativeness are the cultivation of observation and the heightening of the associative power.

The Habit of Observation

Since we build our imaginative concepts out of elements which we have observed, it is clear that the scope of our imagination will depend upon our store of observational experiences.

Unfortunately, many of us are poor observers, and so fail to accumulate adequate stores of such experiences, sufficiently clear and vivid to be drawn upon. Ask a friend to draw, from memory, a sketch of his own front door, or to tell you the exact color of his wife's eyes, or to recall and

whistle a tune that was popular last month, or to describe the pattern of his living-room rug, and he will probably confess embarrassment and defeat. Among the thousands of sights and sounds in a day's experience—some of them very familiar—we note carefully only a few, giving to the rest such scant attention that they do not remain available in our memories for recall. We think we have observed them, and are often much surprised and crestfallen to discover how helpless we are when asked to reproduce them as actual images.

It is entirely natural and inevitable that this should be so. Life is far too complex, too full of experiences, for us to observe and remember them all. We must select and reject, retaining the impressions that interest us most, and allowing the rest to slip away. But there are degrees in such matters. Some people can retain more and clearer impressions than others; and nearly any one can learn to retain more than his naturally lazy habits would ordinarily cause him to retain. It is partly a matter of vigorous self-discipline—a persistent determination to stay awake—and partly a matter of intelligent method, based on analysis of the methods of others.

The things we observe best are the things that interest us most. The woman interested in clothing has an uncanny ability to observe every detail of another woman's costume in the twinkling of an eye, and to remember it for hours, or even weeks; while a mere man could not tell you five minutes afterwards whether the prevailing color of the costume was red, blue, or yellow. On the other hand any normal modern young man can distinguish at a glance the various makes and models of automobiles or airplanes, because he has observed them keenly. A person interested in geography and maps can tell you where he is at any moment on a long journey, and remember places in their proper relation for a long time; while one who lacks that interest will lose all track of his whereabouts and be content to live in a kind of geographical fog. Every one is observing in his own way; but the person who is observing in the largest number of ways is the one whose memory is best stocked with images.

It follows that the best way to cultivate the power of observation is to increase the number and variety of one's interests.

There are people, of course, who deliberately refrain from doing this for fear of diffusing their abilities and losing the power of concentration. From one point of view they may be right. If one cannot take an interest in many things without becoming a superficial dabbler, a mere skimmer of surfaces, it may be wiser for him to stick to his own specialty. But variety of interest is not necessarily diffusion of interest; it is only so when the individual lacks the intensity of mind necessary to give keen, curious, whole-hearted at-

tention to many things—to live the mental "strenuous life," and to become, like Theodore Roosevelt, a jack of all trades and a master of many.

Certainly the actor—whose profession "comprehends the whole system of human life"—must be a passable journeyman of all trades in order to be master of one. He, of all persons, should somehow contrive to take an observant interest in almost everything, especially everything involving human values and affecting the development of character. The person with a single-track mind, and a narrow, intensive curiosity in one field only, may become a master of some trade; but it will not be acting.

Diversity of interest is, therefore, the first requisite of good observation. It is not, however, the only one. A second essential is accuracy.

Not all poor acting is due to the actor's lack of interest in the life about him; some of it is due to amazingly inaccurate observation of familiar things. When an actor acquires the habit of observing freely, but inaccurately, he may develop a kind of lively imagination, but it will be a false imagination. He may have a vivid mental picture of the character or situation, but it will not be a true picture; either it will deceive the audience into a mistaken conception of the character, or they will recognize it as untrue and unconvincing, and it will not deceive them at all.

An actor who does not play golf, for example, may ruin his whole portrayal of a golfer by the way he swings his club, or hands his bag to a caddy. He has seen others do these things, but has not observed accurately how they do them; and every golfer in the audience instantly detects the inaccuracy. An actor who does not smoke (if such can be found) is likely to betray himself by the way he holds or lights a cigar on the stage. An actress who is not a typist may give herself away to every typist in the audience when she pretends to operate a typewriter on the stage. Time and again a player will reveal, not only a lack of accomplishment but a lack of reasonably accurate observation, by the way he or she portrays a doctor or nurse examining a patient, a waiter carrying a tray, a cowboy handling a gun, a tennis player wielding a racket, a housewife sewing or knitting, a mother holding a child, a mechanic handling his tools, or a musician fingering an instrument.

But accuracy in the observation of mechanical details is only part of the problem. Important as it is, it is less so than accuracy in the observation of fundamental truths about human character and behavior.

One of the chief faults in a great deal of professional acting today is that the lesser Broadway actor has too much opportunity to observe Broadway and too little to observe more normal life. His contacts are too largely with other actors, who are at best a little artificial. He observes too many

objective mannerisms, too many professional stereotypes, too many people putting on a front and concealing their inner natures. He observes too few human beings in the more natural and more basic situations of life. In consequence, his acting is often superficially clever, brittle, mechanically accurate, rather than fundamentally sound and sympathetic. He knows very well how people look, how they talk, walk, stand, sit down, get up, read, write, and do a thousand other things in public—especially on Broadway; but he does not always know how they react to the deeper emotional experiences or conflicts of ideas, or how they really feel when they succeed in concealing their reactions from the superficial observer.

To be sure it is often lack of opportunity to observe, rather than inaccurate observation, that accounts for such ignorance. But audiences make no allowance for that. After all, it is the actor's job to observe, and he must find the opportunity. He has no business to portray human beings on the stage if he cannot contrive to learn how human beings think, feel, and act.

It is worth noting that observation is keener and memory more trustworthy when the motor activities are involved. We remember a thing better and more accurately when we have done it ourselves than when we have merely seen others do it. The actor should welcome, therefore, every opportunity to take part in unfamiliar activities; and when actual participation is impossible he should strive to empathize as strongly and freely as possible in observing the activities of others. Those who have felt things empathically will remember them better and recall them more imaginatively than those whose observation has been purely objective. And those who have participated in activities involving a totality of response with sufficient imaginativeness to feel the corresponding emotional repercussions, will remember best of all, because they will have what Stanislavsky calls "emotion memory"—that is, imaginative memory of the emotions as well as of the facts.

THE POWER OF ASSOCIATION

Imagination depends upon two things: the presence of the image in experience, and the associative link by which it is recalled to consciousness. Abundant and accurate observation builds up the stock of experience stored away in the memory, but it does not necessarily insure a free and responsive use of that experience for imaginative purposes. Only the associative mind makes adequate use of its own potentialities in this respect. One may be a keen observer, and may file away a vast number of memory images; but lacking active association of ideas he will keep most of these

treasures in their own pigeonholes, hidden from his consciousness and for all practical purposes forgotten, while he goes on living a placid, objective, day-to-day existence, untroubled by imaginative repercussions. No doubt one can achieve a kind of happiness that way, but he can hardly learn to act.

To become a highly imaginative person, in the way in which actors must be imaginative, one must cultivate a keen sense of the relationship among the things observed, so that one thing will suggest another, and whole floods of images will come surging up into consciousness on the slightest excuse.

This associative power, like the power of observation, is a matter of habit, and can be strengthened in practice. The trouble with most of us is that we pigeonhole our ideas in separate compartments of the mind, keeping one compartment for family, one for business, one for pleasure, and so on, with little or no interrelation. The schools and colleges help to teach us this bad habit by excessive departmentalization. The student learns mathematics in one room from one teacher, history in another from another teacher, and literature in a third, from a third teacher; and he puts each subject completely aside and out of mind as he goes to the next. The result is specialized rather than coördinated thinking. To strengthen his associative powers he needs more comparative or coördinating courses and more conference and discussion; out of school he needs more indulgence in comparative reading and study, more intellectual curiosity, more informal browsing, more literary detective work.

If this seems a bit vague, let me illustrate with some specific suggestions. Let the person who would develop a lively association of ideas go to a library, not to get a book, but to study the cross-referencing system. Let him spend an hour a week on the library catalogue, and another on the periodical indices and readers' guides, just looking up cross references and comparing the various sources and classifications of material. Let him handle the books on the reference shelves, comparing them as to scope and emphasis. Let him look up some words that have bothered him, not in one dictionary, or encyclopedia, but in half a dozen. Let him browse a little in the dictionaries of quotations, of phrase and fable, and especially of similes —for nothing is more stimulating to the associative powers than a good simile. Let him discover the fascination and amusement of comparing synonyms in Roget's *Thesaurus of English Words and Phrases*, and of looking up etymologies. Let him take some event in history, such as the outbreak of a certain war, and study it successively as a problem in chronology, in mass psychology, in the philosophy of history, in economics, in sociology,

in political science, and in military science. Let him read a book or article on the principles of design and find parallel illustrations for each principle from painting, etching, sculpture, architecture, music, literature, drama, scenic art, furniture making, dressmaking, millinery, and landscape gardening. When he has taken, or is about to take, a journey, let him trace it out comparatively on a railroad map, a relief map, and several highway maps; and let him read up the region in a good geography and a good history. In short, let him follow any line of mental activity that forces him to associate ideas which might ordinarily be buried in separate compartments of the mind.

Such a program will make no appeal to the type of Broadway actor who, according to DeWolfe Hopper, "never reads a book unless he has written it himself or is looking to see if his name has been mentioned." But it does provide a method by which an exceptional young man or woman, determined to learn acting thoroughly, may help to achieve the associative power which, coupled with keen observation, tends to enlarge and strengthen the imagination.

IMAGINATION IN CHARACTER STUDY

Valuable as such general exercises may be, the actor will sooner or later have to concentrate more specifically on the imaginative realization of the character he is to play, and of the situations in which the character finds himself.

The most natural approach to this study is a program of self-questioning: Who is this character? How old is he? Where was he born? What were his parents like? In what kind of an environment did he grow up? How would he have reacted to it? Is he introvert or extrovert? Coarse or refined? Visionary or practical? Kind or unkind? . . . and so on, as exhaustively as possible. To some of the questions the author may have given the answer, or implied it. To others, the actor will have to find his own imaginative answers; but unless he asks himself the questions he is not very likely to think of the answers. The difference between an unimaginative and a highly imaginative characterization often lies in the fact that in the first instance the actor has not bothered to ask any questions, but has merely spoken the words set down for him without any curiosity about their background and implications.

In any such program of self-questioning, the actor must be sure to ask subjective questions as well as objective ones. He must know not only what the character has done and what has happened to him, but what he thinks and how he feels about it. He must build up his imaginative concept

in terms of mental and emotional images as well as physical and factual ones. And having formed his concept he must rehearse the imagery over and over again, building his memory of the part imaginatively and perfecting his "emotion memory" as well as his verbal and factual memory.

This is never easy, and is particularly difficult at rehearsals as they are all too frequently conducted. When the actor and his comrades are groping uncertainly for their lines and positions against a restless background of interruptions from the director, changes in movement and position, arguments about this or that, hammering and shouting by the crew, side conferences of various kinds, and endless comings and goings, it takes a tough imagination to remain concentrated and sincere. The young actor, therefore, should make up his mind that he will have to do a great deal of his creative imagining when he is studying his part alone, especially during the earlier weeks of rehearsal.

Some of these problems will be considered more fully in later chapters. For the present we are concerned with the importance and the more general aspects of imagination.

IMAGINATION IN PERFORMANCE

The importance of imagination in acting is by no means limited to its function in helping the actor to visualize and develop his characterization in rehearsal. A lively imagination is also the most essential requisite for a vital, convincing performance.

As already suggested in the discussion of emotion, a great deal of the turmoil over the question of the actor's feeling his part would subside at once if we could agree upon imagination, rather than emotion, as the *sine qua non* of fine acting.

When an actor depicts a character in fear or anguish, it does not matter whether he feels fear or anguish emotionally; if he does, it is the result, not the cause, of his realism. What does matter is that he shall be able to *imagine* fear or anguish, vividly and accurately, and in terms of the particular character he is portraying; and to do it at every performance.

It is obvious that different people reveal the same emotion in different ways. Take for example the emotion of grief. A highly repressed and self-controlled person may register grief by a strong, expressionless countenance. An equally repressed but more intense person may show a drawn expression about the eyes and a tendency to bite his lips. A strongly emotional but inarticulate person may break into uncontrolled sobbing. An equally emotional but loquacious person—of Latin type perhaps—may indulge in loud and voluble lamentations. A nervous or hysterical person may

sob and laugh by turns; and a cynical one may cover his grief entirely by bitter laughter.

The actor who abandons himself to real emotion in performance, is likely to reveal that emotion in just one way—his own. The less imaginative he is, the more completely limited he will be to the playing of one part— that of himself.

On the other hand, an actor whose imagination is vivid in performance can project himself into the character, and can portray that character's way of revealing emotion even though it be entirely different from his own. When he does this successfully, he may feel the emotion himself, in accordance with the James-Lange theory; but he will feel it empathically, rather than personally, and in a limited way, and will be able to preserve his æsthetic distance and his self-control.

The power of a really imaginative actor to stir the imaginations of his audience is out of all proportion to his physical technique. An observant and discriminating friend of mine, who has been an ardent theatre-goer for three generations, in jotting down for me some notes about Sir Henry Irving, said, "It is certainly a tribute to his genius that with a queer voice, queer legs, often awkward gestures, and a funny walk, he could somehow make you forget all this and, as in Charles the First, give you the notion that you were looking at Van Dyke's portrait of him, whereas it was no such thing."

When a play is to be repeated through many performances, the importance of imagination grows. Even if we grant—which I, personally, do not—that an actor may give an inspired first performance by abandoning himself to uncontrolled emotion in a part much like himself, it is still true that he cannot hope to repeat this inspiration with any sort of reliability, for five, or fifty, or five hundred performances. Emotion wears down with familiarity. But imagination builds up; and it is quite possible for an actor to be even more imaginative after several performances than he was in the first. The relief from strain and self-consciousness that comes after several performances tends to free his imagination and give it scope; and the reactions of the audience stimulate his imagination when it is true and check it when it is false, so that his fiftieth or sixtieth performance may well be his most vivid.

To re-state, therefore, the simplest and most important thing that can be said about acting: It is not emotional sensibility, or temperament, or inspiration, that makes an actor; but a lively, flexible, and well-controlled imagination.

CHAPTER VII

The Actor and the Play

U P TO this point I have been discussing, in somewhat abstract terms, what might be described as the philosophy of acting. It is time, now, to consider some of the definite problems faced by the modern actor in beginning work on a particular play.

His first problem is that of the proper attitude to assume toward the play and the production as a whole. Shall he concern himself only with his own part, or shall he accept some responsibility for understanding the plot, theme, and action, and adjusting his part to the author's purpose?

A surprisingly large number of actors, especially second-rate professionals, decline to interest themselves at all in the play as a whole. With some this is a matter of laziness, indifference, or lack of intellectual curiosity. With others it is a matter of misguided loyalty to an unfortunate tradition—a tradition which originated in the old stock-company days, when actors had to learn their parts hastily, from "sides" rather than books, and with so few rehearsals that they had no opportunity to find out what the play was about until the week's run was nearly over. With still others it is a matter of inspired egotism; they concentrate upon their own parts with such unrestrained enthusiasm that the rest of the play seems to them nothing more than unimportant background. With all of these groups the choice is more accidental than logical, and calls for no serious discussion.

THE BLISSFUL IGNORANCE THEORY

There are some actors, however—including some very intelligent ones—who have a definite and conscious theory that it is better not to know too much about the play. They believe that the actor who knows only his own part can remain more consistently within the character; that he is less likely to be betrayed into false emotions and insincerities through extraneous knowledge of what has happened in his supposed absence, or what is going to happen in later scenes; that in his ignorance of what the other characters are thinking, doing, and saying, he can better preserve in his

own character what William Gillette so illuminatingly called "the illusion of the first time."[1]

An opinion so well thought out is entitled to respectful consideration. Certainly there are elements of truth in it. But they are based, I think, upon a very limited conception of the actor's art. They are based, in fact, upon the idea that acting is simply objective impersonation; upon the actor's function as instrument to the exclusion of his function as artist.

Not knowing what the play is about may perhaps help the actor to seem objectively like the character in the same way that being blind or lame may help him to portray a blind or lame character accurately, or being stupid may help him to portray stupidity. But these things do not help him to share with his audience that wise and sympathetic appreciation of the author's meaning which is expected of the true artist. They may help him to read a line or perform an action as the character would do it in real life, but they do not help him to let his audience know, subjectively, what the author desires them to think of that line or action.

In other words, if we are to justify the blissful ignorance theory we must deny the dual function of the actor, and accept the idea that realistic impersonation is the sole end in acting.

Even if we do accept it, it is still doubtful whether the end can be attained in this way. Suppose the actor does try to remain within the character and to be ignorant of whatever the character would not know; he can never be more than partly successful. In repeated rehearsals and performances he is bound to pick up something of what is going on; and at the very least he must know his own lines, and his cues. While pretending ignorance or uncertainty in Act I, he cannot help knowing, in reality, what is going to happen in Act III. The "illusion of the first time" is, after all, illusion, except at the first rehearsal; and it can be maintained only through effective use of the imagination. The actor who can best portray innocence, or stupidity, or surprise, therefore, is not necessarily the one who knows so little of the play that he is really innocent or stupid or surprised about it; it is rather the one whose imagination is so vivid and consistent that he can create at will the illusion of being innocent or stupid or surprised. In attempting to depend upon reality rather than imagination, an actor may succeed only in weakening his imagination.

Despite its plausibility, therefore, I do not hesitate to condemn the blissful ignorance theory as unsound. Assuming that the actor wishes to be, not just an impersonator, but a real actor and a real artist, I believe that he should seek to know as much as possible about the plot, theme,

[1] See his article under that title in *Publications of the Dramatic Museum*, Columbia University.

mood, style, and technique of the play as a whole, and to know it as early as possible in rehearsals.

THE ACTOR AND THE PLOT

The plot of a play is ordinarily the story of a conflict or struggle between two contending forces—one concrete and personal, as symbolized by the hero or protagonist; the other relatively abstract and universal. In a long play there are complicating circumstances which for a time render the outcome of the conflict more and more uncertain. At last a climax is reached and the action takes its final turn for better or for worse. This climax may occur some time before the conclusion, or it may be almost simultaneous with the conclusion.

When the particular force succumbs to the universal and the protagonist is finally defeated, the play is technically a tragedy. Ordinarily a tragedy deals with serious matters of life and death, the more profoundly serious the better. We do not care, as a rule, to endure the disappointment of a tragic ending without the compensating effect of elevation that comes to us in the contemplation of great emotional forces. There is one technical exception to this rule in the catastrophic farce—that is, the play which is technically a tragedy in that the hero meets disaster, but which deals with such absurd caricatures and situations that we do not take him or his troubles seriously, or care what happens to him. Slapstick and pie-throwing farces are frequently of this class. But real tragedy is seldom successful in the middle ground of everyday life and trivial unspectacular struggle. It demands the pity and terror of great crises in the lives and emotions of great characters.

When the particular force prevails over the universal—that is, when the protagonist triumphs over his obstacles or adversaries—the play is technically a comedy. If it deals with serious or dangerous situations it is a comedy-drama, melodrama, or tragicomedy; if it deals with the humorous aspects of life it is a comedy in the more usual sense; if it deals with preposterous absurdities it is a farce or farce-comedy.

There is a great deal of discussion, if not dispute, as to the exact dividing line between comedy and farce; the most commonly accepted distinction is that for comedy both the characters and the situations must be within the bounds of probability, while for farce one or the other (and perhaps both) may be preposterously unbelievable. A still more difficult distinction is that between high and low comedy. One view is that low comedy portrays the clownishness of stupid, ignorant, or low-caste characters, and high comedy the wit and humor of gentility. A rather more helpful idea

is that low comedy is frankly intentional fun-making, and high comedy the seemingly unintentional humor of characters not trying to be funny. But perhaps the best distinction of all is based on the notion that low comedy makes use of extraneous methods, such as exaggerated mannerisms or make-up, distorted voice or language, comic stage business, and the like, while high comedy draws its humorous effects from the actual meaning of the lines, or the essentially amusing situations in which the characters find themselves.

One advantage of the last distinction is that it can be applied to farce as well as comedy. *The Taming of the Shrew*, for example, is often classed as one of the world's greatest farces; but there are two ways of playing it. If the emphasis is all on the physical humor of Petruchio's boisterous antics, and the assumption is made that Katherine is cowed and tamed by the impact of extraneous violence, you have a low farce. But if the director and the players are discerning enough to see, through the lines themselves, that Katherine, unlike any other member of her family or any of her previous suitors, has a sense of humor, and that what really tames her is her discovery of a kindred sense in Petruchio which allows her to join him in laughing inwardly at her own predicament and to share with him the joke on her humorless relatives, the result is what might be called a high farce.

It is part of the dramatist's business to make clear the plot construction of his play, and its comic or tragic intent; to see that his climax is clearly defined, that the action rises to the climax, and descends thereafter; and to strengthen the effect by a certain amount of "finger posting" to foreshadow the ultimate turn of the plot. It is the business of the director to understand these things and to bring them out in the production; and up to a certain point it is his responsibility to see that the actors interpret their parts in harmony with the author's plan.

But the individual actor should share the responsibility. He should understand the nature of the plot conflict, and know with which side his own character is identified. He should know the nature and position of the climax and should distinguish the rising from the falling action. He should understand the author's method of dramatic foreshadowing, and should study how his own playing can contribute to it. He should grasp the factual details of plot and subplot, and should see to it that his own characterization fits in with them. He should note especially, scene by scene, how much the character is supposed to know of what is going on, and should be careful not to anticipate such knowledge. He should comprehend the

plot significance of every line or action in the play, and its possible relation
to his own part. Above all he should note which of his own lines are essential to an understanding of the plot, and should point them up to insure
their being heard and understood by the audience.

THE ACTOR AND THE THEME

More important sometimes than the plot is the theme of a play—the
abstract thought, or message, or philosophy behind the story. Some plays,
it is true, have no themes that can be distinguished from their plots; but
many fine plays, especially of a subjective or a satirical nature, have
themes so different from their plots that they may be totally misinterpreted
if the themes are not understood.

The plot of *Macbeth* is the story of a murder leading to other murders
and to ultimate death for the murderer; the theme is the degeneration of
character under the influence of ambition. The plot of *Hamlet* is concerned
with a young man's effort to identify and punish the murderer of his
father; the theme is the weakening effect of doubt and procrastination.
The plot of Tchekhov's *The Cherry Orchard* is the unsuccessful attempt of
a broken-down family of aristocrats to save their estate from being sold at
auction; the theme is the degenerating impact of social change on character. The plot of O'Neill's *Mourning Becomes Electra* is the story of a New
England girl's effort to avenge her father's murder; the theme would seem
to be the relentless immortality of the Greek Electra.

The theme is ordinarily much more difficult to grasp and analyze than
the plot. One can discover the plot of any ordinary play by reading the
play; but to understand the theme it is often necessary to know something
of the author's attitude and outlook on life, as reflected in his biography
and his other works. Sometimes there is great difference of opinion as to
the author's meaning and the proper interpretation of his theme; and if
he is not living and at hand to settle the controversy, there may be no
perfect solution to the problem. In such cases it is the director who must
ultimately interpret for his particular production; but it is important for
the actor to know the director's interpretation as early as possible, since it
will affect his own interpretation of his part.

It is the theme, when there is one, even more than the plot, which de-
termines the tone of the acting. If the plot of a play is romantic or sentimental but the theme satirical, some of the satirical flavor must creep into
the acting; else the audience will take the romantic or sentimental meaning
and miss the theme altogether. If the plot is trifling or absurd but the au-

thor intends to imply an undercurrent of wisdom or philosophy, the actor must somehow grasp that wisdom or philosophy and help convey it to his audience. It is just another manifestation of the dual function. Objectively he helps portray the plot; subjectively he shares with the audience his appreciation of the theme. .

In a charming little unpublished play by Albert Earl Robinson called *The Week-End of a Pirate*, for example, we have what appears on the surface to be just a medley of naïve romance and farcical absurdity. A swashbuckling pirate of 1726 returns to his home in Jamaica for a week end with "the little woman" in celebration of their twentieth wedding anniversary. He brings with him a young and handsome gentleman whom he has captured, and for whom he hopes to obtain a ransom; but his "latest investment" promptly falls in love with the pirate's pretty niece. The way in which "the little woman" dominates her bloodthirsty husband at home while youthful romance upsets his business arrangements is very amusing and fairly obvious in its farcical intent. But there is an underlying satirical intent which is not so obvious. The theme is really the split personality of the eternal business man—cold-blooded, impersonal, objectively fair, but utterly ruthless in his business dealings, while at the same time so kind and affable at home and off duty that he "wouldn't hurt a fly."

It is easy for the actors in this play to grasp the plot and action, the romance and the farce, and to make the audience laugh at preposterous incidents and witty lines. But precisely because the underlying satire is so sly and unobtrusive, the two casts I have seen work with it were not quite successful in conveying its full import to the audience. The theme is not written directly into the lines, but is merely hinted at by implication, and it could only be felt by the audience if the actors were so keenly amused at the satire as to keep it constantly alive in their own minds, responding to it subjectively as artists while functioning objectively as instruments of robust entertainment. A little rewriting might help, but too much would destroy the subtlety of the theme. Nothing could really make this play "click" but superb theme acting.

Many plays have this baffling thematic quality—most of Barrie's, for example. *Dear Brutus, Mary Rose, A Kiss for Cinderella*, and *The Admirable Crichton* all masquerade as more or less romantic comedies, but all turn on the tragic theme of human incapacity or unwillingness to rise above the problems of life and environment. Actors who miss a Barrie theme may give us an entertaining play, but it will not be the play that Barrie wrote.

THE ACTOR AND THE MOOD

The duty of the actor to understand and convey the mood of his own part is obvious to the most casual theatre-goer, but his duty to the mood of the play as a whole may not be so obvious.

In a play which has a definite theme, the mood may be said to belong to the theme, or to be identical with it. But many a play which has no discoverable theme, has at least a dominating mood, or succession of moods, expressing the author's emotional attitude towards his material. This larger mood or succession of moods is often ignored by the inferior actor, in favor of what he conceives to be the mood of his part.

A good actor will coöperate with the director in bringing out the mood of the play, and the mood of each scene. In order to do so he must understand just what bearing the mood of his character has upon the mood of the scene. In one case he may find that the character he portrays is the instrument of the author's attitude—that the author has somehow identified himself with that character and is speaking through him. In another case he may find that his own character is rather a foil, designed to set off the dominant mood by contrast.

It is the latter case, rather than the former, that calls for the keenest understanding and the highest technical skill. When all the characters in a play, or a scene, share the same mood with the author, it is a very insensitive actor indeed who cannot feel that mood and fit in with it. But when his job is to intensify the mood of a scene by creating a contrasting one, it is not so easy, for that sort of thing must be done with just the right degree of exaggeration.

In *The Show-Off*, by George Kelly, a whole play is built around such a contrast. Aubrey Piper, the principal character, is a jarring note in the lives of the other characters, and in the mood of the author and the audience. To create the right blend of sympathy, annoyance, and ironical amusement in the mood of the audience, the actor who plays Aubrey must exaggerate his boisterous egotism considerably beyond real life; yet he must not carry it to the point of unconvincing farce, nor to the point at which the exasperation becomes painful. The actor who played the part in one of the earliest productions was an old musical-comedy comedian, and he committed both faults. He exaggerated the farcical antics of the character, causing the frivolous members of the audience to laugh inanely at the wrong times; and he made the character so unpleasantly asinine that Amy's love for him became unbelievable. I later saw a comparatively un-

known player do this part with more understanding; he played with enough exaggeration to be funny, and to explain the family's irritation at him, yet he never became entirely unconvincing and he managed to preserve a little suggestion of the glamour and charm which had first attracted Amy to him. Not that Aubrey was a pleasant character in either case; but in the one his mood was entirely independent of the play, while in the other it was intelligently keyed to just the right degree of contrast.

In the professional theatre it is not at all unusual for the star to play in a mood that fails to key in with that of the play. It happened, for example, in *Erstwhile Susan*, the Pennsylvania Dutch comedy based on Helen Martin's novel *Barnabetta*, and originally played by the late Mrs. Fiske. In her production the play was treated as a farcical burlesque, with Susan completely out of key, not only in characterization but in mood of playing; it was theatrically effective, but in no way important or convincing. Since then I have seen three other casts play it in a more restrained spirit, each actor shaping the mood of his part to fit the author's intention, with the result that the whole became fairly human and convincing—just as humorous as in the original, but more sympathetically so, and actually a better and truer play than the text itself would seem to indicate.

A great deal of bad acting is bad because the mood is wrong. An actor must be constantly alert to avoid letting his own mood obtrude on that of the character, or taking his mood from other characters on the stage at the same time, or diluting the character's mood with a hang-over mood from another part. The last danger is one of the weak points in the repertory system. I once saw a production of *Twelfth Night* by a repertory theatre, and was much disturbed at the false mood of the actress playing Viola; she was missing all the humor and whimsy of that rich, delicate part, and playing it like a nun just about to take her final vows. When I learned that she had been rehearsing all day in the part of Saint Joan for a forthcoming production of the Shaw play I understood the reason. On another occasion I saw two performances of the same play a few days apart, and was mystified at the change of mood in one of the actresses playing a comedy part; on inquiry I learned that the actress, a mother in private life, had a dangerously sick child at home. Such influences on mood are fortunately only occasional, but the danger of taking mood falsely from another character is present most of the time in almost every play.

THE ACTOR AND THE STYLE

What is now generally called style in a production, especially in relation to "stylized" setting, is a matter of mode rather than mood. It is concerned

with the characteristic flavor or atmosphere, the external color or rhythm of a play, rather than its inner emotion. It is seen at its best in productions of symbolic plays, fantasies, period plays, genre plays, and especially plays for children.

The stylization may be inherent in the play or in the author's conception of its treatment, as in *The Yellow Jacket*, the imitation Chinese play by Hazelton and Benrimo; or it may be determined by the producer as a special feature of his production, and may not be indicated at all in the text—though it should not, of course, be inconsistent with the text. The Norman Bel Geddes production of *Hamlet* was highly stylized according to the taste of the producer; the same play has been stylized in quite different ways by many other producers, and has been produced number- less times with no particular attempt at stylization. *A Midsummer Night's Dream* has been stylized in many different modes, from the dainty and fairy-like, to the outlandish or grotesque.

The intelligent director today is not content to stylize the setting of a play and leave all other factors to take care of themselves. Rather he seeks a consistent agreement of style in scenery, costumes, make-up, direction, and acting. The increasing prevalence of stylized production is making it more and more necessary for the actor to grasp the purpose and intent of such production, and to learn how to key his acting to a particular mode.

If, for example, he is to play a part in *Androcles and the Lion*, and the producer decides to accentuate Shaw's tongue-in-the-cheek attitude by using grotesquely fanciful settings and costumes in loud colors, it then be- comes the actor's task to interpret his part in a similarly heightened way— to act, so to speak, in loud colors and unbelievable forms, disarming any tendency of the audience to take the play too literally.

This sort of acting calls for imagination, humor, and good taste, and is many times harder than realistic acting. It implies a clear understanding with the director concerning the style or mode of the production as a whole, and an ability on the part of the actor to adapt his acting to it consistently. In a lightly frivolous or broadly satirical play, the difficulties are not so great; but in a play that involves some genuine emotion and character- ization, the problem of sustaining both mood and mode, without detriment to either, is a troublesome one, upon which many otherwise good actors have failed badly.

The presentation of exotic plays, or period plays, involves other ques- tions of technique which may not be thought of as problems in mood or style, but which nevertheless affect the way in which a play is to be acted.

When, for instance, an eighteenth-century comedy like *The Rivals* or *The*

School for Scandal is to be acted, the modern actor finds himself confronted with a technical problem in the handling of asides and soliloquies. Shall these be spoken with the direct, communicative frankness of eighteenth-century technique? Or shall they be covered with a pretense of realism, suggesting that the character is inadvertently thinking out loud? The director must decide, but the actor should know the decision before learning his part, and should develop his whole characterization in a manner consistent with the chosen technique. When a play like *The Yellow Jacket* is to be given in the Chinese manner, the player, before learning his part, should seek to grasp the exotic spirit and precise detail of the Chinese technique, without which such a play would lose most of its interest and charm. And when, on the other hand, a repressed play is to be given with great restraint and simplicity of realism, the actor should grasp the intention early in rehearsals, and adapt his characterization to the more subdued technique.

ACTOR AND DIRECTOR

In other words the actor and the director should coöperate from the first rehearsal, and should seek to understand each other. Some directors, through stupidity or egotism, or perhaps only through lack of time, make this difficult by failing to explain their intentions to the actors; but the good actor will contrive to find out what the director is trying to do, if not by asking, at least by keeping his eyes and ears open. Sometimes, of course, the director himself does not know; in that case there can be nothing but discouragement for the conscientious actor.

When the director has, as he should have, a competent understanding of the play, and a clear idea of the manner in which he intends to produce it, and when the actor accepts his share of the responsibility, seeking from the first rehearsal to help the director realize his conception of the play as a whole, there is no earthly reason why either should conflict with the other; and there is every prospect that the actor, instead of acting an unrelated part, will, in the truest sense, be acting his part of the play.

CHAPTER VIII

The Actor and His Part

IN ADDITION to his study of the play as a whole, the actor has, of course, to consider the mastery of his own part. Here again there is a difference of opinion as to the best procedure. Shall he first memorize the lines and then rehearse for action and meaning? Or shall he postpone memorization until the details of stage movement, business, and interpretation have been worked out? There are clearly certain advantages and disadvantages in each method.

If he memorizes at once, he saves much time at rehearsals, frees himself from the awkward necessity of carrying his book, and shortens the period during which he is foggy-minded about his lines. On the other hand he runs the risk of memorizing hasty misconceptions or misinterpretations along with the part, or of fixing in his mind a mechanical and uninspired reading.

If he postpones memorization until he has had a chance to assimilate the interpretation and to coördinate lines and business he improves his chance of giving a rich, well-rounded, convincing performance; but he slows up rehearsals, hampers himself with the necessity of carrying his book, cramps the work of the other actors, and delays the final timing and polishing of the performance.

In other words, neither method is wholly satisfactory, and neither is equally suited to all conditions. The method to be used in any given case will be dictated partly by the circumstances of that case and partly by the director's preference. In stock company work, for example, when a new play is to be given each week by the same players, and only four or five rehearsals are possible, it is almost necessary that the actors commit their lines before the first rehearsal—certainly before the second. Some directors prefer this method anyhow, and insist upon it even when there is plenty of time; others prefer to take several weeks for careful blocking out, and to delay memorization until the action is clear; and still others, following the method of Stanislavsky or Frank Benson, like to keep their players studying a play informally for months, working out the interpretations

73

slowly and letting the memorization wait until it practically takes care of itself.

For the student actor, the best plan is to experiment with both methods, and with various modifications, thus fitting himself to meet different conditions and the demands of different directors.

MECHANICAL MEMORIZATION

When an actor attempts to memorize an unfamiliar part in advance of rehearsals, it is obvious that he cannot have a very clear conception of it. It is all new to him. There has been no chance to develop a feeling for the play, to visualize the situations and the other characters, or to coördinate lines and action. His best plan, therefore, is to memorize words, not meanings; to commit the text without forming premature, and perhaps false, notions concerning its interpretation.

It is well for the actor to understand this clearly, and to realize that mechanical memorization is an entirely different process from interpretative memorization, to be handled in a different way, and with a different purpose in view. The ultimate objective is, of course, the same: complete mastery of the part. But the immediate purpose is the partial and temporary one of transferring the text from the printed page to the page of memory. It is partial in the sense that it involves, not the whole physical, mental, and emotional personality, but merely one limited function of the brain. It is temporary in the sense that the mechanical words and phrases are to be later clothed in meaning. Such memorization is little more than a makeshift device to free the hands and eyes in the early rehearsals, enabling the actor to read his part from memory more fluently and with less impediment to his movements than if he were reading from the book.

It is unlikely that he will read any more intelligently or feelingly at first from the memory page than from the printed page. It is reading in either case; and reading is not acting. The wise actor will keep this in mind, and will understand that any expression he may give to his reading in the early rehearsals is tentative, to be kept flexible and subject to change as his comprehension of the meaning grows. He will seek to avoid the more or less stereotyped inflections of ordinary reading; and especially to avoid fixing them in his memory in association with the words, lest he fail to shake them off later. Instead, he will try to separate the mechanical process of memorization from the imaginative process of interpretation; to keep them apart in his own mind, and to prevent the one from interfering with the other.

Some actors are fortunate in being able to do this without any trouble,

and later to develop their interpretations in a natural and convincing manner with no trace of false or mechanical reading.

Others have a great deal of trouble. Having once memorized in mechanical fashion they remain mechanical to the end. Or, having sought to give meaning to their lines during premature memorization, they get false meanings or inflections firmly fixed in their heads and seem utterly unable to unlearn them, even when they come to know better. Sometimes they seem to unlearn them in rehearsal, but revert to them under the nervous strain of public performance. Many have great difficulty, also, in coördinating actions with words when the words are learned first, or in changing their coördinations if once learned wrong.

The only way to keep the memory process completely separate from the interpretative process in one's own mind is to exaggerate its mechanical aspects, obliterating all inflections at first, and memorizing in such utterly meaningless monotones that they cannot possibly be mistaken for anything else. If one works in this way at least until the play has begun to develop in rehearsal, he is much less likely to give an ultimately mechanical performance than if he allows himself to memorize meanings before fully grasping them.

At best, however, the mechanical method is desirable only when rehearsal time is very limited, and when the players are especially fitted for it either by talent or training.

Interpretative Memorization

For all ordinary purposes, and especially for amateur or art theatre groups to whom the rehearsing of a play is an artistic adventure and not merely a job, a more gradual process of memorization through interpretation is best.

Such memorization takes time, but in the long run it is easier, more natural, and much more reliable, because it is based on coördination. Lines, meanings, stage movements, stage business, bodily attitudes and facial expressions are worked out together in logical association. Experiments are tried and changes made before the memories become too fixed. Interpretations are enriched and technique perfected all at the same time, and without the studied synthesis that is often noticeable with the other method.

The actor who memorizes in this way is usually far more convincing in performance than the one who memorizes mechanically. Incidentally, he is much less likely to forget his lines. He does not depend upon an auditory memory alone, nor upon a visual memory of the printed page. He depends

upon a combination of memories, associating each line with his stage position, attitude, and gesture, the position and appearance of the other characters, the flow of imagination and empathic emotion, the tempo and cadence of the scene. Should his visual memory fail him at any instant, something in the sound or rhythm of the play, or something in the feeling of the action, will come to his rescue and remind him of his line. If his coördination is perfect, he will find that he can go through his part smoothly and surely even though his mind is tired or wandering. An actor of my acquaintance gave one of the best comedy performances of his life on an evening when he was worried and upset over a private matter and his conscious mind was wrestling with his troubles in a sort of melancholy daze. He could not have done so had he not perfected his coördinations through careful rehearsal and gradual, imaginative assimilation of his part.

Coördination and assimilation are the chief elements in good interpretative memorization. Assimilation means more than possession and retention. Food is not assimilated the instant it is swallowed. It must first be digested, and then, by a gradual process, absorbed into the blood, until it becomes in every sense a part of oneself. In the same way, a role must be assimilated through gradual absorption before it can become a part of the actor in the imaginative sense; before he can feel that perfect assurance without which acting never quite carries conviction. And only when lines, action, and meaning are effectively coördinated can they be so assimilated.

This suggests an important point in relation to methods of study. The actor trying to study lines between rehearsals should not make the mistake of sitting quietly in an easy chair—not unless he wishes to memorize mechanically. Rather he should make his study period a private rehearsal, setting his stage as accurately as the room and equipment will permit, visualizing the other players in his imagination, and going through movements and business in association with the lines. By taking one scene at a time and going over and over it in this way the actor not only learns more quickly, and retains more surely, but he makes progress with his interpretation as he goes.

There are difficulties, of course, chief of which is the laziness to which all normal people in their right minds are addicted. It seems so much easier to sit in a chair and study, especially if one happens to be very fat or very tired. Sometimes, also, the rehearsal method is impracticable because of congested quarters or the danger of annoying other people. The actor who, for one reason or another, is forced to do his studying silently should at least learn to rehearse his coördinations imaginatively—that is, to

visualize stage positions, hear in his mind's ear the voices of the other actors, and go through his own actions empathically in articulation with the lines. By this method an experienced actor can rehearse his part with reasonable vividness while sitting in a chair, or riding on a train or trolley, or awaiting his fate in a dentist's office. To be sure, he is apt to break out into audible or visible manifestations from time to time, and incur the suspicion of being slightly demented. But art demands sacrifices.

I trust that nothing here said in support of interpretative memorization will be understood as an encouragement of unnecessary delay. Just as soon as interpretation and coördination are established, memorization should proceed as rapidly as possible, and should be completed in time for plenty of polishing in the later rehearsals. The actor who delays beyond that point not only jeopardizes his own playing but inconveniences the director and his fellow actors, and is manifestly guilty of poor sportsmanship.

CADENCE

Few actors appreciate the importance of cadence in coördinating lines and business and in mastering a part. Directors say a good deal in the later rehearsals about rhythm and tempo in the larger sense, with special reference to the dramatic values in the more stirring scenes; and most actors fall in with these rhythms eventually, to point up contrasting moods, work up emotional responses, and build climaxes. But cadence, in a simpler and less spectacular sense, can be of enormous help to the actor learning his part, and properly used can add greatly to the smoothness and verisimilitude of the performance.

In the case of plays in verse this is fairly obvious. Any actor who has tried it knows that lines in verse are easier to learn than lines in prose, and that they are easier to recall after an interval. He knows, too, that it is easier to take up cues in verse, and if he has a true sense of rhythm he finds that he is less apt to be too quick or too slow in taking them up. The verse supplies the cadence for him in such a way that he has to be extraordinarily dull to miss it; and having once adjusted himself to it he no longer has to depend on literal memory, but responds to the cadence with body as well as mind, feeling it physically in nerves and muscles.

In a less obvious way the cadence of prose lines can be felt and learned, along with the rhythm of the accompanying movements.

There are at least two reasons why many actors fail to realize this. One is that they learn short cues, literally and objectively, and then listen for them in the tense manner of a runner listening for the starting gun, instead

of feeling the cadence through bodily adjustment. The other is that the one actor who will not learn his lines upsets the cadences in rehearsal and so prevents his fellow actors from learning theirs.

To make good use of cadence all the actors in a scene must coöperate, working out their lines, movements, and business together, and learning the rhythms as soon as possible. The central portions of long speeches may be left until the last, but the cues should be worked out early so that each actor, as he studies his lines, may feel the rhythm with which each cue will come to him, the direction from which it will come, the position and movement of the actor who will give it, and his own movement or attitude as he receives it. He should not permit his memorization to become fixed until this is done; and he should not delay memorization after it is done. To prolong the process unduly is to defeat its very purpose. One of the strongest objections to the Stanislavsky method of unlimited informal study is that in the hands of any but the most talented and experienced players it tends to blur the rhythms. Too many experimental rehearsals fill the actor's mind with so many varied interpretations, and his body with so many different cadences, that they become badly jumbled in his memory, and at each successive rehearsal he becomes less certain which to use, and less certain what to expect from his fellow actors. He "goes stale"—not because he knows his part too well, but because he has absorbed too many different impressions and got himself into a state of restless confusion.

Books or Sides

Because plays are usually produced before they are published, professional actors, from the earliest times, have been accustomed to learning their parts, not from printed books, but from what are often called "sides." These are simply pages of manuscript containing the lines of one part, with a short cue for each speech consisting of the last two or three words of the preceding line—usually with no indication of which character speaks it. Only the prompt copy contains the whole play, and the actor does not know what it is all about until he has attended enough rehearsals to enable him to remember the continuity. The obvious reason for this arrangement is economy; it would be too expensive to have complete copies written out, or typed out, for all the actors in a large cast. But actors who have always studied from sides not infrequently persuade themselves that such is the best way to study. They are often the same actors (mentioned in Chapter VII) who prefer not to know too much about the play.

There are just two situations in which the use of sides is desirable. The first is when nothing else is available, and the second is when speed in memorization is more important than understanding.

The stock company actor who has to memorize in a hurry and is satisfied to use the mechanical method, finds, of course, that sides are not only adequate but advantageous, in that they permit the maximum concentration, with the minimum of distracting interference. When the object is to learn words, not meanings, only the words are needed. The stock actor can usually tell you just how many sides he can memorize in an hour, and it is usually a goodly number. His objection to using a book is the very fact that he may get interested in it and find himself inadvertently reading and digesting the play. If he has to use a book he sometimes guards against this danger by blacking out all lines but his own.

On the other hand, if the actor desires to follow the advice given in Chapter VII, and make a sympathetic and intelligent study of the play, the book is far better than the sides. The sides, in fact, are of no use at all.

It is quite possible to combine the two methods, and some very good actors do so. Using a book for the preliminary study of the play, the actor may block out his part and make notations concerning timing, business, and interpretation, studying these carefully and slowly until he has grasped the meaning and rhythm. Then he may copy off his lines in the form of sides and study them intensively to complete the memorization. This method retains many of the values of the stock company method without its worst dangers, since the interpretations and coördinations are pretty well worked out before the mechanical process begins.

GETTING ACQUAINTED WITH THE CHARACTER

There is, of course, much more to learning a part than mastering lines. Acting is primarily characterization, and its major problem is how to realize imaginatively the character to be portrayed.

The inexperienced actor commonly thinks of his character in terms of lines only, basing his understanding of the part entirely on what he is supposed to say, and estimating the importance of the character by the number and dramatic significance of his lines. This results in some very shallow and very blurred acting.

In real life we are not so easily fooled; we know perfectly well that a person's importance is not to be measured by his loquaciousness. Nobody who is worth knowing talks all the time, even in company; yet he may be no less a personality and no less interesting when he is not talking. Some-

times we can discern his character better from his behavior when silent, or his reaction to the behavior of others, than from his speech—words being as often used to conceal ideas as to express them.

Using the lines, therefore, merely as an introduction to the character, the actor should study, not just what the character says, but what he is; what he is doing and thinking all the time he is on the stage—and, for that matter, off the stage; what his past history and environment have been, and how they have affected his attitude and state of mind.

Some dramatists give the actor a great deal of help in this study by means of character sketches offered as stage directions. Barrie, for example, begins the published edition of *The Admirable Crichton* with two or three pages of stage directions, including a generous character sketch of the Hon. Ernest Woolley, who speaks the opening lines. In *Pantaloon* he gives us a lengthy prologue, in the course of which we become pretty well acquainted with three of the characters before the curtain rises. In *A Kiss for Cinderella* he describes the young probationer in Dr. Bodie's hospital in the following direction: "The attractive girl does her pretty bow to Mr. Bodie. It is one of the few things she does well, and will probably by and by bring her into some safe matrimonial harbour. . . . She is of a nice nature, and would like to be of use, but things slip through her hands as through her mind. . . ." Similar directions flash through the pages of all of his plays, but the gem of the collection is the one in *The Admirable Crichton* concerning a minor character who has not even one articulate line of dialogue: "The page-boy cheers, and has the one moment of prominence in his life. He grows up, marries, and has children, but is never really heard from again."

It is hardly to be expected that the actor who plays the page-boy can convey to the audience a literal knowledge of his subsequent life history by the way in which he utters the cheer. But it is entirely possible that the stimulus to his imagination contained in that classic direction may help him to realize the character more fully, and to make of it not a supernumerary part but a real "bit."

Perhaps this is as good a spot as any in which to emphasize the importance of "bits," and the fact that to the good actor every part is a part, and worthy of his best efforts no matter how brief. In the words of Constantin Stanislavsky, "THERE ARE NO SMALL PARTS: ONLY SMALL ACTORS" —a slogan that is posted in the green rooms of many little theatres, and deserves to be posted in all. There are *short* parts, of course, parts with few lines and brief periods on the stage. But there are no unimportant parts— not in good plays, by competent authors. Every part that is worth keeping

in a play is worth doing well. Incidentally, the brief parts are often more difficult to do well, for the very reason that they supply fewer tangible materials to work with, and so present a more serious challenge to the actor's imagination. If I were doubtful about the abilities of a supposedly experienced actor, I would try him on a bit part.

Unfortunately, not all dramatists are as helpful as Barrie, and in the attempt to get acquainted with a character the actor often has to shift for himself. Some writers even show a disposition to neglect minor characters or become indifferent about them. The writer usually works in his imagination, without visible symbols, and when he has a number of characters on the stage at once he may actually forget some of them for a time. They exist; but they exist much less vividly in his abstract conception than they will later in the eyes of the audience. That is one important difference between drama and fiction. Just as long as a character is on the stage he has concrete reality for the audience, and occupies a share of their attention. Even when he is off stage for a while, he is likely to be more vivid in their minds than a character in a novel who has not been mentioned for some pages, since the spectators have actually seen and heard him, and have a more complete mental image of him than any author could give them in words. But until the play is cast and in rehearsal the author is merely an author; and unless he has Barrie's extraordinary interest in the minor characters he is likely to have left many of them half-finished.

The actor's problem, therefore, even in a minor part, is to get acquainted with the character beneath and beyond the lines, whether the author gives much or little help. He should do what Barrie does for a character, and more, searching every corner of his existence with sympathy and insight. And he should remember that he cannot escape the responsibility by negative playing. A character in a book may fade from the reader's consciousness whenever he is not active, but a character in a play, especially when on the stage, is an integral part of the total effect. If he is not well played at any particular moment he is badly played. If he is not contributing to the integrity of the performance he is detracting from it; there is no neutral zone. There is foreground in drama, and background, but the human part of the background is so near, so real, so concrete, that it never fades into the complete neutrality and subordination one finds in the background of many other arts. If the player's realization of his part is incomplete, his playing will be vague, restless, and negative; and no matter how small the part, nor how well the other parts are played, it will tend in some degree to weaken or blur the effect of the whole. That is the price we pay for the vividness of the theatre.

Believing in the Part

One of the hardest things for the inexperienced actor to do—and even for the experienced actor in some plays—is to develop the necessary imaginative belief in his part. If he is to play a part with conviction, he must have the conviction; and when we remember how unconvincingly some parts are written, we realize that that is asking a good deal of him.

To believe in a part it is by no means necessary to believe in its literal truth or actuality. The play need not be realistic in order to carry conviction. It is true, of course, that an actor accustomed to modern realistic plays would find it harder at first to believe in a part from Shakespeare or Sheridan than in one from George Kaufman or John Van Druten; his mere unfamiliarity with the grand manner would create a difficulty for him. On the other hand, the modern realistic play stakes its merits on objective truth and probability to such a degree that a part in such a play must be highly probable before the actor—and his audience—can believe in it at all.

A part like that of Inspector Donahue in Bayard Veiller's *The Thirteenth Chair* illustrates the way in which a dramatist sometimes makes it impossible for the actor to believe in his part. The Inspector is a foil for the other characters. In some respects he is a typical, or rather conventional, stage detective, hard, businesslike, a little crude, but not a caricature. In order, however, to build up the plot, sustain interest in the mystery, win sympathy for the heroine, and give Madame LaGrange the opportunity to outwit both the murderer and the police, the author makes him scintillatingly clever at one moment and unbelievably stupid the next. The actor trying to develop the part and believe in it is constantly distressed by its inconsistencies and improbabilities. The more successfully he gets under the skin of the Inspector in his clever moments, the more impossible it becomes for him to feel convinced (and convincing) when obliged to appear superlatively dumb.

The same actor may have no trouble at all with a part like that of Sir Peter Teazle in *The School for Scandal*. He can believe in Sir Peter in spite of his silks and satins, and his artificiality, heightened almost to the point of caricature; in spite even of his eighteenth-century technique, his direct asides, and confidential soliloquies. For Sir Peter is at least consistent with himself, and with the author's basic conception of him. He is unreal, but not unbelievable. He is drawn with imaginative sincerity and artistic integrity.

The part of Ruth Wilkins in *Dear Ruth* is a more recent example of un-

believable motivation. She jilts her unromantic but well-meaning and perfectly decent civilian fiancé in order to run away with a romantically impetuous air-force lieutenant, who has been tricked into supposing himself engaged to her by some forged letters from her adolescent sister. The author tries frantically to justify her treachery by making her betrothed appear an ass, and making her so kind and compassionate that she cannot bear to hurt the young aviator's feelings. But if the actress can believe in Ruth when she is being kind and compassionate to a total stranger, she finds it difficult to believe in her when she is being callously treacherous to a man who loves her, whom she says she loves, and whom she has solemnly promised to marry. The more she believes in the romantic Ruth, carried away by a flaming passion of love at first sight, the less she can believe in the Ruth who would calmly pledge herself to marry Albert. If she can play Act I with complete belief in her part, she cannot play Act II with conviction—or vice versa.

Ruth Wilkins and Inspector Donahue might very well exist in real life, inconsistency being all too common in nature; while Sir Peter could hardly exist today. But in drama, as in fiction, it is artistic probability, not scientific possibility, that matters. Most of us, perhaps, do not believe in ghosts, but we can easily believe in ghost stories, if told with imaginative conviction. Conversely, we do believe the outrageous, illogical things we read every day in the newspapers; but we should not believe in most of them if presented as fiction, or as drama. It is not enough for the actor to say, "This character could do these things in real life." He must be able to say, "I can believe in this character doing these things as he is conceived in this play."

Modern critics and audiences often wonder how the absurd rhetorical hokum of many nineteenth-century plays—plays like *East Lynne, The Old Homestead,* or *Fashion,* to say nothing of Boucicault's *After Dark* or *The Streets of New York,* or the early thrillers of Owen Davis—could ever have been played sincerely, and how they could have aroused any true emotions in audiences not completely feeble-minded. Yet we know that our grandparents wept and thrilled over those plays with a frankness and sincerity that is not given to us; and we hope they were not feeble-minded.

The explanation is that the actors of those days did not regard the hokum as hokum. They accepted the exaggerations and sentimentality as traditional conventions of the theatre, as part of the language of expression; and within those conventions they believed in their parts and played them with imaginative sincerity. The audiences felt the sincerity and accepted the hokum, just as our supposedly sophisticated audiences today accept

the less honest hokum of the motion pictures. The reason why modern audiences treat plays like *East Lynne* as burlesques, to be laughed at, is that the actors refuse to believe in their parts. When an actor knows a part is hokum, and plays it as such, it *is* hokum, and is so felt by the audience. When he plays the same part with imaginative sincerity it becomes an entirely different thing, even if written as hokum. It is still possible to move audiences profoundly with some of these old plays in the hands of sincere and imaginative actors; *East Lynne, Camille*, and *The Old Homestead* have all been sympathetically and effectively played in recent years. In the case of the Boucicault plays the strain is perhaps too great; the modern actor would have to be pretty imaginative to believe in those as anything more than hokum. Yet they were once played quite sincerely.

Unless a part is to be burlesqued, therefore, the chief concern of the actor should be to get inside of it imaginatively and to believe in it artistically. This does not mean that he is to lose his self-control in a welter of hallucination—to "be" the character in the almost supernatural sense affected by some temperamental actors, and publicized by their press agents. That sort of thing should have ended for all time with the famous remark of Dr. Johnson, quoted by James Boswell:

"If sir," said he, "Garrick believes himself to be every character that he represents, he is a madman and ought to be confined. Nay, sir, he is a villain and ought to be hanged. If, for instance, he believes himself to be Macbeth, he has committed murder, he is a vile assassin, who in violation of the laws of hospitality as well as of other principles, has imbrued his hands in the blood of the king while he was sleeping under his roof. If, sir, he has really been that person in his own mind, he has in his own mind been as guilty as Macbeth."

Here, as in all problems of acting, the solution is to be found in the dual attitude, properly balanced. If, as artist, the actor can believe in the integrity of his interpretative concept, as instrument he can be convincing.

SELECTION AND EMPHASIS IN CHARACTERIZATION

One other point of major importance, mentioned briefly in another connection in an earlier chapter, should be considered by the actor in learning a part.

Art is not life, but a conventionalized representation or presentation of life. Real life is complex, and full of infinite detail, much of it unimportant and confusing. From this complexity the artist selects significant things, weaving them into a pattern or design, and emphasizing their meaning or beauty through simplification. Unnecessary details are screened out, not

because they are untrue, but because they are insignificant and distracting.

For the actor this means that good characterization is not necessarily photographic realism. He should learn all that he can about the character in every detail of that character's life; but there is no reason why he should use it all. Rather, he should select and emphasize, exaggerating if necessary, those traits or characteristics which will best convey to the audience his artistic conception of the character.

There are several reasons why photographic completeness in characterization is seldom desirable on the stage.

In the first place real people do too many meaningless things; their lives are crowded with unrelated trifles that would merely be colorless and characterless in a play.

In the second place civilized people actually conceal their most important thoughts and feelings behind a mask of self-control, which, copied faithfully, would convey no meaning at all. George Henry Lewes, that shrewd critic of nineteenth-century acting, stated this principle many years ago in the following words: "It is obvious to anyone who reflects for a moment that nature is often so reticent—that men and women express so little in their faces and gestures, or in their tones, of what is tearing their hearts— that a perfect copy of almost any man's expressions would be utterly ineffective on the stage."

In the third place there are certain symbols which, in the course of time, have become so familiar to theatre-goers that they actually convey meanings and emotions more effectively than photographic realism. To quote Lewes again: "It is the actor's art to express in well-known symbols what an individual may be supposed to feel, and we, the spectators, recognizing these expressions, are thrown into a state of sympathy." When a stage character dies, for instance, he gasps out feeble, but perfectly intelligible, last words, and then, at precisely the right moment for dramatic effect he goes limp, his head falls back, and somebody says, "He's gone!" Any doctor or nurse can tell you that most people do not really die that way. But if the actor were to imitate accurately the usual hospital death he would have his audience confused and uncomfortable; they would find it tedious and trying, if not revolting. In the same way, audiences have learned to understand certain obvious and perhaps exaggerated attitudes and facial expressions as registering love, grief, exultation, despondency, pride, indignation, or impatience; while they might be sorely puzzled by the thousand varied and obscure ways in which different people register these emotions in real life—or fail to register them.

Finally, many of the details of real life are so unpleasant in themselves,

or so charged with unpleasant associations, that they tend to destroy æsthetic distance by reminding us too insistently of our own troubles. Such details are best omitted. The landscape artist, sketching a lovely hillside or valley, does not hesitate to omit the telegraph pole or billboard which spoils the view for the tourist—though the same artist, when sketching a city water front, may put in dozens of telegraph poles and billboards as part of the essential composition of that scene. So the actor, portraying a character in a significant mood or situation, should omit all ugly or distracting details, no matter how true to life, if they are not necessary or do not contribute to the desired effect—though he should not hesitate to portray the same unpleasant things when they do happen to be part of the essential thought or characterization.

In short, he should remember that some centrality of purpose, some fidelity to the essential at the expense of the unessential, some selection and emphasis, is necessary to good art; and that such selection and emphasis is what often marks the difference between mastering a part and letting it master him. One of the very best reasons for making the study of a character exhaustive and complete is that he may know what to leave out.

CHAPTER IX

Rehearsing

THE attitude and behavior of a player at rehearsal constitute a pretty accurate gauge of his ultimate success. There are, it is true, actors who loaf through rehearsals with careless indifference, neglecting to learn lines and making themselves generally annoying to their comrades, yet who manage to scintillate in performance, carrying off honors at the expense of those who have worked patiently and sincerely. Such exploits, fortunately, are seldom more than temporary, and do not lead to lasting achievement of an important kind. Sooner or later the triflers get found out; audiences begin to sense their shallowness and grow weary of being fooled by it. In the long run it is the loyal, attentive, coöperative actor who develops the imaginative sincerity essential to honest art.

Initially, the commercial producer has an advantage over the amateur in this, as in many other matters. Holding the purse strings, he can promptly dispense with the services of a beginner who does not take rehearsals seriously, while the director of amateurs, conscious that his players receive no compensation, cannot be quite so hard-boiled. Ultimately, however, the advantage is equalized, or reversed. The commercial manager, interested only in box-office returns, hesitates to dismiss or antagonize an actor who has box-office appeal; and some of the smart triflers have a good deal of that, at least for a time. But serious and well-organized amateur groups, for the very reason that they play for their own satisfaction, do not long tolerate the actor who persists in being a nuisance. They just stop inviting him to play.

That is not to say, however, that the actor in rehearsal should maintain an attitude of deadly seriousness, killing his own and his comrades' pleasure, and reducing the process of learning a play to sour-faced drudgery. Lack of time may force an actor to go at his business with too much intensity and too little joy; and a commercial manager may encourage high-pressure methods in rehearsal on the theory that he pays the actor for his time and is entitled to service. But in the long run the most artistic results in the theatre are achieved when the actor looks upon rehearsals as part of the fun—as a joyous adventure in creative art.

The idea that rehearsing is a tedious job, to be well done only because one is to be paid for it in money or glory, is almost as bad as the idea that rehearsing is just a social pastime, one way of spending a pleasant evening in congenial company. The actor's attitude at rehearsal should be business-like, in the sense that he should be alert, attentive, and coöperative, sub-ordinating his personal superficialities and irrelevancies to the main business of the moment; but at the same time it should be full of group en-thusiasm, the thrill of sharing imaginative or vicarious experience, and the satisfaction of doing something well.

When the players take their rehearsals too lightly, frittering away time in irrelevant hilarity, inattention, and superficiality, the result is sure to be a half-hearted, amateurish production, lacking in clarity and intelli-gence, to say nothing of polish. When, on the other hand, they take their rehearsals too solemnly the result is apt to be mechanical and uninspired.

The ideal attitude at rehearsal is that of the hobby-rider—the person who does something for pleasure, but, because the pleasure is deep-seated and lasting, does it intensely and whole-heartedly. To the true hobby-rider there is no satisfaction in superficial dabbling; nothing connected with his hobby is too much trouble, and what would otherwise be hard work is in this connection merely glorified play. The true actor—amateur or professional—does not sell his energy for a price. He gives his energy because he cannot help it. He strives to appreciate to the full the author's art and meaning, and he enjoys the pleasure of sharing his appreciation with his fellow actors at rehearsal almost as much as he later enjoys sharing it with the audience.

How to Torture the Director

It is astounding how many actors, or people who think they are actors, are willing to antagonize the director and make life miserable for their comrades, by displaying a non-coöperative attitude at rehearsals. The actor who wishes to get himself on the black list need only persist for a short time in one or more of the following iniquities:

1. He may cut rehearsals without permission. In the professional theatre that means a fine or dismissal. In a well-organized amateur theatre it means a complete loss of the director's confidence, and no second invita-tion to play.

2. He—or she—may offer trifling or selfish excuses for nonattendance. "I can't possibly rehearse Saturday night; I'm going to a dance that night" has (fortunately, perhaps) cut off many a budding stage career. People who prefer some other form of pleasure to acting, or even to rehearsing, have a

perfect right to their preference, but they have no place in the theatre; nor have those who cannot appreciate the unfairness to others involved in cutting rehearsals. No matter how brief an actor's part, he should remember that others depend upon him and that they may need the rehearsals even if he does not. He should accept no part unless he is willing to accept the implied obligation.

3. He may come to rehearsals late. That is a sure way to make the director apprehensive that he will come late to the performances also; and every director lives in agonized dread of the night when he will be unable to ring up his curtain because somebody in the cast is missing. A young girl of my acquaintance who claimed to be "crazy about dramatics" was given a chance to try out for a part in a community theatre production. She arrived an hour after the tryouts had begun, saying with a cheerful laugh, "Oh, I'm always late!" It is hardly necessary to add that she did not get a part.

4. He may be present at rehearsals, but so inattentive that somebody has to wake him up when his entrance cue is given; he may be off in another room playing bridge, or in a corner telling the story of his life to the ingenue. If he wishes to make the director exceptionally frantic he may waste further time when called by saying: "Oh, am I in this scene? What page is it? Who has a book? I left mine home!" or by seizing a book, opening it, and beginning to read at the wrong page. And if he wishes to run the risk of being murdered as well as black-listed he may say, when called: "Can't you wait a minute till I finish this hand?" One of the cleverest and most charming amateur actresses I have ever seen, whose services were once in frequent demand, was ultimately black-listed because she just would not be a good sport at rehearsals. Even when they were being held, for her convenience, in her own home, she was always missing when her entrance cue was given; there was an awkward stage wait and a letdown for the other players while somebody went to call her from her knitting.

5. He may indulge in loud laughter or conversation in the wings, or in an adjoining room, while the director is trying to conduct a rehearsal. If he wishes to be especially offensive he may gather two or three congenial souls in a corner and tell smutty jokes; the peculiar sniggering laughter with which such jokes are received is possibly the most exasperating sound to which people trying to think creatively can be subjected.

6. When actually rehearsing, he may drop out of character, and out of position, whenever there is a pause or interruption for directions. The actor who indicates his boredom by sitting down or lighting a cigarette every time the action lags is neither learning to act nor helping the others.

7. He may prove his interest in the work by appointing himself co-director, and telling the director and the other actors a better way of doing things. No right-minded director resents an occasional good suggestion, modestly offered at an appropriate time, but no director and no actor can fail to be irritated at another actor who is continually interfering, especially with suggestions intended to glamorize his own part to the detriment of the other parts and the play as a whole.

8. He may adopt the opposite attitude of complete disinterest in the director's problems: "Tell me what you want and I'll do it. I don't care; it's all the same to me!" He should, of course, accept the decision of the director. But it is one thing to coöperate in a sportsmanlike way with the director's plans even when they seem to him ill-advised, and quite another to reject all interest and responsibility and assume an attitude of surly or casual indifference.

9. He may indulge his desire to be the life of the party by kidding his way through every rehearsal, gagging his lines, making the ladies giggle, jollying the director, and displaying great virtuosity as a comedian in everything but his part.

10. He may seize his hat and go home as soon as his big scene has been rehearsed; or he may interrupt the director at his busiest moment to say, "You won't need me any more tonight, will you? I only have three lines in that last scene, and somebody else can read them." He may easily double the potency of this treatment by taking the ingenue with him.

If anyone supposes that such irresponsible attitudes are to be found exclusively among the rankest of amateurs he need only attend one or two professional or semi-professional rehearsals; or he may read that entertaining book on *How a Play Is Produced*, by Karel Çapek, which describes the insanities of production, not in a cheap commercial theatre, but in the great state theatre at Prague, in the days before Hitler and Stalin wrecked the free culture of Czechoslovakia. Çapek, of course, wrote his book in a spirit of humorous exaggeration; but he could not have written it at all without considerable provocation. Or one may read *The Curtain Falls*, by Joseph Verner Reed, to see how some of our most famous stars behave in rehearsal. I have seen a popular stage and screen star behave like a spoiled child at a Broadway rehearsal, telling a very able director (much older than himself) that he guessed he knew his business all right, and did not need to be told how to act, or when to sit down, or when to get up. Human nature has about the same faults in professional and amateur circles. The chief difference is that the professional director is usually free to express

his feelings with appropriate candor, while the unfortunate director of amateurs is expected to observe a gentlemanly restraint.

TEAMWORK

Let us forget the negative side of the picture, however, and consider what happens when the players maintain the right mental attitude at rehearsals. It is noteworthy that in the gossip among directors the highest praise one hears of an actor is not, "He's a fine actor," but "He's a grand player to work with."

In modern production, especially of modern plays, unity and consistency in the work of the group have come to be thought of as more important than individual virtuosity. The star system is still with us, but the modern star cannot afford to be poorly supported. He may see to it that nobody in the cast is quite good enough to outshine him, and he may insist that certain scenes or lines be cut or revised in order that nothing may detract from the emphasis on his own part; but he must not be caught at it. In the eighteenth and nineteenth centuries the great actor was the one who "stopped the show"—a standard that still applies in grand opera and musical comedy. But in the twentieth-century legitimate theatre, and especially in the non-commercial theatre, we have come to have a more sincere regard for integrity of illusion and imaginative consistency. When an actor stands out vividly we may admire him, but we are apt to deplore the weakness of the others and complain that the play as a whole is not convincing. We like best the actor who can move us, but who nevertheless fits into the play, helping a good, well-balanced cast to achieve a unified impression.

Theodore Komisarjevsky, in his essay on the teaching of acting (in *Myself and the Theatre*), roundly condemns the star system and pleads for teamwork. "There can never be an actor," he says, "great enough to enable an audience to overlook the bad acting of his 'supporters' and capable of interpreting a whole play by himself."

There are those who lament the passing of the good old days in the theatre. Like the Navy men who grow nostalgic about wooden ships and iron men, they sigh for the days of great actors who could stop the show.

As a descendant of two theatre families, I often share this feeling; but as a critical student of theatre history, I am aware of the gains as well as the losses. And the greatest gain of all is the increasing emphasis on teamwork in acting—on plays rather than parts. Many of the great players of other days had a high sense of integrity in their own creative work of characterization. Many of them had high artistic ideals, and would have hated the

organized commercialism and industrial strife of modern show business. Yet many of them would unhesitatingly exalt the art of the actor at any cost to the art of the dramatist or the director.

To take just one example: Richard Mansfield, one of the most successful stars of the last century, won his fame overnight by what George Freedley calls a *tour de force*. In *A Parisian Romance* (1883), in a minor part, he literally, if temporarily, stopped the show. One commentator wrote: "I have tonight witnessed a wonderful event. . . . The actor who played the Baron Chevrial was unknown till tonight. Tomorrow he will be famous. . . . It is the birth of a great career, the coming of a great artist." His biographer, Paul Wilstach, wrote: "Mansfield had come into his own. The superb art of his performance had dwarfed all about it; the play was killed, but he was from that moment a figure to be reckoned with in the history of the theatre."

The play was killed! If there is any virtue in the theatre of today to compensate for the absence of giants, any element of artistic integrity to offset the commercialism and make the young actor proud of his own time, it is that we are apt to think twice before hailing as "great" the actor who kills the play.

Unfortunately there are still backsliders in the commercial theatre, who may well operate for some time before audiences find them out. Not long before this page was written a certain famous star of stage and screen made a western road tour in a rural comedy which, having finished its Broadway run, had already been released to non-commercial theatres in the east. A competent critic who had seen a community-theatre production of the play in Pennsylvania, later saw the star and his road company in Michigan. He reported that the star was very good in the part, but that the rest of the company was much inferior to the community players, and that many of their best lines had been cut out or given to the star; also that several of the parts were conspicuously miscast. He was particularly outraged when the star took his curtain call completely out of character by singing a totally irrelevant song which he had popularized in another production. I mentioned this incident to a friend of mine in Broadway circles, and he laughed. "I happen to know the inside story of that," he said, "for the manager is a buddy of mine. The star did not really want to make the road tour, but consented on two conditions. One was that the better minor players should be fired and their parts recast and rewritten so as not to compete with him in audience response. The other was that he be allowed to sing his pet song for a curtain call in order to boost his royal-

ties." Fortunately such instances are growing less common, though I could cite some others almost as disgusting.

In the art of acting today—if not always in "show business"—teamwork (or team play, as Sir Henry Irving called it) has become a major concern. It is not that teamwork has become more important than individual acting; it is rather that the two have become less distinguishable, and that the excellence of individual acting is now more likely to be judged in terms of teamwork. The best actor is no longer the one whose temperamental outbursts, varying nightly, surprise and startle the other actors out of their composure, scare nervous people into hysterics, and compel tumultuous applause, interrupting the play, as an escape valve for emotional tension. It is rather the actor who, in perfect coöperation with his fellows, can help make a play seem true, vital, or stirring, night after night, with sure artistry and fine sincerity.

The development of such teamwork is the main business of rehearsals. It is true that rehearsing also helps the individual actor to learn his part, and that a certain amount of rehearsing is necessary before he can learn it at all. But his ultimate effectiveness will be greatly increased if he can school himself to think of rehearsals as by, of, and for the group; and to work, not for his own characterization alone, but for group pictures, group action, group rhythms, and total effect.

The right mental attitude at rehearsals is the essential thing. It may help the young actor to cultivate that attitude if he will observe the following specific suggestions:

1. He should be regular and punctual in attendance at rehearsals.[1]

2. He should become familiar with the play as a whole just as soon as possible.

3. He should never fail to go over his part just before a rehearsal, in order to have it as fresh in mind as possible.

4. He should pay strict attention to the rehearsal, whether his own scenes are being rehearsed or not.

5. If not in the scene he should keep off the stage or out of the way, but should watch carefully the development of the other characters, noting everything that may possibly bear upon his own part, and profiting by the instructions and directions given to others.

6. He should keep careful track of his entrance cues, and be ready for his entrances without being called. This not only wins the confidence of

[1] Joan Caulfield, arriving late at her first professional rehearsal, found the entire cast sitting grimly waiting for her, and was made to go around and apologize separately to each member. She says it cured her.

the director but it makes the actor himself feel in the picture; it helps him to "belong."

7. If the rehearsal is held on a bare stage he should make every effort to visualize the ultimate setting, the lights and properties, even the presence of the audience.

8. If the rehearsal is held in a private house or enclosed rehearsal room, he should visualize the actual conditions of the stage. He should strive to imagine the direction and distance of the audience, and to avoid being stifled and repressed by the presence of a solid wall where the audience is supposed to be.

9. He should secure his hand properties as early as possible; if the real ones are not available he should provide himself with substitutes of about the same size and shape, not waiting for the director or stage manager to provide them.

10. In the early rehearsals, when scenes are being blocked out, he should carry a pencil and make careful notes, so that he will have movements and positions to study at home as well as lines, and so that the director will not have to repeat his directions at every rehearsal.

11. In making notes he should keep track of the locations of other characters in relation to his own, so that in studying he can visualize not only his own position but his surroundings. He should not, at the tenth rehearsal, address his lines to the wrong character, or be heard saying: "Oh, am I supposed to be talking to Millicent? Where is she? Oh, are you playing Millicent?" I have heard a veteran professional actor do just that, in almost those words.

12. He should strive to remain imaginatively in character during every moment at rehearsal. In the earlier and more ragged rehearsals, when it is hardly possible to let go imaginatively or to act with freedom and fullness of expression, he should at least try to keep his mind working and to visualize the action as it will be when learned rather than as it is.

13. He should rigidly refrain from lighting a cigarette, eating, chewing gum, or handling properties while rehearsing a scene, unless those actions are part of the scene and are to be done in performance. The actor who cannot rehearse without a cigarette in his mouth whether called for or not, cultivates a false ease in rehearsal that drops away when he has to play without his "crutch." He may even find himself unconsciously lighting a cigarette in the wrong scene of a public performance—perhaps in the wrong play, or the wrong century.

14. When the action does call for such business he should repeat it at each rehearsal with the proper timing.

15. He should strive to grasp the director's conception of each stage picture, to appreciate its composition, and to feel himself as part of it. The actor who can develop a sensitive feeling for stage pictures to such a degree that he will instinctively shift his position a little to balance another actor's movement, yet remain imaginatively in character while doing so, is by way of becoming a really valuable team player.

16. Remembering that his lines are the small part of his characterization, he should study to perfect the necessary by-play to keep him convincingly, though unobtrusively, in the picture. More will be said of by-play later.

17. Finally, he should strive to keep his temper and to remain on the friendliest terms with his colleagues. A congenial group of players, working together in a spirit of good fellowship, not only get more pleasure out of acting, but they give to the performance that extra quality of enthusiasm or delight which redeems many an amateur production in spite of technical imperfections, and often raises a professionally competent performance to the level of art.

There are, of course, no substitutes for talent, training, and experience. You cannot assemble a group of rank beginners or hopeless incompetents and expect them to give a finished and beautiful performance merely because they are congenial and enthusiastic. I hope I have not been understood as implying a belief in such miracles. But granted a reasonable standard of individual ability and experience, it is not too much to say that the ultimate quality of a performance is likely to depend more upon a favorable group attitude than upon individual virtuosity. And rehearsal, even more than performance, is the test of group attitude.

Coördination

The main business of rehearsals, I repeat, is teamwork, and good teamwork rests upon good coördination. The actor must not only coördinate his own lines, meanings, and actions, but must coördinate them with the lines, meanings, and actions of the other players, and with the meanings, actions, and rhythms conceived by the author and the director.

It is evident that this is not an easy matter, and that a single uncoöperative actor can upset the whole scheme rather badly. In a general way, good teamwork is the director's responsibility, but no director can be expected to accomplish it unless every actor does his bit.

In the early rehearsals the actor should seek first to master those difficulties that stand in the way of coördination. They begin with the mechanics of his first entrance. The book tells him, perhaps, that he is to enter

following a certain line, spoken by another character already on the stage. A single experiment, however, quickly proves that if he stands in the wings until he hears that line spoken there is an awkward stage wait while he walks the necessary distance. He must therefore learn an earlier cue to begin his walk, in order to articulate his action with the action already in progress on the stage; and if he has a line to speak, or a reaction to show on seeing the other characters, he must work out the proper timing for that also. But he cannot do these things until he knows the dimensions of the stage, the location of the entrance, the positions of the other characters and the position from which the director wishes him to speak his line or register his reaction. Sometimes these things cannot be known perfectly until the scenery has been set up, and the timing and spacing worked out in a stage rehearsal. But if the actor really uses his head he can always form an approximate notion of the distances, minimizing the adjustments that will later be necessary, and avoiding much of the surprise and confusion that thoughtless actors experience at the first stage rehearsal or the first rehearsal with full settings.

So for all the entrances, exits, and crosses that depend upon spacing and timing. The earlier these problems are solved in rehearsal, or approximately solved, the sooner the group as a whole will begin to feel the cadences that produce good coördination, and the sooner the actor will be free to interpret the subtleties of his part without fear of upsetting the others. What has already been said about cadence in connection with memorization applies in rehearsal, and it covers the giving and taking of cues, and the interrelation of movements as well as the actor's own coordinations of lines and actions.

Common Faults in Rehearsals

In addition to the faults of indifference or irresponsibility already described, there are several common practices in rehearsal which do not, on the whole, contribute to the actor's ultimate success. Some of these are harmless enough in the early rehearsals, but likely to grow into dangerously persistent habits if not carefully suppressed before the polishing rehearsals begin.

One of these is the practice of letting the memory struggle show in the facial expression. When the actor is just learning his lines and having great difficulty in remembering them, he is very apt to display a faraway expression, quite irrelevant to the thought or mood of the character. In extreme cases he even tilts his head back, closes his eyes, and taps his forehead in concentration. When this sort of thing is continued into the later rehearsals

it is almost certain to persist in some degree before the audience. Moreover the habit is indicative of a too-conscious memory process which in itself is bad; and the actor who displays it most consistently is often the very one who has the greatest trouble in learning his lines, and forgets them most often in performance. Such an actor is depending upon brute force of memory rather than meaning and cadence, and he often requires a prompt in the middle of a fluent, significant phrase, when either the meaning or the cadence should have carried him through.

Another bad practice, closely associated with that just mentioned, is the habit of looking inquiringly at the prompter every time one is a little uncertain about lines, and it is bad for the same reasons. A much better plan is to remain in character, hold position, and wait for the prompt; or to signal for it in some unobtrusive way, or even to ask for it in a subdued voice while "following through" imaginatively on the thought and action. Actors who do this learn their lines more quickly and retain them more surely, and at the same time prepare themselves to "cover" more effectively in case they do have to take prompts in performance.

Still another fault, especially with amateurs, is the common practice of looking down at the floor a good part of the time. It originates, perhaps, in the shyness of the beginner, but easily becomes a habit under the adverse conditions of rehearsal, unless one takes pains to overcome it. Amateurs, of course, are frequently compelled to rehearse in private living rooms or parlors, with solid walls where the audiences are supposed to be. It is always a little oppressive to act against a solid wall three or four feet away, and the temptation is strong to look away from it—right or left, up toward the ceiling, or down toward the floor. The right and left turns are limited and controlled by the action of the play; it is uncomfortable to look up at the ceiling for very long; so the easy thing to do when not looking right or left, is to look down. It is possible to acquire the same bad habit even when rehearsals are held on a stage, if the curtain is kept down, or if the director and stage manager habitually sit on the stage, with nobody out front. Some actors, perhaps, fall into the habit in the early rehearsals while reading from their books or sides. In any case it is a habit that must be checked quickly if it is not to mar the performance. A canny director will often check it by using bright footlights in rehearsal. If the actors complain, it is a pretty good sign that they need the treatment.

But by far the worst and most common fault developed in rehearsal and carried over into performance is that abomination of the modern theatre: inadequate voice. When actors mumble through rehearsals in lifeless undertones they are not likely to speak in loud, clear, ringing voices

at the first public performance. And both amateurs and professionals do mumble through rehearsals, though for different reasons. Amateurs do it partly because of timidity and inexperience, and partly because of the same repressive influence already mentioned: that of rehearsing in private homes, with solid walls around them. Professionals do it partly out of laziness, partly out of overconfidence, but mainly out of false pride. A foolish tradition assumes that the actor who knows his business need not extend himself at rehearsal, but will be all right "on the night." Both amateurs and professionals seem curiously sensitive to criticism on the subject of voice, taking it almost as a personal insult; and instead of working to overcome the fault they frequently argue with the director and insist that they "never have any difficulty in being heard when the audience is in." I have heard this defense most often from the very players who do *not* make themselves heard when the audience is in.

The only way to be sure of adequate voice is to develop it carefully and painstakingly in rehearsal. Theatres, even of the same size, vary enormously in acoustic properties, but there are very few of them indeed in which an actor speaking in easy conversational tones can be heard from all parts of the house. Even an experienced actor is seldom heard well on his first few lines in a strange theatre; he has to experiment a bit before he can get his voice adjusted to the proper pitch and placement. If the acoustics are bad and he has been mumbling through rehearsals he will waste a whole scene before he discovers that he must turn on the power; and when he does turn it on he is very likely to shout, and to sound as if he were shouting. It takes practice to speak lines in unnaturally loud tones without letting them seem unnaturally loud. The only safe plan is to assume that the acoustics will be poor, and to rehearse the part consistently in tones that are suited to the character and mood but are nevertheless loud enough to project themselves easily under adverse conditions.

Rehearsing in Costume

When the actor is to wear a costume essentially different from his ordinary street dress, he will find it exceedingly helpful to rehearse in costume as early and often as possible. If the actual costume is not available, or would be too badly soiled or mussed if used in rehearsal, a cheap substitute of similar style and feeling may be used.

There are some actors, and some writers on acting, who protest that such procedure is unworthy of a great actor. To depend on a costume to help him create character, they say, is a confession of weakness; a good actor should be able to act in any costume equally well. This attitude is obviously

a survival from the individualistic, declamatory school of acting, and ignores the James-Lange theory and the principle of empathy. Perhaps an experienced actor could contrive to imagine a character without the aid of costume—or rather to imagine the costume correctly with himself in it; but he could hardly escape some sense of inhibiting awkwardness when wearing an unfamiliar type of costume for the first time. It is to give this awkwardness a chance to wear off that the wise actor rehearses in costume.

If, for example, a young actor is to play his first eighteenth-century part, wearing satin knee breeches, lace cuffs, jabot, periwig and rapier, he is going to feel a little queer the first time he assumes the outfit. If he rehearses in modern dress right up to the final rehearsal he will learn his coördinations in terms of modern dress. When he sits down he will give his trousers a hitch to keep the "knees" out of them. When he stands up he will probably put his hands in his pockets. He will have some ten or twelve pockets, containing handkerchiefs, cigarettes, matches, fountain pen, wallet, memorandum book and a dozen other articles, many of which he will unconsciously finger or make use of as he rehearses his lines and movements. But he will not have a rapier. When he finally puts on the costume he will be disconcerted to find that he cannot hitch up his trousers, that he has fewer pockets, and in the wrong places, that his lace cuffs feel queer and get in the way, that his jabot and collar make it hard for him to turn his head freely, that his rapier is a problem when he sits down and that his stockings refuse to stay up. If he does not become flustered and lose his lines altogether he will at least be awkward and self-conscious, and his acting will suffer badly. He will have to unlearn and relearn a great deal before he can play with ease and conviction.

It is also true that rehearsing in costume is good for the teamwork. To find the actor to whom you have been speaking lines for several weeks suddenly changed in appearance is disconcerting to say the least, and destructive of coördination. A technique of love-making suitable for use with a slim, modern actress in a tailor-made suit may become embarrassingly impossible when she appears in décolleté gown with bodice and hoop skirt; similarly, the friendly slap on the back one has been rehearsing for several weeks may not work out so well when the recipient turns up in spike-studded armor.

Naturally, the actor with wide experience in wearing exotic costumes and with plenty of imagination will anticipate such problems more successfully than the beginner; and for him rehearsing in costume is not nearly so essential. But a reasonable number of costume rehearsals will not hurt anybody, and where there is the slightest danger that the lack of them will

prevent the actor from using his imagination truly and vividly he should at least make an attempt to fake the costume in early rehearsals.

The use of essential properties, unfamiliar elements of costume, and even the more radical features of make-up through at least a part of the rehearsal period is simply one phase of the practice of acting at rehearsals, for which I have already tried to present the case. The actor who is so sure of himself—or so unsure—that he does not like to extend himself at rehearsals will not wish to do any of these things. Nor will he, in all probability, bother to read this book.

CHAPTER X

Reading the Lines

THE most obvious function of the actor is, of course, the reading of his lines.

It is a curious phenomenon that the very phrase commonly used to describe this activity stands for precisely what the actor should not do. We speak of "reading" the lines when we really mean speaking the lines. We say of one actor that "he reads his lines with intelligent understanding," and of another that "his reading is inferior to his acting." What we mean is that the first speaks his lines well and the second does not. As a matter of fact, the one thing that most clearly stamps an actor as inexperienced or incompetent is reading his lines when he should be speaking them.

Few people realize how different the rhythms and tones of conventional reading are from those of spontaneous conversation. Most readers follow elaborate, but stereotyped, inflection patterns—apparently under the misapprehension that these constitute "expression." Actually they constitute a sort of dress uniform for reading as such. So well established and so familiar are these patterns that when someone who has been conversing in the next room suddenly begins to read, even though we cannot distinguish the words we easily recognize the inflections, and say, "That person is reading." When we listen to an inexperienced radio speaker we say to ourselves: "He is not speaking naturally; he is reading from a manuscript." Of course, even the very best radio speakers do read from manuscripts, but they contrive to conceal the fact, and to give the impression that they are speaking naturally. We expect this of them and give very little thought to the means by which they accomplish it, or to the actual differences between reading and speaking.

In the same way, we expect an actor to speak naturally and in character, though we know perfectly well that he is really reciting from memory. When he succeeds, we take it for granted; but when he sounds as if he were reading, we quickly detect the artificiality, and set him down as a poor actor.

When an actor is fortunate enough to escape this fault, and to speak

naturally by reason of innate ability or imagination, he need hardly bother to analyze the differences between reading and speaking. But most actors are not so fortunate, and must struggle against a persistent tendency to fall into reading inflections. For them, a careful analysis of such differences is in order.

WRITTEN AND SPOKEN LANGUAGE

In considering the characteristics of conversational speech as contrasted with those of reading, it is important to realize that we are dealing with two things: the style of the language itself, and the manner of its utterance.

The actual language most of us use in conversation is fundamentally different from that which we write for others to read.

Our speaking vocabularies are, as a rule, much smaller than our writing vocabularies, and limited to more familiar words. In speaking, we use more words of Anglo-Saxon origin and fewer of Latin or French; more short words, and fewer long words; more folk words, and fewer learned or literary words; more slang words and fewer polite words; more current words and fewer archaic or special words. Similarly we use more familiar phrases —more direct, simple, even hackneyed phrases, and fewer involved, picturesque, or figurative phrases.

Our constructions, also, are simpler in living speech than in writing. We use shorter sentences and a more direct word order; fewer complex sentences and more simple and compound sentences; fewer periodic sentences and more loose sentences. Sometimes we do not complete our sentences at all, but leave them half finished, interrupting and correcting ourselves as the impulse strikes us, or finishing with gestures instead of words. In conversation we do not have the time, nor the need, nor the skill to use the studied literary devices with which writers adorn their language.

Obviously it is the business of the dramatist—the realistic dramatist, at any rate—to note these differences, and to write his play in a more or less colloquial style, putting into the mouths of his characters language they might reasonably be supposed to speak. Unfortunately, many dramatists fail to do this, and the actor will sometimes find himself asked to deliver lines that his instinct and experience tell him the character would not really utter. If the play is not too significant as literature, and the director does not object, the actor may be able to ease some of the difficulty by slight changes in the wording or phrasing, though he must beware of the temptation to change the character as well. If the play is an established classic there is a certain obligation to speak the lines as written; and if it is highly literary or poetic the very artificiality of the lines may be a part of the

convention by which it attains dignity and beauty. In such cases the problem for the actor is not how to substitute more natural language, but how to make the poetic or conventional language sound reasonably natural and convincing. To do this successfully he must know how living speech differs from oral reading in manner of delivery as well as in form.

CONVERSATIONAL QUALITY

A conversational quality in delivery includes at least five important characteristics: (1) A much greater variety of inflections than in conventional reading; (2) a more uneven tempo, including pauses of varying lengths; (3) a stronger contrast between accented and unaccented syllables; (4) a liberal use of contracted forms, such as "don't" for "do not"; and (5) a weakening of the vowel in such words as the article "a" or the preposition "to."[1]

The first of these characteristics is very deceptive, for to the casual ear the elaborate inflection patterns of elocutionary oral reading may sound more varied than the less pretentious ones of normal, unaffected speech. The variations in reading, however, are artificial; they may be intricate, and may cover a wide range of pitch, but they do so in a routine pattern, following sentence form rather than meaning, and repeating whenever the form repeats. The variations of true speech, on the other hand, though less extreme in range of pitch, are more spontaneous and unexpected; they express meaning rather than form, and repeat only when the meaning repeats. In other words they represent *real* variety as opposed to an elaborate pattern of monotony.

It is interesting to note that this difference between elocutionary and natural inflections is by no means a recent development. John Rice, in his penetrating book on *The Art of Reading*, published in London in 1765, calls attention to it in these acid words:

Next to the intolerable Cacaphony of the Whine and Cant of the Illiterate, the Monotony of the artificial Declaimer is most disgustful: Not that he may want variety in the Inflections of the Voice; but these are made to succeed each other so regularly, that whatever he be repeating, it seems to be still the burthen of the same Song.

The modern actor—and perhaps even the platform reader—can well afford to learn that expressiveness is not to be measured by the number and extent of the pitch changes, but by their independence of mere form and

---

[1] These words would always be weak in good speech, formal or informal (except when specially accented), but stilted readers are likely to make them strong. The practice, unfortunately, is increasing, especially on the radio.

their appropriateness to the exact shade of meaning to be conveyed. They do not have to be spectacular unless the meaning is spectacular.

The second characteristic of a conversational quality—a more uneven tempo—presents a very similar problem. Tempo, like pitch, can be stereotyped into elaborate patterns, and if unskillfully handled may result in rhythmic monotony or "singsong." In poetic drama a more or less regular pattern of tempo may be an instrument of great beauty. But in prose, a freely varied tempo, not stereotyped, is one of the most powerful means at the actor's command for naturalizing dialogue. When he is obliged to deliver a long, literary speech of the sort that seems hopelessly stilted and unreal, a skillful change of pace and a sensitive use of pauses will do more than anything else to break the speech up into something like real conversation. Even in verse, a variation of tempo that does not destroy the essential rhythm helps enormously to vitalize the dialogue.

The third, fourth, and fifth characteristics may well be considered together.

The degree of contrast between accented and unaccented syllables varies in different languages, but is always greater in natural speech than in conventional or literary discourse. An exceptionally strong contrast is to be found in the English language. In conversational English, accented syllables are not only pronounced with more force than unaccented syllables, but they are made slightly longer in duration. At the same time the unaccented syllables—including the monosyllabic articles, prepositions, and conjunctions—are both weakened and shortened; unnecessary vowels are elided, and familiar forms like "I am," "we have," "she is," and "they are" are contracted into "I'm," "we've," she's," and "they're."

Such variations and contractions do not necessarily make for slovenliness of speech, as some of our less learned and more pedantic school teachers seem to think. They may, of course, be accompanied by slovenliness—by mouthing or blurring of consonants, degradation of accented vowels, or substitution of vulgar for reputable pronunciation—but that is another matter. The most cultivated and skillful speakers, when speaking informally, shorten or elide weak syllables without the least suggestion of ignorance or vulgarity; and the British—who are generally less lip-lazy and more agile in their speech—clip syllables even more than we do.

To speak lines without seeming to read them, the actor must learn to distinguish unerringly between those tricks of speech which mark the ignorant, slouchy, indifferent speaker, and those which represent the natural informality of the cultivated speaker. In the effort to avoid slovenliness he must avoid the opposite vices of bookishness and false precision.

ACTOR VERSUS ELOCUTIONIST

Among amateurs and those attempting to break into the profession, there are two opposite types who have trouble in reading their lines: those who read with too little expression, and those who read with too much. The first type usually improve with experience, but the second type sometimes grow worse. The most persistently unnatural readers are often those who have had so-called "elocutionary" training.

There is no reason why a sound and thorough training in speech by a competent teacher should be a handicap to an actor; but a superficial training by an incompetent teacher is one of the worst handicaps he can have. Unfortunately, much of the training offered under the name of "elocution" is superficial and given by incompetent teachers. There seems to be something about the profession which attracts to it a class of shallow, half-educated people, who talk a great deal about art, and beauty, and interpretation of literature, but who do not know the history and structure of the language, and have no deep understanding of the literature they profess to interpret. Some of them have little social background, mental depth, or scholarship; but they have a great zeal for culture, and seek to spread it by the only means at their command. Lacking wide acquaintance with those who, by environment and tradition, speak well without effort, they have no authority to depend upon except that of the printed page, and that of other elocutionists as superficial as themselves. This explains the chief faults of their teaching: eye-pronunciation and false elegance.

In the chapter on Stage Diction I shall try to set up some more reliable standards of pronunciation. The point here is that the faults mentioned often interfere seriously with a young actor's effort to speak his lines naturally and convincingly.

Among the most flagrant examples of eye-pronunciation common among actors with elocutionary training are: the rendering of the articles "a" and "the" in *unaccented* position as ei and ði:[2] rather than ə and ðə; the similarly overprecise rendering of the infinitive particle and the prepositions "to," "at," "for," and so on, when unaccented; the restitution of silent *t* in words like "fasten," "soften," and "often"; the attempt to take the perfectly reputable [tʃ] sound out of "picture," "fortune," and so on, because it is not spelled *ch;* the similar attempt to take the [ʃ] sound out of "issue" or "ocean" because it is not spelled *sh;* the attempt to put back unpronounceable sounds long elided in good speech usage, as in "clothes,"

---

[2] For an explanation of this and other phonetic symbols see the charts on pages 212 and 213, and the explanation beginning on page 211.

"postscript," or "Wednesday," just because they are still retained in the spelling; and the leveling out of long polysyllables by lengthening and overemphasizing the unaccented syllables. These and many other examples will be discussed in more detail in Chapter XV.

The mistaken notion behind such well-meaning niceties is that the spoken word derives from the written, and that one can establish his claim to education or refinement by proving that he knows how to spell. Unfortunately, many half-educated elocutionists do not seem to realize that in proving their knowledge of spelling they often reveal their ignorance of traditional usage in cultivated speech. Historically and logically the real language is the spoken one; the written is secondary. Written language serves to record and preserve speech, and to transmit it beyond the range of the voice; it does tend to stabilize forms and slow their rate of change, but it cannot dictate changes or prevent them. Even if this were not true off the stage, it would still be the actor's business to present the spoken language, not the written; and nothing can hamper him more in that than a standard of pronunciation based on spelling.

Among the more annoying aberrations of speech growing out of the elocutionist's notion of elegance are the indiscriminate, exaggerated, and often bungling affectation of British vowel sounds in American speech, such as [ɑː] for [æ], or short [ɔ] for short [ɑ]—not only in words where the Londoner uses them, but in others where he does not; the ruthless elimination of final *r* (and even medial *r*), sometimes in places where the Londoner or the New Englander would not eliminate it; the desperate determination to pronounce English long *u* with full diphthongal value [iu], not only in words where it is usual with good speakers, such as "student," "institute," or "duty," but in words where it can be managed only with a self-conscious effort, such as "blue," "true," or "cerulean"; the attempt to recapture foreign pronunciations for words of remote foreign origin long since Anglicized in reputable speech, such as "valet," "boulevard," or "clientele"; and the use of certain pet affectations current among elocutionists and almost nobody else, such as the very special way of saying "girl" (gɜil or geɜl), "really" ('reæli), or "world" (wɜild or hwɜild). Surely the reader has heard these elegant monstrosities.

GOOD ELOCUTION

If elocution could be understood to mean simply utterance—the giving out of words—and good elocution to mean clear, audible, intelligible utterance, the actor should by all means cultivate good elocution. It is not elocution that is bad, but Elocution with a capital *E*—the cult of shallow

Lester Wallack
(1820–1888)

versatile actor himself, he carried on
e fine stock-company tradition of his
ther at Wallack's Theatre. Harrison
rey Fiske called him "the glass of fash-
n and the mold of form."

"Lotta" (Charlotte Crabtree) (1847–1924)
The darling of the pioneer west, she was a minor actress
but a major figure in theatre history, the greatest "barn-
stormer" of them all.

late 9. Popular stars of the post-
ivil-War decades.

Third and most succes-
ful of his family name,
he made Rip popular in
1859 and kept him so for
forty years.

Charming and versatile
daughter of E. L. Daven-
port, very popular in the
seventies and eighties.

Fanny Davenport
(1850–1898)

Joseph Jefferson (1829–1905)
as Rip Van Winkle

Lily Glover

Mrs. E. J. Phillips

Lizzie Harold

Charles Stanley

Plate 10. A long run in the seventies. Souvenir program of *Our Boys*, which ran all summer and fall in the Centennial year, breaking the record for Philadelphia. The program was printed on white satin, a procedure which became a ritual in many theatres for 100th performances. This theatre had strong resident companies for a number of years under the direction of F. F. Mackay. They played standard repertory with the accent on comedy.

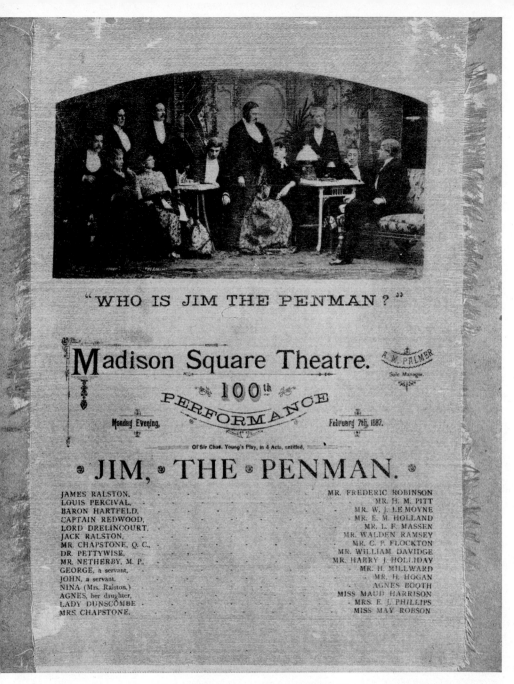

Plate 11. A long run in the eighties. In the seventies and eighties New York, having displaced Philadelphia as theatrical capital, rejoiced in several fine stock companies, notably those of Wallack, Palmer, and Daly. Long runs were not usual in those companies, but *Jim the Penman* was a smash hit, running far beyond the performance here commemorated. The program is printed on satin, with an unusually good halftone for that early date.

Clara Morris
(1846–1925)

J. H. Stoddart
(1827–1907)

May Robson
(1865?–1945)

E. M. Holland
(1848–1913)

Maud Harrison

W. J. LeMoyne
(1831–1905)

McKee Rankin
as Jacques Frochard

Annie Russell

Harry Woodruff

Plate 12. A few Palmer players. The union Square and Madison Square Theatres of A. M. Palmer were training schools for a generation of young actors who played in association with seasoned veterans. Here shown are some of his best-known artists, young and old. Others are mentioned or shown in other connections on Plates 11, 12, 16, 17.

Augustin Daly's stock company in his farce *A Night Off*. (John Drew, James Lewis, Ada Rehan, Charles Fisher, Virginia Dreher, Mrs. Gilbert, Otis Skinner, and May Irwin.)

John
Drew
(1853–1927)

Otis Skinner
(1858–1942)

Ada Rehan
(1860–1916)

Plate 13. The Daly company. Concentrating more on light comedy and farce, Daly's Theatre was also a nursery for stars-to-be.

Mrs. G. H. Gilbert
(1822–1904)

John Drew and Ada Rehan in *The Squire*

Sarah Bernhardt ↑
(1845–1923) →

Plage 14. Foreign stars successful in America. "The divine Sarah," whose voice was "liquid music," acted only in French, with her own French company. Salvini, called by Towse "incomparably the greatest actor I have ever seen," acted in Italian with English-speaking companies. Modjeska, Polish-born, acted in English and remained in America.

Helena Modjeska
(1844–1909)

Tommaso Salvini (1829–1915)
as Ingomar

Constant Coquelin
(1841–1909)

Denis Diderot
(1713–1784)

Sir Henry Irving
(1838–1905)

Ellen Terry as Portia

Plate 15. Masks or faces. Key figures in the famous controversy. It was Coquelin's essay on *The Actor and His Art* in 1880 which revived interest in Diderot's *Paradoxe* (1770), and it was Irving who led the opposition. Coquelin is shown below in his most famous part as Cyrano, and Irving as Shylock. Ellen Terry (mother of Gordon Craig and great-aunt of John Gielgud) was Irving's co-star. Note the old-fashioned grooved stage in the Cyrano picture.

Plate 16. A portrait gallery on cigarette cards. It was quite the fashion, when stage players were idolized as movie stars are now, for smokers and their friends to make collections of these cards, one of which came in each package of cigarettes. Baseball players and pugilists were similarly honored; occasionally even statesmen or authors.

exhibitionism built up by well-meaning but ignorant practitioners who mistake veneer for culture and artificiality for art. The wise actor will keep out of such company and avoid every trick or mannerism associated with the cult.

On the other hand, actors who have had no training in elocution at all, good or bad, are likely to fall into the opposite error. In the attempt to be natural and unaffected they are likely to read their lines in the same inarticulate, mumbling tones that pass for naturalness in real life.

In ordinary conversation, even at close range, we Americans speak none too clearly. Many of our remarks are not heard correctly the first time. "I beg your pardon?" "What did you say?" "Sorry, I didn't catch that?" "Huh?" "Whassat?" "Come again?"—such responses are heard all too often in everyday life. But what becomes of the theatre if the actor does no better? The audience cannot very well say "Huh?" or "Beg pardon?" every time the actor mumbles his words. People who buy tickets for the theatre have a right to expect what they do not expect in everyday life: to hear and understand the speaker clearly in every line, without repetition, and in spite of the greater spaces and distances.

To speak his lines with clarity, meaning, and carrying power, yet without artificiality or affectation—that is good elocution for the actor.

To achieve it he must, of course, have a reasonably strong, clear voice, and good clean enunciation. Suggestions for developing these qualities will be offered in later chapters. But he must also have something a little less tangible: namely, a sense of projection; a keen awareness of his audience without direct communication with them; a power to gauge the exact volume, the exact degree of clarity necessary to reach them without straining or pounding. He must speak his lines openly—not to himself and his fellow actors only, but to the most distant part of the audience—while at the same time he must seem to be speaking them naturally to the other characters in the play.

Good elocution is not shouting, not overprecise enunciation, not painfully exaggerated syllabification, not excessive literalness, not brittle artificiality. Rather it is a subtle, unobtrusive heightening of the natural rhythms and inflections of conversation, in such a way that they become clearer than in real life, and project easily to all parts of the theatre.

Insuring the Key Syllables

One device that is very essential to good elocution is the accurate selection and emphasis of the key words or syllables—those that are especially significant in conveying the meaning.

As already mentioned, English is a language of strong contrasts between accented and unaccented syllables. It is also a language of phrases rather than words. In normal speech we do not hear all the unaccented syllables, or we hear them so indistinctly that we cannot depend upon them for meaning. We may think we hear all the syllables, but actually we hear chiefly the key syllables; and we are able to supply the missing ones because the phrases and their rhythms are familiar to our ears. When an unimportant syllable escapes us we know instinctively what it ought to be from the rhythm and context. But we can only do this when the missing syllables are routine ones; the moment we miss a key syllable we are in danger of losing the meaning, since nothing in the phraseology will necessarily supply it.

In the following sentences, for example, we should certainly have difficulty in grasping the meaning if we heard only the syllables printed and missed the ones indicated by dashes:

You must not —— —— because it —— —— —— all the —— —— ——.
It had —— —— your —— —— —— perhaps, but I assure you it's a ——.
I bear no —— —— for a fair act of ——.
I —— to —— an —— —— —— so he won't —— —— —— again.

On the other hand we could easily make a good guess at the missing syllables in the following sentences:

You must —— do that —— —— —— outrages —— —— decencies.
It —— escaped —— memory —— haps —— —— assure —— —— —— fact.
I bear —— malice —— —— fair act —— war.
I want —— make —— —— pression —— —— won't misbehave —— gain.

They are, of course, the same sentences. All are taken from the dialogue of modern plays.

What makes a key syllable a key syllable? Not the fact that it is an accented syllable, though most key syllables are accented. Not its logical importance; for a syllable may be logically important and yet not a key syllable in the sense in which the term is here used. For example, in the sentence, "The prisoner is not guilty," the most important syllable logically is "not." But if, by chance, that word is indistinctly uttered, or is blurred by a competing cough or sneeze, there is little likelihood that anybody will miss the meaning, because the rhythm of the sentence is so different from that of the contrary sentence, "The prisoner is guilty." In other words, the importance of any syllable as a key syllable depends not only on its logical significance, but on the relation between its meaning and

the context, especially the sentence rhythm. A key syllable is one that is essential to an understanding of the meaning, and that nothing in rhythm or context will supply if it is indistinctly uttered or blurred by distracting sounds.

The obvious method of insuring the key syllables is to go through the part on paper, underlining the syllables that appear to be significant, and then memorizing the lines with the importance of those syllables consciously in mind. But that method is extremely dangerous, for it is almost sure to be mechanical and to result in artificial "pounding."

A far better method is to work from the inside out by trying to sense the importance of the syllables in terms of the meaning, and to feel the rhythms as part of the meaning. Like most problems in acting, it all comes back to the actor's imagination. The actor who is sufficiently imaginative in respect to the meaning of his part will be much more apt to project successfully the syllables essential to convey that meaning than the actor who is only half aware of what it is all about. If the imaginative actor does occasionally let down too much in the force of his utterance, becoming too confidential, he is at least likely to keep the relative values right; and on being told by the director to project more vigorously he is likely to raise the level in proper proportion.

In projecting the key syllables it is extremely helpful to remember that tempo is at least as important as force, if not more so. What is needed to make a key syllable come clear is often nothing more than a retarded tempo, with more duration on the vowel sound, and very little, if any, increase in force. When an *m* or an *n* follows the vowel sound, that also should be lengthened and vocalized with fuller resonance.

WORD EMPHASIS FOR MEANING

A surprising amount of dullness, not to say obscurity, creeps into the reading of many actors through ignorance or neglect of certain simple principles of emphasis.

Apart from the rhythmic emphasis of verse, and from the physical problem of projecting key syllables, there are three common reasons for emphasizing a word or a phrase. The first is its logical or intrinsic importance. The second is the necessity of drawing attention to some contrast or parallelism in which it is involved. The third is the newness of the idea which it injects into the current of discourse.

With the first of these reasons the actor usually has little trouble. He knows enough to emphasize an important noun, verb, predicate adjective,

or adverb which clearly relates to the main thought the character is trying to express; and he knows enough not to emphasize the ordinary run of articles, prepositions, conjunctions, and other utility words.

With the second reason he has a little more difficulty, especially in the first few rehearsals. When contrasts, parallelisms and other rhetorical devices are simple and short, there is little danger of overlooking the proper emphasis; but often they are long and involved, and the words to be compared or contrasted are separated by long subordinate passages. In that case the actor may read them at first without the proper emphasis to bring out the contrasts or parallels. If he goes on to study his part intelligently he will probably discover these devices and give them their proper emphasis before it is too late. The chief danger is that he will not be able to unlearn the false inflections acquired on the first reading; or that he will be too artificial in bringing out the rhetorical devices when he does discover them.

It is the third reason, however, that young actors know least about, and neglect most seriously.

The idea back of every reasonably important word or phrase is either a new idea, appearing for the first time in the speech or scene; or else it is an idea that has been recently mentioned and is being repeated as a matter of back reference. In the first case it calls for a positive emphasis, and a tone of voice that will direct attention to its newness. In the second it calls for no particular emphasis; instead, it should be spoken casually, to reassure the listener that it is the same idea he has already become familiar with, and that nothing new is implied by its repetition. If the actor falsely emphasizes an idea that is not new, or fails to emphasize one that is, he obscures the thought, and perhaps deceives his listeners—not to mention himself—into an outright misunderstanding.

In the following passage (from that charming play, *The Romantic Age*, by A. A. Milne) each of the italicized words or groups of words introduces a fairly important idea for the first time in the scene, or reëmphasizes an old idea in some new connection, or by some contrast or parallelism of thought:

MELISANDE.   It's a *wonderful* night, Mother. *Midsummer* night. I'm not *cold*.
MRS. KNOWLE.   But you *shuddered*. I distinctly *saw* you shudder. Didn't *you* see her, Jane?
JANE.   I'm afraid I wasn't *looking*, Aunt Mary.
MELISANDE.   I didn't shudder because I was *cold*. I shuddered because you will keep calling me by that *horrible name*. I shudder every time I *hear* it.
MRS. KNOWLE.   *What* name, Sandy?

MELISANDE.   There it is *again*. Oh, why did you christen me by such a *wonderful, beautiful, magical* name as *Melisande*, if you were going to call me *Sandy?*

MRS. KNOWLE.   Well, dear, as I think I've told you, *that* was a mistake of your *father's*. I suppose he got it out of some *book*. I should certainly never have *agreed* to it, if I had heard him *distinctly*. I thought he said *Millicent*—after your *Aunt Milly*.

Just how much emphasis each of the italicized words should get, is, of course, debatable. The only purpose in picking them out at all is to force the mind to consider the possible reasons for emphasizing them, or for not emphasizing others.

In the first speech, for example, "wonderful" and "Midsummer" are italicized because they introduce new ideas, but "night" is not, because it has been mentioned in a previous speech of Mrs. Knowle's. "Cold" has not been used before, but has been implied, and might for that reason escape emphasis; but I have italicized it to build up the contrast with "horrible name," which is reaffirmed in the fourth speech. That raises the question whether "cold" should again be emphasized in the fourth speech; I think it should be, not in this case because of newness, but because the reëmphasis is needed to make fully clear the contrast with "horrible name."

In the second speech I have italicized "shuddered" and "saw" because they are new, and have not italicized the second "shudder" because it is a back reference; but this, too, is debatable, for the reason that "shudder" is obviously the most important idea in the speech, and so might bear repeated emphasis. On the other hand, the flighty nature of Mrs. Knowle's thinking seems to come out better if the emphasis shifts to the new element in each of her short sentences.

In the sixth speech the words "christen" and "call" might be emphasized both on the score of newness and also of rhetorical contrast; but the same contrast is carried by the names "Melisande" and "Sandy," and the names themselves are more important than the verbs that go with them. It would be possible to emphasize "christen" and "call" in addition to the words italicized, but that would make the whole speech a bit top-heavy with emphatic words, and might lead to pounding.

Almost any passage of dialogue will involve similar problems in the shading of meaning, with similar opportunities for choice of emphasis. But if the choice be made intelligently in each case, with due regard to the principles explained above, a reasonably clear and colorful reading is likely to result.

I do not suggest that the young actor should mechanize his reading of every speech by underlining each emphatic word and memorizing the

underlining as part of the text. If he did so he would almost surely develop an exaggerated degree of emphasis and a habit of pounding.

On the other hand, every director who has tried to train young actors knows that their most persistent and baffling fault is a tendency to misplace accents for no reason at all, and to memorize the wrong accents before the right ones penetrate their minds. In the passage quoted, for example, amateurs are apt to miss the possible emphasis on "wonderful," "saw," "you," the second "cold," "horrible" (which should split the emphasis with "name"), or "Millicent," and perhaps to put an unnecessary or misleading one on the first "night," "shudder," "see," the second "shudder," the second "shuddered," "mistake," "never," or "said." Any one of these false accents would slightly distort the meaning, and four or five of them would blur the whole passage badly.

What the earnest young player should do is cultivate carefully the habit of being sensitive to the interrelation of ideas, to syntax, to contrast, to parallelism, and especially to back reference or its absence. To that end he should practice frequently the exercise of underlining words to be emphasized in selected passages of varied style—but preferably *not* from parts that he expects to play. They need not, in fact, be from plays at all; they may be from any form of prose or verse, some of the most interesting material for the purpose being discoverable in lyric poetry. Such exercises should be treated as drill work, to limber up the imagination as scales on the piano limber up the fingers, and to be forgotten in actual performance.

Let me repeat that the worst trouble arises from failure to note back reference, or the lack of it. It is due, I think, to the fact that in reading— or reciting—we are under such constant pressure to look ahead and to consider what comes next that we neglect to keep in mind what has already been said, and its relation to what we are saying or about to say. Only by developing a high degree of alertness to back reference can we overcome this difficulty; and there is nothing more important in the curriculum of the student actor.

Teamwork in Reading Lines

There is one phase of the reading of lines that the young actor should never allow himself to forget for a moment. In any other kind of reading aloud, and in most kinds of speaking, the problem is solely, or largely, an individual one. But in acting—except in the rare moments of prolonged soliloquy—the effect of the dialogue does not depend alone on the reading or speaking characteristics of an individual actor; it depends on the co-

ordination of all players involved in bringing out the interrelation of meaning as they speak to, and answer, each other.

That means that the actor must study the delivery of his lines as part of a larger pattern, including his cues, his listening to others, and the effect of their lines on his. In his choice of pitch, or inflection, he must be guided by its relation to the pitch used by the other players. In the matter of tempo, what would seem a slow pace in a duologue with a character having exceptionally rapid speech, might still seem faster than necessary in a scene with a different character. In selecting words for emphasis he must remember that his back references will include back references to words in the speeches of others as well as his own—an exceedingly important point frequently missed by actors who study from "sides" rather than books.

At the same time he must guard against one insidiously bad influence growing out of the fact that he is not working alone. That is the constant temptation to take his pitch or tempo from the other actor by mere thoughtless imitation, instead of choosing it intelligently to fit the character he is playing. This is an extremely common fault with beginners, and does much to spoil otherwise good dialogue. Audience interest in dialogue is greatly heightened by contrasts in pitch and tempo, as well as in timbre, or tone quality. Actors are perhaps less apt to imitate each other in timbre than in pitch or tempo; yet to a lesser degree they may allow almost any characteristic of a fellow player to influence their own reading. An actor playing a refined, highly educated character in a scene with a number of coarse characters may occasionally find himself unconsciously following their tones or pronunciations and failing to maintain the contrast. An actor playing the only American character in a British play—or vice versa —has to watch his reading carefully to avoid a similar temptation. "When in Rome, do as the Romans do," is good advice for a traveler but bad advice for an actor.

THE READING OF VERSE

A good part of what has been said about the reading of lines applies primarily to more or less conversational prose. A great many plays, however, especially from earlier periods, are written in verse. For the player unaccustomed to verse this creates an added problem; though many experienced actors assert that the speaking of verse is easier, once you get used to it, than the speaking of prose. That, of course, is debatable, though there is fairly general agreement on the idea that verse is easier to learn and remember—provided it is good verse.

In speaking verse lines there are two opposite extremes to avoid. The

first is a mechanically singsong reading, and the second is a too-prosy reading.

Singsong reading is distasteful to most listeners, and since it is easy to detect, it is often severely criticized. Schoolteachers trying to teach children to read poetry seem to make singsong reading the unforgivable sin, and hammer at it so incessantly that they induce many youngsters to cultivate the opposite fault.

Singsong reading is not (as many teachers seem to think) the result of too much feeling for the rhythmic quality of the verse. It is the result of too little feeling for the mental and emotional content. The singsong reader grasps only the mechanics of the meter. He does not really grasp the rhythmic feeling at all, because he does not grasp the meaning and emotion; and if the poetry is good poetry the rhythm is inseparable from the meaning and emotion. That is why the poet feels the need to express them rhythmically. Singsong reading is not singsong because it is musical, or songlike, but because it has no songlike quality at all. It is merely mechanically regular, automatic, shallow, meaningless and emotionless—a tinkling sound, but signifying nothing.

A prosy reading, on the other hand, is one that seeks only the literal meaning and throws away the poetry. It never seems to occur to some people that if a poet meant no more than is brought out in a prosy reading he would have written it in prose in the first place. If he chose to put his thoughts and feelings into rhythmic language, it must have been because he expected that rhythmic language to convey something beyond what could be conveyed without it. Yet the chief thing our children are taught in many schools about reading verse is to ignore the rhythm and read it as prose. An excuse sometimes offered for this is that young people do not like poetry unless they can be made to forget the meter and think only of the meaning. If that were true, it would be a possible reason for giving them prose and sparing them poetry; but it is no reason for teaching them to read poetry badly. If they have to choose between meaningless singsong and prosy literalness, they will naturally prefer the latter; but perhaps if they were taught to read imaginatively for *both* music and meaning they would not be so insensitive to poetry.

Good reading of verse is neither one extreme or the other. It is songlike in proportion to the lyrical quality of the verse, but it is never singsong. It is meaningful, but imaginatively and emotionally so, not just factually or literally so. It is rhythmic, in varying degree, from the strongly metrical to the relatively free; but it is never shallow or mechanical. It is not just a

middle course between two extremes, but an organic coördination of two good things: form and content. It does not sacrifice some meaning to capture some rhythm. Instead it combines the deepest and most spiritual meaning with the most moving and satisfying rhythm, both elements gaining by the combination.

If this seems like claiming the cake and the penny too, the explanation is very simple. We do possess both body and mind at the same time; and they do function harmoniously in many ways, without sacrifice of one to the other. If we think of the rhythmic aspects of verse as primarily physical, appealing to bodily response, and the meaning as primarily mental, appealing to the intelligence, it becomes easier to understand how both can operate to the full at the same time. If emotion, as suggested in the chapter on that subject, is an all-overness of response, coördinated through the sympathetic nervous system, it is not difficult to see why a harmonious combination of physical and mental appeal has more emotional depth than either would have alone.

This conception of the problem suggests a technique for studying poetic verse, and for reading or speaking it. In beginning his study, the actor should first seek to find the rhythms by physical means, beating, or stamping, or dancing them out with his body until he has them physically memorized, so to speak. Secondly (with perhaps some overlapping in time) he should direct his intelligence and imagination toward the meaning and mood. The order is not vital, for the objective is a totality of response; but as the rhythm is more likely to be neglected if meaning comes first than is meaning if rhythm comes first, the latter order is recommended as the best approach to a verse part.

When it comes to the actual reading of verse lines, the actor is often troubled by a seeming conflict between meaning and rhythm. He may find, for example, that a unit of meaning runs past the end of a line, and stops in the middle of the next; or that a metrical accent seems to fall on an unimportant syllable, while an important one seems to come in the wrong place to receive proper accent for meaning without upsetting the meter. The solution lies in the fact that the actor is not dependent upon one variable element of expression, but upon several—especially pitch, force, and tempo. Therefore his task is to find, not weak compromises, but strong combinations. If he will remember that tempo is the most important element in conveying the rhythmic effect, and pitch inflection the most important in conveying meaning—with force helping now one and now the other—he will be able to work out a method of balance which will re-

tain both sets of values. But if he has never tried it before, and never even thought about it, he cannot expect to become skillful at it in a week—or even in a year.

The danger of singsong reading is usually greatest in connection with rhymed verse; but even in blank verse (which is unrhymed five-stress iambic verse, and the commonest verse in dramatic literature) the actor is apt to get into mechanical trouble by giving too much attention to the individual line. It is to some degree true of all good verse, and especially true of dramatic verse, that too much emphasis on the line as a metrical unit destroys the poetic feeling. Certainly no great poetic dramatist ever intended his actors to scan separate lines, rather than passages. After all, lines are devices for the eye. The actor, and the dramatist who writes for actors, think of dramatic verse as flowing, emotionally charged dialogue, full of rhythmic beat, but not end-stopped on every line. As often as not, a character speaking in verse begins or ends his speech in the middle of a line; and if he ends it in the middle of a line another character picks it right up and keeps the meter flowing. Bookish scholars have worried a great deal about some seeming irregularities in the scansion of Shakespeare's lines; but most of them are only seeming irregularities, and do not worry the experienced actor at all, because the voice flows right on rhythmically regardless of the printer.

The young actor today has one additional handicap in learning to speak verse lines which his grandfather never faced. That is the blurred rhythmic sense characteristic of our age. Since shortly after World War I there has been a strong tendency in popular song, in dance music, and even in poetry, to abandon the clear rhythms of earlier days and substitute confused, chaotic rhythms, all too expressive of our disordered, disrupted, disillusioned, disintegrating civilization. It began with the restless, nervous, jangling noisiness of the "jazz" age, and resulted at first in overelaboration of rhythms and oversyncopation. Syncopation is temporary shift of accent from the main beat to an offbeat; but when you syncopate too elaborately or too long you simply lose the main beat altogether and the rhythm disappears in amorphous confusion. The most popular type of syncopation for a time was a delayed beat; but it soon degenerated into chronic dragging, and ultimately into the utterly formless maundering which goes by the unhistorical name of "crooning," or into the strange behavior of many modern "dancers," who clutch each other and sway around a ballroom with movements completely unrelated to the music. A whole generation (and more) of young people raised in such an environment could hardly be expected to appreciate the rhythmic qualities of real verse or real music,

much less to be able to act in poetic drama and speak verse lines without blurring the rhythms.

To learn how to speak dramatic verse well, the young man or woman today must first learn how to march, and dance, and sing, and speak verse *on the beat*. He, or she, will do better to learn from the marching band (one of the few hopeful counterinfluences) rather than from the radio crooners. It would be much easier to teach verse reading to a drum-major, or "majorette," than to a torch singer. The student actor should make up his mind that good verse reading is a very different thing from maundering, and that the first step in learning it is frequent, persistent drill—bodily as well as vocal—in clear, simple, basic rhythms. Eventually he will want to speak dramatic verse with freedom and variety; but before he can do that, he must master the normal rhythms which are the basis from which freedom and variety start.

CHAPTER XI

Comedy

A FINE piece of comic acting is so entertaining and delightful to watch, and usually seems so spontaneous and effortless, that the young actor is apt to fancy himself as a comedian and to suppose that comedy is the easy road to success. Veterans know that comedy—especially high comedy—is far harder to act than tragedy, and good comedians harder to find than good serious actors.

Wisecracking, loud-mouthed "funny men" are, to be sure, very plentiful, especially on the radio and the screen, and they have no difficulty making the moronic millions laugh at ancient jokes, topical gibes, or lacerations and degradations of the language. Their success is less often due to their skill and originality than to the high percentage of nitwits in their audiences, and to the fact that most people will laugh at what they know is supposed to be funny even when it is obviously strained. Call it good nature, or politeness, or call it the herd instinct to conform, but without it many of our professional zanies could not make a living. I do not mean to suggest that there is no place in the art of acting for low comedy or clever buffoonery; but much of what passes for comedy in these days is not acting at all. Real comedy is never too plentiful in our theatres, and real comedians to make the most of it are unfortunately rare.

With imagination, sympathy, intelligence, and sincerity, a young player of very little experience can often do surprisingly well in a serious or tragic part, especially if the play itself is well and sincerely written. For success in comedy, however, he must have something else. Either through talent or training he must have a highly skilled technique, and above all he must have that mysterious quality which theatre people call "the comedy sense."

NATURE OF THE COMEDY SENSE

The comedy sense is not easy to define, though its absence is painfully easy to detect. Many an otherwise promising young player, with plenty of intelligence, and even with a certain kind of dramatic imagination, seems hopelessly inept in comedy. He may have alertness, literary under-

standing, a keen enjoyment of acting, and an undoubted sense of humor, and yet fail dismally to project the comedy to the audience. He may be consciously aware that he is failing, and not know what to do about it; and this may happen to actors of considerable experience as well as to beginners.

One of the most reliable non-professional actresses of my acquaintance works under a constant handicap through her lack of an accurate comedy sense. In the part of Mrs. Malaprop, for example, she had difficulty in getting results after several weeks of rehearsal. An indefatigable worker, she had her most important speeches recorded, and brought the records to me for study and criticism. To help her, I took motion pictures of her, in costume, speaking the same lines, so that she could both see and hear herself. She was desolated.

"I'm not funny a bit!" she said. "When I read those lines to myself they seem full of humor, and I laugh at them every time; but nobody is going to laugh at them if I say them *that* way. They're deadly. I know they are. I can see it, and hear it, and still I don't know what is wrong."

Working word by word and line by line, we tried to find out what was wrong. We found, among other things, that her pace was too even, and that she was missing many opportunities for contrast; also that she was "pounding" the Malapropisms in such a way as to suggest, not the character's pride in her fancied erudition, but the player's consciousness that the words were being misapplied. She corrected these and many other faults, and I am happy to report that in the end she played Mrs. Malaprop very well indeed; experience and persistence bring results, even in the arts. But it was very exasperating, especially to her, to realize that a player with a naturally accurate comedy sense could have spoken those lines effectively with one quarter of the effort. The baffling thing about it is the fact that the lady in the case really has an exceptionally keen sense of humor, and is, off the stage, the most entertaining conversationalist I have ever had the pleasure of knowing. She has an endless fund of amusing anecdotes, which she relates so comically as to keep her friends in a constant state of humorous appreciation; and she does it without the slightest effort.

If this were a unique and abnormal experience I should not have set it down. It is, unfortunately, a typical experience among those who enjoy comedy and like to act in it, and I could cite many similar cases. Intelligence and a keen enjoyment of humor just do not necessarily imply a comedy sense in terms of theatre. Conversely, some of the best stage comedians are known to be serious or even melancholy souls, not at all

funny off the stage. The comedy sense, as the term is used in the theatre, is a very special talent or accomplishment, not identical with, nor to be confused with, the sense of humor.

It must, of course, *include* a sense of humor, even though it be a reticent one; an actor could hardly convey the humorous implications of his part to an audience unless he had first grasped them himself. Indeed, our pleasure in the work of a good comedian lies partly in the comfortable feeling that he fully understands the author's humorous intent, and enjoys sharing it with us. At the same time we prefer that he shall not be too obvious in his enjoyment; that he shall not try too hard to be funny; that he shall not "push" or "pound" his lines, or laugh too hard at them himself. In short, we expect him to project the humor to us with just the right balance between impersonation and appreciation—in other words, between empathy and æsthetic distance.

Without attempting a categorical definition of the comedy sense, I would venture the suggestion that it includes at least the following elements:

1. A confident, easy ability to function on two planes at once, as artist and instrument.
2. A strong, but subtle, feeling for thought-sharing as opposed to exhibitionism.
3. A keen sense of humor.
4. A lively sense of projection.
5. A delicate sense of timing.
6. A sharp sense of contrast.
7. A reasonable amount of restraint.

These do not begin to cover all the details of technique by which comic effects are achieved in the theatre, but they do indicate the more important psychological principles involved. The first two of them have already been discussed at some length in earlier chapters; the last five need, perhaps, some further explanation.

THE SENSE OF HUMOR

The sense of humor itself is not so difficult to understand. It is usually explained as the recognition of incongruity—the discovery of something out of place or out of proportion with the normal or natural or expected order of things. When very important matters are so seriously out of place that we cannot maintain our æsthetic distance, the effect is apt to be disturbing rather than humorous; but when the incongruities are trifling

enough to be viewed with detachment, the effect is humorous, and the more fantastic the incongruities the more humorous they seem.

There is nothing either humorous or tragic about a normal human face, with two eyes, two ears, a nose and a mouth, of the usual size, arrangement, and proportion. But when a cartoonist distorts a face by making some of the features larger or smaller or more crooked than usual he creates an effect that may be either humorous or revolting depending upon the spirit in which it is done and the degree of painfulness in the distortion.

If you behold a person with an abnormally long, or colorful, or bulbous nose it is apt to strike you as humorous—the more so if he does not seem too sensitive about it and is willing to joke about it himself. There are professional comedians who find some such happy affliction a great asset in their efforts to be funny; in fact there are some who could never have been mistaken for comedians at all but for a preposterous nose, or cauliflower ears, or crossed eyes, or an ear-to-ear mouth. Crossed eyes are thought to be especially comical in a professional funny man, but most of us do not see the humor in them when they occur in a four-year-old niece or granddaughter. If you encounter a friend with a black patch or a blood-stained bandage over one eye, you are instantly concerned, and inquire anxiously what has happened to him; if you encounter him, instead, with an equally incongruous but less alarming blue-black-and-green "shiner" you are very apt to laugh boisterously and make facetious (if not altogether original) remarks.

In other words, the sense of humor is based upon a sense of incongruity, but not all incongruity is humorous. Whether it strikes us as humorous, pathetic, tragic, or merely annoying, depends upon the relationships that control our attitude towards it. Hence the common observation that humor and pathos are closely related. The same incongruity may strike us as humorous one moment and pathetic the next; it may even strike us as humorous and pathetic at the same time, since the painful and absurd aspects may be so interwoven as to seem inseparable. Much of the best and most lasting humor in literature is of this mixed type; lyric poetry, for example—such as that of A. E. Housman, or Sarah Teasdale, or James Stevens—abounds in rueful smiles and comic tears.

If the sense of humor rests upon the recognition of incongruity or disproportion, it follows that the person most likely to have a true sense of humor is the person with a just sense of proportion—with what is often called a sense of values.

Distorted, unstable, or one-sided people are generally humorless, or they are characterized by a warped, unhealthy, and frequently unkind

form of humor. Such people laugh readily at crudities or cruelties; at obscenity, bad manners, or the painful misfortunes of others. True humor does not thrive in countries where reciprocity and fair play are not understood; where men consider a one-sided form of conduct—such as the persecution or "liquidation" of opponents, the seizure of power by force, the suppression of free speech, or the use of forced labor—a great crime in others but a great virtue in themselves. In such countries you will find humorless sadism, insincerity, and bad manners masquerading as humor. The newspaper cartoons of Germany and Spain for the last two generations, and more recently of Soviet Russia, are good examples.

True, sound, healthy humor is found at its best in those countries and those periods in which men generally honor the rights of others, believe in fair play, reciprocity, individual freedom with corresponding responsibility, and majority rule tempered by consideration for the opinions of the minority; and it is best appreciated by well-balanced persons who see things in true perspective, who have no distorting obsessions, no exaggerated notion of their own importance, or of man's importance in the universe. The world would be a happier place if everybody had a true sense of humor, or if only those who had were permitted to achieve leadership.

So much for the nature of humor. But a keen sense of humor implies both the humor and the keenness. To a just sense of proportion must be added considerable mental agility, a lively awareness of what is going on, a discriminating alertness in spotting incongruities when they occur. Even a well-balanced person can only be said to show a keen sense of humor when his mind is fully awake and alert, with all parts functioning. Perhaps that is why some persons with a good sense of humor in social life seem to lose it on the stage; perhaps something in the unfamiliar situation provokes self-consciousness and inhibits certain mental functions, while others— the memory function, for example—are abnormally active. This may or may not be good scientific theory, but it suggests an approach to the problem which I have found useful in baffling cases of weak comedy sense.

THE SENSE OF PROJECTION

Some attention has already been given to the element of projection in relation to the devices of exaggeration and signaling, all three being important in general acting technique on the subjective side of the dual function. All three are particularly important in comedy technique, and in a larger sense projection may be said to include exaggeration and signaling.

The comedian must learn, however, that projection does not mean ex-

hibitionism; nor does it mean forcing, pushing, or pounding the humor. The worst thing any comedian can do is to try too hard—or at any rate to be caught doing so. Even his exaggeration must not be too obviously intentional; and his signaling must not be so frantic as to suggest a lack of confidence in the intelligence of the audience, or in his own ability to convey the humorous intent.

Good comic projection is permissive, rather than imperative or persuasive. It does not say to the audience, "Laugh, you lunkheads, laugh!" It does not say, "Please laugh, friends; I'm trying so hard to be funny!" Rather it seems to say, "Okay, friends, your ears are not deceiving you; that's what the author meant to say, and it's just as funny as you think it is, so go right ahead and laugh!" People in a theatre are eager enough to laugh, but they are also a bit fearful of misunderstanding something and perhaps laughing at the wrong place. They may even be afraid to laugh at the right place lest they miss an important line by doing so. The function of good projection, and especially of the projected laugh signal— such as the lifting of the eyes straight front, described in Chapter IV— is to give them a familiar and instantly recognizable green light.

Perhaps the most important element in good comedy projection is that often spoken of as "following-through." The good comedian, like the good golfer, tries to think his stroke through to the very end, and even a little bit beyond. He must be careful, of course, not to overdo it—not to be tempted into obviousness, or into "mugging." But the actor who fails to follow through on humorous lines, dropping his voice too soon, or changing his manner, or turning away at the critical instant, only succeeds in concealing or blurring the author's comic intent and killing legitimate laughs to no purpose whatever.

For example, consider the moment in *You Can't Take It With You* when Penny, wrestling with her problems as a playwright, interrupts Mr. De Pinna on his way to the fireworks laboratory in the cellar, and says, "Mr. De Pinna, if a girl you loved entered a monastery, what would you do?" Mr. De Pinna hesitates an instant and replies, "Oh, I don't know, Mrs. Sycamore . . . it's been so long." It is his exit line, and he is anxious to get back to his work, so the temptation is strong on the actor to turn away as he says the line and go out. But there is a nice bit of humor in that line, seasoned by a touch of pathos, and if the actor turns away too quickly and too casually he kills the line and spoils the laugh. To share the comedy with his audience he must pause just long enough on the last part of the line to follow the thought through before turning away. This may best be done in such position that the audience can see his face—an easy thing to

manage naturally in this case, since he is about to exit right when Penny
calls him from left, and the interruption catches him in medial position,
with ear cocked left, feet still aiming right, and face front. I have chosen
this example because it also illustrates the opposite danger. If the actor
pauses just a little *too* long, or points up the nostalgic suggestion too senti-
mentally, or strains too obviously for the laugh, he violates the character
of Mr. De Pinna, sacrifices the integrity of his imagination, and becomes
just a mugging actor. Good comedy acting is precisely that kind of tight-
rope-walking; you can fall off any minute on either side.

For another example of following-through, take the moment in Lonsdale's *The High Road* when Lord Trench, about to make a comically
indignant exit, pauses at the door and says, "I wish to say I have had a
damned insulting evening." For best effect, the line must be said with
pompous deliberation, including a slight pause after "say," and followed
through imaginatively. The actor must not hurry the exit, and the audience
must be able to see his face until the last word is spoken. In this case,
however, good following-through does not preclude his beginning the turn
an instant before the last word is out, so long as the turn is deliberate and
does not cut off the final syllable, for the exit itself is inherently related to
the thought expressed and is hence really a part of the following-through.

The technique of following-through is not confined to exit lines, however,
nor even to final lines. Many of the most critical moments calling for it
are to be found in medial lines, just before a significant pause, a sharp
contrast, a quick shift of thought, or a hurried afterthought. In the last
two cases especially the actor is likely to be caught off guard through his
anticipation of the change (which he knows is coming, though the character
does not) and to neglect the following-through.

For example, in the last moments of *The School for Scandal*, Sir Peter
Teazle says, "And may you live as happy as Lady Teazle and I intend
to do." Spoken as punctuated, the line is conventional, and has no particular comedy value. But if Sir Peter follows through on "Lady Teazle
and I" as if the thought were complete in his mind and ought to have a
period after it, and then adds the last three words as a hurried afterthought
to ward off the reaction of amusement which he suddenly sees coming,
he not only gets a laugh—he gets two laughs crowded into one. Whether
Sheridan so intended it I cannot say, though his making Sir Peter add the
last three words at all shows a lively consciousness of the fact that the
couple had *not* lived very happily up to that moment. In any case our
broken reading is good comedy, and it is in no sense cheap or insincere
because it is more imaginatively true to Sir Peter's character and to the

mood and spirit of the play than the duller reading which throws the laugh away.

There is one type of comedy in which the following-through technique is particularly essential. That is the type which rests upon our amused observation of what happens to characters who are themselves never intentionally funny, but react sincerely (with an allowable measure of exaggeration) to their experiences, no matter how preposterous. There are elements of this type in most of the best comedy. There are many examples of it—along with some unfortunate lapses—in *You Can't Take It With You;* enough, perhaps, to explain its Pulitzer Prize. The Russians, in their somewhat infrequent experiments with comedy, have given us some excellent examples, and the finest one I know of is Gogol's *The Inspector-General.* In scene after scene of that delightful comedy the humor stems from the fact that each character is following his own thoughts through with great intensity and many resulting incongruities; and at the final curtain—perhaps the funniest final curtain in all theatre history—each character falls into an attitude which expresses the concentrated distillation of his state of mind, and holds it till the curtain is down. At least that is what Gogol wanted, and asked for in a careful written statement; he begged and pleaded with the actors to think out their attitudes and hold them without wavering until the curtain was down, and after the first performance he tore his hair at their failure to follow through.

Whatever the type of line or situation, the actor should think of following-through, not as a device of cheap trickery to force a laugh unfairly or insincerely, but as a reasonable and necessary form of insurance against the blight of obscurity or dullness. Good comedy is a delicate thing, the least mismanagement of which destroys half the pleasure of watching it; and much of the very best comedy is ruined in performance by the inexperienced actor's failure to follow through.

Good projection also includes sufficient heightening of voice and manner, and sufficient clarification through selection and emphasis to overcome the difficulties of space and distance; but enough attention has already been given to those points.

THE SENSE OF TIMING

A good sense of timing might conceivably be thought of as part of a good sense of projection. Good timing is certainly an important part of following-through, as in the case of Sir Peter's line already cited. If he hurries on to the afterthought just a mite too quickly he spoils the follow-through and the audience misses the point; whereas if he delays a fraction of a

second too long the audience beats him to the first laugh, killing the after-thought and the better laugh that should come with it. Bad timing could ruin any one of the examples given in the last few pages.

Just what constitutes good timing one would hardly dare say. Mark Twain, in his interesting essay on how to tell a humorous story, says that everything depends on the skillful use of the pause, especially the final pause just before the denouement. But there are many kinds of pauses, and many subtle variations of tempo besides actual pauses; and the endless variations of plot, situation, character, and action on the stage make the actor's problem of timing much more complex than the storyteller's. No simple formula, no set of formulas, could possibly cover it. In one line a comedian gets a happily comic effect by hurrying the tempo; in another by slowing it down. In one case a skillfully managed pause brings out a humorous meaning; in another a similar type of pause seems to kill the humor entirely. In some cases the timing must give the audience an opportunity to laugh; in others it must deny that opportunity while the player hurries his lines, keeping one jump ahead of the laugh until the audience nearly chokes with pent-up mirth. For the true comedian every humorous line is a new problem in timing.

In general it may be said that more good lines, both comic and serious, are made ineffective by timing that is too rapid than by timing that is too slow.

True, if one thinks of the rapid-fire pace maintained by some of our high-pressure funny men, that statement may seem like a strange one. But there is a practical reason for the present cult of mile-a-minute wisecrack-ing. Humor that is ground out to order, "Monday through Friday," mainly by disguising warmed-over jokes in new slang or fresh distortions of voice or language, has to be rattled off fast so that the listener will laugh before he has time to think; otherwise he will discover the staleness, or the strain, and realize that the stuff isn't very funny after all. Fast timing is the only effective camouflage for moronic humor, and never in the history of the world has there been such a deluge of moronic humor as we have at present.

In real comedy, however, where the humor has some degree of subtlety or profundity, even perhaps of originality, the actor can usually achieve a richer, fuller enjoyment for himself and his audience by taking enough time to "suck the juice out of it," so to speak. Comedy will always call for a faster average pace than tragedy, and certain scenes—like some of those in *The Inspector General*—will call for an exceptionally rapid pace. Never-theless, the biographies of successful actors, both comic and tragic, cite

many examples of good effects achieved by taking plenty of time and refusing to be hurried into blurred or meaningless utterance.

This does not mean that the average pace should be slow; still less that it should be uniform. Indeed, it is just as important to speed up the subordinate and non-critical passages—the passages that present no subtleties or chances of misunderstanding—as it is to bring out the full values of the essential passages. Nothing kills the comedy spirit more effectively than unnecessary "dragging." Good timing, therefore, means taking enough time to clarify meanings, point up imagination, and allow for the full impact of wit and humor; but it does not mean wasting so much as a fraction of a second. Good timing is always varied timing, partly because variety is pleasing in itself and an aid to lively attention, and partly because varied timing is the best means of heightening contrast and revealing incongruities. A delicate sense of timing and a sharp sense of contrast are closely related indeed.

If the young actor does not have a naturally accurate sense of timing—as most do not—there is only one thing for him to do. That is to train it by experiment. Taking each comedy line or situation as a special study, he must try it out with every conceivable variation of tempo. He must try it fast, and try it slow; try it with slow start and rapid finish, and with the reverse; try it without pauses, and with; try pausing just before the main point, and just after it. If he can arrange to record his experiments and play them back for study, so much the better; but he must not be trapped into the common error of listening only to his own words and inflections, and not to his *meanings*. In other words, he must not get so interested in the mechanics of expression as to forget that they are only the means, not the beginning and not the end. Important as timing is, he must realize that it cannot be completely isolated, even for study, but must be considered in its relation to all other elements of expression—pitch, force, timbre, and so on. And he must understand that the problem of timing is a problem in the coördination of voice, gesture, facial expression, pantomimic action, movement, and every other conceivable element of expression; it is not a problem in vocal expression alone.

A slowly timed movement accompanied by a rapidly timed line may produce an effect of incongruity quite appropriate to certain comic situations; a rapid movement accompanied by a slow line may be equally comic, but convey an entirely different meaning. Rapid timing on a low pitch is very different in effect from rapid timing on a high pitch. A pause in line just before a movement may suggest a shade of meaning quite unlike that suggested by a movement just before the pause. A bit of timing that is just

right on a line spoken straight front may be all wrong if the line is spoken on a turn to right or left. The permutations are endless.

Does that mean that they are hopeless? That the young actor should give up all attempt to study them, and rely on sheer luck, or genius, or that mysterious thing that lazy people call "inspiration"? It certainly does not.

It does mean that he should realize from the first the enormous complexity of good comedy technique, and accept the fact that it cannot be coldly and scientifically synthesized. He should make no attempt to reduce it to a set of rigid rules. But there is no reason why he should not study it with care and curiosity, in the effort to discover the causal relationships involved as an aid to intelligent self-criticism. The more knowledge he accumulates about why this piece of timing was effective and why that one was not, the less frequently he will get into trouble through bad timing. The emphasis must be on the "why," however—not just the "what." After all, though the possible variations in technique are infinite, the reasons for success or failure are not nearly so numerous, and most of them can be learned through alert observation and experience.

Some of the most difficult and interesting problems of timing, especially in comedy, are to be found in scenes that have very few lines, or none at all.

Such scenes, when logically appropriate to the action, well conceived and well acted, furnish some of the most delightful moments in comedy. One reason for this is the fact that the eye is generally quicker and sharper than the ear, so that most people can grasp visible humor better than humor conveyed in words. But there is another and perhaps more important reason. When the actor conveys the humor in words everybody subconsciously feels that it is the author and the actor who are being clever, not the audience; whereas, when no words are spoken and the humor is perceived in the physical attitudes, actions, and facial expressions of the actor, each observer somehow feels that he has detected it for himself, through his own superior discernment and cleverness—a very pleasant and harmless form of egotism which most people enjoy enormously without quite understanding why. There may be a touch of vanity in it, but it is pretty closely related to the creative impulse which makes us all want to share imaginatively in the work of the artist, and thus makes the living theatre a more vital group art than the movies can ever be. Small wonder that those scenes which give it free play have a special kind of effectiveness with audiences.

If examples are needed, consider the opening scene of *The Professor's Love Story*, by J. M. Barrie, in which the professor sits at his desk for nearly

five minutes without uttering a word, yet tells us most amusingly by his actions that he is in love and does not know what is the matter with him; or the scene in Fagan's *And So To Bed* in which King Charles, discovering a flageolet in his lady-love's apartment, realizes that Mr. Pepys must be there, looks suspiciously at the window drapes, the bedroom door, and other possible hiding places, and finally spots the chest in which the audience knows that Mr. Pepys is hiding; or the scene in *The High Road* in which Lord Trench, having voiced his disapproval of cocktails and indignantly refused one, silently watches Lady Minster enjoying hers, and slowly yields to the temptation to try one himself; or the scene in *You Can't Take It With You* in which the Kirby family, arriving for dinner on the wrong night, stand frozen in the doorway at the amazing tableau that confronts them; or the scene in the same play in which Grandpa Vanderhof, about to start a game of darts, is suddenly tempted by a choice of targets; or the final scene already referred to in *The Inspector-General*.

In the latter scene (as in all curtain scenes) the timing is largely in the hands of the prompter and curtain puller, though the Gendarme does have a responsibility in timing his entrance, announcement, and exit, and Karobkina has a very critical responsibility in timing her little giggle, which is the signal for the shift from one tableau to the other. In the remaining examples the timing is almost entirely in the hands of the actors, subject, of course, to the director's instructions. In *You Can't Take It With You*, the entrance of the Kirbys stops the show, and nobody has much control over the timing until the audience quiets down enough for the actors to proceed; their worst difficulty is to retain their composure through the long laugh, and to resist the temptation to resume their lines in too much of a hurry. Those who have actions to perform rather than lines can resume a little sooner, since people can still see, even when they are laughing too hard to hear anything. A wise director will not let this sort of interruption last too long, for an audience that has laughed itself out feels let down and is less responsive thereafter. He will probably suggest that the actors resume speaking the instant they feel that the peak of the laugh has been passed (or even sooner, if the laugh is unreasonably long) moving their lips or faking lines, if necessary, until they can make the correct lines heard.

The four other examples mentioned all involve difficult problems of timing for the individual actor. In each case the most obvious difficulty is the temptation which all actors feel to distrust themselves in silent scenes and hurry on to the spoken lines. The inexperienced actor feels it most acutely, of course; he feels it with particular embarrassment at rehearsals,

when there is no audience out front to give him even a silent reaction, and
the few people present, if listening at all, are impatient to get ahead with
their own scenes. If the director tells him to take his time and play the
scene for its full comedy value, he is likely to protest that he cannot feel
the timing with no audience there to respond, but "will be all right when
the audience is in." If the director still insists that he do the best he can,
he is apt to study the timing mechanically, never quite believing in it;
and in the end he may have to study it all over again when the audience
is really in. So much emphasis in rehearsals is necessarily concentrated on
learning lines and taking up cues promptly, that the actor feels rather
guilty if he consumes any appreciable time without speaking. He has a
horrible fear that if he does so in performance the people out front will
think he has forgotten his lines, and begin to laugh at him instead of with
him. If he is an actor of some experience he may have the even more horrible fear that the prompter will think so too, and begin throwing lines at
him prematurely—which is about as disconcerting as anything that can
happen to an actor. If he is a thoroughly experienced comedian he may
conquer these fears, but will be aware of another danger not so obvious to
the beginner: the danger that a too-zealous effort to hold the audience without lines will tempt him into overacting.

In the delightful opening scene of Barrie's worst play, the Professor
tries to write, but his mind wanders. So do his eyes—toward an empty
chair at a typewriter desk nearby. He gazes dreamily at it for a time, recalls himself with a start, and resumes his writing. But the pen seems to
drag, stalls again, and the dreamy look comes back. He tries to shake it
off, looks puzzled and distressed about himself, remembers his pills, and
gets a pillbox out of the drawer of his desk. Absent-mindedly lodging his
pen over his ear, he reaches for a glass of water, swallows a pill, and me-
thodically washes it down. Again he tries to resume his writing, but cannot
find his pen; he makes a patient search for it all over the desk and on the
floor, looks completely baffled, and finally gets another one from the
drawer. He dips it in the water instead of the ink and tries to write, blames
the trouble on the pen and gets out a new one. He dips this one in the ink
and then stares into space for the inspiration that does not come. His eye
falls on the pillbox, then shifts to the clock, and again he is puzzled; has
he taken that overdue pill or not? He decides not, and takes another. And
so it goes, for as long as the actor can sustain it successfully and the audience can take it. It must be over thirty years since I saw George Arliss
do that scene, and I have neither seen nor read the play since; I remember
nothing about the rest of the play except its general inferiority and that

awful wheatfield scene (one of the worst ever written by a master hand) yet the opening scene has remained vividly in my recollection as one of the most appealing bits of comedy I have ever seen.

Obviously the actor who distrusts himself in such a scene is under great temptation to rush the timing; but if he does, he will falsify both the character and the situation. The Professor is not in a hurry. To sustain the scene, the actor must, of course, be intelligible; his silences must have meaning, and they can only have meaning for the audience if they have meaning for him—vivid, imaginative meaning. So long as his silent business is clear, amusing, varied, and well timed, the audience will take a surprising amount of it without impatience. But even after he has learned to take his time, he is still under a constant temptation to overplay the business in the fear that it may not be clear enough. He is very apt to make the dreamy look too dreamy, the start too violent, the worried look too intense, and the search for the pen too frantic; he is apt to take eight pills instead of two or three, or lose five pens instead of one or two. In that case the scene will go sour; but it will not be the fault of slow timing.

In the cocktail scene of *The High Road*, Lord Trench, having previously established his character as that of a charmingly cantankerous old Tory, scolds his cousin Lady Minster—his hostess—for offering him the indignity of a cocktail. It is not that he is an abstainer; rather, he belongs to the age of port and brandy, and resents such upstart modernism. While he is still scolding, the butler arrives with the drinks, offering them first to Lady Minster, who takes one, and then to Lord Trench, who frowns suspiciously and says, "What's that?" "That, milord," says the butler, "is a gullet washer." Lord Trench waves him away with a pained expression, while Lady Minster explains that she really meant him to try a side car. The butler apologizes and departs, leaving the drink and the shaker on the table; Lady Minster sips her drink with evident enjoyment, while Lord Trench turns away and paces the floor in annoyance, casting occasional glances at her, and feeling increasingly sorry for himself. She catches his eye, holds up her glass, and says, "It's lovely! Good luck, darling!" and takes another sip. He snorts and turns away, but in a moment he is edging toward the table, while she pretends not to see him. After some vacillation he goes so far as to pick up the cocktail and smell it, very much as one might smell a can of fish to see if it had spoiled. He starts to put it down, but evidently it does not smell as bad as he expected, and he hesitates. It is the psychological moment, and Lady Minster—this time without even catching his eye—says, "Go on, drink it. It won't hurt you." He glares at her, but she isn't looking at him. Again he hesitates, then takes a little

sip, and studies the taste, with one disapproving eye still on her. She looks up with a smile and says "Well?" For a few seconds he does not answer, then says, "Not bad!", and smells the thing again. Judicially he takes another sip, contemplates it, says, "No, not bad!" and drinks the rest down. "So that's a gullet washer!" he says; and she replies sweetly, "Yes, dear." He sets the glass down, looks thoughtfully at it, and repeats, "So that's a gullet washer!" He pauses a second, looks severely at her, and says, "*Short* drink!"

If the timing and contrasts have been right, that line turns the chuckles and titters into a joyful shout of laughter from the audience.

There is much more to the scene, in the course of which Lord Trench has two more gullet washers, becomes unexpectedly affable, and finally goes out carrying a fourth one carefully concealed under the flap of his coat. But I have given enough to illustrate the timing problem, and a great deal more indication of the timing than will be found in the text.

In this scene the temptation to hurry on to each line before getting the most out of the intervening business is felt even more strongly by Lady Minster than by Lord Trench; her waits are every bit as important as his, but because she is not the one who "carries" the scene it is harder for her to feel the timing—especially in the rehearsals. It is particularly important that she shall not say, "Go on, drink it!" until he has actually picked up the cocktail and sniffed at it; and that she shall not say, "Well?" until after he has actually tasted it. She must be careful, also, to sip her own drink slowly, showing enjoyment and making it last; otherwise she will be left with nothing to do before Lord Trench has had time to work up his business of being tempted.

For him, that is the difficult part of the timing. Having just denounced cocktails and refused one, he cannot very well change his mind at once; he must take time to be convincing. For an appreciable period after his refusal he must give no hint of the slightest intention to change his mind; yet he must not prolong the delay to the point of boring us. When he does begin to waver, it must seem to come about accidentally—not because he wants to be tempted, but because he keeps seeing that drink on the table, and noticing Lady Minster's enjoyment of hers. He must begin with the merest suggestion of temptation (for which the bright members of the audience will be eagerly watching), quickly rejecting it, and turning away in annoyance at his own weakness. He must have quite a battle with himself before yielding, but the ebb and flow must be varied in style and tempo, and not carried to the point of painful repetition. So drastic a reversal of intention could not be made convincing at all but for the fact that we al-

ready know Lord Trench, and realize that he has got himself into difficulty by declining a drink at the very moment when—being Lord Trench—he most needs one. The timing of the whole scene may be based on that.

It may occur to the reader that all these examples are exceptional, and that the young actor may never have to play a professor in love or an English gentleman who has refused a drink. Granted. But if he ever expects to be a comedian he will have to play many scenes that depend more upon well-timed actions than upon lines; many scenes in which he will have to convey, through action and facial expression, amusing truths about a character which that character does not himself realize; many scenes in which a character is seen arguing silently with himself and losing the argument; many scenes in which the words say one thing but the timing and the action say another. Constant study of such scenes brings resourcefulness and sureness of touch, in timing as in other things. It calls attention to principles that can be applied in hundreds of other cases; principles often absurdly elementary in themselves, yet commonly overlooked —such principles, perhaps, as the following:

1. Take time enough to be imaginatively intelligible and convincing.
2. Do not take time enough to drag the action or bore the audience.
3. Vary the timing, to sustain interest and bring out contrast.
4. Do not vary it so pointlessly or so suddenly as to confuse the mind or strain the attention.
5. Avoid timing that cuts off a laugh, unless a better laugh is right on its heels, and the two can be built up into a double-decker.
6. Avoid timing that obviously waits for a laugh.
7. Give the observer time to use his own intelligence in seeing the point.
8. Do not hold him back, once he has seen it.
9. Take time to think the character's thoughts, and follow them through.
10. Do not take time to falter over them, muddle them, or add extraneous thoughts of your own; do no woolgathering unless it is the character's.
11. Remember that timing is teamwork, except when the actor is alone on the stage; and sometimes even then, since it may involve cues for entrances, offstage effects, and so on.
12. Remember that all timing is relative; that what may be too fast for Act I may be too slow for Act III; that what is too fast at the beginning of an act may be too slow at the end; and that what is right for one audience may be too fast or too slow for another.

And that brings us to the final point about timing, namely, that in the end success or failure is not measured by theory or principle, but by results—that is, by audience response.

Here is another reason for really acting at rehearsals, not just saying lines; another reason for inviting a few new listeners to rehearsals now and then, to test audience response; another reason why Broadway producers send a play to the "dog" towns for a couple of weeks before the New York opening. The most skillful and experienced comedian, rehearsing in an empty theatre, can never be quite certain whether his timing is effective. He can make a good guess, and he can be alert to modify his timing when performances begin; but if he has had no audience at rehearsals he will meet many surprises on opening night, and on several successive nights also, and will have to make many adjustments.

Even on a long run he may have to make minor readjustments almost nightly. "How are they? They sound dead," an actor waiting in the wings may say to a comrade just coming off stage. The reply may be, "Slow on the uptake, but they'll laugh if you give them time." Or it may be, "Quick on the uptake, but light. You can hardly hear them, but they're getting it." Or it may be, "Dead? They're extinct! Not a laugh in the house. I tried rushing them and they didn't even snicker. I waited for them and they went to sleep. You'll have to trip over the rug if you want to get a laugh out of that gang!" How to gauge each audience is the actor's constant concern, and a large part of the problem lies in the timing.

My old friend who so greatly admired the imaginative power of Sir Henry Irving also told me of a slip in timing made by that actor in the trial scene of *The Merchant of Venice*. "In this same scene," he wrote, "I once saw Irving make a miscalculation. Gratiano had made his smart crack about wishing his wife was in Heaven, if Antonio might escape the Jew. Of course there was a laugh, and Irving, who had one of the best lines to follow, "These be your Christian husbands!", delivered the line just a few seconds too soon, when the people had not recovered from their first laugh; and so, instead of a roar, there was just a trickle of laughter. On other nights he waited properly, and the line made its expected big hit."

THE SENSE OF CONTRAST

If the sense of humor rests upon a sense of incongruity, it follows that a sharp sense of contrast will help the comedian to convey humorous effects.

Incongruity is the contrast between what is and what should have been; between what is unexpectedly out of place or out of order and what is normal or expected. Incongruities are not always obvious, especially to dull minds; it is the humorist's contribution to perceive them—to see things from a humorous angle, and give them a humorous twist by heightening the contrasts. There is no point in his trying to force humor out of

material that is essentially dull; but there is a good deal of point in his discovering hidden incongruities that really exist but have escaped the less observing. That, I think, is what is generally meant by the statement that the best humor is manner rather than matter.

Many of the incongruities written into comedies by witty authors are lost by poor actors through lack of the sense of contrast to bring them out. An author, working slowly and carefully over a humorous passage, sees the contrasts clearly in his own mind, and hopes he has made them clear in his words. A reader, reading the same passage at leisure, with freedom to choose his own pace and to reread when necessary, can usually figure out the humorous intent, on the second or third reading, if not the first. But people in a theatre cannot regulate the actor's pace to suit their own intelligence, and they cannot ask him to stop and repeat when they miss the point. If he fails to bring out, through adequate contrasts, the full value of the humor, they will either miss it altogether or get it in a washed-out, lukewarm version, comparable with a black-and-white photograph of a colorful painting.

Of the two catastrophes, the latter is really the more serious. When an actor muffs a point completely, nearly everybody realizes the fact and blames the bad acting; but when he gives us the washed-out, lukewarm kind of thing we are likely to get just enough of the meaning to suppose that we have got it all, and to misjudge the play entirely. Much fine theatre, both serious and comic, is lost that way, and thousands of people are misled into supposing they have seen the best when they have seen something less than that. Like those who think they have seen great paintings because they have seen the colorless photographs, or those who think they have read Shakespeare because they have read Lamb's *Tales from Shakespeare*, they never know what they have missed.

To put it simply, the actor with a sharp sense of contrast does not miss very much himself, and so does not permit his audience to miss very much. He gives them the picture in full color.

To take another example from *The School for Scandal*,[1] Sir Peter's first and most famous soliloquy begins:

SIR PETER.   When an old bachelor marries a young wife, what is he to expect? 'Tis now six months since Lady Teazle made me the happiest of men, and I have been the most miserable dog ever since! . . .

This is direct exposition, spoken communicatively to the audience, the character stepping out of the play, but not the actor out of character. It

---

[1] For a detailed study of the comic effects in that play, see "A Laugh Analysis of The School for Scandal," *Quarterly Journal of Speech*, November, 1930.

is, of course, a priceless bit of humor, and an audience will smile or chuckle at it if it is spoken with ordinary intelligibility, even with no particular change of tone or pace. But if its full comic impact is to be felt, the actor must make the most of the contrasts. Having just entered, he may speak the first sentence to the audience with a nervous glance off stage, a tone of exasperation, and a rueful expression suggesting that he has just retreated in disorder from a quarrel with his lady. Then, after a slight break, seeming to feel that having said so much to the audience he owes them further explanation, he may take a step forward, and begin his next sentence in an expository tone. As he reaches the phrase "happiest of men" he may brighten up a little in tune with that phrase (for in spite of all, he does love the lady); then, with a sudden catch of breath, a fall of countenance, and a quick deflation of manner, he may turn away sheepishly on the words "and I've been the most miserable dog ever since!" The sharp contrast in facial expression, tone, and tempo will bring out the humor as good seasoning brings out the taste of good food.

There are numerous opportunities for similar contrasts in the later parts of this soliloquy, as on the words "Yet I chose with caution . . . ," or the words "I doubt I love her . . . ," or, "However, I'll never be weak enough to own it!"; also in Sir Peter's later soliloquy at the end of the second quarrel scene, when he watches Lady Teazle's exit and then explodes into the following passage:

SIR PETER.   Plagues and tortures! Can't I make her angry either! Oh, I am the most miserable fellow! But I'll not bear her presuming to keep her temper: no! she may break my heart, but she shan't keep her temper! (*Exit. Curtain*)

Here the effect is greatly enriched if Sir Peter, after saying the first eight words in angry annoyance, breaks suddenly on the second syllable of the ninth word ("either"), wilts completely, turns away, saying "Oh, I am the most miserable fellow!" in a tone of crushed futility, and then breaks again into an even more violent tone as he hurls the rest of the speech at the audience and storms angrily off.

It is extremely important to understand that such contrasts, though I have recorded them in terms of counted words, are not to be studied in such terms originally. They are to be felt out in terms of mood and manner; they are to be discovered through imaginative study of character. The point is not that there should be contrasts, but that they should be the right ones, soundly and honestly humorous. In these same passages there is danger of another and totally mistaken kind of contrast, very commonly indulged in by third-rate actors. I refer to the mechanical contrast achieved

by pounding words. The good Sir Peter will contrast imaginatively the feeling of being "the happiest of men" with the feeling of being "the most miserable dog." The poor one will contrast the word "men" with the word "dog," and get only a false, artificial emphasis, without real humor. In a similar way he will contrast the word "love" with the word "bear," and fail to contrast Sir Peter's sheepish feeling in acknowledging that he loves his wife with his baffled irritation on the words "or I should never bear all this!" Listen to inferior actors trying to play comedy anywhere, and you will hear them pounding rhetorical contrasts right and left, but missing opportunities to bring out contrasts in imagined feelings and changing moods.

Reference has been made earlier in this book to "the illusion of the first time." Contrasts in imagined mood and feeling help enormously to preserve this illusion, while mechanical or rhetorical contrasts in word emphasis have precisely the opposite effect. Rhetorical contrast is, in fact, one of the surest ways of destroying the illusion of the first time, because it keeps reminding the listener that the actor has memorized the words in advance, and has his attention focused on them rather than on the character's feelings. When studying to achieve humorous contrasts, therefore, the actor should ask himself, not "Which words shall I contrast? Which should go up in pitch? Which down? Which should be strong, and which weak?", but rather, "What mood does this passage suggest? When does it change, and how? How would a character who felt that way sound, and how would his voice and manner change when his mood changes?" If he can answer these questions, and others like them, imaginatively—and if the playwright has done a good job—he is quite likely to achieve the illusion of the first time.

Sir Peter Teazle's contrasts are largely quick changes from one mood to another. The character of Mrs. Candour, in the same play, illustrates a different sort of contrast, rather more difficult to bring out. It is a contrast between what she says and what she does. In her first gossip scene she retails five choice bits of scandal, each followed by a virtuous deprecation of those who spread scandal; the series ends with the words, "But do you think I would report such things? No, no! Tale bearers, as I have said before, are just as bad as tale makers." An inexperienced actress is apt to gush through both sets of lines, contrasting only the pitch and tempo, but not the mental attitude, and giving the impression that the character sees through her own duplicity and rather expects everybody else to do so; the result is the rather mild, somewhat resentful amusement we feel at hypocrisy, but no lively mirth. The real comedienne will perceive the deli-

cate contrast between the imagined mentality of the incorrigible gossip and that of her *alter ego,* whose protestations of innocence are so effusive that they almost convince herself; and she will bring out the contrasts by speaking the protestations as if she expected them to be believed. The result will be a crescendo of appreciation, mounting through five degrees of response, from a chuckle to a hearty laugh. I have seen it happen. The first method conveys only artificial, rhetorical humor; the second conveys a more human and penetrating kind of humor, and raises the scene to a higher level of art. The difference is all in the depth and subtlety of the contrasts.

If an easier and more obvious example is wanted, it may be found within one of Mrs. Candour's lines—the one ending, "But Lord! there's no minding what one hears; though to be sure I had this from very good authority!" Even a second-rate actress should see that a sharp contrast is called for at the semicolon, expressed, probably, in a quick change to a lower pitch and volume, a faster tempo, and a more breathy quality of voice, suggestive of a more confidential attitude.

The close association between timing and contrast has already been emphasized. It is well illustrated in the cocktail scene from *The High Road.* When Lord Trench, after tasting the drink, says "Not bad!", the humorous effect is enormously heightened, first by the delayed timing, and second by just the right contrast between his words and his facial expression. A thoughtless actor would be apt to do the obvious thing: he would taste the drink, brighten up with a surprised smile, and say "Not bad!" That would be crude farce, untrue to the character. The competent comedian will delay his answer a few seconds after Lady Minster says "Well?", to increase the tension, maintaining his self-righteous expression and casting a defensive sidelong glance at her before answering; just as he says "Not bad!" he will avert his eyes from her with a slight scowl on his face, and only the slightest suggestion of a twinkle in his eye. His expression leads us to expect a disapproving answer, and when the answer belies the expression we enjoy the incongruity hugely, recognizing at once that it is genuinely humorous and sincerely true to Lord Trench's character. Of course he will relax a little on the next speech or two, but only a little; he will retain some of the defensive attitude, and will adopt a tone slightly approaching indignant accusation on the words "*Short* drink!" The contrast between that tone and the prophetic implication of the words is highly amusing. After the second "gullet washer" he can begin to thaw out a little more rapidly, but even then the contrasts must be subtle rather than crude.

One of the most difficult types of comedy is that in which a humorless

character serves a humorous purpose. It is difficult because the actor must contrast two interpretations of the same event or situation—the author's and the character's. The author finds it amusing, and hopes that the actor and the audience will see the humor; but the character sees nothing funny about it. That deprives the actor of some of the usual means of conveying humor. He must be extremely careful not to spoil the integrity of his characterization by any overt signs of his own amusement, so he cannot make his contrast directly between his own interpretation and the character's; he must do it by more subtle implication. One way of doing it was suggested in an earlier chapter; that is, by exaggeration. By making the character seem even more lacking in humor than is quite believable in real life, he places the latter in contrast, not with himself, but with a normal expectation. The best effects, however, are achieved by teamwork, in which two or more actors heighten the contrast between humorless and humorous characters by exaggeration in opposite directions, and by playing up the reaction of each to the other.

Shakespeare loved to contrast humorless and humorous characters; there are many examples in *The Taming of the Shrew, Twelfth Night, The Merry Wives of Windsor*—even in *Hamlet,* where the tragic protagonist has an unmistakable sense of humor, but his sententious would-be father-in-law has none. One of the most interesting cases may be found in *A Midsummer Night's Dream,* where Egeus, the father of Hermia, is one of the most humorless characters ever drawn. He is an irate, sputtering, ineffective old man, so ridiculously unable to control his own daughter (in an age when that was supposed to be unusual) that he has to drag her before the duke and beg for help—a procedure that would be impossible for anybody with the capacity to laugh at himself. No actor can play Egeus effectively unless he himself has a good comedy sense; but he must give no hint that Egeus sees anything funny about anything. A good Egeus is greatly aided by a good Lysander, a good Hermia, and particularly a good Theseus; though it is unfortunately quite unusual to see either Egeus or Theseus well played. The reason, of course, is that this play provides so many longer and more obvious comedy parts for the first and second leads, the eccentric comedian, the first and second old men, and a couple of extra character men, that nobody is left to play Egeus and Theseus except bit players or walking gentlemen. Yet these parts are extremely important in setting the comedy key in the opening scene; and being less obvious in their comedy than many others, they are more difficult to play. The necessary exaggeration of Egeus is hampered by the fact that most acting editions of the play (based on nineteenth-century prompt books) cut out some of his

best monosyllabic sputterings as written by Shakespeare. They may be found in the First Folio, or in any authentic edition based upon it; the wise director will put them back, and the competent actor will make much of them. When the humorless Egeus that Shakespeare conceived is thrown into contrast with the pert humor of Hermia, the swaggering wit of Lysander, and the wise, tolerant, affable, yet mischievous humor of Theseus, the point is made.

A similar contrast between the humorous Lysander and the humorless Demetrius runs all through the play, and gives us a clue as to why Egeus prefers the latter as a son-in-law. The old man just cannot understand the mercurial bantering of Lysander, and so resents him; but he takes more kindly to Demetrius, in whom he sees his own kind.

It would be possible to take almost any page of good comedy, classic or popular—particularly high comedy—and study out a dozen possibilities of humorous contrast, varying greatly in style, implication, and degree of subtlety. A great deal of practice in doing so is excellent education for the comedy sense, and helps the player to achieve in time a keener perception of incongruities and a greater facility in making them clear to an audience, with less effort and more spontaneity. But the actor should remember that detailed, conscious analysis, while often necessary as training and self-discipline, is not ultimately the proper basis of creative art. He should be advised to do his intensive study on parts he does not expect to play, at least in the immediate future; or on parts he has already played, not quite to his own satisfaction; or on a part he has been rehearsing for some time with disappointing results. He should avoid the highly analytical approach to a new part which he is scheduled to play, seeking rather to grasp it naturally and imaginatively as a whole, at least in the early stages; and falling back on conscious, corrective analysis only when the more instinctive, spontaneous, creative method has failed. Even then he should avoid sitting in an uncreative mood and asking himself analytically, "What ought I to do about this?" He should get up and do it; try it this way and that way and the other way, note the effect on himself and others, and then ask himself, "Which was best, and why? What was lacking? Where did I go wrong? Or did I?"

THE SENSE OF RESTRAINT

One more component of the comedy sense deserves brief mention before we leave the subject—namely, the element of restraint.

Nearly everybody appreciates the danger of overacting—including many actors who get caught at it themselves. Overacting is a common

fault of the inexperienced actor, but it is typically the fault of the earnest, eager actor—not the stupid, lazy, or indifferent one. Now and then it does arise from egotism or vanity (in which case it is a problem in character education rather than art), but more often it arises from the actor's distrust of his own ability to be clear, or his underestimate of audience intelligence, or his bad judgment in selecting the wrong elements to receive the emphasis. The "pounding" so often referred to in this chapter usually arises from the latter cause, and is one of the worst enemies of the comedy sense. The remedy, as we have seen, is better study and analysis. But overacting generally is a sign of underconfidence.

The actor who himself really understands, in an alert, imaginative way, what the character is doing, thinking, feeling, and saying, need have little fear that he will not be understood by others. Audiences are amazingly keen at catching meanings, even when underacted, and they enjoy the compliment to their intelligence implied in underacting, or in restraint, as much as they dislike the insult implied in overacting. And the actor will do well to remember that the collective intelligence of an audience is far higher than the average intelligence of the individuals composing it—which is fortunate, for on occasion the individual intelligence may be pretty low. What happens is that the brighter, quicker individuals catch on first, and by telegraphing their appreciation through collective response lead the slower and duller ones to see the point and join in the fun. That is one reason why so many people who are too feeble-minded to read books for themselves individually can enjoy plays or movies quite well. It is not only that the actors do some of their thinking for them, but that their fellow listeners do the rest. When the actor overacts, they are unpleasantly reminded of the fact that he is talking down to them; but when their fellow listeners register collective appreciation of a restrained piece of acting, even the densest individuals think they have caught the point for themselves, and are grateful to the actor for giving them the opportunity to be so bright.

Restraint is to be desired in almost all acting, but is especially important in comedy. When a piece of tragic acting is unrestrained (short of obvious insincerity) we may be sufficiently moved to share the character's emotions sympathetically, even though we are a little embarrassed and uncomfortable about the sensationalism. But comedy is rather more objective, and when a comedian overacts we are more likely to catch him at it, and we resent his trying to make the situation seem funnier than we think it is, and funnier than we believe he really thinks it is.

A good rule of restraint for the comedian is: Be sure you have discovered

every shade of humor in the character, the situation, the lines, and the action; then let the audience enjoy discovering it too. Permit them to get it, but never try to force it on them.

INHERENT AND EXTRANEOUS COMEDY

In attempting to distinguish between high and low comedy earlier in this book, I mentioned the fact that high comedy is usually developed out of the essential incongruities inherent in the meaning of the text itself, while low comedy is often achieved extraneously through absurd mannerisms, exaggerated make-up, outlandish costumes, and the like. Whether or not this is an acceptable distinction between the two types, it is an important distinction for the comedian to keep in mind, for it often marks the difference between good and bad comedy, as well as high and low.

Not that I mean to condemn low comedy. There is certainly a place for low comedy, just as there is a place for farce. This tragic world of ours desperately needs the tonic effect of good hearty laughter; and low comedy, in the hands of good actors, is one of the most effective means of inducing it. I will even go so far as to say that good low comedy, informed by the genius of a great buffoon, may be very high art indeed. One has no need to be ashamed of enjoying it. Among my choicest memories of the theatre I count the low comedy performances of Wilfred Clarke as Grumio, John Bunny as Bottom, Maclyn Arbuckle as Old Bill (in *The Better 'Ole*), LeRoi Operti as Launcelot Gobbo, Martyn Green as Koko, Perdue Cleaver as Bunthorne, and Sidney Greenstreet as Dogberry—along with the music-hall skits of Vesta Victoria, the screen clowning of Charlie Chaplin, and the inspired waggery of Balieff in the *Chauve Souris*. The healthy mind can derive keen pleasure from low comedy when it is well done, and when it either stands by itself, or is naturally and honestly called for by the lines— as it is, for example, in the last scene of *A Midsummer Night's Dream*.

But in a half-century of theatre-going I do not recall a single instance in which I felt that good low comedy had been spoiled by being played too high; on the other hand I can recall innumerable cases in which good high comedy was spoiled by being played too low. Time and time and time again I have seen a second-rate comedian take a fine high-comedy scene, miss all its real humor and humanity, and turn it into bad buffoonery for the sake of a quick, easy laugh from an undiscriminating audience.

For example, I once saw what was supposed to be a first-rate company in *The School for Scandal* just a few days after I had closed a production of the same play, so that every word and meaning was fresh in my memory. In the first act alone I counted eighteen legitimate high-comedy laugh

lines that missed fire because the players failed to discern their real humor and threw the laughs away. The worst offender was the Sir Benjamin Backbite, who read almost every line with a complete lack of understanding, getting no humor out of it whatever, and then tacked on an effeminate gesture and an asinine falsetto giggle in order to force an unearned laugh. The audience (consisting largely of people obviously unfamiliar with eighteenth-century high comedy) thought he was quite a card; but his performance was cheap vaudeville, with Sheridan twenty miles away. The Mrs. Candour got most of her laughs out of a ridiculous headdress with a wobbly feather, but missed the essential humor in all the contrasts described earlier in this chapter, and many others. Fully half the actors in the company, unable or unwilling to play for the inherent high comedy, chose low comedy methods instead. Looking back over my old programs, I could cite a hundred similar cases.

As everyone knows, there is plenty of gorgeous buffoonery in the Gilbert and Sullivan operas; but it is recorded that Sir William roundly berated an actor in the original production of *The Mikado* for burlesquing one of his scenes to the extent of rolling on the floor. "But they laughed at it," the actor protested. "Of course they laughed at it," Gilbert replied. "Anybody can get a laugh by falling down or throwing a pie. But it had nothing to do with your lines!" It is worth noting that the lines Gilbert wrote were— to use the words he himself chose in reprimanding another actor for poor enunciation—"perhaps not altogether without merit."

What makes so many actors cheapen their art in such fashion? Some of them, no doubt, are just too stupid or superficial to understand high comedy at all, and so are forced to fall back on the more obvious devices of buffoonery. They know they are expected to be funny, and have no resources for doing so except by clowning. Others, perhaps, are too lazy to work out the more subtle and difficult techniques of high comedy, and prefer the easier methods of the clown—or rather the methods they think are easier. It is true that bad low comedy is easier than any sort of high comedy, but really good low comedy is just as difficult as good high comedy. It is always easy, as Sir William Gilbert pointed out, to get some kind of a laugh; but it would be well for the young comedian to ponder the difference between the physical laugh that comes easily and automatically, almost against the will, often accompanied by a touch of derision and followed by a touch of shamefaced resentment, and the whole-hearted, unashamed laugh that intelligent people give to what they honestly think is funny. Lazy people often fail to realize that what is easier to get may well be an inferior article.

But it is not only the stupid or lazy comedians who "play it low." Many who are neither simply yield to the temptation to do what they know will get immediate and sure-fire results. Many just do not believe in Hamlet's advice to the players; they are perfectly willing to make the judicious grieve as long as they can make the unskillful laugh—even by imitating humanity so abominably. They know (for it is the first thing a comedian learns by experience) that audiences will always laugh more audibly and readily at physical or visible humor than at cerebral humor; that if you cannot make them laugh at ideas you can always "trip over the rug."

Knowledge of this psychological fact, used with judgment and restraint, is of great service to the comedian, as it is to the writer of comedy. At the same time it is a constant temptation to both; and used *without* judgment and restraint it is the worst pitfall in comic acting.

When a dramatist has ably conceived a piece of honest, robust low comedy, bearing its proper and logical relation to the purpose of the play, there is no reason why director and actor should not make the most of its low comedy aspects, and enrich it with well-conceived and appropriate comic business. I have mentioned the last scene of *A Midsummer Night's Dream*. The mere fact that Shakespeare gave us in that play six clowns (so called in the First Folio), instead of the usual one or two, would be sufficient evidence of his low comedy intent, even if we did not have the idiotic lines of "the most lamentable Comedy and cruell death of Pyramis and Thisbie" to prove it. Surely the internal evidence of those lines justifies such traditional bits of physical humor to accompany them as Quince's business of painting blood on the dagger, Pyramis's business of falling with the dagger under him, so that, after he is supposedly dead, he has to roll over to let Thisby[1] find it, and Thisby's business of falling so heavily on her lover's corpse that it grunts. This is not spoiling high comedy to make low comedy. It is getting the most out of what is already unmistakably low comedy, with the help of wittily amusing business honestly consistent with the lines. I feel quite confident that Shakespeare himself would have approved such business; it is even possible that some of these bits date back to Shakespeare's own company—though I believe that in the older version of the second item Thisby never does find the dagger, and has to kill herself with the scabbard instead.

But when an actor chooses to ignore the inherent humor of high comedy and substitute physical humor not essentially related to the lines, he is doing something very different indeed—something that could hardly be

---

[1] Usually spelled "Thisbe" in modern editions, but Shakespeare spelled it indiscriminately as "Thisby," "Thisbie," and occasionally "Thisbe."

approved by Shakespeare, Sheridan, Gilbert, or any other real humorist.

The student actor, therefore, if he wishes to learn the high art of comedy and not merely to be a professional fool, should give heed to the kind of laughter he is to provoke. Let him learn, by all means, the devices of low comedy, and the possibilities of physical humor in its proper place. But let him also realize that, mental or physical, the best humor is that which is truly inherent in the dramatist's purpose and consistent with the lines of the play. And let him frequently remind himself that, although tripping over the rug may make the unskillful laugh, the author's words may be "perhaps not altogether without merit."

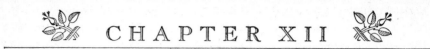

CHAPTER XII

Tragedy

THERE is a popular notion that tragic acting is a higher and more difficult art than comedy, calling for more physical and emotional endurance, a richer imagination, and a greater measure of genius. Such a notion is not hard to explain; there are several reasons for it.

The first reason might be called the tradition of obligatory thanks. When a comedian succeeds in amusing us we feel comparatively little sense of obligation. We laugh, of course, and if the scene is very funny indeed we may break into spontaneous applause, but more to express pleasure than thanks. We somehow take it for granted that the actor is having a good time too. But when a tragedian enacts a scene of pain and sorrow we feel that the poor fellow is earning his living the hard way, and that we are obligated to express our thanks in generous applause. The more often this happens, the more habitual the attitude becomes.

A second reason is the press agent. When the press agent is promoting a comedy, he can tell us with enthusiasm how entertaining it is, and how we are going to roll in the aisles with laughter. But when he is trying to sell us a tragedy, and is a little afraid we shall find it too depressing, he does not dwell on the painful aspects; he diverts our attention with praise of the acting. He tells us in words of awe what a great artist the star is, how he has dedicated himself to his art, what a magnificent portrayal he is giving, and how utterly exhausted he is after each performance. If the star happens to be feminine, he dwells also on her beauty or glamour, and drops hints about the number of great men who have been her lovers, and the private tragedies that have haunted her life and enriched her genius.

A third, and perhaps more universal reason, is the harrowing quality of tragedy itself—especially for those who are seeing the particular play for the first time. If it is reasonably powerful and well acted, we are deeply moved, and experience empathically much of the sorrow and suffering portrayed by the actors. Watching a tragedy thus becomes something of an ordeal, no matter how much we appreciate its beauty; and if watching it is harder work than watching a comedy, we naturally jump to the conclusion that acting it is harder work than acting a comedy.

Actually neither is easy, though both, to a real actor, are fun. I do not mean to suggest that great tragedians are not great artists, or not worthy of their hire. I merely wish to suggest that the overpowering odor of sanctity which so often surrounds great tragic acting is partly myth and partly bunkum; that tragic acting is not something mystic, occult, or metaphysical —not a matter of inspired insanity or ecstatic self-deception. Acting is acting, and theatre is theatre, however the subject matter of the moment may range from the ridiculous to the sublime.

Tragic acting does, of course, draw a little more heavily on some abilities than comedy, and not so heavily on others. As indicated in the preceding chapter, it usually makes less demand on technical skill, because it more often deals with the simple, basic emotions and conflicts of life, while comedy more often deals with its subtleties and complexities. On the other hand, tragedy makes more demand on emotional concepts and their visible and audible symbols. Both demand sincerity of imagination; comedy demands it largely in terms of wit, humor, and understanding, tragedy in terms of feeling and sympathy. Comedy centers on human follies and foibles, arousing such lighter emotions as amusement, exasperation, surprise, and the like; tragedy centers on human crises and crimes, arousing fear, grief, hatred, anger—what William James called "the coarser emotions."

If the reader doubts the assertion that it is easier to find untrained actors who can act tragedy passably than untrained actors who can act comedy, he may find the explanation in the universality of emotion. One has only to observe the news films of strike riots, of the homeless and hungry in Europe, of mothers watching their delinquent sons being tried for rape or murder, of the survivors after a train wreck, of hysterical Jews trying to crash the Palestine blockade, of gold-star mothers receiving the caskets of their returning soldier dead, or of India's Hindus and Moslems shouting for each others' blood, to realize that human beings who can express fear, grief, hatred, joy, or violent excitement are a dime a million. It is inevitable that some of them should be able to express such emotions mimetically without much special training.

One may well ask if there is not a "tragedy sense," as important to the tragedian as the "comedy sense" is to the comedian. I believe that there is; but I do not think it is as rare as the comedy sense, nor technically as complicated and difficult to learn. It is more a matter of sincerity than of finesse. That does not mean, however, that the tragic actor is exempt from the necessity to learn and perfect his art. For highest achievement he will need just as much study and experience as the comedian; but it will be

concerned rather less with technique and rather more with the basic nature and purpose of tragic drama.

THE NATURE OF TRAGEDY

The mere portrayal of grief, fear, hatred, and disaster does not of itself constitute tragedy in the dramatic or theatrical sense. Such things may be painful to contemplate, as they certainly are in the news films and newspapers, but they are not necessarily effective as tragic art.

In Chapter VII the distinction between comedy and tragedy was discussed in terms of plot conflict. Comedy was there defined, in its broadest sense, as drama in which the particular interest of the protagonist triumphs over the universal forces or obstacles set up against him; and tragedy was defined as drama in which the particular interest succumbs to the universal forces, and the hero or heroine is overwhelmed by catastrophe.

It is quite possible, however, to construct a plot which meets this definition in a literal way, detailing the struggle and defeat of a protagonist, and yet to suggest very little of that inner sense of tragic beauty which we expect in the theatre. It is equally possible to have a play which is a comedy in plot construction but a tragedy in feeling, like Paul Green's *The House of Connelly;* or to have a tragic theme treated in a spirit of playful comedy or gentle satire, as in Barrie's *Dear Brutus* or *The Admirable Crichton.*

The actor must know how to analyze tragic action in terms of both plot and theme. But even beyond that he must know how to capture—or help capture—the curious blend, or balance, or resolution of emotions by which we feel simultaneously despair and resignation, horror and beauty, surprise and inevitability, indignation and satisfaction of poetic justice, castigation and exaltation. The spirit of tragedy lies much more in such things than in mere plot construction. Their attainment is not always possible for the individual actor alone; that necessitates teamwork, not only with his fellow actors, but with the author and the director as well. At times it may necessitate his playing in a different key himself in order to furnish the dramatic contrast intended by the author, just as football teamwork may require one individual to do the blocking while another carries the ball.

It is natural that we should think of tragedy very much in terms of the protagonist, since the plot turns on his struggle and downfall; unfortunately that often leads us to think of the tragedian solely in terms of the star who plays the leading role. There is much more to tragedy than that; and the student actor should remember that he is likely to act many minor parts in tragedy, some identified with the interests of the hero and some

with the opposing universal forces, before he ever gets a chance to act the hero's part himself.

Basically, there are two types of tragedy: the elevating and the depressing. In my own philosophy the former is the greater and the more lastingly popular; but doubtless this is, at the moment, a minority opinion, for the second type appears to prevail in modern taste. Of course ours is not primarily an age of tragedy at all; our real preference is for comedy. History shows that such a preference is normal in those periods of prosperity and extravagance in which the theatre is most highly commercialized as entertainment. The taste for tragedy has flourished chiefly in those periods when the theatre has been consecrated as a public observance of national or religious festivals, as in the golden age of Greece; or when a national art has just begun to emerge in a period of new-found security following turmoil, as in Elizabethan England. In an age like ours, those who seek mere entertainment ordinarily choose comedy; while tragedy is thought of mainly as a museum exhibit from the past, or as an up-to-the-minute vehicle for agitation, propaganda, or protest—in other words, as an instrument of sociology or politics rather than art. Tragedy so motivated is much more likely to be depressing than elevating.

The distinction is not solely one between the relieved and the unrelieved; between the heroic or romantic and the stark. *Macbeth, Hamlet,* and *Romeo and Juliet* are highly romantic in spirit, richly poetic in style, and relieved by varying degrees of comic contrast; while the *Electra* of Sophocles and the *Medea* of Euripides are implacably horrific and unrelieved from start to finish. Yet the Greek and the Elizabethan have more in common with each other than either has with such modern plays as O'Neill's *Desire Under the Elms,* or Green's *The House of Connelly,* or Steinbeck's *Of Mice and Men.* All these—and a hundred others—are powerful plays, but they point down, not up. One comes away from them impressed, but not ennobled. Shakespeare and Sophocles both give us that purging of the spirit through pity and terror which Aristotle called the essential beauty of tragedy; they permit us to go home with a sense of elevation, a feeling that we have seen life at its peak, both good and evil, and are better men or women for the experience. Most of the moderns give us, instead, a look into the sewer or the charnel house; we go home feeling degraded, not elevated, and a little ashamed of having busied ourselves with such disgusting aspects of the human race.

To make a slightly more specific comparison: *Electra* and *Hamlet* have remarkably similar themes except for the sex of the protagonist. Each

deals with the avenging of a father's murder on the father's widow and her lover. *Hamlet* has variety, ebb and flow of passion, romantic color, comic relief, memorable imagery, numerous quotable gems of thought, and immortal poetry. *Electra* is inexorable, almost to the point of monotony; it is all in one direction; there is no ebb and flow, no doubt of the outcome, no flicker of comic relief. The one is entertaining, the other harrowing; yet both make us feel that we have been in the presence of great crises in the lives of great (if not always good) human beings. Both give us emotional "lift." But now compare *Hamlet* with *The House of Connelly*. We find another, though equally striking, similarity in these; each deals with the scion of a crumbling house, and his struggle to reclaim it in the face of his own weakness and vacillation. Both are ably and sincerely written. Theoretically, *The House of Connelly* is rather a tragicomedy than a tragedy, since the hero does not die but merely marries out of his class; and there is even a faint hint that the new blood may in time regenerate the family. In total feeling, however—at least as I saw it acted in New York—it is not only tragic but profoundly dispiriting. I happened to see it at a matinee, and to see *Hamlet* in the evening of the same day; and the difference was staggering. I came away from *Hamlet* deeply moved, but feeling cleansed and regenerated. I had come away from the modern play feeling horrified and contaminated.

In making this comparison I intend no disparagement of Paul Green, or any other author of serious or tragic drama who writes in the modern idiom. Paul Green is a sensitive, compassionate, deeply sincere writer, warmly attached to the beautiful aspects of southern life and tradition, but profoundly disturbed by the rotten core he sometimes finds in the apple. He is only one of hundreds who write in deep perturbation of spirit about the hidden sins and sorrows of humanity, the regrettable, painful, ugly aspects of life. I do not think they generally mean to be degrading; they mean to be truthful, and they hope, somehow, that the truth will be uplifting. That is the modern creed in all the arts—a sadly mistaken creed, as time will tell, for it is not truth which makes better ideals, but ideals that make new and better truths. Whereas the Shakespeares and Rembrandts and Beethovens presented beauty creatively, the moderns choose to present ugliness critically—and sometimes, I regret to say, uncritically. Like the surrealists in painting and the exponents of dissonance and disorder in music, the modern writers of tragedy are the inevitable result of an age in which literacy and science have far outstripped ethical and æsthetic stability; an age of confusion, wallowing in a slough of abnormal psychology and waiting for atomic destruction.

The actor who would achieve success in the idiom of our time must, I suppose, learn to wallow too. But he need not wallow all the time. He may note the fact that both types of tragedy still draw audiences in the modern theatre, though only the depressing type flourishes in current writing, and the elevating type is seen chiefly in the revival of old plays. As a matter of fact, there have been five or six Broadway productions of *Hamlet* since the one that ran concurrently with *The House of Connelly*, and as I write this paragraph Shakespeare's *Antony and Cleopatra* and Euripides' *Medea* are playing to full houses in New York. What this indicates for the student actor is plain. If he wishes to prepare for a versatile career he must learn how to play, or play in, both types of tragedy. He must point his tragic sense up, or down, as the play demands.

Depressing Tragedy

Apart from questions of structure and technique, the spirit of most modern tragedy is essentially the spirit of clinical realism. A certain measure of exaggeration is, of course, expected, as in all theatre, but rather less than in the older tragedy. In general, the author is not saying to us, "This is the wonderful, heroic world of the past," or "This is the noble, mystic, terrifying world of the gods." He is saying to us, "This is the sordid world we live in, with all its dirt and rottenness laid bare."

There is something curiously anomalous about the attitude of the typical modern writer. When he comes out with a particularly horrifying tale of insanity, promiscuity, perversion, treachery, robbery, exploitation, or murder, and some brash critic too newly from "the provinces" dares to accuse him of vilifying humanity through a distorted picture of life, he almost invariably defends himself (or his admirers defend him) by saying that he does not mean to imply that all life is like that. "This is just a specific case," he says, "based upon an actual incident in my home town. I don't say that everybody is a thief, or a murderer, or a homosexual pervert. I only say that such things exist, and that it is the artist's business to tell the truth about them." Yet it is precisely this type of clinical realism which *does* seem to imply that our world is like that. By its very convincingness in the presentation of one case it seems to imply that there must be many more. In the heroic tragedies of other days there is no such implication. We accept *Electra*, or *Macbeth*, or *Medea*, or *King Lear* as something colossal and unique. We know there is only one *Hamlet*, though he may be variously interpreted to us, and here and there a lesser man in a lesser position may exhibit some of his traits. But when we see *Of Mice and Men* we exclaim in horror, "So that's what migratory farm laborers are like!"

and we begin to think of all the morons and imbeciles in our own neighbor-hood and wonder whether they are potential killers like Lennie. When we see *The House of Connelly* we shake our heads and say, "Isn't it awful about all those decaying southern families with their mulatto servants who are their own half-brothers and cousins!" And when we see *Desire Under the Elms* we say, "So the New England farmers are all adulterers, too!" Of course the authors make no such assertions; but in the modern tragedy of degradation the spirit of such implication is almost universally accepted. Where the tragic writer of the past said, "Here is something horrible, as-tounding, exceptional!" the modern writer seems to say, "Here is some-thing foul, but, I assure you, quite real and usual."

What does all this mean to the actor?

That depends, naturally, upon his objective. If his ultimate desire is to please his own soul through mastery of his art, it may mean one thing. If his aim is merely a good salary and box-office appeal on Broadway, it may mean another. I use the word "may" because the matter is after all one of taste and convictions which the individual must decide for himself. He has a right to his choice, as I have to mine. Some very honest and thought-ful people believe that the contemplation of sewage is a finer and truer art than the contemplation of the gods; and the actor who feels that way may well please his own soul by precisely the same kind of art that is most in demand at the Broadway box office. The actor who feels otherwise may conceivably please himself best by refusing to act in the depressing kind of tragedy, or by acting in it only with a little more of the spirit of elevation and purgation than is inherent in the play. He may not be able to get away with that on Broadway, but it is being done quite successfully in many of our college and community theatres. Again and again a non-commercial theatre director will take a play of this type, delete some of the obscenities and profanities, tone down or cut out a few episodes, change the emphasis here and there, use a less realistic tone and method, and with the aid of more kindly (if less expert) acting produce a less sensational and less de-grading but perhaps more moving play. Participation in such a produc-tion can be more satisfying to a certain kind of actor than participation in the latest Broadway clinic. But for the actor who is concerned only with money and fame (and who does not wish to cast his lot with Hollywood), the best advice is doubtless to conform to the mode of Broadway and play down, not up.

Do I malign Broadway? I do not think so. Broadway, of course, is many things, for many kinds of people. It frequently patronizes a *Hamlet*, a *Medea*, or an *Antony and Cleopatra*, not to mention such harmless things

as a *Life With Father* or a D'Oyley Carte repertory of Gilbert and Sullivan; and it frequently refuses to support a well-meaning but confused discussion masquerading as a play, such as *This Time Tomorrow*. But it can always be relied upon to support any play that gets advertised on the grapevine as the most daring piece of sewer-raking yet attempted, or the most shocking to the people of Boston or Philadelphia.

Not long before these words were written, a certain play destined for Broadway had a trial run in Philadelphia, where many of my friends saw it. One of them, a lifelong theatre-goer of catholic tastes, who never misses anything, good or bad, and who is not easily shocked, told me it was quite the nastiest thing he had ever seen on the stage—well written, but more offensively indecent than *Tobacco Road*. He added, "It will be a big hit on Broadway, of course!" Another friend, a sophisticated modern young lady studying the theatre arts quite seriously in preparation for a career on the stage, wrote in a critical report on the production: "The psychological study is sensitively done, but [the author] succumbs to box-office sensationalism many times. Sex is made unnecessarily predominant. The dialogue and action is often crude to the point of being revolting. . . . The policy of shocking the customers usually pays off at the box office, but I feel that the author sacrificed finely drawn characterization for a cheap thrill." A third friend, a professional psychologist who has spent many years in the scientific study of pornography, told me it was an obvious exploitation of a good basic idea in terms of unnecessary obscenity. "I see no excuse for it," he said, "but since it plays up two seductions, a rape, and a case of homosexuality, it is bound to be a sellout in New York." The Saturday before it opened in New York I happened to be in the lobby of the theatre trying to get tickets for another play that was just closing. I had to stand in a long queue of people eagerly buying tickets for the new play, which was already sold out for six or eight weeks in advance. There was great excitement among them, and their remarks were most illuminating: "I hear it's a hot one!" . . . "They say it was censored in Providence!" . . . "My cousin saw it in Philly and he says it doesn't leave much to the imagination!" . . . "How do you suppose it got by in Boston?" . . . "I hear he rapes her right on the stage!" . . . and so on. Nobody seemed to know—or care—whether it was artistically a good play; but it was certainly something you mustn't miss! When it opened, the critics all said it was a good play, and some said it was a great play. The *Times* said it was the most distinguished play in several seasons, and that its phenomenal success was proof of New York's good taste. Not having seen the play, I venture no opinion as to its merits, but the statement that its "success"

was proof of New York's good taste was sheer nonsense, for the New York theatre-goers (with a few exceptions) had not yet seen it; they had merely bought tickets for weeks and weeks ahead on the strength of dirty rumors from Boston and Philadelphia. They always do.

All this may seem like a digression, but it concerns what is after all a major problem for the young actor or actress today, especially for the one reared far from New York but dreaming of a career in the professional theatre. It will inevitably affect his or her decision whether to go on with acting at all; whether to seek a career on Broadway or be content with avocational activity in a community theatre somewhere; and whether to conform or protest when his associates choose to play down rather than up. It will profoundly affect the inner spirit of his acting, especially in serious or tragic plays.

If he accepts and approves the modern idea that tragic acting should shock, depress, and disturb, not exalt and cleanse, he will have to teach himself certain approaches to the study of a part quite different from those ordinarily required for heroic tragedy.

First of all he will have to accept the idea that ugliness, not beauty, is the aim of tragedy. Translated into terms of empathy and æsthetic distance, that means more empathy—especially unpleasant empathy—and less æsthetic distance. It means more factual realism, not necessarily without selection, but with more deliberate selection of the ugly and distressing elements rather than the beautiful or symbolic ones. In portraying death, for example, he will not conform to the accepted conventions, but will feel perfectly free to imitate nature in any of its horrors—drooling blood, retching, gasping, rolling the eyeballs, twitching, screaming, or just staring glassily into space, as the case may be. In portraying war he will not think in terms of blood, sweat, and tears—much less of glory and unselfishness; he will think in terms of futility, of bestiality, of spattered brains and guts (what a fascinating idea for the technicians!). In portraying the relations between man and woman he will of course think only in terms of those behavior patterns which least distinguish man from the so-called lower animals.

Secondly, he will have to accept a certain spirit of sadism which creeps into the modern type of tragedy. When a writer's purpose is to plumb the depths of human degeneracy, to shock, and (perhaps) to reform, he wants it to *hurt;* and the actor will serve him best by making it hurt. It will not quite suffice for him to exaggerate the horror; after all, both types of tragedy exaggerate. To carry out the purpose of some modern writers I think he must actually learn to *enjoy* making it hurt. That is what I mean

by the sadism of it; and I have felt that spirit in much modern acting as well as in modern playwriting.

Thirdly, he will have to decide in each case whether the play under consideration is chiefly motivated by the idea that ugliness itself is entertaining, or by the author's desire to teach a lesson or preach a sermon.

If the former seems to be the case, he will have to learn to understand and share the mentality of those people who get real enjoyment out of visiting morgues or dissecting rooms, or collecting obscene pictures, or witnessing executions. He will have to learn the technique of heightening such pleasure by sugar-coating it with elements of picturesqueness, charm, or daring; and the still more subtle technique of treating shocking things so casually as to make them seem commonplace. This technique makes a pseudo-sophisticated audience feel at peace with its conscience and rather pleasantly blasé, and is very popular on Broadway. He will also have to discover the fact that the entertainment of such people is the real motivation of at least some authors whose press agents proclaim that their purpose is to expose evil, or tell the truth about life, or achieve high "social significance."

On the other hand, if he can satisfy himself that the play is sincerely intended to teach or preach, his problem will be somewhat different. The tragedy which is depressing solely because the author is trying to make evil look as black as possible obviously needs no sugar-coating. It may need the emphasis on ugliness, and it may need the sadism—though I have known plays with neither that still managed to exert a healthy social or moral influence. There is one point, however, on which the young actor should not allow himself to be confused: Just in proportion as a play exists to teach or preach it ceases to be pure art. Such purposes, as we have seen, are historically respectable and quite honestly in the direct line of æsthetic evolution, but they are much earlier in that line than pure art; and when what has been a pure art turns back to those purposes it is certainly turning back—back to something more primitive, something culturally and artistically inferior, however necessary or desirable as a matter of social expediency. When the dramatist and the actor turn preacher, they may become very good preachers, but they should not expect to be thought of as artists, or ranked artistically with those who give themselves wholly to art.

If the actor is to help the socially minded playwright teach a lesson by tragic example, he will do well to study the chief reasons for success or failure in that kind of teaching.

Failure is likely to result from either of two quite opposite faults. One

is excessive exaggeration—the kind by which the contrast between good and evil is so obviously overdrawn and distorted that only a childishly naïve mind could take it seriously. The other is excessive sugar-coating, by which the evil to be condemned gets glamorized instead; even the most earnest writer is sometimes tempted into this fault by the desire to hold attention and make his lesson interesting.

Success is correspondingly dependent upon just enough exaggeration to make the picture of evil forbiddingly impressive without making it unbelievable. It is no easy matter for author, director, or actor to steer this critical middle course—still less for all three. The task is most critical for the actor, since he is the one who actually reaches the audience, and, so to speak, has the last word. If the author wobbles a little, a good director may steady him; if the director slips off the course, a good actor can compensate for it to some degree by toning down or building up. But if the actor, with or without the director's approval, slides off either way, the damage is done—at least for that performance.

In this, as in so many of the actor's problems, it is the inner feeling and attitude, rather than the superficial technique, that counts. The actor who thinks the problem through clearly, making up his mind firmly as to just how much of his purpose is didactic and how much æsthetic, and then seeks to carry it out imaginatively and sympathetically, is quite likely to achieve the right feeling and to choose the right amount of exaggeration, distortion, ugliness, or sadism to accomplish what the author had in mind. But like the comedian working for laughs, he will have to do it a little differently for each audience.

Perhaps it will help him to assume the most effective teaching attitude if he recalls the fact that most human beings like to be taught but do not like to be preached at; or more accurately that they are willing to be taught provided they do not catch the teacher at it. The more childlike they are, the more exaggeration or distortion they will accept without realizing that they are being preached at. The more sophisticated they are, the more sugar-coating they will require if they are to swallow the lesson at all.

But the actor—and every other artist with a desire to teach or preach— should bear in mind the vital difference between sugar-coating a lesson and sugar-coating the evil which is the subject of the lesson. The latter is neither good preaching nor good art.

ELEVATING TRAGEDY

The older and more exalted type of tragedy originated in public ceremonials of religious or tribal or national significance. The spirit of elevation

is a direct inheritance from the festival or "feast-day" tradition almost inseparable from such ceremonials.

It would, of course, be a mistake to think of the great tragedies, like those of Sophocles or Shakespeare, as still belonging to the era of religious or tribal instruction, or as written for propagandist purposes. Like painting and music, the art of tragedy did not reach its full stature of greatness until it came out of the church and the school and became an art in the pure sense of the word—an expression of creative imagination in the search for beauty.

Long after it had become an art, however, it clung to the traditional association with matters of larger public concern—with the doings of the gods, or of nations, or dynasties, or kings, or nobles, or highly exceptional people; or with matters symbolic of the deeper and more universal human experiences.

There is an interesting parallel in the history of painting. In its earlier stages most important art was religious in significance; but long after it had ceased to be exclusively so, great painting continued to be generally exalted in feeling. When no longer dedicated to religious fervor or political idolatry, the painter with a passion to express great beauty still thought in elevated terms; he did not ordinarily content himself with ten-by-twelve pictures of specific places or people; he thought rather in terms of great murals for public buildings, or canvases large enough to be hung in palaces, museums, or art galleries. True, the man who painted the famous mural of "The Last Supper" also painted the rather small "Mona Lisa"; yet he put into the latter something that has kept it in a public gallery for centuries (except when somebody stole it for a time). There are many exceptions, and there are conflicting opinions even about the best in art, yet something of the grand tradition still lingers in painting. A very fine painter may paint small studies of pleasant landscapes or interesting people—for practice, for amusement, or for sale—and in so doing may now and then produce a real work of art; but when he has a profound or noble or stirring thought or feeling to express he usually works in larger terms. The people who go to see paintings in museums and galleries still expect to find something big—if not in actual size, at least in concept; they expect to be stirred, impressed, and (except in a museum devoted exclusively to modern art) ennobled.

So for tragedy. Since tragedy normally deals with death and disaster (which many people still take seriously, and think of as universal), it has retained, even in the face of the current sewer-raking vogue, at least some association with the heroic tradition, and some parallelism with the tradi-

tion of great painting and great music; and people still go to see one of the older tragedies in much the same mood as that in which they visit an art gallery or attend a symphony concert, for an adventure in poetic exaltation.

Shortly after seeing Judith Anderson in Robinson Jeffers' version of Euripides' *Medea*, I came across a published note by Mr. Jeffers, in which he described his experiences in making the translation. He said that he had been shocked to discover in the Greek original just as much cruelty and hatred and love of harrowing detail as in any modern horror play. I could hardly believe my eyes, and was ready to break out in protest, when he went on to say that what distinguished the Greek play was its sheer poetic power, and that that was what he had tried to recapture. That made me feel better; and I am happy to say that I think he succeeded. Whether we call the thing poetic power, or elevation, or exaltation, or idealization, or universality, or just beauty, it is very ancient and persistent, though missing from much that is called art today.

It is not mere accident that has caused grand opera to associate itself largely with tragic themes—some of them as horrific and harrowing in detail as anything from Euripides or O'Neill. Though a hybrid art, at times disconcerting to lovers of drama and lovers of pure music alike, grand opera is peculiarly fitted to maintain the heroic or festival tradition. The nobility of the music preserves the elevation of the theme; so much so that it sometimes enables us to retain a sense of poetic and tragic exaltation in a music drama which, judged as a play without the music, would be promptly condemned as cheap melodrama.

A thoughtful actor, studying the place of tragedy among the arts, may well ask in some surprise why there is not a similar correlation between the noble and the tragic in pure music, especially symphonic music. There are, to be sure, a considerable number of short compositions which strike a tragic note; but with the exception of the *Pathetique* and one or two lesser examples, the major symphonies are practically all tragicomedies rather than tragedies. They have their ups and downs, with moments of confusion, danger, pathos, or despair, alternating with moments of peace, or ecstasy, or frivolity; but they almost always end in a stirring crescendo of triumph, suggesting the victory of the human spirit over its trials and torments. Ought we to conclude that the composer of symphonies would improve and ennoble his art by turning to tragedy (as Tchaikovsky thought for a brief period)? Or should we counsel the dramatist to turn from tragedy to tragicomedy as a better means of achieving triumphant exaltation? And how is it that the great symphony with its triumphant

ending and the great tragedy with its final catastrophe have such a similar effect in purgation and elevation of spirit?

The answer to the first two questions is, No. The answer to the third is an important lesson for the actor as well as for the dramatist.

Tragedy only achieves its purgative exaltation when so conceived and executed that the concrete physical disaster is offset by a certain sense of spiritual triumph. No matter how horrible the fate of the individual protagonist, if we discern in the balance and resolution of spiritual forces a measure of inevitability and poetic justice, upholding the dignity of mankind as a whole and the beauty and integrity of his ideals, we feel a compensating sense of vindication. As the symbolic individual who has sinned or erred goes down to defeat, the collective spirit of all mankind, felt in the abstract, seems to triumph. The things we believe in have once more been proved true. This is precisely what happens in a great symphony, except that it happens directly in the abstract. The composer does not have to set up a concrete protagonist and make a human sacrifice of him in order to justify our spiritual victory; the collective human spirit *is* the protagonist, struggling through a series of changing moods and abstract experiences to an ultimate mood of spiritual triumph. This mood is essentially the same as the mood of exaltation generated by great tragedy, though the machinery for generating it is simpler and more direct. But it is only in the tragedy of elevation that we can feel this analogy; the tragedy of depression is quite different, though it has its own analogies in the work of our more chaotic modern composers.

This is not a book on music, or on the arts in general. It is a book on acting; and the point for the student actor in the last few pages is simply that if he wishes to act in heroic tragedy he must look far beyond the facts of the plot or the specific traits of the character. He must grasp and feel sympathetically those universal overtones which great tragedy shares with great music and great painting. How to do so is not a problem in the narrower aspects of technique, but a problem in breadth of understanding and scope of imagination.

Recalling his dual function, the actor *as instrument* must be able to imagine accurately the thoughts and feelings of the character he represents, not to mention the appearance and physical actions; but *as artist* he must go beyond these, and even beyond his personal attitude towards the character and the play, and must grasp its significance as an expression of universal human experience. As instrument he may be writhing in the agony of death as the curtain comes down, or weeping over the death of another, or laughing the mocking laugh of a Mephistopheles; but as

artist he must be feeling that larger triumph of the human spirit and sub-jectively sharing it with his audience.

Obviously no one actor can do this by himself, even if he is playing the lead. It is a matter of teamwork, to which each actor must contribute according to his part. And a good team is not just a group of individuals, each playing his own position brilliantly. A good team is welded together by a group spirit, a common loyalty, a peculiar something which makes it transcend itself and "play better than it knows how." For a team of tragic actors, that something is the group sense of a universal implication behind the tragedy—of the triumph of eternal verities behind the defeat of the protagonist.

It is this group awareness of the larger implications in tragedy which seems to me the most essential part of a "tragedy sense," if there is such a thing. In its absence a heroic tragedy may very well become just as de-pressing and painful as a clinical tragedy, without the excuse of being truthful. In its presence even the filthiest and most disgusting clinical tragedy may rise in dignity at least a degree or two.

Since the problem is a group one, the main responsibility is naturally on the director; but the director can accomplish little unless each actor does his share. No one actor could achieve the effect of purgative exaltation by himself, even in a leading part; but one actor could easily spoil the team-work by failing to sense the overtones, and therefore playing too objectively and independently. This, it seems to me, is one of the major dangers of the so-called "Stanislavsky system" (as set forth in *An Actor Prepares*), with its excessive emphasis on the individual actor and his search for "inner realism" of characterization. An actor may be a very good actor indeed in the degree of imaginative intensity and human truth with which he por-trays his character, and yet be a thorn in the flesh to the director who is trying to achieve an overall effect of poetic justice or grandeur in the play as a whole.

A young actor studying the Stanislavsky system should by all means keep in mind the thought that it represents a highly specialized concept of acting appropriate to the low-key dramas for which the Moscow Art Theatre is chiefly famous. In dramaturgical concept, or in technique of production, or both, the series of plays associated with Stanislavsky stands for something distinct from the plays of other nations and other periods, and even from other plays of the same nation and the same period. When the Moscow Art Theatre company was playing in this country in 1923, one of our most distinguished professors of drama, after seeing their repertory, said to me, "They just aren't like other people; they take their fate with

hopeless resignation, and don't fight back." That spirit would seem to be the precise opposite of the spirit in most heroic tragedy.

Whether the remark is true of the Russian people as a whole is debatable, though the spectacle of a nation of 200 millions ruled body and soul by a tiny well-organized minority party would seem to bear it out. But it is certainly true of the effect conveyed by Stanislavsky's productions as we saw them in 1923. It is interesting to note that Tchekhov himself was distressed by some of it, and complained bitterly in letters to his wife[1] during the production of *The Cherry Orchard* (in 1904) that Stanislavsky was stupidly misunderstanding his play, and filling it with tears, melancholy, and despair, when he had intended it as a comedy, full of hope for the future. The merits of the controversy do not concern us here. The point is that the concept of tragic acting implied in *An Actor Prepares*, however suitable it may be for the peculiar effects sought by the Moscow Art Theatre, is not necessarily suitable to all kinds of plays, and least of all to heroic tragedies with poetic exaltation.

In Greek tragedy much of the implication of universal overtones was conveyed by the words—and perhaps by the dance patterns—of the chorus. In later tragedies we often find a similar function performed by a smaller and less obvious chorus, or by a prologue or narrator, or by a minor character serving as the author's mouthpiece in somewhat the same way. The actor assigned to a chorus or mouthpiece part should have little difficulty in feeling the overtones and pitching his acting in the right key.

As a rule, also, the actor playing the hero or protagonist can readily sense the import of the whole, since the centrality of his character forces him to study the whole play, keeps the director working with him, and requires him to be in at the death, so to speak.

It is the actor playing a minor character, a by-plot character, a foil, a servant, a messenger, or a "comic relief" character who is most likely to play off key; and it is in some such part that the young actor is likely to have his first experience in tragic acting. He will be expected to learn his art by doing the more difficult thing first—bad pedagogy, perhaps, but customary, and perhaps inevitable.

The problem is especially acute in the matter of the so-called "comic relief" character, for which an actor is sometimes cast primarily because he is a comedian rather than a tragedian. This fairly common practice may be one reason why so many sensitive critics have deplored the bad taste of our great tragic writers—even Shakespeare—in cheapening their noblest plays by the injection of irrelevant buffoonery. One may choose to

[1] Published in Princess Toumanova's biography of Tchekhov (1936).

believe that the Drunken Porter in *Macbeth* and the Gravediggers in *Hamlet* were bits of irrelevant buffoonery thrown in as a sop to the groundlings; but such things are irrelevant buffoonery only if the actors make them seem so. Properly acted, their purpose may be less that of comic relief than that of contrast, intended to heighten the irony or poignancy of the scene by throwing it into relief—relief in the sculptor's sense of the word, not the escapist's. This is what we do when we season our food by adding a spice of sharply contrasting taste, not to divert our attention by an irrelevant effect, but to heighten the overall flavor through contrast.

There is no reason why an actor with an excellent comedy sense should not also have an excellent tragedy sense; and there is no reason why both should not operate at the same time. That is a phase of the actor's "dual function." But there is no use denying that actors who can handle that particular phase adequately are pretty rare, perhaps because the need for them is so little realized; and that the few who can measure up to it are more likely to be found playing leads than gravediggers and porters. I have seen seven or eight Macbeths, all but one fairly good; but I have seen only one good Drunken Porter. I have seen two mediocre Hamlets and seven or eight good ones, but only two good Gravediggers, and only one of them with a full sense of the tragic overtones. I do not mean to imply that the latter was not funny. As instrument he was the funniest of the lot. So was the one good Drunken Porter. But whereas a mere comic playing the Drunken Porter always seems to be saying, "Come on, folks, relax! Forget the play and your troubles and let's all have a good laugh!", the artist who is both comedian and tragedian seems to be saying, *as artist*, "Look at this ridiculous fellow I'm pretending to be; what a rowdy he is! But he doesn't know what you and I know. He hasn't the faintest notion what goes on in the King's bedchamber. Let's laugh while we can at his roaring folly, but let's not forget that the preposterous knocking that annoys him so comically is really a symbol of doom!"

Is this asking too much of the actor? Is it impossible for him to suggest such opposite things at the same time? If so, then our whole conception of the dual function is impossible, and the best actors for generations have been working under a delusion. But it is not impossible. Real actors do it right along. They are constantly telling us one thing objectively, and another thing subjectively. This just happens to be one of the more difficult cases. An actor with a deep simultaneous appreciation of both comic and tragic values can make us feel an overpowering sense of impending and inevitable disaster, and make us laugh at the same time. Call it telepathy or call it technique; it is the essence of good acting.

One could go on discussing and analyzing the nature of tragedy almost indefinitely, but perhaps we have covered enough to suggest the actor's problem. It is not a problem to be reduced to rules and formulas, nor is it a problem to be occultized in a semantic brain storm of mystic terminology. It is a problem for intelligent, straightforward, persistent, thoughtful study.

Before the student is abandoned to his own devices, however, he should be cautioned against three of the most treacherous pitfalls into which inexpert tragedians can tumble. These might be called the "tragic moan," the "tragic strut," and the "tragic pose."

THE TRAGIC MOAN

The tragic moan has many varieties, but essentially it is the tendency to fall into a conventional vocal pattern or rhythm, as a means of expressing a somewhat vague emotion, in the absence of a clear, vivid awareness of specific meanings. It is not unlike the sweetly sad lilt in which a rather shallow type of clergyman keeps assuring us that what he is saying is very compassionate and very holy, whatever it may actually mean. It is really a variety of that "elaborate pattern of monotony" common with shallow oral readers and discussed in that connection in Chapter X. It is perhaps commonest in the speaking of verse, but most annoying to the listener in the speaking of prose.

Sometimes it takes the form of a plaintive whine, suggesting an abused or discontented attitude; sometimes it is sweetly melancholy; sometimes it is artificially orotund, or self-consciously noble; sometimes it is indignantly resentful; but most frequently it is monotonously rhythmic in a tone of kindly sympathy—so much so that the actor's friends nudge each other and say, "There he goes again, singing his lines!"

The tragic moan, especially in its last-mentioned form, is most likely to afflict an actor who is accustomed to playing rough or boisterous parts in comedy or melodrama, and who, confronted with a more serious or sympathetic part, feels a sudden need to tone himself down to a more restrained but more emotional mood. The tone he chooses may be appropriate enough for certain lines or situations; the trouble is that, being ill at ease in unfamiliar emotions, he is apt to overdo a good thing and let it grow upon him as a mannerism. The fault is not common with very bad actors; it occurs most frequently with those who have enough imagination and enough sense of the tragic overtones to realize that some suggestion of tragic mood is needed, but not enough experience in tragic acting—or in self-criticism—to keep out of a vocal rut.

Almost any form of the tragic moan may have its proper place in some passage or situation where it really fits the meaning. The point is not that the actor should rule any one of them out of his vocabulary, but that he should take pains not to let any one of them grow upon him as a habit, to be used monotonously for *any* meaning just because it has *a* meaning which may not be *the* meaning. The actor in process of acquiring this habit is seldom aware of it. He is not trying to build up a mannerism, still less to be monotonous. In fact, his tendency to fall into unnatural inflection patterns and elaborate singsong rhythms is unconsciously motivated by his desire to avoid monotony; but like the type of reader so "disgustful" to John Rice in 1765 he arrives only at "the burthen of the same song."

Fortunately, the modern actor has available an excellent method for overcoming this difficulty. He need only make a practice of having his speeches recorded and listening to the playback five or six times, and if he is really an actor he will soon cure himself.

THE TRAGIC STRUT

The tragic strut is not nearly so common a fault nowadays as it used to be when the schools of "elocution and dramatic art" were at the peak of their influence, and a more bombastic style of acting was in vogue. It still occurs, however, with some frequency in poorly directed amateur or second-rate professional companies, and much less frequently on Broadway —though occasionally in very high places. John Gielgud, no less, gave us several examples in his *Hamlet*, and one glaring example in his first entrance as Jason in the Jeffers version of the *Medea*.[2]

It is a rather forgivable fault, at least in its motivation, for it does indicate a feeling on the part of the actor that he must do *something* to distinguish tragedy from comedy and to give it elevation. Seeking to portray a character imagined as bigger or nobler than himself (if only in the scale of his villainy), he makes the understandable mistake of supposing that it can be done by external exaggeration—by lengthening his stride, puffing out his chest, making spectacular pivots, and so on. There are times when any one of these things, in moderation, may help; but again it is a matter of overdoing a good thing, and depending too much upon it. It is a fault less frequently noted among rank beginners with no theatre experience than among those who have seen a good deal of second-rate acting in cheap stock companies or class B movies.

Historically, the tragic strut is inherited from the days of more or less

---

[2] Mr. Gielgud played Jason only for the opening weeks, Mr. Dennis King succeeding him for the New York run.

artificial poetic drama, performed on platform stages or deep forestages, where the actor had little help from lights or scenery, and felt small but conspicuous at the center of converging sight lines. It has a close association with the traditional rules of stage movement, especially those concerning footwork and turns,[3] and is to some degree an exaggeration and exploitation of those movements. But it has other manifestations, especially among those unaware of the older traditions. It represents, perhaps, a more or less natural impulse, based upon the mimetic instinct, a heroic cast of imagination, and a somewhat defensive reliance on exaggeration—what the psychologist calls "overcompensation." It is clearly observable in the mimetic play of children, before they are old enough to have had theatre-going experience, but not before they are old enough to have formed some heroic concepts from hearing fairy stories, looking at "comic" strips, and listening to such radio exaggerations as "Superman."

On the whole, it is a more harmless and less persistent fault than the tragic moan, rather more likely to be checked in time by the actor's self-criticism, the kidding of his friends, or the vigilance of the director. The one thing which may tempt the actor to make it a habit is false praise from "the unskillful" (who, alas, are often "the general") while "the judicious" grieve too silently.

THE TRAGIC POSE

The tragic pose bears a close analogy to the tragic strut, and is sometimes almost indistinguishable from it. But it also has some variations of its own, stemming perhaps from different sources. It is somewhat more likely to be found in otherwise good productions, and in the work of otherwise good actors.

The main root, I think, lies in the tradition of pure beauty in tragedy— a laudable tradition in itself. A certain amount of decorative formalism in movement and posture has been associated with tragedy from the earliest times; it is at least as old as the choric odes and dithyrambs out of which Greek tragedy evolved. The symbolic groupings and rhythmic movements of the Greek chorus were certainly examples of tragic pose; but presumably they must have been legitimate and satisfying ones. There have been many examples since, in which well-designed stage pictures or sculptural posings of characters (whether prescribed by the dramatist or worked out by director and actors) have contributed to the symbolic and decorative beauty of tragedy, without detriment to its dignity or sincerity. So long as a symbolic pose is usefully symbolic, or a decorative pose decora-

[3] See Chapter XVI. See also *The Art of Play Production*, p. 118.

tive *without distraction*, no harm is done. Certainly tragedy would seem to call for more of such posing than comedy, and heroic or poetic tragedy for more than clinical tragedy. No actor should be discouraged from striking a pose at a moment when that pose most effectively expresses the meaning or feeling and at the same time most effectively suggests the dignity or beauty of the tragic overtones.

The trouble begins when a director who is more of a painter or sculptor than a dramatist gets more interested in visual formalism than in meaning, and starts to run wild with his groupings and posed pictures; or when an actor who has been looking in the mirror too much, or reading too many reviews praising his grace of movement, begins to fancy himself as a living symbol of tragic beauty rather than as an interpreter of thoughts and feelings.

To be sure, a moderate amount of natural vanity does an actor no great harm; it may, in fact, help him to conquer his timidity, and perhaps without it few people would venture on the stage at all. But a little too much of it, approaching egotism, readily leads to an excess of tragic pose. When an inexperienced actor, or one making his first venture in a tragic part, falls into the trap, it is not hard to explain. Nor is it, as a rule, very hard to correct. He has only to be convinced that vanity is making him pose, and the same vanity will make him wish to avoid being caught at it again.

But the tragic pose, like the tragic strut, sometimes appears in high places, where it can hardly be explained as a result of youthful vanity or inexperience. In such cases it must doubtless be explained as a good impulse unconsciously overdeveloped, or as an honest overenthusiasm for sculptural beauty as an expression of tragic style.

The amount of tragic posing which an audience can accept without being aware of it as a distraction is enormously variable with the period, the country, and the type of play. A great deal more was accepted and expected in the "palmy days" of the nineteenth-century theatre than is generally acceptable today—yet not so much that Edwin Forrest could escape the charge of excessive posing from some critics in his own time. My actor-grandfather, who knew Forrest at the height of his fame, thought that he overdid the tragic pose, and much preferred the acting of Macready, who did not. In my own youth, at the turn of the century, I saw a good deal of tragic posing by such actors as Robert Mantell, E. H. Sothern, and Ben Greet, not to mention a horde of lesser ones who acted the subordinate parts in their companies. It is possible, however, that some of the individual posing of actors in the past stands out in our memories because there was less attention paid to the posing of groups. The present ascend-

ancy of the director (dating roughly from the spread of Gordon Craig's ideas after 1911), and the consequent emphasis on teamwork, has brought about more group posing in the interest of the stage picture as a whole; and the developments in modern stage lighting and design have created new possibilities of unified theatric effect in the interest of beauty and symbolism. This means that we are relatively less apt to notice the posing of the individual actor when he is part of a well-posed picture or sculptural group; but it also means that the actor—more than ever before— can ill afford to indulge in exaggerated individual poses which detach him from the group and distract our attention from the total effect.

Near-perfection breeds perfectionists, and when a production is almost perfect, marred only by something well done that should not have been done, our disappointment is the more acute. For me, John Gielgud's Hamlet—which in other respects might well be rated the best of our time —was spoiled by the tragic pose. The irony of it is that the poses themselves were beautiful, both individually and in relation to the sculptural group. Mr. Gielgud read the lines with amazing fluency, poetry, and understanding, and also with remarkable (if somewhat studied) variety and originality. His movements were stunningly graceful, and dramatically appropriate to the lines, and his poses, considered separately, were beyond criticism. But all evening it was just one beautiful sculptured picture after another, with the actor moving swiftly and surely from one to another, holding it long enough for the beauty or symbolism to sink in, and then moving swiftly to the next. The effect upon me was that I could not keep my mind on Hamlet, the character, for marveling at Gielgud, the sculptor —a sculptor being his own model rather than an actor being his own instrument of characterization. Imaginatively, I never lost myself for five minutes in the play.

It is interesting that Mr. Gielgud also directed the *Medea* in which he played Jason. The same quality of conscious sculptural formalism was evident in this production, and the same perfection of beauty and symbolism. But the conscious formalism was much more appropriate and satisfying in the Greek play than in the Elizabethan, *Hamlet* being after all an introspective play of human psychology in which we lose a good deal if we cannot keep our minds on the character. The most obvious use of the tragic pose in the *Medea* was the formal posturing of the three women of Corinth, to whom Mr. Jeffers entrusted the duties of Euripides' chorus. Since they represented not so much real people as an abstract symbol of public conscience reacting to the tragic overtones, formal posing did not seem out of place with them. But plenty of conscious poses were assigned

to other characters—droopy tombstone poses to the Nurse, statuesque ones to Creon, and a kaleidoscopic variety of tragic attitudes to Medea herself, ranging from the prostration of abandoned grief to the crouch of a tigress. It is a curious fact that all these members of the company, even the chorus women, seemed able to carry out the formalism with less self-consciousness than Mr. Gielgud himself. Miss Anderson, as Medea, had more planned poses than all the others combined, yet she managed to keep our minds—and apparently her own—on the monumental passions of the character against any distractions originating in the poses themselves. Perhaps the explanation is that the actors who did not have to direct accepted the poses contrived by the sculptor-director, but still remained actors at heart; while the director, playing a relatively minor part, could not forget his problems as a sculptor.

In any case, the lesson for the young actor is plain. There is little likelihood that he will do the wrong thing as superbly as Mr. Gielgud, or draw as much praise for it from undiscriminating critics. But there is plenty of temptation for him to do the wrong thing badly, or to overdo the right thing in the course of his apprenticeship. Let him remember that there is nothing wrong with a tragic pose *per se*, but that there is everything wrong with any device of technique or habit or impulse which distracts attention from the essential thought or feeling or purpose of a work of art.

It is a sad comment on the insidiousness of the tragic pose that another great actor, who had nine-tenths of the equipment to make him the greatest actor in American history, and who is fondly remembered by his admirers as the "Sweet Prince," should be widely remembered by his critics as "The Great Profile."

In warning the young actor against the tragic pose, I should like it clearly understood that I am referring to an honest error or defect of technique, rather than to the much-too-common trick of "upstage" posing by which certain actors—including another equally famous Hamlet of recent years—intentionally "hog" the stage for their own aggrandizement. That is a defect of character, not technique; of ethics, not art; and as such is out of our province.

CHAPTER XIII

Reaction and By-Play

THERE is one general phase of the actor's art that is commonly neglected, and yet extremely important. Passing reference has been made
to it in several previous chapters, especially in relation to teamwork; but
it deserves a good deal of concentrated study by the young actor, if only to
protect him from the influence of a popular misconception.

The misconception is that acting consists almost exclusively of speaking
prescribed lines and executing prescribed actions, and that between such
assignments what the actor does is unimportant. No one familiar with the
modern theatre really believes that, literally and completely; to do so he
would have to be very stupid and unobservant. Yet so much of the emphasis in popular discussions of acting falls on the lines and the accompanying action that it is easy for thoughtless actors to slip into a habit of concentrating on their own lines and cues, and neglecting their reactions to
what others say or do, and their by-play when not in the foreground. Their
mistake is perfectly natural, for those phases of the actor's art are the least
conspicuous. Neglect of them is greatly encouraged by the conditions
usually present at rehearsals; there are so many interruptions and distractions, so many waits and repeats, that the actor is constantly tempted
to relax between lines, light a cigarette, and forget that he is in the play
at all until the director tells him to resume speaking. Several weeks of that
sort of thing can easily lull an actor into a state of indifferent listening
and half-hearted reaction, if not into a state of complete confusion.

It is possible that the prevalence of the misconception is partly due to the
persistence of an older tradition, going back to the days when plays and
acting were more formal and declamatory than at present. Leading actors
then paraded to the center of the stage, or of the forestage, subordinate
actors kept more in the background, the lighting was often poor, especially
in the background, and people paid much less attention to the reactions
of the minor characters. The leading actors were given long, eloquent
speeches, which held attention by their own style and content, and were
generally less dependent for effect upon the reactions of those spoken to

than is the rule today. For the most part, the minor actors at least were not expected to go much beyond the actions prescribed for them.

There is a widely accepted belief (not, perhaps, conclusively proved) that the actors of Shakespeare's day entered out of character, did not begin to act until they reached the acting area, and dropped out of character when not actively involved in the lines. This belief finds some support in the fact that Shakespeare often reminds his actors of the need for reaction by having the speaking character describe the reactions of another. When Othello says,

> Honest Iago, that look'st dead with grieving,
> Speak, who began this?

we know, and presumably Iago is reminded, that he is supposed to be looking crushed. When Macbeth perceives the ghost of Banquo, and Lady Macbeth says to him,

> Why do you make such faces? When all's done
> You look but on a stool. . . .

we should be much disappointed—and the actor much embarrassed—if he had failed to make the faces. And when Mark Antony, come to bury Caesar, says to the crowd of citizens,

> O, now you weep, and I perceive you feel
> The dint of pity . . .

we understand clearly that even the minor characters have been expected to react.

Warren Smith, in a fascinating and exhaustive dissertation on the stage directions in Shakespeare's lines,[1] calls attention to a great number of such directions. He is somewhat troubled by the fact that these regularly come after the reactions they describe, not before, and he is therefore loath to interpret them as cues reminding the actors addressed how to react. He prefers to explain them as devices to clarify for the audience reactions which are important to the meaning, but which some of the customers might miss by reason of poor lighting, bad sight lines, or distance from the stage. If Elizabethan actors did have a habit of dropping out of character when not speaking, it is possible to assume that Shakespeare committed essential reactions to the lines because neither he nor his audience had any hope that the actors would perform them. That seems an extreme view. I prefer to believe that they merely had a tendency to neglect their reactions,

[1] Ph.D. thesis at the University of Pennsylvania, 1948.

Joseph Jefferson as Bob Acres

Mrs. John Drew as Mrs. Malaprop

Plate 17. A famous revival of 1896. An all-star production of *The Rivals*, with many veterans in favorite parts. Mrs. Drew had been playing Mrs. Malaprop on and off for forty years, and Jefferson had made Acres almost as popular as Rip. The script, of course, was the Jefferson version, with Julia (Sheridan's original heroine) left out altogether. Francis Wilson, here shown in a minor part, was a popular eccentric comedian, with a most remarkable skill in projecting his soft, nasal voice. Julia Marlowe, then the wife of Robert Taber, later married her co-star, E. H. Sothern.

Francis Wilson as Fag

Robert Taber as Jack

Julia Marlowe Taber as Lydia

W. H. Crane as Sir Anthony

Richard Mansfield (1857–1907)
as Baron Chevrial in *A Parisian Romance*

Robert B. Mantell (1854–1928)
as Macbeth

Plate 18. Stars of day before yesterday. The versatile Mansfield became one of the most popular and prosperous actor-managers. Mantell and the Sothern-Marlowe team kept Shakespearean repertory popular on the road until the road disappeared; all three lacked variety, but were fine in some parts. Gillette, a distinguished actor of somewhat limited range, left us the stage version of Sherlock Holmes and a famous essay on *The Illusion of the First Time.*

William Gillette (1855–1937)
as Sherlock Holmes

E. H. Sothern and Julia Marlowe
as Romeo and Juliet

Frank Bacon (1864–1922)

White

George M. Cohan (1878–1942)
in *Dear Old Darling*

Plate 19. Stars of yesterday. Frank Bacon reached stardom only in his old age, but broke the long-run record in his own play *Lightnin'*. Cohan—actor, songster, dancer, and playwright—had amazingly expressive hands and feet. Mrs. Fiske had expressive hands but was jerky and unexpected in both speech and gesture. Maude Adams was a special favorite in Barrie's plays.

Maude Adams (born 1872)
in *The Little Minister*

Mrs. (Minnie Maddern) Fiske
(1865–1932)

Hugh Miller as Alfred
Jingle in *Pickwick*

Right:
Charles McNaughton as
Sam Weller and Bruce
Winston as Tony Weller
in *Pickwick*

White

Wilfred Clarke (son of
J. S. Clarke) as the Grave-
digger in *Hamlet*. His
brother Creston was an
excellent Hamlet.

Plate 20. Comedy old and new. Upper left: A well-known bit of
low comedy relief in tragedy. Above: Delicious character
comedy out of Dickens. Lower left: High comedy in a serious
play ("When I wrote that, God and Robert Browning knew
what it meant; but now only God knows!"). Lower right: One
of the teams best known as Mother and Father Day turns to
something different as a pair of shiftless Cajuns in Louisiana.

Brian Aherne and Katharine Cornell
in *The Barretts of Wimpole Street*

Vandamm

Dorothy Gish and Louis Calhern
in *The Great Big Doorstep*

Vandamm

Plate 21. *Unforgettable characterizations*. Above: Katharine Cornell as Mary Fitton in *Will Shakespeare*. Upper right: Tyrone Power as "the drain man" in *The Servant in the House*. Below: Jeanne Eagels as Sadie Thompson in *Rain*. Lower right: Richard B. Harrison as De Lawd in *Green Pastures*. Right: Rollo Peters as Romeo—the best Romeo the author has ever seen.

John Barrymore

John Gielgud as Hamlet

Plate 22. Some leading players of our time. The Barrymores, with their brother Lionel (who is perhaps best known as a film actor), represent the third generation of the Drew-Barrymore "royal family"; the fourth generation is now being heard from. John Gielgud, a grandnephew of Ellen Terry, has had top success in both England and the United States. Eva LeGallienne, daughter of a famous poet, has done distinguished work both as an actress and as directress of several repertory companies.

Ethel Barrymore as Miss Moffat
in *The Corn Is Green*

Eva LeGallienne as Queen Katharine
in *Henry VIII*

Plate 23. Unforgettable scenes superbly acted. Above: Daniel Poole as Abraham Lincoln receiving his impeachment summons from General Grant in *If Booth Had Missed*—a fine piece of restrained emotional acting. Below: Walter Hampden as Cyrano in the spectacular, swashbuckling duel-in-rhyme scene of his own production.

Plate 24. Players of the Moscow Art Theatre. Constantin Stanislavsky and some of his leading associates at the time of their American visit in 1923. Upper left: Portrait of Stanislavsky. Upper right: Stanislavsky as Gaiev in The Cherry Orchard. Left: Olga Knipper-Tchekhova (widow of Tchekhov) as Masha in The Three Sisters. Lower left: Ivan Moskvin as Epikhodov in The Cherry Orchard. Center: Maria Ouspenskaya as Charlotta in The Cherry Orchard. Lower right: Vassily Katchalov as The Baron in The Lower Depths.

and needed frequent jacking up if the dramatist was to be sure of getting at least the more essential ones out of them.

It is quite true that a cue coming after the reaction it describes is of no help to the actor at the first rehearsal or two, or even at a performance if he does not know his part. But it does embarrass him to have been caught off guard and to have missed an important reaction clearly stated in the lines. It disturbs him even at the first rehearsal; and after he has missed the same reaction at two or three rehearsals, and been laughed at for it, he begins kicking himself for his own lapse. At that point he goes over the passage carefully, figures out an earlier warning cue, and swears a big oath that he will get that reaction next time or bust; and by the time performances begin he usually knows it better than anything else in his part. Many scholars have thought that by making such exacting requirements of his actors in the lines, and committing them in advance to precise reactions, Shakespeare was being very hard on them. Actors know that he was being hard on them in early rehearsals only to be easier on them in performance, by leaving them in no doubt about what was expected of them and giving them the strongest of all mnemonic aids through fear of disgrace. Whether that was his conscious purpose I do not presume to know; nobody could know without more information about the customs of the time, the exact stage arrangements, the position and duties of the prompter, and whether he read the lines ahead of the actors (as he has done in many European theatres at various periods). I do know that it works that way today, not only in Shakespeare's plays, but in all plays having similar reaction cues. There is nothing that so hurts a modern actor's pride as being caught a second or third time failing to register a reaction mentioned in the lines. He not only feels guilty of incompetence, he feels hypocritical at being credited with acting which he obviously hasn't done. That hurts. I have heard young ladies say "Damn!" at that who wouldn't say it for a mashed thumb. Even the actor who habitually declines to act at rehearsals will make an exception for the cued reaction.

The sum of all this is that the cued reaction is the easy part of the problem.

Modern acting, however, calls for many reactions that are not mentioned in the lines, and not even hinted at. With its bright lights, imaginative consistency, and unity of teamwork, the modern theatre calls for the actor to stay in character all the time, and to react in some way, if only negatively, to everything that happens while he is on the stage. That presents a much more difficult problem for him than the few indispensable reactions called for by Shakespeare's cues. It would not be an exaggeration to say

that a very considerable part of good modern acting lies in effective re-action and by-play.

For purposes of study, it is convenient to think of reaction under two separate classifications, as foreground reaction and background reaction.

FOREGROUND REACTION

Foreground action, including reaction, is not necessarily forestage ac-tion. Though it does frequently take place down stage, it may now and then occur up stage, or at one side, or on a stairway or balcony. By fore-ground action is meant simply that which logically and properly occupies the focus of audience attention at any given moment; and foreground reaction is reaction within the same focus. The focus of attention is most often on the main characters, but shifts freely from one character to an-other and from one location to another with the demands of the plot and meaning.

There is a vital difference between foreground and background action, which every actor should keep everlastingly in mind. Foreground action is meant to attract and heighten attention to the main flow of thought, while background action must never divert or weaken it by distracting it from its proper focus. The distinction applies with equal force to re-action.

For the reasons already mentioned, foreground reaction is rather less of a problem than background reaction. More of it, for one thing, is taken care of by the author, through direct description or indirect suggestion. Shake-speare's cued reactions are all foreground reactions; his calling direct atten-tion to them necessarily makes them so. They indicate the dramatist's feeling that the character addressed belongs, at the moment, in the focus of attention. The young actor should realize, however, that there are many more opportunities for foreground reaction than are specified in the lines, even by Shakespeare; and he should be alert to discover and make the most of them.

The problem is largely one in good listening, the importance of which can hardly be exaggerated. Good listening is obviously not to be expected from the actor who is woolgathering, or who is listening mechanically for his next cue instead of listening imaginatively to the meaning. There are actors who actually fear to listen imaginatively, because, as they say, it distracts them and makes them miss their cues. That can happen only when they have learned their cues in terms of meaningless words, and not in terms of coördinated thought, feeling, and cadence. If they have learned their listening and their reactions along with their cues, as part of a co-

herent, rhythmic flow of meaning, they are not likely to have that trouble.

Normally, the focus of audience attention is on the character who is speaking. But there are moments in many plays when what the speaker says is much less important for itself or for its effect on the speaker than for its effect on another character. It is at such moments that foreground reaction becomes of greatest importance. Sometimes the speaker himself shifts attention to the listener (even in the absence of a reaction cue) by turning toward him or showing interest in his expected reaction. Sometimes there is no reason for him to do so; and sometimes it would be decidedly out of place—as, for example, when the speaking character is not supposed to be aware of the other's reaction, though the audience is. In the latter case, there is a problem for the director, who must so place his characters that the focus of attention may shift at the proper moment without being openly passed over by the speaker, and must see to it that the actor who is to react carries out his assignment. But a good actor in that spot can help enormously in pulling the attention away from the speaker and pointing up the significance of his own reaction.

The difficulty of doing this varies considerably with the distance between the two characters. When they are close together there is danger that the reaction will seem overdone; but when they are far apart there is danger that it will escape notice altogether. A good working rule for the reacting player is this: If, at the moment of reaction, he is well within the visual field of those looking at the speaker (say within thirty inches of him), he should react with restraint, using facial expression rather than movement, and just enough of that to convey the idea. But if he is on the opposite side of the stage from the speaker he should react with a sharp body movement (preceding his line if he has one), and with enough conspicuousness to catch attention and draw it across the stage. This is hard to do without some danger of "hamming" it, but is sometimes quite necessary. The rule must naturally be modified to suit the type of play, the character's own nature, the size of the stage and the theatre, and so on, and of course to fit the specific meaning. It must also be modified proportionately for conditions between the two extremes. But it is still a useful rule.

There are many lines which do not necessarily suggest or demand reactions from the characters addressed, but which are nevertheless improved by them. A line which is slightly obscure, or dull, or colorless, can often be brought to life and made interesting and intelligible if the actor addressed points it up by a clear reaction. Every actor should remember that a listening audience faces many difficulties in the effort to follow the lines—

bad acoustics, distance from the stage, coughers and sneezers, wrigglers and whisperers, unfamiliarity with the actors' voices, and the like—and that any line spoken without special force, or not foolproof in its clarity, is sure to be missed by some. Everything he can do to support its meaning by his visible reaction helps the audience to utilize both senses at once, and so greatly improves the chance that the line will be understood. People often really hear a line but are not quite sure they have heard it correctly; instinctively they watch the character spoken to, and if his reaction confirms their hearing they feel reassured. Conversely, if his reaction is blurred, unintelligible, false, irrelevant, or missing altogether, they are left in a worse fog than if they had not heard the line at all. It is part of the actor's job to help the audience over such difficulties by helping his fellow actors to make their lines understood; it is his duty as a member of the team.

Like almost every good thing, this technique carries its own temptation to excess. Nobody wants to see an actor listening with unbelievable eagerness to the most commonplace remarks, hanging on every word and frowning, or smirking, or bobbing his head with painful exaggeration. Nobody likes people who do that in real life. That kind of listening defeats its own purpose; it distracts the listener's own attention from the speaker to himself, and distracts the attention of the audience from the meaning of the words to the strange behavior of the listener. There are actors who make this mistake habitually in their zeal to appear animated and alert, and to convince themselves that they are acting every minute of the time. One can forgive them for their good intentions, but they are in the same class with the readers who repeat exaggerated inflection patterns to the point of monotony in the belief that they are being expressive.

There are also actors who exaggerate their listening reactions quite intentionally, as a means of drawing attention to themselves and building themselves up professionally. That is just a particularly cheap and shoddy form of the practice described in the last chapter in connection with upstage posing, and like it is not so much an error in technique as a defect in ethics.

THE DOUBLE TAKE

A somewhat special, but highly popular, type of foreground reaction is known to actors by the general trade name of the "double take." It has many forms, but essentially it is a delayed reaction, taking its name from the fact that it seems to come in two impulses—a false reaction followed by a corrected reaction.

In its most familiar form it is a slightly flippant device, common with funny men, and undeniably overworked by them, with the result that it is often sneered at by superior critics as a cheap kind of trickery. But when a device is persistently popular and generally effective, it is always well to take the sneers of its critics with some caution, and to consider whether they do not grow out of its abuse rather than its use.

Since the double take frequently involves a spoken response as well as a visible reaction, it is apt to be thought of as a technique in reading lines. Now and then it is actually written into the lines, as when a character asks a catch question and the person addressed thoughtlessly answers "Yes"—and then hastily corrects it to "No!" This form, with variations, is very popular with "patter" comedians; and since it can be conveyed by the voice without the help of facial expression it is heard a good deal on the radio. But the psychological principle underlying the double reaction applies in many less crude and less hackneyed forms, and in many that are completely silent.

Basically, the double take is a device for pointing up meaning through contrast; which accounts for its usefulness in comedy. There are several reasons for its effectiveness. In the first place it has a sympathetic quality of homely naturalness, since in real life many of us are heedless thinkers, or have slow reaction times, and are often caught off guard and obliged to make hurried corrections; that makes it easy for us to empathize in the double take. In the second place, a hurried correction is justifiably a little more emphatic, or picturesque, or exciting than a simple expected reaction, and therefore sharpens audience attention. In the third place, the slight delay permits even a relatively slow-witted listener to perceive the falseness or inappropriateness of the first reaction, and to anticipate the second one; when it comes he experiences that delicious sensation of having beaten the character to it through superior alertness—a pleasant enough sensation for anybody, but especially so for the slow-witted. Finally, the dramatic impact of the true reaction is considerably heightened by contrast with the false lead given first. This is really the essential function of the device.

In a sense the double take is a tiny little drama in itself, with its own plot structure. The cue line gives us the exposition of a situation, arousing expectation and curiosity. If the true reaction were to come at once, the drama would be over before it began. But instead the false reaction gives us an unexpected complication, a fresh doubt, a threat of disappointment; it may last only an instant, but in that instant it generates a heightened anxiety as to the outcome. Then, lo! the hero comes through with the

correct reaction, everybody is relieved, poetic justice is satisfied, and the thumbnail drama is over—all, perhaps, in a second or less.

The double take has many variations. For one thing, it varies in time; usually it is almost instantaneous, but now and then it works quite slowly. Sometimes the exposition is not a single cue, but a gradual build-up of a false line of thought, followed by a sudden realization of its falseness. Sometimes the false reaction is instantaneous, and the realization is gradual. Sometimes the false reaction is unspoken and the true one spoken; sometimes these conditions are reversed. Sometimes neither is spoken. Frequently the purpose is purely comic; sometimes it is dramatic, and occasionally it may be deeply tragic.

Let us consider a few examples. Several have already been given in other connections, especially in the chapter on Comedy. Sir Peter Teazle's hasty afterthought on the words "intend to be," mentioned in the discussion of following-through, is really a kind of double take—a reaction of complacency (in this case to his own line), followed hurriedly by a corrected reaction of self-consciousness, expressed in the added words as well as his manner. Several of Lord Trench's reactions in the cocktail scene have elements of the double take—notably when he draws in his breath to comment on the drink in a manner which his expression suggests will be unfavorable, delays an instant, and then says, "Not bad."

For an example in which the false reaction is unspoken and the true one spoken, note the following lines from A. A. Milne's charming comedy, *Mr. Pim Passes By:*

GEORGE. What are you doing?

OLIVIA. Making curtains, George. Won't they be rather sweet? Oh, but I forgot—you don't like them.

GEORGE. I don't like them, and what is more, I don't mean to have them in my house. As I told you yesterday, this is the house of a simple country gentleman, and I don't want any of these new-fangled ideas in it.

OLIVIA. Is marrying for love a new-fangled idea?

GEORGE. We'll come to that directly. None of you women can keep to the point. What I'm saying now is that the house of my fathers and forefathers is good enough for me.

When Olivia adroitly turns the subject from curtains to young lovers (in her campaign to get George's consent to their niece's engagement), the slower-witted George is caught off guard. The lines give only his considered reply, but any actor worthy to play George would see that a slight false reaction is needed first to give it its proper impact. The false reaction is unspoken, and consists merely of a follow-through on his previous manner,

suggesting that he is about to answer in the same tone. But as he draws his breath to do so, his wits catch up with him, he pauses an instant, and says, "We'll come to that directly" in a different tone, completing the double take. Incidentally, in this case George may even achieve the effect of a *triple* take by saying the first clause in a tone of subdued annoyance, and then changing a second time to a louder and more exasperated tone on the words, "None of you women can keep to the point."

For an example of a double take in which the first reaction is spoken and the second one silent, we have only to turn to Sheridan again. When Sir Peter explodes with his famous line in the first quarrel scene:

SIR PETER. Ay—there again—taste. Zounds! Madam, you had no taste when you married me!

his first reaction is an outraged follow-through on his own line, lasting just long enough for the audience (and Lady Teazle) to see the joke; then, just as they catch their breath to laugh he sees it too, and suddenly breaks to the corrected reaction of confused embarrassment at his own slip of the tongue—a silent reaction, though we can readily imagine the words he may be saying to himself.

For an example of a double take in which neither reaction is spoken, I am reminded of a scene in the original production of *Strictly Dishonorable*, a frothy comedy of the Prohibition era by Preston Sturges; it was superbly cast, and bits of it have stuck in my memory nearly twenty years for the precision and restraint with which they were acted. In the scene in question, Patrolman Mulligan (played by Robert Bunce Williams) was facing the audience while another character at his left shoulder was trying to wheedle him into something or other not altogether favorable to a third character in the play, a gentleman from East Orange, N. J. Mulligan's only reaction at first was a slowly growing expression of good-natured skepticism; then the speaker, seeing the need for strategy, slyly referred to the third character as "that Orangeman," and went on talking about him. The expected reaction came, but with precisely the right amount of delay to make it an effective double take; and when it came, it was not a spoken one, and not even a sudden start or turn, but a subtle change of expression from good humor to comic belligerency. The actor did not even alter the direction of his gaze, but his smile faded, his brow knitted slightly, his eyes began to burn like hot coals, and his eyebrows and eye shadows seemed to merge into dark circles of thunderous animosity. It was a beautiful piece of restrained comic acting, and a good example of the double take in one of its less hurried and less obvious forms. I am sure that any

reader who can remember *Strictly Dishonorable* will recall that bit with a chuckle.

Another example of the slower and more restrained double take, this time with a highly tragic effect, may be found in that smash hit of the 1880's, *Jim the Penman*. The effect in question, which is the climax of the play, had much to do with turning what, on paper, looks like a third-rate piece of melodramatic literature into a first-rate piece of living theatre, so powerful in its emotional appeal that it broke the long-run record of its day, was summoned to Washington for a "command" performance, and has been revived professionally several times since—notably with an all-star cast in 1928. The play is concerned with a mysterious series of forgeries, and the climax is a scene in which Mrs. James Ralston (played originally by Agnes Booth, and in the 1928 revival by Cecilia Loftus) comes to the silent realization that her own husband is the wanted criminal. The climax is skillfully built up by preceding events, and comes late in the play. Several people are present, and James Ralston is doing some of the talking, while his wife is silent. When the scene begins, she has not the faintest suspicion of her husband, though the audience has. As she listens to the conversation she puts two and two together, while the audience watches her silent reactions. Her first reaction is slow, a mingling of interest, puzzlement, confidence in her husband, detachment—everything but suspicion. When suspicion dawns, it does so with a crushing impact, amounting to certainty almost at once. What makes it a double take is that the change of reaction from the mistaken one to the correct one is a slightly delayed reaction as the observer times it; that gives him a sense of foreknowledge tragically confirmed. His profound sympathy for the wife is greatly heightened by the fact that he knows the blow is going to fall a little before she does, and can see it fall with his own eyes. The whole play thus turns, not on a spoken line or a positive action, but on a foreground reaction.

It is immaterial whether these varied examples are all to be called double takes; the point is that they all involve the same psychological principle, and illustrate the variety with which that principle may be applied. Perhaps very few actors analyze the principle and think the problem through logically. Many good actors arrive at it through an instinctive feeling for what is artistically effective; many poor ones arrive at it by imitation of others. It is when they arrive at it by bad imitation, or when they work it to death, that they bring the double take into bad repute. Properly used, it is one of the most important tools in the actor's kit, as useful to him as oil to a painter or rosin to a violinist.

BACKGROUND REACTION

There is no great mystery about background reaction. The reason it is rather more troublesome than foreground reaction is that it is likely to be neglected most of the time, and then correspondingly overacted when the need for it is realized.

Since background reaction is usually a group problem, the responsibility is initially on the director. Every experienced director knows the exasperation of watching a dozen players stand about listlessly with poker faces when a main character is saying or doing something which the author meant to startle, or surprise, or alarm, or shock, or amuse, or please the other characters present; and every experienced actor has seen a director tear his hair and implore his players to "React! for God's sake, react!"

In justice to the players it should be said that their failure to react is often due less to stupidity or bad acting than to wandering attention—superinduced in many cases by the rehearsal conditions described a few pages back. After several performances before audiences they frequently learn to build up their reactions intelligibly, if only by imitating those of the audience. The director's particular worry is to get enough out of them at rehearsals to insure an intelligible first performance.

That is not to say that background reaction is all that it should be, even at the tenth performance. Some actors do not react enough; others react too much, distracting attention from foreground to background. Some react to the objective meaning in a detached way, much as the audience reacts, but without thought of their individual characters and their relation to the event; or they react simply as a chorus, not as individuals. Worst of all, they often react mechanically, according to the director's instructions but without creative imagination.

There are many scenes in which the things said and done in the foreground are of such a nature that all the background characters will react to them with the same emotion—all equally shocked, or astonished, or delighted, as the case may be. Even then, however, the individual actor should remember that we do not all show the same emotions in the same way. He should ask himself, not how the average citizen would react to such a situation, or how he would react himself, but how the character he is portraying would react. That seems childishly elementary, but it is astounding how many actors fail to think it out.

A particularly fine example of the problem occurs in that final tableau of *The Inspector-General* described in the section on timing. With minor exceptions, all the characters on the stage when the Gendarme makes his

announcement experience the same emotion—one of utter consternation and frustration. They have spent their efforts and their money entertaining and bribing the wrong man, and now that the real inspector has arrived they are back where they started, with much less prospect of success. But they are all sharply drawn individual characters, and show their reaction in varied ways.

So anxious was Gogol to make this clear that he wrote out a special series of instructions to the players, the most important part of which follows:[2]

The last scene is especially important for its effect. The turn of events is no joke to these people; it is dead serious, almost tragic. The Town Governor is especially tragic. For this clever grafter to find himself fooled by a youngster, a mere nobody, is crushing; when the announcement comes he simply turns to stone.

Everyone in the final picture should have a special pose and facial expression suited to his character, and showing the degree of fear or astonishment felt.

The signal for the change of positions can be the exclamation of Korobkina which comes right after the announcement.

The positions are as follows:

In the center the Town Governor, arms apart, head back, mouth slightly open, eyes wild with fear and astonishment.

To the right are his wife and daughter, looking at him with fear.

After them, the Postmaster, simply converted into a question mark, facing the audience.

Farther on the same side, the Superintendent of Schools, white and frozen stiff.

On the left, Zemlyanika, eyebrows raised, his fingers at his mouth, as if he had burned himself.

After him the Judge, almost sitting on the floor, his lips forming the words, "There you are!"

Farther on the same side, Bobchinsky and Dobchinsky, looking at each other with mouths open and index fingers raised.

The rest are distributed on either side, half of them expressing astonishment, the other half trying to catch the expression on the Governor's face. All are immobile. Karobkina and a couple of others can assume an ironical "serves-you-right!" expression.

It is not often that a dramatist gives his players as much help as this. But there are many plays indeed which call for group reactions expressing more

[2] Translated by Benjamin Rothberg, for the edition published by the Walter H. Baker Co., Boston. An illustration of the scene included in the same edition is reprinted in *The Art of Play Production*.

or less uniform feelings, but expressing them in highly divergent ways according to character. There are also many plays in which different characters react differently because they are feeling different emotions; their reactions differ in content as well as style. It will be noted that the scene just discussed contains an example of this also, for several of the women, Korobkina, and perhaps Khlopova, are more cynically amused than horrified, and react differently for that reason, while one or two others are merely curious or uncomprehending, and react hardly at all.

The actor playing a background part, or a main part temporarily shifted to the background, should constantly remember his obligation to stay imaginatively in the picture; not just to "react" when the director yells at him, but to react all the time in terms of the character and the situation, toning it down when necessary for subordination of background, but keeping it imaginatively true. He should constantly remind himself of a fact mentioned earlier in this book—namely, that in the theatre even the background is never wholly out of attention. A novelist, wishing to concentrate on certain characters, can describe their actions and quote their words in such a way as to control attention at will. The reader may be vaguely aware that minor characters are present, but if the author does not mention them for a while they fade out of emphasis almost completely. The painter can do the same thing by brightening the colors and sharpening the outlines of his foreground, and at the same time painting his background out of focus in more subdued colors and hazier outlines, blurring it just enough to discourage unwanted attention, yet retaining enough suggestion to give it meaning as part of the whole. All this is much more difficult for the dramatist and the stage director, because of the efficiency and adaptability of the human eye. When the observer is watching a foreground character at a distance of, say, 30 feet, a background character at 40 feet is still fairly within his depth of focus; and whenever there is the slightest temptation for him to shift his glance to the background character he instantly and automatically adjusts his focus to the correct distance, opens his pupils to compensate for any reduction in the lighting, and sees the background character in clear detail. The director may discourage this to some degree by careful choice of costumes, skillful grouping, and clever lighting, but he can never control it as surely as a painter or a novelist. This means that proper subordination must be accomplished psychologically rather than visually, and must be accomplished largely by the actor. It means that the actor is never insignificant while on the stage, and that his reaction must be right if it is not to be wrong.

To meet this challenge the actor must do two things: he must remain so

completely in character all the time, and so true in his reactions, that whenever audience attention strays to him accidentally he will seem an integral part of the picture and the story; and he must keep his acting under such restraint that it will never distract attention to him improperly or unnecessarily.

There is nothing technically abstruse about all this. Most of the problems can be solved with intelligence and imagination plus a little will power. The one thing that may cause the most difficulty—apart from real incompetence—is the fact that the actor can never quite see himself as others see him in relation to the stage picture of which he is a part. That is where the director comes in. But the director can do little to balance and perfect the reactions until the actors really begin to act; and that is another reason for acting at rehearsals. Too often what happens is that the director works desperately at rehearsals trying to coax enough background reaction out of unimaginative players to give the play unity and clarity, only to find that as soon as the audience is present some players begin to overact obtrusively, throwing the whole thing out of balance again. The actor should seek, therefore, to work up his reactions as early in rehearsal as possible, adjust them to the satisfaction of the director, and then stick to them without laxity on the one hand or excessive enthusiasm on the other.

There is one other point about the difference between foreground and background reaction that ought to be mentioned before we leave the subject. Since foreground reaction is intended to attract attention, it must be projected; which means that the actor must select such changes of expression or attitude as can be seen and understood by people sitting far back in the audience as well as by those near the stage. But since background reaction is *not* intended to attract attention, but only to be right for those who happen to see it accidentally, there is no need to select expressions and attitudes that will project. They must be right for those sitting near enough to see them, and they must not be false or misleading for those sitting far away; but they do not have to be clearly visible to everybody. The actor who remembers that is less likely to be tempted into excess.

It may come hard to a vain or self-centered actor to subordinate himself in this way, but unless he can learn to do so properly he is of no earthly use to the team. An actor who cannot subordinate when in the background is quite unworthy to be trusted with foreground parts. The essential philosophy of good reaction rests on the premise that we are acting plays—not parts.

BY-PLAY

The term "by-play" is frequently used to describe background action which is not strictly reaction—that is, action not directly provoked by what the foreground characters are saying or doing at the moment.

There are many ensemble scenes of mixed activity and animation in which the actions of background characters are seemingly unrelated and the only unity is to be found in an overall effect of variety or in the totality of mood created. There are also scenes in which most of the characters are reacting to foreground events, but a few are conducting minor activities of their own, apparently indifferent to the focal interest. It should not be thought, however, that good by-play is ever truly irrelevant. It may be seemingly irrelevant, in the sense that it has no direct connection at the moment with foreground words or action, but unless it fits in to the overall concept of significant truth which the dramatist is trying to create it is not good by-play. There must be a certain logic in the presence of the character at that time and place, in his attention or inattention to what is going on, and to his choice of occupation at the moment; and there must be a strong sense of appropriateness about the whole business. In other words, good by-play may be literally irrelevant, but must be artistically relevant.

Almost every play has some by-play either written into it or indirectly suggested by the dramatist, and many opportunities for good actors to enrich it by adding more. But there are some plays, or scenes in plays, that are largely dependent on by-play for their effectiveness. *You Can't Take It With You* is almost an orgy of by-play, dealing as it does with the activities of a large family the members of which simultaneously carry on a dozen varied and picturesque hobbies. *The Inspector-General* is full of highly pertinent by-play, some of it calling for improvised lines as well as action. The first act of *The Admirable Crichton*, with its animated tea scene, calls for an exceptional amount of by-play. The dinner scene in *Erstwhile Susan*, the Okie invasion in Saroyan's *Love's Old Sweet Song*, the third act of *Stage Door*, the third act of *The Cherry Orchard*, the second act of *The Farmer's Wife*, and the subway scene of *Two on an Island* are other good examples.

The chief hazard in by-play is fairly obvious. It has even more serious potentialities for distraction than ordinary background reaction, not only because it has no direct relation to the main thought and action of the moment, but because it puts the actor performing it so much on his own that he is tempted to overelaborate. Dramatists seldom give more than a fraction of the by-play they envision as part of the general effect, and di-

rectors are usually so busy taking care of foreground problems and essential background reaction that they have little time to work up rich by-play for all the subordinate characters. Many directors feel, also, that it is better for the actors to work up much of their own by-play; it keeps them interested, stimulates their creative imagination, and makes the ensemble work more spontaneous. But for that very reason the actor must be careful not to overdo it.

In one sense, by-play is merely a subtler form of background reaction, lacking its direct relevancy but having the same function as part of the total effect. For that reason it is best for the actor to think of it as bound by the same limitations. It is intended to complete the picture for those whose attention accidentally wanders from the foreground, and must be good enough to enrich their enjoyment when that happens; but it is not intended to distract attention from the foreground, and must not be permitted to do so. To be sure, there are some bits of by-play much more important than others, and many gradations between; and there are moments when an author actually wants audience attention to skip about from one bit of by-play to another in order to achieve a totality of impression—as in several of the ensemble scenes just mentioned. Good by-play is fun for the actor and gives him much valuable experience, even in minor parts; and he should aim to perform each bit with the greatest possible excellence short of obtrusiveness. But he should never forget that he is part of the team. An actor whose enthusiasm for his own bit of by-play tempts him into exaggeration and overemphasis is precisely like a football player whose assignment is to run interference, but who tries instead to grab the ball from his own team-mate and run with it himself. Most football players know better, but there are a good many actors who do not.

Careful timing is just as important in by-play as in any other phase of acting, and is especially helpful in steering the middle course between too little and too much. A piece of by-play which may seem perfectly appropriate and unobtrusive at a moment when the main action lags or pauses will seem glaringly distracting at a moment when the main character is speaking an important line. In the tea scene of *The Admirable Crichton*, for example, there are moments when the servant-guests are being greeted and seated, other guests are still to arrive, and nothing very significant to the plot is happening; yet, as Barrie says, "the scene is now an animated one." That suggests a great deal of by-play—pouring tea, carrying cups to the guests, passing cakes, shaking hands, chatting and laughing in little groups, and so on. The housekeeper and the French chef, for example, may have a little friendly argument growing out of the fact that the former

disapproves the servants'-tea idea, while the latter approves and is having a grand time. He tells her so in French, perhaps; she reminds him that Crichton disapproves, and he laughs loudly and tells her that Crichton is a snob. This is only one of several playlets going on simultaneously, and it does not matter whether any particular member of the audience hears it or not. But it matters a great deal that it shall be timed to be heard, if at all, only in the intervals between more important events, and that the chef's laugh shall not occur at a moment when it may kill an important entrance or distract attention from an important line.

A vital element in the timing of by-play is to bring the emphasis up and tone it down gradually. A piece of by-play breaking out suddenly is more distracting than one that has built up slowly; and one that has captured audience attention and then stops too suddenly creates a fresh distraction that is even more serious because the audience recognizes the heavy hand of intention.

In the tea scene just mentioned it is very important that the conversation between Crichton and Lady Mary shall be clearly heard, since it foreshadows the theme of the play; and to that end the by-play of the other characters must be toned down during it, both in sound and movement. But in one all-star revival a few years ago the actors painfully overdid the director's obvious instructions to tone it down. The instant Lady Mary addressed Crichton they all froze, and their voices ceased like a radio suddenly shut off. The result was to distract attention from the two principals more effectively than if it had not been toned down at all. A good director would have suggested a gradual toning down, beginning some lines ahead, and never carried to the point of unbelievable silence and immobility; and good actors would have done it that way unless a bad director insisted otherwise. They would also have built up again gradually after the most important lines had passed.

At another point in the same scene Barrie deliberately breaks into those key lines (doubtless to avoid the suspicion of pointing them up too intentionally) by letting Lord Brocklehurst create a diversion. He has been trying to entertain Tweeny, the giggling kitchen maid, and we suddenly hear him saying:

LORD BROCKLEHURST (*Desperately to* TWEENY). And now tell me, have you been to the opera? What sort of weather have you been having in the kitchen? (TWEENY *gurgles*) For Heaven's sake, woman, be articulate.

He seizes her cup, marches across to Lady Mary, who refills it, and marches back with it to Tweeny. Barrie gives him no follow-up line, and Lady Mary

and Crichton resume their conversation. A poor actor as Brocklehurst
would fail to lead up to this scene with appropriate by-play; he would
stand gazing meaninglessly at Tweeny until he heard his cue (or worse yet,
converse with her privately and out of character) and then break out suddenly with his absurd line. After bringing her the second cup of tea he
would hand it to her and promptly freeze. A good actor would anticipate
the scene by some quiet by-play, building it up so gradually that attention
would not shift to him prematurely, but in such a way that when his
scheduled lines did attract attention the observer would realize that he
had really seen the business developing out of the corner of his eye. After
the business he would follow through with diminishing by-play until
Crichton and Mary had recaptured the attention, and, more quietly, for a
few lines beyond that.

In all this, to be sure, the director has a major obligation; but the director
is helpless unless the actors come through. There is no more important
phase of the actor's art than the creative management of by-play within
ever-changing limits of proper subordination. And there is no phase which
is more generally in the hands of those actors whose youth and inexperience
limit them to subordinate parts.

One final warning about by-play, however: The modern vogue of the
Stanislavsky System has led to a serious overemphasis on improvisation
in acting. Improvisation has its proper place in the imaginative training
of the actor, and the more of it he does in the classroom the better. It has
its place, also, in the early rehearsals of a play, and especially in the working up of by-play. How else, indeed, could by-play be invented, if not prescribed in detail by the author or director? But a growing skill and facility
in improvisation is the greatest temptation in the world for the actor to
overdo his by-play in actual performance. Improvisation before an audience is fatal; once it becomes a master instead of a tool, it is the surest
possible device to make the actor forget the play, forget his teamwork, and
go wild in the exploitation of his own part. One of the worst headaches in a
director's life is the problem of holding down the actors who, in working
up their by-play, have discovered the joy of improvisation and been carried away by it. At the slightest suspicion that he is falling into that error,
the young actor should take himself firmly by the ear and teach himself
to do his improvising only in the early rehearsals, and to be constantly
on guard against the temptation to improvise at the expense of proper
subordination.

CHAPTER XIV

The Actor's Voice

THE importance of an adequate, flexible, and well-controlled voice as an instrument of acting is so evident as to need no emphasis. Equally evident is the fact that a single chapter in a book on acting is no place for a general treatise on voice training. Any comprehensive program of such training would require years of study and application, an extensive text (possibly several of them), and above all a competent teacher giving individual criticism and instruction. Any young actor whose voice is less than adequate should begin such a program early in his career.

The purpose of this chapter is merely to point out a few of the special objectives and limitations which may affect the problem of voice for the actor as distinguished from the singer, the crooner, the orator, the teacher, or the clergyman; and perhaps to suggest a few useful wrinkles in voice projection and hygiene especially applicable to theatre work.

ONE VOICE, OR MANY?

When a prospective orator or concert singer, or, to a lesser degree, a prospective opera singer sets about training his voice, the problem is relatively simple. His objective is one voice: his own; and he wants to make it as good a voice as he can. The singer wants above all else to make his voice musically beautiful—clear, resonant, and pleasing. He will not object to flexibility, and if he is training for opera he will need flexibility in order to convey a variety of emotions; but it will still be his own voice, in his own range. If he is a baritone he will sing only baritone parts, and while his public will value some evidence of personality it will not expect one baritone voice to be markedly different from other baritone voices.

But the actor, and especially the character actor, faces a different and far more complex problem. Desirable as it may be for him to have a resonant, pleasing voice in straight parts, that is not his chief concern. He will, of course, need a voice free of bad habits and distracting faults, one that does not grate on the ears or suggest inappropriate states of temper. But it need not be a supremely beautiful voice in the musical sense; it will, in fact, be more useful if not too beautiful, since an excessively beau-

tiful voice may hypnotize an audience into admiring the tones rather than listening to the play—a situation acceptable in grand opera and endurable in some of the more formal poetic plays, but extremely undesirable in the general run of good theatre. What the actor needs to develop is a voice that is highly adaptable to a variety of uses, and so managed as to withstand fatigue, and even abuse.

In other words he needs many voices, for he must portray many people. A voice that would be too harsh or cold for Manson in *The Servant in the House* might still be too smooth for Yank in *The Hairy Ape.* A woman's voice that would be ideal for the flippant, vivacious Maria in *Twelfth Night* might very well lack the depth and sympathy for Viola's "She never told her love," in the same play. One of the finest voices I ever heard in the theatre in respect to fullness and richness of tone was that of Robert B. Mantell. It added considerably to his robust playing of Macbeth; but as he could not (or did not) change it, it seriously distorted his playing of Hamlet, and made his attempt to play Romeo little short of ridiculous. One can hardly believe in that boyish lover if he booms his lines in barrel-chested tones suggesting the grand organ in a cathedral.

The most beautiful feminine voice I ever heard in the theatre was that of Sarah Bernhardt. She was able to vary it sufficiently to give some suggestion of characterization; but since she played only in French, and in the French tradition of conventionalized vocalization, she was not expected to vary it as much as a modern American actress would be expected to do. It was after all the voice of a personality actress rather than a versatile character actress. On the other hand the late Alice Brady, generally credited with one of the best voices in American theatre history, was exceedingly versatile. Her voice was magnificent, with deep, moving tones that contributed greatly to the tragic power of *Mourning Becomes Electra;* yet she could play youthful comedy parts with enough change of tone to suggest plenty of humor and vivacity. In other words, it is not impossible for a fine voice to be also a flexible voice; but of the two things the latter is the more important.

The ideal voice for the actor is one that can be varied, not only in the manner necessary to suggest different moods and emotions in the same person, but in the more difficult manner necessary to suggest different persons. Nearly any actor can contrast two moods of the same character, especially if that character is really himself; but it is not so easy to contrast two different characters in the same mood. The hardest task of all is to differentiate the voices of two characters not very sharply contrasted,

and therefore in danger of being played without any differentiation at all. In the type-casting world of the commercial theatre that does not matter much; but in a community or repertory theatre where the same audience sees the same player in many different parts it matters a good deal. In such theatres, deliberate miscasting often seems the only solution unless the actor can learn to change his voice enough to achieve reasonable versatility. For the young actor planning a stage career, the only wise procedure is to cultivate as many voices as possible without undue strain, and to get them under perfect control.

This whole problem raises again the issue of objective impersonation versus personality in acting. One need not go so far as to advocate the complete submergence of the actor's personality as artist in each new character, with a new voice for each, completely unrecognizable as coming from the same artist. After all, it is convincing suggestion that we want, not absolute deception. But with most actors there is little danger of the latter. Too often an actor's voice is so unmistakably and persistently his own that we never think of the character at all, but only of the actor in a succession of new plays. The actor whose own voice is not particularly distinctive has a decided advantage, since it is not so likely to be obtrusively recognizable when heard in different parts. It is the actor with a strikingly unique voice—good or bad—who is least likely to manage a reasonable degree of character differentiation. A distinctive voice may, of course, be a temporary box-office advantage, versatility being in rather less demand than personality. For the one-voice actor, however, a certain amount of type-casting seems inevitable, if he is to remain an actor at all; and the actor who is always bitterly complaining about being "typed" would do well to consider whether his own lack of variety in voice control is not partly responsible.

VOCAL HYGIENE

Before considering ways and means of developing such variety, let us give some attention to the care of the voice. If the young actor will learn his vocal hygiene first, he will later be able to go farther in the direction of variety and flexibility without danger of damaging his voice through strain and abuse.

One phase of the problem is largely in the hands of the doctors, and unfortunately they do not seem to have been able to do much about it. Medical science has so far had little success in its effort to conquer the common cold, and has failed completely to conquer the chronic head catarrh which

afflicts so many Americans, especially in the damp cities of our eastern coastal region—the region in which most professional actors and a great many non-professionals must use their voices.

The common cold, if it does not render the actor's voice temporarily unusable and compel him to cancel his appearances, at least alters the quality of his voice and destroys much of its flexibility. There is, so far, no perfect protection against colds, but there are some matters of common-sense hygiene which, in most individuals, do tend to reduce their frequency. While it is traditional to blame colds on exposure to drafts, dampness, and low temperatures, avoidance of such exposure is probably not the most important consideration—besides which it is impossible in drafty theatres. Far more important is avoidance of certain predisposing factors which weaken resistance to colds. Opinions differ as to what those factors are, and they probably vary with different people; the young actor who seems unduly prone to take cold should certainly consult his doctor. But as a general rule he is not likely to weaken his resistance to colds by avoiding long hours, lack of sleep, excessive fatigue (especially nervous fatigue), excessive use of alcohol and tobacco, and excessive indulgence in sweets (especially candy). He may, in most cases, considerably strengthen his resistance by keeping his system on the alkaline side, by taking plenty of fresh air and healthful exercise, and by getting his proper daily share of vitamins A and D. My own experience suggests that the last item is particularly important.

Avoidance of colds is only the first hurdle in vocal hygiene. Avoidance of strain is almost equally important. The two problems are to some degree interrelated, for they involve a sort of vicious circle; a throat that has been strained and irritated is usually more predisposed to infection, and a throat already infected with cold is much more subject to irritation or strain. Chronically strained voices seem especially subject to frequent colds, while carefully trained voices, kept in good condition and never strained, seem much less so, though not by any means immune.

Unfortunately, a great deal of the damage done to human voices by unhealthy strain is done in youth, often before the individual has any notion of becoming an actor. It is not often done in infancy or childhood (unless as the result of disease or injury), for children are relatively uninhibited, and so use their voices more naturally. They may yell and scream and make such a din that nervous adults feel certain they are ruining their voices, but so long as they do it freely and instinctively, without self-consciousness, little harm is done. At a later stage, however, after

inhibitions have been acquired, voices are often severely damaged by unnatural or unaccustomed strain.

Young voices, especially male voices, are particularly subject to injury at the time of adolescent change. Boys who run with older and tougher boys, or who sell newspapers in tough neighborhoods, often affect hoarse, precociously masculine tones as a kind of defensive mechanism, and often seriously damage their voices by it. Both boys and girls strain their voices by singing beyond their proper range, by singing or shouting when they have colds, and by playful imitations of screen or radio comedians who offer shrill, raucous, nasal voices and coarse diction as a substitute for real wit and humor. But worst of all, hundreds of thousands of girls and boys permanently ruin their voices shouting themselves hoarse at football and basketball games in misguided loyalty to school or college. School authorities who should know better too often encourage this vicious practice; or at the very least permit it to go on without warning the youngsters or their parents of its dangers. It is true that a healthy, carefully trained voice, intelligently used, may be able to repeat a well-designed school cheer—one that uses only resonant vowels, avoiding diphthongs and harsh consonants, especially *r*—several times in an afternoon without serious strain, just as a well-trained singing voice can produce loud operatic tones without undue fatigue. But there are few well-designed school cheers, and few trained voices among the rooters. The untrained voice, subjected to such abuse, frequently goes hoarse in the first ten minutes; yet the owner, goaded on by school spirit or false pride, forces himself to go on yelling for two hours or more in painful, croaking tones, irritating the membranes and straining the delicate muscles of the throat until they are sore and inflamed, thus inviting infection, and laying up future trouble for himself. Voices that have been treated in such fashion often later turn out to be dull, colorless, coarse, wooden, inelastic, unresponsive, hard to control, easily fatigued, and abnormally predisposed to colds and other diseases. No doubt it is folly to hope that school authorities will ever do anything to lessen this evil. But perhaps here and there a drama teacher may be able to slip a word of warning to boys and girls who would like to act.

Most of the causes of strain so far mentioned are really avoidable. The young actor (or prospective actor) who makes up his mind not to strain his voice unnecessarily need only observe a very simple rule: Whenever there is the slightest sense of irritation, tension, or fatigue in the vocal organs—stop! The presence of these symptoms is a sure sign that the voice is being improperly used. In healthy, natural voice production there is no

such strain. Luckily, nature has given most of us remarkably good vocal apparatus, which will withstand a great deal of fatigue, and even some abuse; but it is not foolproof. When mistreated, it rebels. Like any other set of muscles, however, the vocal muscles need exercise, and a voice that is regularly and properly used is much less sensitive to strain than one that is half atrophied from non-use.

Vocal exercise, therefore, should be frequent; and within safe limits it should be varied. In good voice production there is considerable muscular activity in the region of the diaphragm, and the heavy muscles involved can stand a good deal of it; but the throat should be relaxed, and free of any sense of tension. The best exercises are breathing exercises to liven up the diaphragm and increase the breath reserve, followed by simple exercises in the intonation of vowels, varying in pitch, but kept well within the individual's natural range. It is well known that many of the best stage voices are relatively low in average pitch; and the actor—or actress—whose normal voice is at all shrill will do well to work for lower tones. A few basic exercises are given at the end of this chapter, but they are intended chiefly to help keep normal voices in condition. A voice that is in any way defective, either congenitally or as the result of strain or disease, is a problem for the specialist, and the student actor is urgently advised not to try correcting it himself.

FINDING THE VOICE FOR THE PART

In adjusting his voice to a new problem the actor, as contrasted with the orator, teacher, or preacher, has one serious disadvantage and one great advantage.

The disadvantage grows out of the fact that in most cases he wishes to find a voice not quite his own, and in some cases a voice very different from his own. Almost any other speaker will start to prepare a speech with the expectation of using his own voice as naturally as possible, without conscious thought about it, and with his mind on the subject matter. The actor, as a rule, cannot start that way. Even if the new part does not call for a very odd or peculiar voice, and permits him to use his own timbre, it will still not follow his own natural style in words and sentence rhythms. That means a certain unavoidable strain on his voice in making the initial adjustments, and a very considerable strain if the part is much unlike himself and calls for a radical change of voice.

The advantage (which fortunately counteracts the disadvantage to some extent) is that the actor has several weeks of rehearsal in which to get used to his part and learn the proper management of his voice. He can

begin gently, experiment cautiously, to find the best type of voice for the character and the best ways of placing and controlling it. Having found the best voice he can learn it thoroughly along with his part, so that in performance he does not have to subject his voice to the continuing strain of uncertainty or unexpectedness. A singer knows that he is much more likely to irritate his voice when sight-reading than when singing something thoroughly familiar. In the same way an actor is more likely to have trouble with his voice when he is not perfectly sure what is coming next than when he has words, meanings, rhythms, tones, and timbre thoroughly coördinated and memorized. This is still another reason for acting at rehearsals, and also for using full voice.

Now and then an actor will try out a character voice early in rehearsals, find it a little uncomfortable yet suited to the character, and decide to use it; but for the sake of saving his voice in rehearsal he will fall back on his natural tones, thinking to shift to the character voice only when necessary for actual performance. This is a serious mistake. Apart from the fact that the element of self-consciousness inherent in the last-minute change will lessen the spontaneity of his playing, he is taking a very foolish chance of straining his voice when he does change; he may even go hoarse in the middle of the first performance, or bring on a coughing spell, temporarily paralyzing his vocal cords and forcing him to create a stage wait. If an assumed voice is too irritating to the actor's throat to be used in rehearsals, it is too irritating to be used at all, and he should experiment at the earliest possible moment to find something better. Having once found it, he should use it consistently in the remaining rehearsals, get it under control, and make it second nature by the time the audience is in.

Fortunately, many of the strains which seem so alarming the first time an actor tries out a fresh vocal experiment turn out to be temporary. They may be due only to the unfamiliarity and uncertainty of the experiment rather than to any real difficulty in the voice itself; and after a few readjustments they may iron themselves out gradually—provided the actor proceeds cautiously, does not force his voice, and quickly discontinues any vocal pattern that is persistently uncomfortable.

In seeking the best voice for a new characterization, the actor should remember that there are many possibilities, and that if one combination does not do, another can be found that will. The voice has many variables —pitch, force, tempo, timbre (or tone quality), rhythm, and enunciation— and each can be varied in a number of different ways. Pitch, for example, can not only be raised or lowered, much or little, but its inflection pattern can be varied within the word, within the phrase, and within the clause

or sentence. As a rule it is safer and easier for the actor to change several elements slightly, thus arriving at a new combination, than it is to change just one variable, and overdo it.

An actor having to play an aged character, and noting that aged voices are often high-pitched, is apt to pitch his own too high for comfort and for secure control, at the same time maintaining his normal breathing rhythms and inflection patterns, with the result that the listener notices the inconsistency. He would do better to raise the pitch just enough to carry the suggestion, and at the same time to alter his breathing rhythms to suggest the shortness of breath and quavery uncertainty of the aged voice; also to slow the tempo, reduce the range of pitch variation, and perhaps simulate the peculiar enunciation that goes with false teeth. A planned synthesis of this kind may seem somewhat artificial, and is not to be recommended if the desired effect can be achieved more naturally; but after all any change of voice is artificial, and if it does not come right without conscious planning it is better to plan it well. The point is that if the planning is done early in rehearsals, in coördination with lines and action, in a manner that does not involve too much strain, some of it will stick and become almost automatic by the time the actor knows his part well enough to throw himself into it with full freedom and imagination.

In selecting a character voice, the actor is often tempted to rely too much on changes of pitch or timbre, and to neglect the less obvious possibilities in variation of tempo, force, and rhythm. He is also apt to think of a change in pitch as merely a shift to a lower or higher average pitch; whereas many of the most effective character changes are in the pitch pattern, or sentence tune. Two voices of the same average pitch may seem very different in character if one combines rising inflections with accelerating tempo within each sentence, while the other combines falling inflections with retarding tempo. Changes of timbre also are more effective when combined with other elements. A rough or harsh voice combined with a lowered pitch suggests coarseness or stupidity; combined with a high pitch it suggests nervous exasperation and lack of poise. Incidentally, a change from a normally smooth voice to a rougher or harsher tone is always the riskiest change, because it carries the maximum chance of irritation. A change to nasality is usually much less of a strain. Nasality also can lead to very different effects depending upon its coördination with other elements. Combined with low pitch it seems to suggest the adenoidal type of stupidity; combined with a high pitch it may suggest a complaining spirit or a weak will. Combined with harshness it may suggest a coarse, ribald kind of pseudo-smartness. In the latter combination it is irritating

to the vocal organs, but the irritation comes more from the harshness than from the nasality. Combined with a touch of singsong rhythm, nasality suggests mournfulness; in tragedy, it accentuates the tragic moan, but with a suggestion of weakness.

The permutations and combinations are almost infinite. If the actor will use common sense and resourcefulness early in rehearsals, there is no reason why he cannot find a suitable voice, slightly different from his own, for any character he is really fitted to play; and to do so without having to rely on excessive distortion of one element, with consequent strain. But as surely as he waits until the last rehearsal and then tries to change his voice, he will have trouble.

EMOTIONAL OVERTONES

The function of emotion in acting has been sufficiently discussed in other connections; but the function of the actor's voice in suggesting emotional content and generating emotional response in the audience should here be emphasized.

Two voices may be heard at different times uttering the same words, both of them clearly and intelligently, yet one of them may stir the listener to vibrant emotion and the other may leave him respectfully cold. What makes the difference? When we say that one voice has emotional overtones, we mean rather more than the sound engineer means when he says that a fundamental tone has certain harmonic or disharmonic overtones. He is referring primarily to timbre, in terms of composite pitch. No doubt the pattern of physical overtones does play a large part in determining emotional response, but in a more figurative sense the emotional overtones include the whole subtle pattern of pitch, force, tempo, and rhythm, as well as timbre. The elements affecting emotional response are so many, and the variations so intricate, that it is doubtful whether much can be done to control them by conscious synthesis. It may be perfectly possible to symbolize a character's identity, age, and general temperament by a simplified conscious selection of vocal traits, but to convey a sincere impression of emotion the coördination must be less mechanical and more imaginative.

There are actors here and there who manage to overdo the vocal suggestion of emotion—like those who practice the tragic moan—and who need toning down rather than toning up. But the majority of inexperienced players, and some experienced ones, need a good deal of toning up. Their voices, for one reason or another, seem to lack the flexibility and responsiveness to stir emotional empathies in the audience.

One of the reasons was mentioned in the discussion of vocal hygiene—namely, the colorless, wooden quality of voice resulting from habitual strain. A strained voice tightens up and loses its elasticity; and elasticity is particularly important in suggesting emotion. Another reason is the common form of inhibition growing out of shyness, timidity, false modesty —a temperamental unwillingness to "wear the heart on the sleeve." This is quite understandable in beginners, and not altogether a bad sign, for it betokens a sensitive nature which, properly developed, may eventually make a good actor; but nobody can go very far as an actor until he can conquer the inhibition, at least on the stage. Another reason is just plain inexperience in using the voice emotionally; it afflicts those who make a habit of repressing or concealing their emotions in everyday life, and cultivating calm, judicial voices. Such persons, especially if they come late to the stage, find it very hard to shake off the habit. But the most troublesome reason of all, because it is a continuing or recurring one, is the distraction which is so common during rehearsals, when the actor's vocal habits are being formed. Nobody can put much sincere emotional quality into his voice when the director and the prompter are constantly interrupting, stage carpenters are hammering, electricians fiddling with the lights, and so on. Having repeated his lines so many times under these conditions, he finds it hard not to memorize them in half-hearted unemotional tones. Some of these may wear off in performance, and emotional overtones may develop under the influence of audience response; but not, as a rule, until several performances have been wasted. The situation is especially serious for the amateur, who may rehearse a play fifteen to twenty times, but perform it only three or four times—perhaps only once. After several years of such experience in the same ratio, he will have used his voice so many times under conditions unfavorable to emotional overtones, and so few times under favorable conditions, that it would not be strange if he actually got worse instead of better. Dare I suggest that this is still another reason for acting at rehearsals, as imaginatively and sincerely and whole-heartedly as possible?

Unfortunately, there is not much that the individual actor can do to correct the distractions and confusion of rehearsal. But there is something he can do to counteract the effect on his own voice, and to increase its flexibility and emotional responsiveness. He can set aside a few minutes a day for vocal exercises, including exercises specifically designed to enrich his emotional overtones. In addition to such basic breathing and vocalization exercises as are listed at the end of this chapter, he can employ a simple and very effective technique to widen the range of variation in his voice

and at the same time to heighten the kinesthetic associations between vocal tone and emotional content. That technique is nothing more than abundant reading aloud of varied emotional material, with intentional exaggeration of emotional response, but with no audience present. Lyric poetry offers the widest range of different emotions, most directly expressed, and in the most concentrated doses; but the choice need not be confined to that. Some prose, some passages of scripture, some excerpts from drama, and what not, may be mixed in. Selections should be chosen to represent as many shades of emotion as possible: joy, fear, grief, anger, excitement, compassion, horror, amusement, bitterness, sarcasm, discouragement, love, hatred, despair, enthusiasm, and so on. Several unlike emotions should be included in each day's exercises, but not too many; enough to teach flexibility in the change of mood, but not enough to confuse and blur the sensibilities. On every selection the greatest possible care should be taken to find the correct mood, and to express it accurately and sincerely.

Remembering that he is alone, with nobody to laugh at him, and that what he is doing is just an exercise and not a pattern for public performance, the actor should throw himself into the reading with as complete an abandonment to whole-hearted emotion as possible. He should give his imagination full play, and lay the emotion on thick, carrying it to the point of considerable exaggeration, far beyond anything he would dream of using before an audience. If his normal voice is exceptionally repressed, he may well carry the exaggeration at first to the point of burlesque; since a highly repressed person who fears to let true emotion creep into his voice will often have much less fear of burlesque emotion. Once he has begun to loosen up, however, he should lay aside any element of ridicule, for after all his ultimate objective is to develop sincere emotional overtones, not mock ones. They may still be exaggerated beyond anything he would wish to use in public, but they should be imaginatively true to the character and the situation.

Daily sessions of this kind will usually bring considerable improvement in emotional overtones in a few weeks. They cannot, of course, overcome deep-seated dullness or woodenness of tone due to strain, fatigue, or disease —though they may mitigate it slightly. But they can do wonders to overcome the ordinary faults resulting from inhibition or inexperience.

VOICE PROJECTION

The problem of projection in the theatre has already been discussed from several angles, in relation to the actor's subjective rapport with the audience, to good elocution in the reading of the lines, and to the nature of the

comedy sense. In the matter of voice projection all of these things are relevant, for there is a psychological element in voice projection as well as a physical one. But the physical problem of voice projection needs attention too.

Almost any reasonably healthy young person can make himself, or herself, heard in a large theatre, if only by shouting. There are exceptions, of course, even to that. Now and then one finds a young man—or more often a young woman—with a longing to act, but with a voice so faint and breathy that it cannot be comfortably heard halfway back in the smallest theatre. Such cases are not necessarily incurable, but a young person in that state should put aside all notion of acting until a competent vocal teacher has had a chance to do something about his voice, and he has made enough progress to show that a cure is possible. Most young people, however, *can* make themselves heard; the question is, *do* they? And can they do it without shouting? Shouting is not acting, and the student should set early about the task of learning to project his voice without seeming to shout.

The first problem is adequate breath support—that is, an adequate flow of breath, so applied to vocalization as to support the tones firmly. People who have led sedentary lives for many years with little occasion to use their voices publicly, are seldom able to support their tones adequately the first time they try to act. This is rarely due to insufficient lung capacity. More often it is due to acquired habits of laziness in the muscles involved in breathing, which leads to shallow rather than deep breathing, and chronically inadequate breath reserve. People who do most of their talking in easy chairs get into the habit of using undertones requiring very little breath support, and of starting their sentences on half-empty lungs rather than full ones. When such a person is suddenly called upon to speak in public, he will start with the lungs half empty, and his voice will lack firmness and body. If warned to take a deep breath he can usually do so only with self-conscious effort; and then, instead of using the breath to support the tone, he will let it go again just before starting to speak, and start on half-empty lungs after all. Sometimes, under prodding from an instructor, he will make five or six unsuccessful attempts before he finally succeeds in getting a sentence started on a full breath.

A person who has got into that wretched habit can get out of it only by persistent effort, applied through carefully controlled daily exercises. He can never get out of it just by trying to remember to breathe deeply when actually playing—or rehearsing—a part; that will only distract his attention from the meaning and ruin his acting, without helping the voice. In

this or any other problem of habit correction it is absolutely essential that the corrective measures be organized as special exercises to be done in regular and frequent, but special, periods, and never allowed to distract the mind from its creative activities.

A second problem, closely related to that of breath support, is that of breathiness in vocalization. It is the combination of breathy tone with inadequate breath support which accounts for many of the worst cases of inaudibility. But even a speaker who has adequate reserve breath and starts each phrase on a full breath may still produce weak, blurred tones if he wastes his breath. A breathy voice is simply one in which the breath is applied faster than is necessary to produce a clear tone, with the result that the tone is blurred by the rush of wasting breath, and the lungs are emptied sooner and more frequently than is necessary or desirable. That is why breathlessness, or shortness of breath, is so often associated with breathiness of tone. You cannot waste your breath and still have plenty in reserve for longer sentences; and you cannot dilute a vocal tone with a hiss of surplus breath without losing the clarity and firmness of tone needed for efficient voice projection.

The correction of breathiness is neither complicated nor mysterious; but it does take time and persistent application. It is all a matter of learning the kinesthetic difference between a breathy tone and a clear one, and then practicing clear ones until they become habitual. A clear tone, although much louder and easier to project than a breathy one, uses amazingly little air. What comes out of the mouth is sound vibration, not flow of air. There is a very simple test for breathiness of tone: a lighted match or candle held close in front of the open mouth. If the tone is breathy it will cause the flame to dance around, or even to go out. But a clear tone may be poured through the flame with enough volume to fill the Metropolitan Opera House and the flame will burn serenely on without a flicker. A little practice with this test will soon teach the student actor the difference between clear and breathy tones in terms of their sound, their carrying power, and the way they feel to him in production. He will be astonished to note how long one good breath will last on a clear tone. It is said that Caruso once sang 266 separate notes on one breath; he could not have done so if he had wasted any of it on breathy tones.

In social conversation, breathy tones often convey a sense of quiet modesty or refinement, and that may be one reason why many people, especially women, and especially people who are a little shy, get into the habit of breathy speech. On the stage, a suggestion of breathy tone may sometimes be desirable to convey an implication of modesty or shyness in a

character; but it should never be carried to the point of ruining the projection. An actor who has cleared his voice of all habitual breathiness can always recall some degree of breathy quality when he needs it for some special purpose in characterization; but an actor who is a slave to the habit of breathiness is helpless when clear tones are needed.

Next to breathiness, perhaps the most frequent cause of poor projection is failure to direct the voice to the place where it should go. Many actors have the distressing habit—deplored in an earlier chapter—of looking down too much; and their voices are frequently lost in the footlight trough or the orchestra pit. Others do too much of their speaking across the stage, in profile to the audience; or they speak up stage whenever addressing characters farther up stage than themselves. This is especially bad when the stage is set with wings and borders, for the open spaces in such a setting permit the sound to go off into the wings or up into the flies instead of out into the auditorium. Even with a box setting, there may be sound pockets on either side and above, made by the slight projection of the tormentors and the teaser; sometimes those elements have gaps behind them to provide room for lighting units, but permitting some escape of sound into the wings and flies. An actor talking straight across the stage usually has little conception of how much projection he is losing by it. The trouble is that his voice sounds just as loud to him as if he were speaking straight front—or even louder; and if he is speaking up stage it sounds a great deal louder, because it bounces back at him from the walls and ceiling of the set. In modern naturalistic acting it is not practical to have all lines spoken straight front; but the actor must realize that whenever there is good reason to direct a line across stage or up stage it must be at least 20 percent louder (and perhaps as much as 60 percent or 80 percent louder) to be heard as clearly out front as a line directed that way—and this in spite of his own illusion to the contrary.

Whenever possible—which is a large part of the time—the actor should project his voice towards the audience, not always necessarily at the same angle, but generally at such an angle as to make the sound travel freely to all parts of the house. A good rule is to keep it up a little higher than would seem necessary, since the maximum absorption of sound usually takes place in the sea of heads on the main seating floor; and to keep it at such an angle as to miss the sides of the proscenium frame. The best angle, both horizontal and vertical, must be found by experiment, and differs greatly in different theatres. So, of course, do the acoustic difficulties. A ceiling with cross beams, for instance, will catch some of the sound and bounce it back

at the actor so that he thinks he is speaking louder than he is, while people sitting at the back of the auditorium have difficulty hearing him. A vaulted or domed ceiling, if smooth and not too high, helps distribute the sound efficiently; but a hard surface, especially a flat one, creates reverberations, and a broken up ceiling absorbs much sound. The worst acoustics known to me in a hall intended for play production and ordinary public address are those of Irvine Auditorium, at the University of Pennsylvania. The ceiling is high and vaulted, with many segments sharply divided by deep ridges so that each segment becomes a separate pocket to trap the sound; if the architect had set out to design a hall on the principle of the Maxim silencer he could hardly have done better. Commercial theatres, especially the smaller ones common in New York, are usually better designed and easier on the actor trying to project his voice; but there are many school and college auditoriums, clubhouses, and halls, occasionally used as theatres, which are models of bad acoustics.

In the worst of these places no actor can project his voice successfully without raising the actual volume, if not to the point of shouting, at least to the point at which a perfect illusion of naturalness becomes extremely difficult. It is therefore wise for the student actor to keep building up his vocal reserve power much beyond his immediate needs, and also to learn all the little tricks in the actor's trade which help him in voice projection.

One of these is to keep his pitch flexible so that he can modify it when necessary to fit the characteristics of a particular theatre—not enough, of course, to falsify a character or a mood, but enough to ease an otherwise difficult effect here and there. There is no recipe for this; it is just a matter of careful experiment in rehearsal. But it sometimes happens that a key word which reverberates and gets lost on a certain pitch, or which is unduly absorbed, will come clear a half-tone higher or lower.

Another is to adjust his tempo slightly in order to avoid the reverberation period of the theatre. This is the problem that train ushers have to wrestle with in its most exasperating form when they announce trains in the huge reverberating vaults that we build for railroad stations; in such extreme cases the speaker must wait for all the reverberations of a word to die away before uttering the next word at all. Happily, actors are not asked to play—and should never attempt to play—in such impossible places; but even in regular theatres there are slight differences in reverberation period which skillful actors will take into account, though sometimes quite unconsciously.

Another is to manage his movements and business in such a way as

to project the largest possible number of his lines—especially his most important lines—directly to the audience, yet with the least possible suggestion that he is doing it on purpose.

The most useful device for accomplishing this is the pull of opposite forces, right and left, with a resultant force between them, an example of which (from *You Can't Take It With You*) was given in the chapter on Comedy. In that example a character moving right was stopped by a question from the left; instead of answering without turning, or turning completely to the left to answer, he stopped in his stride, turned only halfway to the left while his posture still suggested that he was going right, and answered the question with his face front and his voice projected straight to the audience. The same principle is involved whenever an actor contrives to have one force (such as a piece of business or an intended movement) pulling him in one direction, while another force (such as a cue from another player, or the need to indicate the character addressed) is pulling him in the other, the resultant force being halfway between. The device not only enables him to project his voice directly to the audience, but does so without the slightest suggestion that he is doing it intentionally; properly managed, it seems like the most natural sort of accident. Thus a character looking out a window at right or left, and turning halfway back to speak to somebody in the room behind him, projects his voice straight front; so does one warming his hands at a fireplace at right or left, or sitting at a desk against the side wall, or primping at a mirror, or dusting a mantelpiece, or looking for a book on a shelf, or pouring a drink at a sideboard, or looking at a picture on the side wall. The device is one of the most useful bits of everyday technique in acting, and it is a poor director who does not teach it to the beginner in his first part.

In real life we do not always stare directly at everybody we speak to or who speaks to us; but the inexperienced actor seems obsessed with the notion that he must do so on the stage. If he is sitting on a sofa facing the audience, and a character up stage to his left speaks to him, he seems to feel that he must rotate his head like a weather vane to the left, at considerable risk of spraining his neck, until his nose points directly at the other character; or if his neck is too sore from previous attempts he may squirm around on the sofa and sit sidewise for the same purpose. This is entirely unnecessary for convincing naturalism, and it is highly detrimental to good voice projection. All that is needed is for him to tilt his head slightly back and to the left, and deflect his eyes a little more so, and the audience gets a perfectly clear illusion that he is talking to the character concerned; while at the same time his voice is projected well out into

the auditorium—a little to his left, but high, and at an efficient angle for good distribution. The same technique, with minor variations, will serve when he is sitting at one side of a table talking to a character on the other side; or even when he and another character are standing and talking at stage center. He should remind himself frequently that in nine stage situations out of ten direction may be indicated just as clearly by tilting the head as by turning it, and with far less sacrifice of good voice projection.

ENUNCIATION

Clear enunciation may well be thought of as a problem in stage diction, but it is so vitally related to good voice projection that it seems best to discuss it here.

A good deal has already been said about some phases of the problem in connection with the reading of lines. Good elocution, in one meaning of that term, is identical with good enunciation. Clear enunciation, as distinct from good pronunciation, is a relatively simple matter. That does not mean that it is easy; nor does it mean that it is unimportant. But enunciation is not so much a matter of technical knowledge, or of controversial standards, as of good sense and persistent application. Clear enunciation is merely clarity of utterance. It is the articulate phase of voice in action. Like any other good thing it may be overdone, in the sense that one's enunciation may be too self-conscious or too precise to be convincingly natural and free from distraction. Short of that, however, it is largely a matter of practice and skill in making one's utterance heard and understood.

Nevertheless, there are a few basic principles, and a few special wrinkles, in connection with stage enunciation that might well be given some attention.

The first and most important is that good enunciation for the theatre is good enunciation of the spoken language *as it is*, and not as some literal-minded bookworm thinks it ought to be; and it is good enunciation of what the particular character would say in the given situation. It has nothing to do with printing, and it is no part of the actor's job to teach the audience how the words are spelled or to prove his own knowledge of spelling. Too often an actor attempts to achieve good enunciation by taking words and phrases apart visually and exaggerating the enunciation of unaccented syllables and connective particles (such as the article "a" and the preposition "to"), throwing them out of their proper relation to the accented syllables and calling audience attention to the least important parts of the

language rather than the parts that carry the main thought; or he gives equal and artificial value to all the syllables, accented or unaccented, in long words like "extraordinary" or "unparliamentary"; or he ties his tongue into knots trying to pronounce difficult sounds indicated in the spelling but long since elided in ordinary speech, like the *th* in "asthma" or "clothes,"[1] the *st* in "postscript," the *h* in "Philharmonic," the *t* in "waistcoat" or "postpone," and so on. Some of these were mentioned in connection with the reading of the lines, and more will be discussed in the next chapter. The point here is that a theatre audience is not interested in spelling; it is interested in getting the thought, in terms of the character and situation. Any clarification of speech which helps to project meaning without falsifying character or distracting attention is desirable. Any clarification which exaggerates normally subordinate sounds or syllables is not.

Considered as a problem in voice, good enunciation is largely a matter of uttering the accented syllables with enough clarity and with sharp enough differentiation of the vowels to carry well, and pronouncing all the consonants *normally pronounced in speech* with as much clarity as is consistent with the characterization—plus a slight margin to compensate for distance and acoustic difficulties. In many cases, a slight lengthening of the accented syllables is desirable in order to differentiate the vowels more clearly or to overcome reverberation periods; and also to permit enough flow of tone to convey mood and feeling.

This is not to say that unaccented syllables are to be left out of consideration altogether. Except when necessary to portray character, unaccented syllables should not be allowed to become quite as blurred as they are likely to be in ordinary conversation, nor should they be elided altogether except in positions where they would regularly be elided in cultivated speech. Many actors lose their unaccented syllables, especially at the ends of words, by dropping the volume on them; this may be due to depletion of breath, or to a mental lapse in failing to follow through. The cure is not to lengthen unaccented syllables or overparticularize them, but to practice better breath support, remembering that it is not necessary to starve a syllable of breath in order to keep it short and subordinate.

There is one trick known to experienced actors which is very helpful in keeping the unaccented syllables clear, and that is a general habit of using [ɛ] and especially [ɪ] for the short vowels in preference to the more relaxed

---

[1] See the entry on "clothes" in Kenyon and Knott's *Pronouncing Dictionary of American English*.

vowels, [ʌ], [ə], and [ɜ].² The habit should not be carried to excess, but actors who have some measure of it are likely to be found among the winners of Academy awards for good diction, and among those rated by the public as easy to understand. The reason is that the high front vowels carry more easily than the indeterminate vowels, and that even when very short they help to clarify adjacent consonants. For example, ˈkrɛdɪt usually carries better than ˈkrɛdət; ˈflɑrɪd better than ˈflɑrəd; ˈætɪtjud better than ˈætətud; fɪlɪˈdɛlfjə better than fələˈdʌlfjə; ˈbæskɪt better than ˈbæskət; ˈkwɑntɪti better than ˈkwɑnədi; dɛˈbri: better than dəˈbri:, and so on. Any actor attempting to modify his unaccented vowels in this way should be extremely careful not to lengthen or overemphasize them; and of course he should be careful not to indulge in any form of clarification out of character.

One other trick of the trade may be useful, and that is simply a little extra care in following through on final consonants, including *s, t, m*, and especially *n*. A good strong *n* helps carry tone, and is another characteristic usually noted in those who win awards for good diction.

A useful general rule in relation to enunciation—to be interpreted, of course, with judgment, and with some exceptions—is that in accented syllables it is the vowels which are most often critical in their effect on clearness, while in the unaccented syllables it is the consonants.

The most important rule of all, however, is one that applies to the whole problem of voice, and to many other things, and that the reader must be weary of by now: Work it all out early in rehearsals, but do not think about it when the audience is in.

EXERCISES

It is important that all exercises for improvement of vocal habits should be done *as exercises* in separate periods set apart for the purpose. They should be done daily, with great regularity, but the daily periods should be short, that they may not become burdensome. Vocal exercises should be done in fresh air, and the best time for them is when a study period is being interrupted for the purpose of airing the room. They should be done slowly at first, with great moderation, and never carried to the point of strain or discomfort. Many good exercises, when done for the first time by a person unaccustomed to them, may cause a slight giddiness or shortness of breath. That is a sign to stop and rest; but with practice the effect will wear off. The student should take his time and not force matters, and he should not wait until he is working on a part before starting to correct a faulty voice.

² See again the chart in Chapter XV.

1. *To wake up a lazy diaphragm.* With the mouth closed, inhale a comfortably full breath; then exhale and inhale small amounts of air in rapid succession, very much as a dog pants, but through the nose, not the mouth. After six or eight cycles release the breath, rest, then repeat. When it gets easier, increase the number of cycles, but do not be in a hurry to do so. Remind yourself that the muscles that are doing this work are the ones that should bear the strain when you are speaking in a large theatre. Keep the throat relaxed.

2. *To encourage deep breathing.* With the mouth closed, inhale slowly in a succession of very short "sips" (but through the nose), packing each sip into the lungs on top of the previous ones, and closing the glottal valve after it to hold it in. Continue until the lungs are comfortably full; hold it a second or two, and then release the air. Rest a few seconds, and repeat. Keep the throat relaxed.

3. *To cultivate central control.* Repeat the "sipping and packing" exercise, but on exhaling open the valve gently instead of suddenly, exhaling very slowly, and controlling the flow by means of the body muscles and not by constricting the throat. Repeat several times. Then try the sipping without the packing; that is, hold each increment of breath with the body muscles without closing the valve, but without letting any air go until the lungs are comfortably full. Then exhale gradually as before. Keep the throat relaxed.

4. *To build up breath reserve.* With the mouth closed, inhale evenly and deeply, but fairly quickly; then exhale slowly, but only to the point of letting what you think is half of the air go; then quickly replenish to full capacity, and repeat three or four times. Then release the reserve, rest a while, and repeat. After several weeks on this exercise, try letting only one-third of the air go before refilling the lungs. Keep the throat relaxed.

5. *To support the voice.* After all the above exercises have become familiar and easy, modify Exercise 4 by vocalizing on the one-third exhalation. At first, use a simple sound of [a] or [ɔ], without inflection. After that grows easier, begin varying the pitch within the middle range of your voice. Then try a connected phrase or short sentence (five to eight words). Change the material frequently. Remember always to start the vocalization on the full breath, and to replenish before repeating. Do not be afraid to work the diaphragm hard, but keep the throat relaxed.

6. *To decrease breathiness.* First practice the test with a lighted match, as described in the text of the chapter. Then practice vocalizing breathy and clear tones alternately, on the same vowel sound. After several days of this change the vowel. After several days with each common vowel try them over again with a slight change of pitch. After some weeks, begin using words, phrases, and finally sentences, always alternating breathy tones with clear tones, but gradually increasing the frequency of repetition on the clear tones, and decreasing it on the breathy ones. Keep the throat relaxed.

7. *To lower habitual pitch.* Choose an easy sentence with a fair number of sonorous vowels in it and some implication of a sympathetic mood. Say it over

several times in a normal pitch for your own voice, with enough volume to project in an average theatre. Then try intoning or chanting it at about the same average pitch. Repeat several times, trying to fix the pitch in mind; finding it on a piano may help. Then deliberately lower the pitch one full tone, and repeat the intoned sentence several times at the lower pitch. Then try to speak it on the lower pitch. Try a different sentence each day. Do not attempt to lower pitch more than one tone for at least a couple of months after starting this exercise, and do not expect quick results. Keep the throat relaxed.

8. *To improve resonance.* With the lips moist and very lightly closed, choose an easy middle pitch and hum it on the sound of *m* (*not n*), keeping the tone as far forward in the head as possible so that the bones of the face vibrate and the lips tingle slightly. Practice this until it is well mastered. Then change the pitch occasionally. Then try it with three-note or five-note exercises in easy intervals. After several weeks of this, try opening the lips occasionally, after beginning the tone, so that the hum turns into an open tone, but without otherwise changing the placing of the resonance. Keep the throat relaxed. (Some of the world's best singers have claimed that this exercise, with some elaboration, is the only one needed to develop a good vocal tone.)

CHAPTER XV

Stage Diction

THE problem of stage diction is one of the most complicated and technical that the actor has to face. Strictly speaking, "diction" means the choice of words, and the actor, of course has little to do with that. But he has a great deal to do with the choice of word forms and sounds, and the term "stage diction" is here used in the popular sense to cover his choice of inflections, rhythms, tempos, intonations, and especially pronunciations—in short, of those elements that give character to his words as distinct from audibility. We have no concern here with the controversial question of what standards of pronunciation the American people ought to recognize in the schools or use on the street; but we have a proper concern with what standards the actor should learn as part of his art.

Clearly there are two problems involved, not just one. The first is what standard to use for straight parts or in straight plays—that is, plays that call for no special peculiarity of diction as portraying period, nationality, or special locale. The second is how to choose the right pronunciations and intonations for plays that do have such peculiarities—period plays, English plays being acted in America, plays set in foreign, or regional, or provincial backgrounds, or calling for local dialects.

Each of these problems has many phases. A classic play may call for a somewhat different standard from that acceptable in a more popular type of straight play. A play on a universal or cosmopolitan theme may call for more (or less) localism, according to its nature. A play in verse may call for a more formal style of diction than a prose play. The varieties of local or dialect plays are legion. And of course there are special problems for individual actors, since a straight play may include one or two dialect characters, and a regional play may include some who do not speak the local dialect.

It is normally the director, not the actor, who must make the decision in such matters. It is he who must say whether an English play is to be done with British or American pronunciations and intonations, and to what

degree. In classic plays, translated plays, and period plays, it is he who must decide whether to attempt such diction as would be expected on the New York or London stage, or to conform to the local dialect in the town where his theatre is located—or to steer a middle course. In other words, it is the director (with perhaps an executive council to advise him) who must shape the policy.

But it will do no good for a director to shape a policy unless the actors can carry it out. It is the actor's job to know enough about stage diction, and to have enough facility in controlling his own, to give the director whatever standard or level he calls for. Almost any actor can speak the dialect of his home town. The question is, can he speak a more cosmopolitan kind of English, suitable for plays not local in their setting? Can he speak English suitable for a characteristically British play—a Shaw play, a Barrie play, a Milne, or Maugham, or Lonsdale play, for example? Can he speak a sufficiently cultivated kind of English for a poetic play? And can he do a Yiddish, or Irish, or Italian, or French, or Pennsylvania Dutch, or Yankee, or Hoosier, or Cracker, or Cajun, or Brooklyn dialect when called upon? The ability to do regional or foreign dialect may be rather a special talent, not necessarily expected of every actor; but every actor—unless he is content to be permanently typed in his own home dialect—must be able to achieve a standard of diction suitable for non-local plays, and even for classic and poetic plays, if not as they are done in New York, at least as they are done in the best theatres of his own part of the country.

A real mastery of good stage diction can be achieved only by years of serious study, and an adequate text on the subject might well fill several large volumes. All I can hope to do in this chapter is to offer the student a few basic suggestions as to how to go about it, and point out a few of the most common difficulties.

The first and most treacherous difficulty arises from the fact that most of us sadly confuse the written and spoken languages; we keep altering pronunciations to fit spelling, or misspelling to fit pronunciations—though we know well enough that English spelling is not consistently phonetic, and complain a good deal about it. The actor, of course, studies his part from a written or printed text, and then has to translate it into pronunciation. A good director may give him some help on pronunciation, but in many cases he has difficulty because he has begun with visual images, and because his ear is poorly trained. He is almost sure to be influenced by the spellings, and the spellings are not phonetic.

PHONETIC REPRESENTATION OF SPEECH SOUNDS

A serious student of speech—for acting or for any other purpose—cannot too strongly be urged to begin his study by mastering at least the rudiments of the International Phonetic Alphabet, a system of symbols that do correspond to vocal sounds, and by means of which any pronunciation of any word can be recorded accurately on paper. Though the "I.P.A." (as it is commonly called) looks very strange to a person seeing it for the first time, it is not really difficult. Anybody with a high school education and enough intelligence to make any kind of an actor could certainly gain a working knowledge of it in a couple of weeks. The advantage of learning the I.P.A. lies not only in the fact that it enables the actor to take notes on pronunciation in symbols that stand for sounds, and always for the same sounds, but also in the fact that it teaches him to *think* in terms of speech sounds rather than in terms of the fantastic spellings that belong to the printed language. It is both a useful tool and a stimulus to the cultivation of a good ear for speech; and to an actor the latter is invaluable.

A working knowledge of the I.P.A. does not, of course, mean an exhaustive knowledge of all the variant and intermediate symbols, gradation marks, special signs, and so on, used by phonetic scholars in what they call "narrow" transcriptions, intended to record with scientific precision all the minor variations in speech of interest to linguistic specialists. That would involve years of study, much of it with laboratory instruments, and would require a knowledge of other languages. A working knowledge for the actor means a sufficient knowledge of the basic symbols (for English and American sounds only) to enable him to look up a word in a modern pronouncing dictionary without feeling like a fool; or to set down his own idea of how a word is, or ought to be, pronounced, in terms of symbols that are sufficiently accurate for what the phonetician calls a "broad" transcription—that is, an approximate one.

A serious student should certainly own at least one text on phonetics, based on American practice, such as the one by Kantner and West. If he hopes to attain any proficiency in British speech he might well invest also in the standard text by Daniel Jones. He should by all means own a copy of Fowler's *Modern English Usage* (one of the most useful books on any reference shelf); also at least one good pronouncing dictionary, and preferably two—one for American standards and one for British. Kenyon and Knott's *Pronouncing Dictionary of American English* is a good one for the former, and Daniel Jones's *An English Pronouncing Dictionary* is best for

the London standard. Both of these use the I.P.A., though with very slight differences which will be pointed out later in this chapter.

The charts furnished herewith will give the student at least some idea of the phonetic system, and a key by which to understand the symbols in most common use (some of which have already appeared in this book, and more of which will be used later). The charts are largely self-explanatory, but the student should be cautioned about one or two possible sources of confusion.

First of all, he should resolutely put out of his mind all relation between speech sounds and English spelling—especially all attempts to interpret English spelling phonetically. In the I.P.A. a single sound (vowel or consonant) has a single symbol, which always stands for the same sound; but if the student will look over the chart he will see clearly that almost every such sound used in English has several different popular spellings—also that we often spell a single vowel with two or more letters, and a diphthong with one, which is confusing to say the least. Historically almost every spelling has a reason, but phonetically many of them are preposterously misleading. Popular confusion on the subject begins in the schools with the outrageously untruthful statement that "the vowels of English are *a, e, i, o,* and *u*, and sometimes *w* and *y*." Those are letters, not vowels. As the first five are pronounced by the teacher making the statement, only one (the *e*) is a single vowel, and phonetically that is not [e], but [i]; the others are diphthongs (glides involving at least two distinguishable vowels). Phonetically, the five are [ei], [i], [ɑi], [ou], and [ju]. For the true vowels of English, of which there are many more than five, the student should consult the Key Chart. He should remember also that the ones given on the chart are only the principal ones, and that intermediate ones are possible, though less common. As for *w* and *y*: when pronounced separately they are whole words, 'dʌbəlju and wɑi. As sounds, *w*, or [w], is a shortened [u] used as a consonant; and *y* is sometimes the vowel [i], sometimes the diphthong [ɑi], and sometimes the consonant [j]. It is all perfectly simple and consistent if one thinks of sounds, not letters.

Unfortunately international phoneticians do not always agree on every detail (though they agree infinitely better than international politicians). When the student uses the Daniel Jones dictionary, for example, he will find several variations from the general practice of phoneticians elsewhere. Two or three of them may be confusing at first. Jones uses the symbol [i] for the vowel in words like "sin," "bit," and "kick," instead of the more accurate [ɪ] (which he himself uses in "narrow" transcriptions); and to

INTERNATIONAL PHONETIC ALPHABET
KEY CHART OF PRINCIPAL SYMBOLS FOR SOUNDS IN ENGLISH

VOWELS

[i] f*ee*t, *ea*t, sk*i*, P*e*te, s*ie*ge, b*e*

[ɪ] f*i*t, p*i*n, d*i*d, s*ie*ve, k*i*ck

[e] v*a*cation, prostr*a*te (short; unstable; tends to glide into [ei])

[ɛ] p*e*t, b*e*d, t*e*n, l*ea*ther, m*a*ny, t*e*ll

[æ] p*a*t, b*a*d, t*a*n, l*a*ther, n*a*nny, b*a*ck

[a] (between [æ] and [ɑ]; common in New Eng. on words like c*a*r, b*a*rn)

[ɑ] *a*h, f*a*ther, *a*rm, *o*tter, b*a*lm, t*o*t

[ɒ] (between [ɑ] and [ɔ]; common in Eng. on words like g*o*t, s*o*rry, n*o*t)

[ɔ] t*a*ll, g*a*wky, P*au*l, b*o*rn, *a*wful

[o] *o*bey, n*o*tation (short; unstable; tends to glide into [ou])

[ʊ] p*u*ll, w*oo*d, c*ou*ld, w*o*man, l*oo*k

[u] p*oo*l, w*oo*ed, d*o*, thr*ou*gh, L*u*l*u*

[ʌ] b*u*t, s*u*n, c*o*me, r*ou*gh, *u*p, m*u*d

[ə] sof*a*, ov*e*r, *a*bove, *u*pon (weak)

[ɜ] c*u*r, b*i*rd, m*y*rtle, c*o*lonel, k*e*rnel (does not include the *r*; heard best in Eng., with *r* omitted)

[ɝ] c*u*r, b*i*rd, m*y*rtle (includes slight *r*, as in cultivated U. S. For strong *r* write [ər] or [ɜr]

DIPHTHONGAL GLIDES

[iɜ], [iə], [ɪɜ], or [ɪə] id*ea*, *ea*r, p*ie*r, op*iu*m (heard best in Eng. on *ea*r, etc.)

[ju] or [iu] *u*nion, c*u*te, be*au*ty, f*ew*, *you* (the [j] is shorter than the [i])

[ei], [ɛi] or [ɛɪ] *a*pe, s*a*me, b*ai*t, w*ei*gh, s*a*ne (often wrongly written [e])

[ai], [ɑi] or [ɑɪ] *I*, p*i*ne, t*y*pe, *ai*sle, sl*eigh*t, n*igh*t, t*i*me

[ou] or [ʌu] *o*ver, h*o*me, *ow*n, be*au*, n*o*tice (more diphthongal in Eng. than U. S.)

[eɜ], [eə] or [ɛə] *ai*r, c*a*re, p*ea*r, m*a*yor (more diphthongal when *r* is elided)

[ɑu], [au] or [æu] *ou*t, kr*au*t, c*ow*, b*ou*gh, t*ow*n (triphthongal in some dialects)

[oi], [ɔi] or [ɔɪ] j*oy*, *oi*l, v*oi*d, n*oi*se, c*oi*n (confused with [ɝ] in Brooklyn)

[oə] or [ɔə] b*oa*, N*oa*h, *oa*r (esp. Eng.; common in N. Y. on m*o*re, f*ou*r, etc.)

CONSONANTS

[p] *p*ay, o*p*en, u*p*; (labial, voiceless)

[b] *b*ay, a*b*ove, jo*b*; (labial, voiced)

[m] *m*ay, a*m*ong, a*m*; (labial, nasal)

[t] *t*en, i*t*em, i*t*; (alveolar, voiceless)

[d] *d*en, i*d*ea, o*dd*; (alveolar, voiced)

[n] *n*ay, i*nn*er, o*n*; (alveolar, nasal)

[k] *c*all, a*c*t, *k*i*ck*; (velar, voiceless)

[g] *g*all, a*g*ate, ba*g*; (velar, voiced)

[ŋ] si*ng*er, lo*ng*, i*nk*; (velar, nasal)

[f] *f*un, go*ph*er, tou*gh*; (labio-dental, voiceless)

[v] *v*im, o*v*er, lo*v*e; (labio-dental, voiced)

[ʃ] *sh*oe, o*c*ean, wi*sh*; (pal. sib., voiceless)

[ʒ] vi*s*ion, a*z*ure, mira*g*e; (pal. sib. voiced)

[j] *y*ou, *y*es; (short [i] as consonant)

[w] *w*ar, *w*itch; (short [u] as consonant)

[h] *h*ow, *wh*o; (aspirate, normally voiceless)

[l] *l*ie, he*l*lo, be*ll*; (lingua-alveolar, voiced)

[r] *r*ay, a*rr*ow, ba*r* (as in most of U. S.)

[θ] *th*in, e*th*er, ba*th;* (lingua-dental, voiceless)

[ð] *th*is, ei*th*er, ba*the*; (lingua-dental, voiced)

[s] *s*in, fu*ss*y, bu*s;* (sibilant, voiceless)

[z] *z*oo, fu*zz*y, bu*zz;* (sibilant, voiced)

[ř] (Scotch trill) co*rr*n, ba*rr*n.

[ɾ] (one-tap trill) ve*r*y, so*rr*y, American; (as in Eng.)

[tʃ] *ch*ur*ch*, i*tch*y, *c*ello; (voiceless)

[dʒ] *j*ewel, e*dg*e, *J*ello; (voiced)

[hw] *wh*en, *wh*at, *wh*ich; (Old Eng. *hw*, now heard chiefly in eastern U. S.)

CHART OF VOWEL POSITIONS

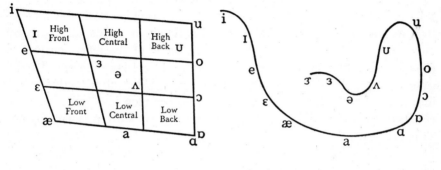

A   B

These figures show diagrammatically the positions toward which the tongue tends to concentrate on each of the common vowels. The speaker is assumed to be facing left. Thus [i] is the extreme high front vowel, [u] the high back, [æ] the low front, and [ɑ] the low back. *A* is the usual diagram, but gives a slightly false impression, since the tongue does not move in straight lines and turn corners. *B* is suggested as an alternative concept; if the student will pronounce the vowels in *B* in a continuous flow of breath, beginning with [i], his kinesthetic sensations will seem more in keeping with *B* than *A*. Both diagrams ignore lip, jaw, and lateral tongue movements. Note that the relaxed vowels ([ɜ], [ə], and [ʌ]) fall into the central position, which is what the tongue does when relaxed.

distinguish the sound in "seem" or "free" he uses the same symbol plus the phonetic lengthener [ː] (practically a colon) and makes it [iː]. Thus for "keen" he writes kiːn, and for "kin" he writes kin; whereas almost any other phonetician in the world would write kin for "keen" (or kiːn if he wished to emphasize its length); and he would write kɪn for "kin." Jones also uses [e] for the sound in such words as "get," "ten," or "weather"; and he uses the symbol [ɛ] (which Kenyon and Knott use for the sound just mentioned) almost exclusively for the first element in the diphthong [ɛə] as heard in such words as "air," "bare," or "mayor" (especially as the Londoner says them, omitting the *r*). These are the chief

oddities in the Jones method; but he is perfectly consistent about them, and once the reader has caught on they do not lessen the usefulness of his dictionary. It should be understood, of course, that Jones gives only the London, or southeastern English standard, and that he is no guide to the pronunciations of Scotland, Lancashire, or Devonshire, much less of the United States. Nevertheless, that is the standard of the English stage, and of English actors, many of whom are heard regularly on our stage and screen.

The chief oddity in the Kenyon and Knott dictionary—shared, I regret to say, by some other American phoneticians—is the blanket use of the symbol [e] to cover everything from the short vowel in the first syllable of "vacation" to the unmistakable [ei] diphthong in words like "away," "shame," or "sleigh." This is done in the name of simplification, but is grossly misleading to the young actor trying to cultivate an ear. The [e] sound is naturally short and unstable; if prolonged at all it tends to glide into [ei] or [eɪ]. These sounds are extremely common in English, and are normally found in long syllables, which is why they are popularly called "English long *a*" (at least when they are spelled with that letter); but they are normally diphthongs. Few, if any, Americans say ə'we for "away" (though Britishers may occasionally do so); they say ə'wei or ə'weɪ or ə'wɛɪ. But Kenyon and Knott, like Jones, are generally consistent in their sins, and if the actor using their book will just remember that their [e] should, in accented syllables, usually be read as [ei] or [eɪ], he can go on training his ear.

Just as in using Jones the reader must allow for the London bias, in using Kenyon and Knott he must allow for a midwestern bias. Most American phoneticians today reside in the middle west, and in dividing all American speech into three parts, "Eastern," "Southern," and "General American," they assume that midwestern speech is General American and the other two minority dialects. By Eastern they mean the speech of New England to the Hudson River Valley. By Southern, they mean the speech of "Dixie." But whenever a pronunciation current in the north central states differs from that current in most of New York State, Pennsylvania, New Jersey, Delaware, or Maryland, or the mountain states, the southwest, California, or the Pacific northwest, it is the corn-belt pronunciation that they label "General American," and the other is labeled "Eastern," "Southern," or left out altogether. Perhaps an unbiased pronouncing dictionary is an impossibility, as a complete one certainly is. But at this writing the two mentioned are the best available in I.P.A., and the most useful to a student actor trying to develop an ear.

In addition to the lengthener [ː] already mentioned, the student should know one or two other supplementary marks commonly used in phonetic transcription. Most important is the accent mark [ˈ], which always *precedes* the accented syllable (contrary to practice in most popular dictionaries). A secondary accent is indicated by a similar mark inverted [ˌ], also preceding the syllable. A small dot or very short vertical line beneath a consonant indicates that it is vocalized as a syllable even though no separate vowel is heard; thus "pickle" may be written as ˈpɪkl̩ rather than ˈpɪkəl if the [ə] is too short to be heard; and "open" may be ˈopn̩ rather than ˈoupən if very short. A nasal quality is indicated by the symbol [˜] over the vowel affected; thus mæ̃n is nasal, but mæn is not. No capital letters are used in phonetic script, and no punctuation marks appear in the dictionaries, though a simplified system of punctuation is used in transcribing whole sentences and paragraphs. It need not concern us here.

Before the student is left to his own resources in the further study of I.P.A., a word or two should be said about the vowels, and especially the glides. In this connection, he should make himself familiar with the accompanying Chart of Vowel Positions.

The distinctness and quality of a speaker's vowels profoundly influence the impression he makes on others—on or off the stage. In Britain it is widely said that nobody can expect to rise economically above four pounds a week unless his vowels are reasonably pure. There is a hint in this for the actor who wishes to be convincing in portraying cultivated characters. A study of the vowel positions in conjunction with the Key Chart of symbols will eventually help one to distinguish between pure vowels and distorted or diphthongized ones.

It is the glides and diphthongs that make most of the trouble. A diphthong starts with one vowel and ends with another; but unless there is a perceptible hiatus between, it glides from one position to another through intermediate positions, even if very rapidly. For that reason it is easier to understand them by thinking of them as glides rather than as pairs of separate sounds. Some, like [ɑi], glide forward and up, along the main line of pure vowel positions. Some, like [au], glide back and up. Some, like [iə] and [oə], glide from a strong front or back position to a relaxed or central position. Several people making what they think of as the same sound will differ slightly as to where they begin a glide and where they end it. Thus the sound popularly called "English long *i*" as in "time," may vary in different regions or individuals as [ɑi], [ai], [æi], [ɑɪ], [aɪ], or even [æɪ], and still be recognizable as meant for the same sound. Besides differing in their points of beginning and ending, diphthongs also differ in their

duration, and in the duration of their elements. Thus the effect of [ɑu] is quite different when the [ɑ] is long and the [u] short from what it is when the [ɑ] is short and the [u] long.

It is well to keep in mind that dialectal differences are most often to be found in the length and position of diphthongs, and in the tendency of certain vowels to glide into diphthongs, or for certain diphthongs to shorten into single vowels. There are differences in the consonants too, but they are generally simpler and less elusive.

SOME REGIONAL TRAITS AS POTENTIAL DISTRACTIONS

For many young actors the most urgent and practical problem in stage diction is not how to learn immediately a perfect standard for the New York or London stage, nor how to learn special dialects, but how to tone down their own most conspicuous regional and other peculiarities enough to "get by" with audiences (and directors) outside their own regions. Thousands of regional traits, noticeable to phoneticians, seem perfectly acceptable in other regions and generally pass unnoticed by the casual listener; others seem loaded with special qualities of potential distraction. A few contribute to the difficulties of clear projection.

Phoneticians often amuse themselves by asking a victim to read aloud (perhaps before a recording microphone) a sentence which includes the three words "Mary," "marry," and "merry." An astounding number of careless speakers from many regions pronounce them all alike with a sound somewhat closer to ′mæri than ′mɛri. The traditional pronunciations, of course, are approximately ′meəri, ′mæri, and ′mɛri (in England, ′mɛəri, ′mæri, and ′mɛri). If people wish to break down these distinctive words into a single confusing one, they have a perfect right to do so. The only point here is that there is an obvious advantage to the actor in being able to differentiate them as a matter of clear projection to the audience— which he can easily do without distraction, since the traditional pronunciations are familiar everywhere, even to the people who do not bother to use them. That may not be true in another fifty years if the midwestern dialect really does become "General American," for in that dialect there is a tendency for most vowels to move towards the [æ]. Thus the front vowels move back, and ′ligəl becomes ′lɪgəl, sɪt becomes sɛt, and ′peərənt becomes ′pærənt; while the back vowels move forward and tɔːk becomes tɑːk, ′wɔːtər becomes ′watər, and so on. If this tendency is carried to its logical conclusion there will someday be no vowel left but [æ].

Though regional variations are countless, those which may seriously embarrass the actor by making themselves distracting to his audience are

fortunately not very numerous. He is more likely to draw attention to his speech by two or three characteristic regional tags repeated a number of times in one evening than by ten times the number of minor variations used once but not repeated. A few years ago he need hardly have worried at all unless heading for the New York stage; but since the advent of talking pictures and network radio, people in the most remote towns and villages have become familiar with the diction of the foremost American and English actors, and while they are not yet ready to approve such diction among the home folks in town meeting, they have come to associate acting with a kind of diction much more cosmopolitan than their own. In the larger cities and their suburbs audiences readily spot any marked provincialism in an actor, unless it happens to be the local one— and sometimes even then.

To mention the dialectal traits of any region that are most likely to be noticed in another region is, of course, to risk criticism and controversy, if not assassination. Nevertheless, it may be useful to the student of acting to know what some people, at least, do notice in that respect; and with this thought in mind I shall take the risk.

An actor who hails from New England is most likely to call attention to himself in any other region by his tendency to substitute [a], or even [æ], for [ɑ] (especially before *r*, though he hardly pronounces the *r*), in words like "car," "hard," or "barn"; by using [a] or even [ɑ] where most Americans use [æ], in words like "past," "half," or "laugh"; by inventing (probably through false linkage) an imaginary *r* in "idea"; and by the way in which he drops his *r* in other words—not by the *fact* that he drops it, for the Londoner, the New Yorker, and the southern American do that also, but by the degree to which he drops it and the effect on adjacent vowels. The Londoner drops it more completely, saying mɔɪ for "more," but the New Englander is likely to say mɔɪə, with just a suspicion that the very short [ə] really implies an *r*. The New Yorker might say moə or 'mowə, and the Southerner might say moɪ or moɪə. In positions where the *r* is followed by another consonant, or preceded by an *a*, the New Englander is likely not only to drop it but to modify the preceding vowel in a characteristic way. Thus he might say hæɪd, bæɪn, wʌɪk, and fʌɪst;[1] whereas the Londoner would say haɪd, baɪn, wɜɪk, and fɜɪst, and most Americans would say hɑrd, bɑrn, wɜrk (or wɝk), and fɜrst (or fɝst). In some parts of New England a hard palatal voice is also a common trait, with just a suggestion of nasality. It fits in easily with the prevailing [æ]

---

[1] The position of the vowel in these words as heard in New England is really neither [ʌ] nor [ɜ], but something in between, almost like a lengthened [ə].

before *r*, but is not so universal. Many a New Englander would be spotted *only* by his [æ] or [a] before *r*.

An actor from New York City might have almost any speech characteristics, cosmopolitan or provincial, since that city is one of the most polyglot spots on earth. New York phoneticians can recognize dialectal differences between Brooklyn and Manhattan, or Manhattan and the Bronx, not to mention the many foreign accents, and the great differences in social levels. But an actor raised in New York, with no special foreign accent, and with average schooling, might be noticed elsewhere for two or three rather typical traits. He might drop his *r* with the peculiar diphthongization of the preceding vowel which gives fɔə or fɔwə for "four," bɔəd or bɔwəd for "board," nɔəθ or nɔwəθ for "north," keiə for "care," hiiə or hijə for "here," and so on. If Brooklynish, he might confuse [ɔi] and [ɜr] to the extent of saying gɜil and wɜid (if not gɔil and wɔid) for "girl" and "word"; and conversely he might say ɜil (if not ɜrl) for "oil." If he had mixed a good deal with immigrants he might be caught occasionally substituting a [t] or [d] for a [θ] or [ð], and saying what he tɪŋks of dɛm bʌmz. He might even be caught inserting a [g] after [ŋ] to say 'sɪŋgər instead of 'sɪŋər, or 'hæŋgɪŋ instead of 'hæŋɪŋ; or substituting [s] for [z] to say bɪ'kɔs for bɪ'kɔz. New York schools teach more diction than most schools, with more cosmopolitan standards, and one result is that the young New Yorker sometimes attracts attention less by poor diction than by surprisingly high-class diction not yet quite convincingly assimilated.

The Philadelphian acting in any other region is most likely to make himself noticeable by a combination of nasality with excessive, drawling diphthongization. He is not content to say mæən for "man," bæənd for "band," or tæaun for "town" (as the Londoner might do); he says mæ̃ən, bæ̃ənd, and tæ̃aun. He lengthens many vowels, with or without a glide, and frequently with a relaxing of the adjacent consonant; thus 'wɔitər becomes 'wɔiədṛ, 'sætərdi becomes 'sæ̃ədərdi (or even 'sæ̃ərdi), 'æftər becomes 'æ̃əfdər, and 'ɔrdmɛri becomes 'oərdə,neəri (with the [d] often degenerating into a glottal plosive heard through the nose). He is likely to be lazy about his medial *t*, saying 'mɛnəl for 'mɛntəl, and 'mər,ɛstɪŋ for 'ɪntrəstɪŋ; and he is likely to lengthen unaccented syllables even more than most Americans, and to use more secondary accents in polysyllabic words. He has a few odd local pronunciations like 'wʌnəmeikər for "Wanamaker" and 'skukḷ for "Schuylkill." He may say strɛnθ for "strength," though he is not alone in this. He is almost sure to pronounce his *r* at full length, but without the hard palatal tone and exaggerated jaw action of the west.

Two very characteristic Philadelphia habits are a short ɑm (not ɑɪm) for "I'm," and a non-diphthongal ɑr for "our."

An actor with a Pennsylvania-Dutch background will probably have shaken off such extremes as 'wɛri for 'vɛri or 'vʊmən for 'wʊmən before attempting to act in another region; but he may still have a trace of the [f] for [v] in words like 'ofər for 'ovər or 'ɛfər for 'ɛvər. He is most likely to be spotted when he says sɪtʃə'eiʃən instead of sɪtʃju'eiʃən or sɪtʃə'weiʃən, and grædʒə'eiʃən instead of grædʒju'eiʃən or grædʒə'weiʃən.

An actor from Baltimore may show slight traces of southern speech, and may possibly use the London biːn for "been" instead of the more usual American bɪn. His most characteristic badge of origin is the way he says 'bɔəldɪˌmoə. Baltimore and Washington are borderline regions between north and south, and actors from either are likely to have traits not particularly local, though the Washingtonian can usually be spotted by the way he says 'wɔrʃn̩dn̩.

An actor from Virginia or the Carolinas is most likely to call attention to himself in a northern or western theatre by a certain softness of speech that persists even when the vowels are normalized. The so-called southern drawl has been overadvertised; there is some drawl in the deep south, but rather less in Virginia than there is in Philadelphia. What is heard from Norfolk to Nashville is rather a soft slurring of certain sounds. From Washington south, the *r* begins to disappear again, especially in final position, with substitution of a diphthongal quality somewhat like that of New York, but without the suggestion of an inserted [w]; thus the Virginian may say fɔə or foə, but hardly fowə. He may lengthen the [ɛə] diphthong into something like [æijə], and say 'ouvə 'ðæijə for "over there." He is likely to place some diphthongs a little farther back than most Americans, somewhat as the British do, using [ai] or [ɑɪ] rather than [ai]; thus he may say tɑɪr or 'tajə rather than tair for "tire," and 'ɑɪrɪs (or even 'ɑɜrɪs) rather than 'airɪs for "iris." In some cases he may substitute a lengthened single vowel for a diphthong, such as [ɑː] for [ai]; and "tired" may become tɑːrd, "I'm" may become ɑɪm (longer than the Philadelphia ɑm), and his eggs may be bɔːld rather than "boiled." Both "high" and "how" are likely to become hæː. But the hardest thing for a southerner to shake off (and one hates to have him do so because it is so pleasing to most ears) is the tendency to run words together which accounts for part of the softness. When he says his cheerful 'hæːɪəːju even a "damyankee" feels friendly, though he himself would probably say hɑu'ɑrju or hɑu'ɑːju. But if the actor says 'hæːɪəːju on the stage in anything but a southern part he is pretty sure to call attention to himself.

An actor from the deep south might be a little slower in speech, and would have minor differences of interest to the phonetician; but in general his giveaway traits would be much the same. In parts of Louisiana one hears, curiously enough, the same confusion of [ɜr] and [ɔi] common in Brooklyn, but it is not so noticeable in New Orleans. The French and Spanish influences in that city, and the "Cajun" dialect of the bayous are rather too special to concern us here.

Chicago, like New York, is highly varied in its speech patterns, and an actor from that city would not be easy to identify. Apart from the German and Scandinavian accents, the speech one hears on the streets in Chicago sounds to an eastern ear much less like the extreme midwestern dialect than like the urban speech of Cleveland, Detroit, or Pittsburgh, or even Philadelphia or San Francisco. But midwestern speech away from the cities has certain characteristics that are extremely noticeable to people of other regions. Several of the most typical seem connected with a lively, but tense, circular action of the lower jaw; it affects the character of the *r*, and of many vowels. The substitution of a short [ɑ] for the more traditional English [ɔː] in words like ˈdatər, ˈɑθər, or ˈwatər, comes much more readily to speakers whose jaws move tensely and produce the hard, rounded, palatal *r*. So does the substitution of a hard [æ] for the traditional [ei] or [eə] in words like ˈpærənt, ˌværiˈeiʃən, and ˈkærfəl. The Easterner who says ˈdɔɪtɜ, ˈɔɪɵɜ, ˈwɔɪtɜ, ˈpeərənt, veəriˈeiʃən, and ˈkeərfəl, and the Englishman who says ˈdɔɪtɜ, ˈɔɪɵɜ, ˈwɔɪtɜ, ˈpɛərənt, vɛəriˈeiʃn̩ and ˈkɛəfl̩ do so much less with the jaw and much more with the lips and tongue. What this all amounts to is that the midwestern actor may call attention to his speech in another region as much by his visible jaw movement as by his speech sounds. There are, however, a few pet midwestern pronunciations that have special potency to distract audiences in other regions. People who have got used to ˈpærənt for "parent" and ˈmæri for "Mary" are still brought up with a jolt when they hear ˌværiˈeiʃən; or when they hear mɛlk instead of mɪlk, ˈɑfl̩ instead of ˈɔɪfəl (for "awful," not "offal"), and especially when they hear bɛn for "been," instead of the more traditional American bɪn. The Londoner, of course, says biːn, but bɪn is usual in western and northern England as well as in the United States, and has three hundred years of respectability behind it; bɛn is largely a recent corn-belt version, though isolated examples can be found in other regions and periods.

Actors from the south central and southwestern states are likely to have southern and midwestern pronunciations mixed, in proportions corresponding to distance south and west, with a certain rugged breeziness of

tone increasing with the distance west; but there are few special traits to spot them as from particular states in the minds of listeners not expert phoneticians. A Texan might be noticed for turning [æ] into [ai] or [ɑɪ], especially on the common word "pass," which becomes pɑɪs.

West of the Rockies speech habits are dictated largely by where a person or his parents came from, much of the population having been there only a generation or two. One hears eastern, midwestern, and southern pronunciations in the same regions, but little that is distinctly far-western. There is comparatively little New England speech on the west coast, but plenty of New York speech, especially in Los Angeles and Hollywood; and a Philadelphian feels somewhat less like a foreigner in San Francisco than in most parts of Indiana, Illinois, Iowa, or Wisconsin. Fusion is taking place in the far west, and the result seems likely to be something more deserving of the term "General American" than the more extreme dialect of the middle west.

In these very brief and sketchy notes I have not by any means attempted to cover all the regional traits one hears in a mixed company of untrained actors, nor perhaps all the important ones. Certainly, no two people would agree on any selection of the ones most likely to draw critical attention from a mixed audience. But I hope the notes will suggest to the student actor—at least through comparison and analogy—the sort of problem he has on his hands if he wants to shake off the most obtrusive features of his own dialect in order to act straight parts somewhere else.

The Snare of Eye-Pronunciation

Regional pronunciations are not the only pitfalls for the actor to avoid in developing his stage diction. Slovenly enunciation is another, remedies for which were discussed in the last chapter. But even more distracting than slovenly enunciation is over-precise enunciation, to which some attention was given in Chapter X; one of its worst forms is eye-pronunciation.

Eye-pronunciation is usually well intentioned. The perpetrator is trying to be clear and correct; he just does not know speech standards as well as he knows spelling. Often he has the spelling before him, but has no acquaintance with the spoken word, and falsely assumes that the spelling is a reliable guide. I once knew a youth who said 'ɔɪri instead of ə'rai for years because it looked that way in the spelling and nobody ever told him he was wrong. In sight reading one often uses eye pronunciations of unfamiliar words because he has no time to look them up; but there is no such excuse for the actor. He has from six days to six weeks in which to

look them up, and pronouncing dictionaries exist for the purpose—based on speech standards, not spelling.

Eye pronunciations used to be largely individual, and to spread slowly, if at all; but since the advent of radio they have been spreading rapidly, and influencing popular speech a good deal. Radio announcers—most of whom are young and rather superficially educated—have to read most of what they say from script, and do not always have time, or realize the need, to look up pronunciations. A network announcer may guess at a pronunciation on the basis of the spelling, and next day a million uneducated people are using it. There have been some curious examples. For centuries the word "parliament" (Middle English "parlement," from the French) was pronounced 'pɑːləmənt or 'pɑrləmənt by all Britons and all educated Americans; the *i* in the spelling was silent, and only a very ignorant American would use the eye-pronunciation 'pɑrliəmənt. But in 1940 I was astounded to hear a B.B.C. announcer say 'pɑːljəmənt; in 1947 five out of nine B.B.C. announcers (supposed to be the best educated in the world) were saying it, and millions of other people in Britain and America were imitating them. A more familiar example is the word "often," which for generations was pronounced 'ɔfən by cultivated people on both sides of the Atlantic (including Major General Stanley in *The Pirates of Penzance*, who puns on the identity of "often" and "orphan"), and only a few simple-minded souls who had just discovered the spelling attempted to pronounce the *t*. But now the radio announcers, aided by half-educated school teachers, have induced millions to do so. There is no more logical reason to reintroduce the *t* in "often" than in "soften," "listen," "hasten," "fasten," or "glisten."

Almost every eye pronunciation is an interesting phenomenon, but there is no room here to discuss others at length. It may be useful to the student, however, to see a brief list of some typical ones often heard from poorly trained actors and radio announcers and readily spotted by listeners who know better. Such a list follows, classified to suggest other examples by analogy:

A. Unaccented particles, prepositions, pronouns, and auxiliaries, normally weak, but often mispronounced with strong vowels under the influence of spelling. Most of them are correct enough in the strong form when there is any reason to accent them.

Spelling	Eye-Pron.	Normal Pron.	Spelling	Eye-Pron.	Normal Pron.
a	ei	ə	nor	nɔr	nər, nr
the	ði	ðə	than	ðæn	ðən, ðn

Spelling	Eye-Pron.	Normal Pron.	Spelling	Eye-Pron.	Normal Pron.
to	tu	tə, t	that	ðæt	ðət, ðt
at	æt	ət	not	nɑt	nət, nt
for	fɔr	fər, fr	my	mɑi	mɪ, m
from	frʌm	frm	you	juː	jə
of	ʌv, ɑv	əv, v	your	jur	jər, jr
till	tɪl	tl	am	æm	əm, m
and	ænd	nd, n	is	ɪz	z
as	æz	əz, z	are	ɑr	ər, r
an	æn	ən	have	hæv	hv, v
but	bʌt	bət, bt	has	hæz	hz, z
or	ɔr	ər, r	had	hæd	hd, d

B. Words in which normal sound changes have long since taken place (chiefly through influence of diphthongs on consonants) but are not reflected in the spelling, leading eye-pronouncers to think they must correct history.

Spelling	Eye-Pronunciation	Normal Pronunciation
issue	ˈɪsju	ˈɪʃu or ˈɪʃju
fissure	ˈfɪsjur	ˈfɪʃur or ˈfɪʃər
passion	ˈpæsjən	ˈpæʃən
ocean	ˈousjən	ˈouʃən
picture	ˈpɪktjur	ˈpɪktʃər or ˈpɪktʃur
future	ˈfjutjur	ˈfjutʃər or ˈfjutʃur
nature	ˈneitjur	ˈneitʃər or ˈneitʃur
fortune	ˈfɔrtjun	ˈfɔrtʃən or ˈfɔrtʃun
literature	ˈlɪtərəˌtjur	ˈlɪtrətʃər or ˈlɪtərətʃur
actual	ˈæktjuəl	ˈæktʃuəl

C. Words in which tongue-twisting combinations of consonants, long since elided in normal cultivated speech, are heroically put back by the eye-pronouncers.

Spelling	Eye-Pronunciation	Normal Pronunciation
clothes	klouðz	klouz
clothesline	ˈklouðzlain	ˈklouzlain
clothestree	ˈklouðztriː	ˈklouztriː
asthma	ˈæzðmə	ˈæzmə
asthmatic	æzðˈmætɪk	æzˈmætɪk
postscript	ˈpostskrɪpt	ˈpouskrɪpt

Spelling	Eye-Pronunciation	Normal Pronunciation
postpone	ˌpost'poun[2]	po'spoun
waistcoat	'weistˌkout[3]	'wɛskət
Wednesday	'wɛdn̩zde	'wɛnzdi or 'wɛnzdɪ
calmly	'kɑlmli	'kɑːmli or 'kɑːmlɪ
solemnly	'saləmnli	'saləmli or 'saləmlɪ

D. Nautical and other vocational words with traditional pronunciations simpler than the spellings. Eye-pronunciations of these are especially distracting to people familiar with the vocations.

Spelling	Eye-Pronunciation	Traditional Pronunciation
boatswain	'boutswein	'bousn̩
gunwale	'gʌnweil	'gʌnl̩
mainsail	'meinseil	'meinsl̩
topsail	'tɑpseil	'tɑpsl̩
forecastle	'fɔrˌkæsəl	'fɔksl̩ or 'foksl̩
leeward	'liːwərd	'luərd
lanyard	'lænˌjard	'lænjrd or 'lænjərd
lanthorn	'lænɵɔrn	'læntərn
clapboard	'klæpˌbɔrd	'klæbərd
leghorn	'lɛgˌhɔrn	'lɛgərn
plait (hair)	pleit[4]	plæt

E. Pairs of words with identical spellings but different meanings and pronunciations, often confused by the eye-pronouncers.

Spelling	Pronunciation No. 1		Pronunciation No. 2	
slough	slau	(bog)	slʌf	(to shed)
bow	bou	(weapon)	bau	(to nod)
bowman	'bomən	(archer)	'baumən	(No. 1 oar)

[2] *The American College Dictionary* (1948) recognizes the eye-pronunciation of this word as prevailing.

[3] *The A.C.D.* thinks this the majority pronunciation in America; but to most Americans it is an unfamiliar word. The American word is "vest." People who normally call the article a "waistcoat" pronounce it in the traditional way. Others are apt to guess at an eye-pronunciation.

[4] The word "plait" has several meanings, but in the familiar one of braiding the hair it is a very old word. English dictionaries give only the traditional pronunciation, and Webster's *International* agrees when the meaning is the one indicated. The *American College Dictionary* gives only the eye-pronunciation, but says that it means "to braid or plat the hair," thereby recognizing the traditional pronunciation but changing its spelling. The student who is curious about such things will find this a good word to play with. He should look it up in every available dictionary, including Fowler, Jones, Webster, the *Oxford*, Kenyon and Knott, and the *A.C.D.* The only point here is that he should not use the eye-pronunciation of "plait" when the character would say "plat."

Spelling	Pronunciation No. 1		Pronunciation No. 2	
mow	mau	(hayloft)	mou	(to reap)
row	rau	(quarrel)	rou	(line of units)
sow	sou	(to plant seed)	sau	(lady pig)
lead	liːd	(a clue)	lɛd	(a metal)
aye	ɑi	(yes)	ei	(always)
dingy	ˈdɪnʒiᵇ	(dusky)	ˈdɪŋgi	(v. of dinghy)
bass	beis	(a singer)	bæis	(a fish)
tear	tiːr	(nature's eyewash)	teɘr	(a spree)
ensign	ˈɛnsən	(naval off.)	ˈɛnsain	(Br. army)
lieutenant	luˈtɛnɘnt	(Br. navy)	lɛfˈtɛnɘnt	(Br. army)

(Many place names with identical spellings also have different pronunciations in different states or countries. Eye-pronouncers often slip on Cairo, Newark, Greenwich, Milan, Berlin, Calais, Derby, Helena, and so on.)

These are just a few of the eye-pronunciations that most often trap the unwary. The remedy for the actor is to put no trust whatever in spelling as a guide to pronunciation, and to put no trust in the people who do. With the aid of a good pronouncing dictionary, used before he starts memorizing his lines, he can avoid the difficulty if he will take the trouble.

In the matter of looking up unfamiliar words or disputed pronunciations most students need less urging and less help, and there is no need to give space to that problem here. The student is strongly advised, however, to read the highly entertaining and informative entry on Pronunciation in Fowler's *Modern English Usage*. It is addressed to the ordinary citizen, and the actor may have some need to command a higher standard of speech than his neighbors on the street. But he should be on guard against the false elegance referred to in Chapter X of this book.

The Snare of False Elegance

Elegant affectations do not arise exclusively from false teaching by undereducated elocutionists. They are also quite likely to arise from the actor's misplaced zeal for good diction. Even though he may have no expectation of acting professionally in New York or London, he naturally wishes to learn how to play cultivated or cosmopolitan characters as well as local or proletarian ones; but he does not always realize how thoroughly

---

⁵ It is always a question whether words ending in *y* or *ie* should be rendered phonetically with [i] or [ɪ]. The latter is generally considered more accurate as representing British speech, but the *American College Dictionary* uses it regularly to represent American practice. The British sound is normally a little lower and more retracted than the American. The issue is a very minor one in relation to these lists.

one must assimilate real cultivation, including good diction, before he can act it convincingly. A cultivated actor can always drop back into a provincial part and play it with some understanding, but an uncultivated one cannot assume cultivation on short notice. Whether it is intelligence or just atavism, a gentlemen can usually imitate a hoodlum (on or off the stage) better than a hoodlum can imitate a gentleman. That is not to imply that any student actor is a hoodlum; if he were, he would of course not be reading these pages. But many potentially fine actors have not been fortunate enough to learn cultivated diction in the nursery or the elementary school, and in their laudable ambition to acquire it for themselves they must be warned against the danger of mistaking the imitation for the reality, and giving themselves away by tricks of false elegance. Let us consider some of those already mentioned, and some others.

The American actor, even when playing a British character, should be especially cautioned against reckless and indiscriminate substitution of [ɑ] for [æ]. It is true that many cultivated speakers, both British and American, sometimes use [ɑ] or [a] in cases where an uncultivated speaker might use [æ], [æə], or [æ̃ə]. It is also true that [a] is frequently preferable to [æ] on the stage in non-dialectal plays. There is far less prejudice against these vowels in this country than there used to be before our millions came to know the speech of Ronald Colman, Claude Rains, Greer Garson, Charles Laughton, Herbert Marshall, Vivian Leigh and Sir Laurence Olivier as well as they know that of Lionel Barrymore, Katherine Hepburn, Tyrone Power, Lana Turner, or James Stewart. The danger of false elegance is not in using [a] with judgment, but in using [ɑ] where cultivated speech normally uses [a]; or by using either [ɑ] or [a] where cultivated speakers (including those in Britain) use [æ]. The actor who says hɑɪnd for hænd or bɑɪnd for bænd merely reveals his affectation and his ignorance of cultivated speech. The actor who says 'fɑɪnsi or 'fɔɪnsi for 'fænsɪ is not using a cultivated London or Boston pronunciation, but a burlesque symbol of affectation from the London music halls. When one hears a B.B.C. announcer talk about 'tʊmi 'dɔɪsiz dɑɪns bæənd, one realizes the danger of assuming that British speakers use [ɑ] wherever most Americans use [æ]. They do not; nor do cultivated American speakers.

An actor, let us say, from Philadelphia, accustomed to saying 'æ̃əftər, læ̃əst, and hæ̃əf pæ̃əst, will almost surely be accused of false elegance if he tries to say 'ɑɪftər, lɑɪst, and hɑɪf pɑɪst. He would do better, even in a British or New England part, to say aftɝ, last, and haɪf past; and even that might be hard to do convincingly at first. It might be easier to begin his training by eliminating only the nasality and the diphthongs, and say-

ing 'æftɝ, læst, and hæf pæst, keeping the vowels clean and dry. Later he might work back toward [ɑ] as experience made it more comfortable.

There are only a very few common words in which an American actor can change [æ] to [ɑ] and sound convincingly like a Londoner or a Bostonian instead of a silly ass (which, by the way, the Londoner pronounces æɪs when he means a donkey, and ɑɪs when he means an affected human making a donkey of himself!). He might manage plɑɪnt for "plant," kɑɪnt for "can't" (not "cant"), dɑɪns for "dance," ɑɪnt for "aunt" (not "ant"), and perhaps hɑɪf for "half" and lɑɪf for "laugh" (though hɑɪf and lɑɪf are safer). On most words pronounced by Americans with an [æ] he should hesitate to go as far back as [ɑ] lest he overdo it and say [ɒ] or [ɔ].

A similar problem arises with the so-called "short *o*," which in American usage is generally a short [ɑ], as in "got," "not," "on," "congress," and the like. For many years the elocutionists have been urging the theory that it is more refined to substitute an [ɔ] in all such words—except, of course, the ones like dɔg or 'bɔstən in which many Americans already use it and which are thought to be more refined if pronounced dɑg and 'bɑstən. But while some people are exerting themselves to say nɔt and gɔt as the English are supposed to do, regular listeners to the B.B.C. know that the English are rapidly abandoning those pronunciations in favor of nɒt and gɒt, and that many of them are now saying nɑt and gɑt as Americans do. The lesson in this for the actor accustomed to using [ɑ] for "short *o*" is that he had better not go beyond [ɒ] in pursuit of the supposedly elegant [ɔ]. One thing he can safely do, however, is to keep the vowel short, being sure to say dɔg rather than dɔɪg, and gɑd, gɒd, or gɔd rather than gɔɪd (which is low caste on either side of the Atlantic).

The ruthless elimation of the [iu] or [ju] diphthong in English "long *u*" in favor of a plain [u] is so offensive to most cultivated ears that there is good reason to retain the diphthong wherever it is reasonably natural. That makes for good diction on the stage as elsewhere. But in attempting to force the [ju] where it is too difficult the unwary actor may expose himself to the charge of false elegance. The diphthong is traditional, normal, and easy to pronounce after [b], [d], [f], [g], [h], [k], [m], [n], [p], [s], [t], [v], and [z], but a little more difficult after [l], very difficult after [r], and practically impossible after [w]; after [ʃ], [ʒ], and [j] the first element of the diphthong is hardly heard, being absorbed in the consonant. This means that the actor can say 'bjuro, 'djuti, 'fjutʃər, 'regjulər, hjudʒ, kjut, 'mjuzɪk, nju, pjur, æ'sjum, 'stjudənt, rɪ'vju, and rɪ'zjum without suspicion of false elegance. If he says 'buro, 'duti, 'futʃər, 'rɛgələr, hudʒ, kuɪt, 'muzɪk, nuɪ, puɪr, ə'sum, 'studn̩t, rɪ'vu, or rɪ'zum he will seem slightly demented

in some cases and just "general American" in others, but will give no impression of elegance, real or false.[6] On the other hand, if he says ljur, blju, klju, flju, or 'ljunətɪk he is likely to sound slightly ill at ease; and if he says 'rjumər for "rumor," rjuː for "rue," trjuː for "true," and sɪ'rjuliən for "cerulean" he is almost sure to be thought affected. He may even choke himself. However, we must not forget that it is stage diction we are considering, and these symbols of false elegance may be just the thing to portray an affected character.

So, likewise, are some of the uncalled-for attempts to restore foreign pronunciations to words originally foreign but so long a part of our language as to have well-established English pronunciations. Half the words in our language once belonged to other languages, and it is foolish to suppose we should now restore their original sounds. The most common attempt of the kind occurs on a word fairly common in plays—the word "valet," which has been a perfectly good English word (pronounced 'vælɪt or 'vælət) for some four hundred years; but a great many people who have learned that the French have a similar word mispronounce it 'vælei, which is neither English nor French. There is no more reason to say 'vælei (or even 'va'le) than to start saying næ'tjur for "nature." There are many other words on which people with a little learning try to show off their linguistic ability: "restaurant," "boulevard," "clientele," "avoirdupois," "envelop," "frankfurter," "Munich," "piano," "piazza," "data," "vice versa," and so on. There is no need to extend the list. Foreign words not yet fully Anglicized are, of course, another problem, on which the actor may get all the help he needs from the pronouncing dictionaries and from Fowler.

Another very common pitfall for those trying to be elegant is too much zeal in pronouncing the [hw] sound inherited from the Anglo-Saxon and reflected (backwards) in the spelling of "what," "which," "when," "whether," and so on. Many cultivated Americans do still pronounce that sound (though the British are rapidly giving it up and saying wɒt, wɛn, and the like); and it does no harm when used in moderation on the right words, by people who come by it naturally. But when a Philadelphia announcer gives the 'hwɛðər forecast for the hwiːk he quickly betrays the falseness of his elegance. An actor who talks about 'hwɪtʃkræft in Salem or a 'hwɪntər at hwɔrm sprɪŋz would call less attention to himself if he aban-

---

[6] *The American College Dictionary* (1948) recognizes one of these pronunciations (that of "assume") as prevailing American speech. To my ear it still sounds inelegant. In any case the alternative pronunciation would not sound like an affectation on the stage.

doned the attempt altogether, and said wɪtʃ for both "which" and "witch,"
and 'weðər for both "weather" and "whether."

But the most vexing problem of all for those seeking to better their stage
diction without affectation is what to do with the *r*—when to pronounce
it, when to elide it, and how. The two most frequent blunders are dropping
it too completely and dropping it in the wrong places.

There can be no doubt that the strong, long *r*, as heard in many parts
of this country is an ugly sound in its own right, and that it does not
conduce to an impression of cosmopolitan elegance and refinement of
diction. Phoneticians call it the "dog letter" because when lengthened it
is a kind of growl; when hardened by tense jaw action and palatal tone it
suggests a kind of snarl. The closest approach to it in Britain is the Devon
r, which is rounded and fairly hard, but seems to bounce off the hard
palate with more resiliency than the American *r*. The Scotch and Irish
trilled *r*'s, though quite as regional and quite as noticeable as the American
r, do not seem to be as offensive to cultivated ears, even in this country.
There is, therefore—quite apart from regional limitations—a reason for
mitigating certain extreme types of *r* sounds as a matter of good stage
diction.

In southeast England and in parts of New England the *r* is almost completely elided in certain positions—notably in final position, or in closed
syllables where it is followed by another consonant. It is not elided in
medial position between two vowels, but is very much shortened and
lightened, with a one-tap trill in London, and a close approach to it in New
England. This is difficult for most Americans west of the Hudson, and our
seekers after unaccustomed elegance often betray themselves by substituting a [w], and saying 'meəwi for "Mary," or æ'mɛwɪkən for "American"
(which may be better than ə'mʌɪrəkən, but is still not cultivated speech).
Others betray themselves by eliding the final *r*, but retaining a full Philadelphia or midwestern *r* in medial position; and still others do so by eliding
the final *r* but failing to restore it by linkage when the following word
begins with a vowel. The Britisher accustomed to saying ðɪs jiəɪ and
'ouvə hiəɪ, says ðɪs jɛɪ rəv greis and hjɛ rɪz ðə njuz. The imitator not
raised on silent *r* would probably say ðɪs jiə ʌv greis or ðɪs jiə wʌv gweis,
creating an awkward hiatus or a false *w* in his effort to avoid the *r*. Anybody trying to be elegant can drop a final *r* (at least when he remembers
to do so), but only a person born to it or with a thoroughly trained ear can
put it back by linkage in the proper places. The matter is greatly complicated by the fact that many good speakers link the *r* only on familiar

combinations of words where the thought-linkage is close, and refrain on
certain other combinations where the thought is more formal or unexpected.

In view of these difficulties, the student actor seeking to improve his
diction should be advised to proceed gradually, and not to attempt a complete elision of final *r;* but rather to mitigate it by shortening it and touch-
ing it as lightly as possible. He will do well to practice this in both medial
and final positions. If he cannot manage the one-tap trill, he will find that
he can come close to it by that method; and if he shortens and lightens the
sound in all positions he will make satisfactory progress toward a cultivated American standard that will not sound too utterly improbable to
the folks at home, nor too offensive to more cosmopolitan listeners.

It is to be hoped that nothing here said about the dangers of false elegance will add to the hysterical fear of affectation which afflicts so many
Americans, or discourage the student from making an intelligent and
reasonable effort to master good stage diction. There is no affectation in
acquiring better speech than one may have blundered into by accident.
All speech is acquired. The only affectation is in doing it badly; in parading
insincerely a mastery that one has not really acquired; in pretending
knowledge where there is only ignorance. The actor should certainly try
to free himself from his worst provincialisms, whatever they are: eastern
or western, urban or rural, crude or snobbish (and who is there who is
without sin in such matters?). He should certainly try to get rid of habitual
nasality, habitual hoarseness, hardness, or roughness of tone, and habitual
slovenliness as distinct from normal informality of conversational style.
He should certainly try to avoid confusing normal single vowels with
diphthongs, or with each other, and to be sure that he is not a slave
to excessive [æ] or excessive [r]. Above all he should strive to educate
his ear.

Two modern devices are available to help him do this: the radio and the
recording machine. He should use the latter at frequent intervals to check
his own speech and compare it with others. He should use the former
constantly, but discriminatingly, to gain a wide listening experience, especially in hearing good diction of many sorts, and in comparing dialects.
He should by all means include much short-wave listening, which too
many people ignore because of impatience at irregular reception or tuning
difficulties, or because of prejudice against anything foreign. On the regular
broadcast band he will hear much good diction and more that is very bad—
some of it intentionally bad. On the short waves he can also hear much

bad diction (not to mention bad diplomacy) on American propaganda broadcasts to foreign countries. But if he listens often, to many countries, he will hear more kinds of English than he can hear on the regular band. From the B.B.C. he will hear not merely the London announcers with their Oxonian vowels and intonations, but all varieties of English speech, good and bad, from Wiltshire, Devonshire, Gloucestershire, Wales, East Anglia, Yorkshire, Lancashire, Scotland, and Ireland. He will hear speech of all cultural levels, from the King and the Prime Minister down to the lowest crooner with a hotel dance band, and many shades of middle-class, cockney, or provincial speech in between. By comparing all these, and all varieties of American speech, with the diction of English-speaking announcers and commentators in Paris, Rome, Stockholm, Bern, The Hague, Moscow, Leopoldville, Brazzaville, Montreal, Quito, Melbourne, and Delhi, he will learn something difficult to learn in any other way: namely, how to distinguish between the provincialisms of Britain, America, or any other country and the cosmopolitan qualities of good English diction as heard round the world.

THE PROBLEM OF DIALECT

When an actor is confronted with a part in a dialect play, or a dialect part in an otherwise straight play, he has a problem to which the ordinary criteria of good stage diction do not apply.

There are really two problems. The first is whether to attempt a complete and faithful rendition of the dialect in all its detail, realistically satisfying to people familiar with it, or to attempt no more than a selection of the more outstanding characteristics by way of suggestion. There are manifest dangers in either policy, and the first is possible only when time and ability permit. Since the choice is usually the director's problem rather than the actor's, and is discussed at length in *The Art of Play Production*, I shall not repeat the discussion here.

The second problem is the actor's: how to acquire, in the time available, the degree of dialectal quality demanded by the director.

This problem cannot be solved from recipes or lists of words in a textbook, especially if the director is asking for some measure of completeness. Nor can it be solved at all in the time allotted for a production unless the actor has one of three qualifications: a previous knowledge of the dialect concerned, an exceptional talent for dialects, or a considerable apprenticeship in the critical analysis of dialects. The first is a matter of happy accident or of type casting, and so need not be discussed. The second is a

matter of good luck, but is seldom adequate unless supported by some knowledge and study as well. The third is the one which the actor can really do something about.

One way of going at it is to make a list of the dialects most often found in plays—Irish, Yiddish, Scotch, Italian, Pennsylvania Dutch, British, Mexican, and so on—and then try to master each one and build up a repertory of dialects, ready for any emergency. This method is not to be recommended. It may occasionally meet a situation, but it has the great disadvantage that it tends to pigeonhole all dialects into a few special forms, and to make the actor too rigid each time he tries to apply one. All of these dialects, and many others, vary enormously in different sections, different periods, and different individual characters, and if the actor is to avoid stereotypes and cultivate flexibility he would do better to choose another method.

A much better method is to train the ear as sensitively as possible by listening critically and comparatively to as many different dialects and shades of individual variation as one can discover, on the radio, in dialect recordings, on the stage, in talking pictures, and (best of all when possible) in actual travel; by recording as many of them as possible, either phonographically or phonetically, for frequent restudy; and by practicing, not a few stereotypes, but as many shadings of accent, vowel quality, tone, and rhythm as time permits. The object should not be to master any one dialect as a preconceived entity unrelated to any particular part, but to develop a high degree of familiarity with dialectal variations, and a high degree of kinesthetic adaptability. When assigned a part, he can then bring such knowledge and flexibility to bear on the specific job of learning the right shade of dialect for that particular part. If he has no fixed idea about the dialect beforehand, he is much more likely to do a sincere, imaginative piece of character study, with the dialect included as part of it.

The subtlety and complexity of the dialect problem is well illustrated in a play like Drinkwater's *Bird in Hand*, which is an English play, but would lose half its charm and meaning if played in only one dialect. The innkeeper speaks a thick Gloucestershire dialect, reflecting his rugged provincial independence and strength of character. His wife, a former circus performer, speaks a modified cockney, smoothed out by her travels and her contacts with the cosmopolitan entertainment world. Their daughter speaks the "received English" she has learned in school; so does her lover, the squire's son, with just enough difference to suggest his higher social background, but not enough to suggest that she is not good enough for him—a very important point in the theme of the play. The sardine

salesman speaks unabashed cockney, the upstart business man speaks a plausible but specious imitation of Oxford English, and the squire speaks the real thing.

An actor who had just one British accent, cut and dried, would have a hard time adjusting himself to such a play. He would have similar difficulties with Shaw's *Pygmalion,* or Galsworthy's *Strife,* or Barrie's *A Kiss for Cinderella,* or Phillpotts' *The Farmer's Wife.* But an actor who had trained his ear by listening to all shades of dialect to be heard on the B.B.C., analyzing the differences, socially, geographically, and phonetically, and practicing them experimentally with his own voice, might have the flexibility to do quite well in one of these plays after six weeks of concentrated and imaginative study. To be sure, the method is not foolproof; nor is it of much use to the actor working in stock on five rehearsals and a week's notice. The point is simply that it is better to soak in a specific dialect after the part is assigned, than to soak in the wrong one ahead of time and then try to apply it forcibly where it does not quite fit.

With these thoughts in mind, I shall make no attempt to catalogue the dialects an actor ought to study, or to systematize the pronunciations he should be familiar with. But if the student is to follow the advice here given and listen analytically to dialectal differences whenever he gets the chance, it may help him to have a few key suggestions as to what to listen for.

In respect to American regional dialects, he should listen especially for just those peculiarities mentioned earlier as likely to betray regional background.

In all study of dialects, he should train himself to listen with particular care to the variations in diphthongs and to any substitution of diphthong for single vowel or vice versa. These matters are not only highly important in shading dialect, but they are so subtle that most people never notice them; one of the chief indications that a student's ear is getting keener will be his increasing sensitivity to diphthongal peculiarities. He should also train himself to listen carefully to significant differences in vocal pitch and quality, inflection patterns, tempo patterns, and rhythms, and to the way in which they are coördinated with pronunciations. One may get every pronunciation phonetically correct, and yet miss the flavor of a dialect altogether; and conversely, if he does get the flavor, he can afford a few errors in specific pronunciations without detriment to the characterization. In all his listening experience he should remember that it is just as important to learn what *not* to do as what to do. Audiences are much more apt to notice sins of commission than sins of omission. If an actor is trying to do an Irish accent, people will hardly notice his missing some of

the opportunities to be positively Irish; but they will quickly notice it if he tries to give them some Yiddish, or Scotch, or Pennsylvania Dutch traits by mistake. In this, as in many other phases of the actor's art, he should remember that audience imagination is always willing and eager to work with him just so long as he does nothing to distract or shatter it. How *not* to remind his listeners that he is not what he seems is the essence of his problem.

In listening to British dialects, the actor should pay special attention to the varying values of *a*, *o*, and *r*. He should note the words in which the Londoner says [ɑ], [a], and [æ], and which of those that take [ɑ] in London take [æ] in Devon, in the Midlands, or in Scotland. He should note what classes and types of people are most insistent on the [ɑ]. He should listen carefully to the cockney's supposed substitution of [ai] for [ei] (as in "piper" for "paper"), and note that he seldom really says [ɑi], but rather [ai], [æi], or [ɛi]; and that the chief point is the lengthening of the glide, especially the last part of it. He should analyze the shadings of [ɑ], [ɒ], and [ɔ], in words like "not," "on," and "sorry," and their correlation with social class. He should compare the various sounds for long *o* with the American sounds, and note that the usual symbol [ou] does not cover the most extreme Oxonian pronunciations, which run closer to [ʌu], or even [ɛu]. He should note the peculiar shading of the *a* in words like "all," "audience," and "call"; the [ɔ] shades toward [o] (precisely the opposite of the midwestern tendency). He should listen very carefully indeed to the different types of medial *r*, analyzing the difference between the London one-tap trill in words like "very" or "sorry" (which American journalists with Anglophobic wit but poor hearing jestingly spell "veddy" and "soddy"), and the Welsh, Irish, and Scottish trills (all different); also between the medial *r* of rural England and that of our middle west. He should study the map of England, and note how the final *r*, elided in London, begins to reappear in Wilts, gets stronger in Dorset, becomes very pronounced in Devon, and begins to trill in Wales; also how it begins to reappear north of London. In all such regional observations, however, he should note the tendency of the better educated in all regions to conform more closely to the London standard when away from home, or when speaking to strangers. Many Britishers are really bilingual, speaking the home dialect easily at home, but the "received English" when traveling. He will note that cultivated people in Britain, as in America, frequently shorten their diphthongs, though they seldom confuse them with single vowels. But he will also notice that the cultivated speaker frequently betrays his original

Plate 25. American tragic acting at its peak. Alice Brady in the powerful final scene of *Mourning Becomes Electra*. But for her untimely death shortly after this production, Alice Brady might well have come to be rated the greatest American actress. Starting as a tomboy comedienne in silent films, she went on to play a great variety of parts, comic and tragic (most of them in trashy or second-rate plays) doing them all well. Her deep, sympathetic voice, sincerity of imagination, versatility, and charm outshone most of the parts assigned her, and did much to make her Lavinia more unforgettable than the play itself despite its five-hour strain on the nerves.

Plate 26. Characterization in make-up. Above: Two scenes from *Victoria Regina* showing Helen Hayes in her remarkable transformation from the young queen (with Vincent Price as Albert) to the old queen. Lower left: Maurice Evans as Falstaff in *Henry IV*. Below: Vassily Luzhsky, of the Moscow Art Theatre, as Firce in *The Cherry Orchard*—a masterpiece, in both make-up and acting.

Vandamm

Left:
Alfred Lunt and Lynn Fontanne ("The Lunts") in *Reunion in Vienna*, one of the long series of sophisticated comedies ridiculing monogamy which their deft, politely salacious style of acting has done so much to popularize. They are really quite versatile, but audiences have come to think of them as typed in this genre.

Vandamm

Vandamm

Plate 27. Husband-and-wife teams, on and off stage.

Right:
Howard Lindsay and his wife, Dorothy Stickney, as Mr. and Mrs. Day in the most popular comedy of the recent past, *Life With Father*. The Lindsays have also re-created the same characters in a sequel under the title *Life With Mother*.

Plate 28. A distinguished revival of Greek tragedy. The *Medea* of Euripides in a new adaptation by Robinson Jeffers, directed by John Gielgud (who, as shown here, also played Jason for the first few weeks), with Judith Anderson as Medea in a magnificent, bloodcurdling piece of acting. Upper left: Medea pleads with Jason, who is adamant. Above: Medea in one of her most tigerish moments. Lower left: Medea shows Jason the bodies of their children, whom she has slain to punish him, loving them, but hating him even more deeply.

Plate 29. Outstanding characterizations of recent years. Above: Wesley Addy as a galvanic Hotspur in *Henry IV*. Upper right: Ingrid Bergman as Mary Gray in *Joan of Lorraine*. Below: Oscar Homolka as Uncle Chris in *I Remember Mama*. Lower right: Leo Carroll in his sensitive performance of the name part in *The Late George Apley*.

Plate 30. Reaction and by-play. Scenes that pose interesting problems for the actors not speaking at the moment. Above: Entrance of the Kirby family in *You Can't Take It With You* (note Mr. Kirby's reaction to the picture and Mrs. Kirby's to Kolenkov's T-shirt). Left: Entrance of the Grand Duchess in another production of the same play. Left, below: Fishkin tells his story, in *Jim Dandy*, while Molly illustrates his words in pantomimic modern dance. At bottom: Two scenes from *Love's Old Sweet Song;* left: The Okie children, after man-handling the writer, attack the pitchman; right: The pitchman outdoes the *Time* salesman, but gets very spotty response, varied according to character.

Plate 31. *Some memorable characterizations by non-pro-fessionals.* Above: Phyllis Beidler as Electra (Pennsyl-vania State College). Upper right: Jean Milne and Wil-liam Whitney as Widow Cagle and Pap Todd in *Sun-Up* (Players Club of Swarthmore). Right: Stafford W. Parker as Papa in *Papa Is All* (Players Club of Swarthmore). Lower left: Marian Brill as The Actress, with J. Kirk Merrick as The Actor, in *The Guardsman* (Plays and Players, Philadelphia). Lower right: Philip R. Whitney as the frustrated Fishkin in *Jim Dandy* (the original ver-sion, not the published one) (Players Club of Swarth-more).

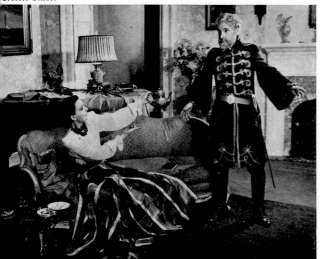

Plate 32. The preacher tries to practice. Above: The author as Sir Toby Belch (two sketches by Helen L. Evans). Upper right: More thinly disguised as Bottom the Weaver. Lower left: As Sir Peter Teazle. Below: As Inspector Donahue in *The Thirteenth Chair* (a particularly foggy piece of acting).

background by failing to make a complete substitution of London diph-thongs.

The actor need hardly be told that some words in common use in both countries have entirely different pronunciations in Britain from those current in the United States. But until he achieves a very sharp ear indeed he will miss many of them by reason of their unfamiliarity. Though my own ear is fairly sharp, I had to listen three times to a recording of Winston Churchill before I could identify a certain word which he passed over very rapidly. It was "trait," which, as I was well aware, the British pronounce trei; but my American ears are so accustomed to hearing it as treit that it just did not register with me. That word is one of the very few foreign words that have been Anglicized in America and not in Britain, the opposite being the rule. The British pronunciation of "schedule" as 'ʃɛdʒul or 'ʃɛdjul sounds strange to American ears, but has the advantage of retaining the two syllables; the American 'skɛdʒul tends to become 'skɛdʒuwəl—an uncultivated pronunciation if there ever was one. The British lə'bɒrətri for "laboratory" is a synthetic pronunciation invented by phoneticians, and strangely enough it seems to have taken hold, though not by any means universally accepted in England. On one occasion I heard a B.B.C. announcer introduce the world-famous physicist Sir Oliver Lodge, saying that he would speak from his lə'bɒrətri; Sir Oliver then began to talk about the pleasures of working in his 'læbərətʌri. The synthetic pronunciation is now standard, however, on the London stage, and is often heard on Broadway. All these examples are so sharply different from common American usage that they need cause little confusion to the actor, once he has learned to identify them, and they may help him to portray a British character.

Somewhat more troublesome are the variations on words like "again," "against," "either," and "neither." Both ə'gein and ə'gɛn are at least 300 years old, and respectable in both countries; ə'gein is more common in southeastern England and less common in America, while ə'gɛn prevails in Devon and other counties, and in most parts of America. Both are found in Shakespeare. The cockney form is ə'gæin. The word "either," as suggested by its phonetic spelling, was 'eiðər in Middle English, later changing [ei] to [i:] in cultivated English, as did many words with the [ei] sound in earlier days. The cockney 'aiðər did not come from 'i:ðər, but from the older 'eiðər, by the same change which made 'leidi into 'laidi. A dictionary published in London in 1787 says that the word is sometimes pronounced "eyether" by "certain classes," but recommends "eether" as preferred by

the better educated, and as used by that master of English speech, David Garrick. Nevertheless, the cockney form now prevails in London and on the New York stage, though the Devon man still says 'iːðər.

There are hundreds of other oddities to fascinate the student actor as his ear improves—the Devon gwein for "going" (closely parallel to the gwain of our southern states); the distinction between 'mɛdsn̩ (the drug) and 'mɛdɪsn̩ (the science); the use of [i] where Americans use [ɛ] in words like "æsthetic," "æsthete," and "Æschylus" (isˈθɛtɪk, 'iːsθeit, 'iːskɪləs); the Scotch gɔːf for "golf"; the usual 'glæsjə for "glacier"; and so on. But he should remember, also, that there are other matters to study besides pronunciation.

Listening for differences in sentence intonation, rhythm, and voice quality, the actor should note the characteristic difference in pitch between Lancashire and Yorkshire; the nasal quality in Lancashire (rather rare in Britain); the soft raspiness of the rural male voice; the firm, determined, pushing of tones in the west country, with a jaw action a little like the Midwestern, but with a diaphragmatic quality in place of the palatal hardness; the peculiar palatal bounce in Devon; the guttural quality of much cockney speech, and its occasional nasality (quite different from that of Lancashire); the tendency of nearly all British speech to more lively inflection patterns than those of this country, and especially to more rising inflections; and the remarkably clear, resonant quality of the typical cultivated British voice. A confirmed short-wave listener who knows no Spanish, French, or Portuguese, can instantly distinguish a B.B.C. broadcast in those languages from a broadcast originating in Havana, Lisbon, Paris, or New York, by the tone quality of the announcer's voice—that is if he is British, as he usually is.

In listening to Irish accents the actor should distinguish carefully between the Irish brogue heard from American comedians in the Bowery theatre tradition, and the speech of educated Irishmen as heard from Dublin or Belfast; and between either and the "beautiful speaking" of the Irish peasant folk as heard in the Abbey Theatre plays of Yeats and Synge, and occasionally on the short waves. He should listen not only for the quality of Irish vowel sounds and the Irish *r*, but for the more subtle and significant influence of Gaelic sentence rhythm and idiom on English word patterns.

In listening to Australian and Canadian speech he should compare the elements of British speech surviving in those countries, and the curious ways in which they have been modified by local conditions and by American influences. He will note that in Australia it is the cockney influence

that seems to have survived best, while in Canada the Scotch seems more tenacious. Though French is a factor in Canada, and many people are bilingual, the English seems little affected by the French; but it is strongly influenced by midwestern American.

In listening to English-speaking announcers and commentators to whom the language is not native, as heard from short-wave stations in all parts of the world, he must, of course, make great allowance for individual differences depending on where the particular speaker got his training. It is part of the fun to try and figure that out. But what he should listen for most keenly is the common denominator of cosmopolitan English—that is, the group of characteristics that seem to be accepted by the neutral foreign linguist as neither British nor American, but English in the language sense. The impediment of a slight accent and of some unfamiliarity with provincialisms and colloquialisms causes these international speakers to reveal to us many of the curiosities and inconsistencies in our own language, and many of our own peculiarities of utterance. One often learns much about what is narrowly British, or narrowly American, by hearing a Frenchman, Italian, or German speaking good cosmopolitan English, and especially by listening to all of them and many others, including the Scandinavian—and the Chinese.

Perhaps this is enough to give some hint of the many significant things the student may listen for, and that may help him to train his ear. Before ceasing and desisting, however, let me add that there is one listening experience available on the B.B.C. which the American actor really must not miss. That is to hear radio plays including both British and American characters *all played by British actors*. When he hears how American speech sounds to others, he will get a most salutary shock. Of course he may laugh it off, or assert indignantly that the British actor is stupid or deaf, or unfamiliar with American speech, or just unfair; and it is perfectly reasonable that he should make the same reservations that a British listener should make when he hears an American actor trying to do a British accent. Nevertheless, it will prove one of the most beneficial phases of his ear training. The famous couplet of Robert Burns loses some of its rhyme but none of its force if we substitute the word "hear" for the word "see."

The study of speech habits and standards is a fascinating one, and its usefulness to the actor is incalculable. There is no reason why an actor should not be interested in it for its own sake, or why he should not have his own tastes and preferences. But *as an actor* he must keep reminding himself that his concern is not with which is right, but with which is which.

CHAPTER XVI

Bodily Action

THE importance of the actor's voice and diction as instruments to convey meaning and feeling is in no way lessened by the fact that he also uses bodily action and gesture for the same purpose. The eye is often quicker and more alert than the ear, and more useful in establishing certain communicative understandings between actor and audience, and in clarifying humorous intentions. On the other hand the ear is perhaps more sensitive to certain emotional overtones and poetic values; and of course it is the ear to which the actual text of the play is chiefly directed. It would be silly to argue that the eye is more important than the ear, or vice versa. Both are indispensable. The actor must appeal to both—sometimes to one or the other separately, but most of the time to both at once—and he is likely to be most effective when he has equally good control over visible and audible expression, and great skill in coördinating them.

PANTOMIME

Meaning portrayed in terms of bodily action—traditionally known as pantomime—has a long and significant history. I have mentioned its possible use by primitive man as a means of communication antedating articulate speech, with the latter perhaps developing out of the accompanying grunts and cries. This aspect of pantomime has never been lost, for whenever two human beings who do not speak the same tongue have need to communicate with each other, they are sure to resort to some kind of "sign language" (not omitting the grunts and cries); and in certain regions where this happens frequently—as where there are many small tribes with separate dialects—sign languages have sometimes become highly codified and much more widely distributed than any one spoken language. This suggests the idea that pantomime (like music) may sometimes transcend the limitations of spoken language and be more easily, directly, and instinctively understood than any code of word symbols.

Dramatic pantomime is older than the theatre itself; it is found in the ceremonial rites and tribal dances of primitive peoples everywhere. It is often rhythmic, and is associated with musical accompaniment and ul-

timately with words, and is part of the common origin of music, dancing, and poetry. Ceremonial dancing is after all largely pantomime—a language of rhythmic action, codified and exaggerated, for the expression of religious, epic, or lyric feeling. It would be difficult to say when it ceases to be dancing and becomes acting; perhaps it would be truer to say that it has been both from the start. It would certainly be safe to say that the pantomimic concept of acting is older than the concept of acting in terms of articulate speech. Through the ages, the close association between dancing and pantomimic acting has likewise never been lost. It permeates the history of ballet; and what is loosely called "the modern dance" is not modern at all, but is rather a return to more direct pantomimic action in dancing—less formally rhythmic than the classic ballet, more contemporary in its idioms, and much closer in its essential nature to the instinctive sign languages of primitive peoples.

In the huge theatres of ancient Greece much of the subtlety of verbal expression common in our intimate playhouses, and even some of the more restrained accompaniment of action and gesture, would have been wasted. The telling of the story (already, in most cases, familiar to the audience) was entrusted to the chorus, who sang or recited the poetic words in unison, and illustrated the meaning with broadly formalized movement, rhythmic enough to be thought of as ceremonial dancing, yet intelligible enough to convey simple emotions and attitudes of mind clearly to large audiences. The essential elements of pantomime—simplification, exaggeration, and codified symbolism—were doubtless present in choral action before the individual actor entered the picture. Further simplification and exaggeration may have been the chief motives for his introduction; and though the megaphone-like mask may have enabled him to achieve some of it in terms of voice and words, there is reason to believe that a large part of his function was pantomimic; that is, to illustrate the action visually while the chorus told the story. The large size of the masks, their exaggerated expressions, the symbolic contrasts of costume, and the various devices for making the actor seem taller were all helpful in making his pantomime effective over long distances, provided the simplification and exaggeration were broad enough.

In the liturgical drama of the medieval church it was pantomime which made intelligible to the illiterate masses the Biblical stories which they could not read for themselves, and the Latin words of which many of them could not understand. When the drama came out of the church and the guilds gave their cycles of miracle plays on wagons or street corners, pantomime still remained essential for the same reasons, and for the addi-

tional reason that words were even more likely to be lost in the confusion and turmoil of outdoor production, while broad, exaggerated pantomime could still be seen and understood.

Much of the work of the vagabond players in medieval Europe was pantomimic for similar reasons. Since the strolling players wandered from country to country they often had to transcend language difficulties as well as the distractions of street-corner acting, and they could do so more effectively with pantomime than with words (though words were by no means excluded). Their pantomimic tradition carried through into the *Commedia dell' Arte*, or comedy of improvisation, and from that into the more sophisticated comedy of Molière in France and also into English pantomime, the heritage of which still endures in the Christmas panto-mimes for children. Modern teachers of acting who make a religion of improvisation, and who point to the *Commedia dell' Arte* as the supreme example of its effective application, often forget the relative importance of the pantomimic element in that form, and the relative subordination of the words. For the very reason that pantomime is more simply codified than articulate language, it is more readily improvised and more readily understood, with or without the accompaniment of words.

What does all this mean to the student actor today? It means that if he wishes to master his art, he will do well to give considerable study to the history of pantomime, and especially to those elements of simplification, exaggeration, and codified symbolism which give it its range and power. Up to the present century no actor would have needed to be told this. The modern concept of individualistic naturalism in acting stems largely from the "free theatre" movement in Europe, and the innovations of Belasco in this country, both dating roughly from 1887. All through the seventeenth, eighteenth, and nineteenth centuries, most actors gave a great deal of study to codified bodily action, not merely for use in silent pan-tomime but for illustrative use in conjunction with their declamation of lines. Not all of them, especially in England and America, were willing to accept the rigid codes of teachers like Delsarte; and it would be hard to imagine a young actor today accepting the Delsartian system at face value. But it should be part of the actor's training at least to know that such things have been.

François Delsarte (1811–1871) started out to be an actor, but by reason of bad vocal training is said to have ruined his voice. Cut off from success in his chosen profession, he turned to the analysis of technique; eventually he became the most highly advertised teacher of acting and oratory in France, and profoundly influenced elocution, if not acting, the world

over. "After several years of diligent study," his biographer informs us, "he discovered and formulated the essential laws of all art; and, thanks to him, æsthetic science in our day [c. 1882] has the same precision as mathematical science." That would seem to have been a considerable achievement, to say the least. The modern student may distrust the result, especially after reading the details of the system;[1] but he ought not to be ignorant of the extent to which action and gesture, as well as vocal tone and inflection, have been codified in the past.

An even more startling example illustrating codified pantomime is to be found in an old book[2] now unfortunately out of print and very hard to find; it not only lists and describes an exhaustive catalogue of bodily attitudes alleged to symbolize every conceivable mood and emotion, but provides no less than one hundred line cuts to illustrate them. The charm of the illustrations is not lessened by the fact that the model portrayed is a somewhat ponderous gentleman with a very large moustache and a Prince Albert coat. If the student can locate a copy of that book in a library some-where, he will find an hour or two spent on it an illuminating and educational experience. Much of it will seem very naïve and amusing; but he should not forget that the fundamental concept of codified pantomime on which that sort of teaching was based is several thousand years old, while the modern tendency to laugh off all codes and conventions is younger than the memory of living men. No doubt the nineteenth century, in its eagerness to perfect the traditional language of pantomime, reduced it to absurdity; but that does not lessen the truth that bodily action, simplified by selection, moderately exaggerated, and codified in accordance with wide human experience, provides a language of expression more universally intelligible than words, more easily projected in large theatres, and more nearly proof against distraction.

How much codified pantomime should a young actor attempt to learn today? And where shall he learn it? Shall he go back to the Delsarte system or to any similar elaboration of the past? Shall he study the formal pos-turings of the Greek theatre, or of the miracle plays, or of Shakespeare's time, or of Garrick's, or Forrest's, as far as they can be reconstructed from the plays and from contemporary references or illustrations? Shall he study the pantomimic codes in the traditional dances of the Chinese, the Hindus, the Balinese, the Fiji Islanders, the Bechuanas, the Zulus, the Aztecs, the Hopis, the Seminoles, and so on, wherever the anthropologists

---

[1] They may be found in *The Delsarte System*, by M. L'Abbé Delaumosne, translated by Frances A. Shaw (1882).

[2] *Lessons in Acting*, by Edmund Shaftesbury (c. 1885).

and archeologists can give him help? And should his study be purely objective, or should he aim to acquire and make use of such pantomimic symbolism himself?

Clearly, the last objective would be absurd, except in rather limited applications. While he might well find certain forms of bodily action sufficiently universal in their symbolism to be just as useful to him as they have been to the Greeks, the Chinese, and the Hopis, most of it would be too much colored by time and place to be utilized in the modern American theatre except for special purposes in exotic plays. But a comparative study of pantomime in all ages and places would teach him to distinguish between what is special and what is universal.

He will certainly be more surprised at the similarities than at the divergencies. Rhythmic movements, especially, are extraordinarily similar the world over, perhaps because human bodies are much the same; for example, he will find some of the ceremonial line dances of the Fiji Islanders or the Bechuanas amazingly like the precision dancing of the "Rockettes" in Radio City Music Hall (though it may be doubted whether the religious symbolism is identical). He will find many differences in the actions which symbolize racial or national traditions or the special conditions of life in specific times and places; but he will find great universality in the attitudes and gestures symbolizing such basic experiences as joy, fear, hunger, mirth, anger, supplication, anxiety, respect, scorn, grief, and so on.

For the study of universal pantomime, however, the actor will find another source much nearer at hand; and I hope he will not think I am going to start this book all over again if I refer him once more to the behavior of young children.

Childhood Pantomime

Since the child repeats in some measure the developmental history of his race, the actions and gestures by which he conveys thought and feeling are apt to follow instinctive and universal patterns, many of them very old. At the same time, children are the most contemporary of human beings; they have no respect for old patterns that no longer fit the conditions of present environment, and are quick to adopt new ones to fit new conditions.

When I was a child, for instance, much mimic play centered about the driving of horses, and "horse lines" were among the commonest toys. The child who wore them pantomimed the actions of a galloping or trotting horse, while a companion mimicked those of his driver, urging him on with

cries of "Giddyap!" and applications of an imaginary (or perhaps a real) whip. A present-day American child would probably not know what "horse lines" were for if he saw them; but he would know how to pantomime the driving of a tractor or a tank, or the zooming of an airplane, and he would certainly know all about pointing bazoukas and Tommy guns in people's faces. Objective or descriptive pantomime changes with the times—as do manners. But the pantomime expressing universal emotions changes very little. The child who is frightened cringes in much the same way now as always; the one who is pleased jumps for joy in the same way; the one who is embarrassed turns away with the same shy, sidelong look; the one who is startled or excited has the same open mouth and popping eyes; the one who is thwarted stamps out his temper in the same way, and the one who is proud of some achievement struts in the same way. And while the actions of adults vary slightly on geographical and racial lines, it is noticeable that the untaught actions of children have a striking similarity, whether the children be English or American, Russian or Japanese, white, black, yellow or red.

By checking his observation of childhood pantomime against his study of historical pantomime and of the codified pantomime described by Delsarte and other elocutionists, the young actor should seek to decide for himself what is really useful. He will hardly need to be told that the highly technical codification set up by those who would reduce all art to rules must be taken with reservations; he may even find that some of it is made intentionally elaborate and complex in the interest of professional mysticism. On the other hand it will not do for him to pooh-pooh it all, and assume that his own genius and common sense will infallibly dictate the best posture or gesture to express every meaning.

He should remember two very important facts. The first is that some bodily actions are so universally and instinctively expressive of certain emotions or attitudes of mind that they never seem to lose their communicative significance. The second is that some actions, whether instinctive or not, have been so long identified in the arts with the expression of certain emotions that they have symbolic usefulness as a more or less conventionalized sign language. Both of these facts must be interpreted with judgment, and with due regard to related truths.

For example, the fact that some bodily actions are universally and instinctively expressive of certain emotions does not alter the related fact— already mentions in other connections—that individuals differ considerably in their ways of expressing the same emotion. It will usually be found, however, that the impulse to bodily action in the expression of a basic

emotion is felt in much the same way, even by unlike individuals, and that
the chief difference in their behavior lies in the degree and kind of inhibition or distortion which they bring to bear on it. Thus, a bodily attitude of cringing may be the instinctive and universal manifestation of
fear; but a timid person will cringe much more than a brave one, and a
well-disciplined one may not cringe visibly at all; yet the actor portraying
such a character will be truer to life if he can contrive to imagine both the
impulse to cringe and the inhibition which suppresses it. In the same way,
the impulse to weep is universal; but different people, and even different
races, vary greatly in the way in which they yield to it or fight against
it. Theoretically, it should be easy for the actor to represent inhibited
grief pantomimically by doing nothing; by just not weeping. Actually he
will be more intelligible and effective if he first learns how to show grief
in the uninhibited way, then in a more formalized pantomimic way, and
finally by adding whatever degree of inhibition is suitable to the character.
To show repression he must repress his pantomime; but he cannot repress
what is not there.

Without attempting to formulate a pantomimic code for ourselves, or
to set up rules of bodily action, let us review what has been said of the
three essentials already mentioned: Simplification, exaggeration, and
codified symbolism.

SIMPLIFICATION

Simplification, or selection of essentials, has been frequently discussed
in this book as a fundamental principle of art; and it is equally fundamental as a matter of effective communication. If human beings, in their
variety and resourcefulness, contrive a dozen different actions or gestures
to convey the same basic idea, no one of them can be as easily and unmistakably understood by as many people at as great distances as would
be the case if only one simple action were universally employed for the
same purpose. That is why actors, for many generations, have found
it best to depict death in only two or three simple and obvious ways, rather
than in the hundred different ways known to doctors and nurses.

The great flexibility and variability of the human body as an instrument of expression can be an actual disadvantage, at times, in making
it more difficult to simplify and select actions artistically. The student
actor is strongly urged to study the bodily actions of marionettes, especially
in the hands of skillful, artistic operators. Marionettes have certain ca-
pabilities in exaggeration denied to human actors—such as leaping twice
their own height to express joy or fright—but they also have many more

limitations than real actors in the number and character of their movements. These limitations have a real value artistically, since they compel
a degree of selection and exaggeration that human actors would ordinarily
neglect. I recall very vividly a production of *The Taming of the Shrew* by
the Tatterman Marionettes in which the character of Baptista, father of
Katherine and Bianca, came alive for me much more effectively than he
had ever done in the many stage productions I had seen. It was achieved
almost entirely by a change in his manner of walking. Baptista is naïve,
puzzled, impatient, and utterly humorless in his eagerness to get his older
daughter safely married, and the marionette reflected this by a jerky,
confused, rather clumsy way of walking. But when Petruchio comes to
his rescue and Katherine is at last off his hands, he is almost absurdly
pleased and self-satisfied, and the marionette portrayed it by developing
a jaunty swagger in his walk which pointed up and illuminated the lines
amazingly. A human actor might have achieved a similar effect by simplification and exaggeration; but most actors do not. The five or six human
actors I had seen play that particular part had missed the opportunity
completely.

Let us repeat that the detailed realities of life are so numerous, complex,
varied, and often meaningless that some kind of selective simplification
becomes necessary for ordinary clarity in communication, and still more
necessary as an instrument of significant art. Pantomimic artists and pup-
peteers have realized this for at least two thousand years; but beginners
in art—including the art of acting—do not ordinarily realize it, and sometimes fight against it and refuse to realize it when told about it by their
teachers and directors.

Perhaps the commonest fault of the beginner in acting is bodily fidgeting. It takes many forms, such as bobbing the head, pushing it forward,
or leaning forward at every spoken line; backing away after finishing a
line; "teetering," or shifting the weight restlessly and unnecessarily from
one foot to the other; fiddling with hand props unnecessarily; and what
most directors call "stage wandering"—that is, continually shifting position from one spot on the stage to another for no reason at all.

The first principle of all good stage movement and business is: No action
without a purpose. Good directors not only observe this principle, but
they try hard to teach it to their actors. Unfortunately it is a hard lesson
for most young actors to learn. There seems to be some strong impulse
in the human mechanism to expend surplus energy in random motor activity, and young people, especially, have a good deal of surplus energy. At
the same time they have less experience of life to guide their selection of

activity, and less practice in controlling their impulses. In many cases it is practically impossible for a young actor to control his fidgeting through sheer exercise of will power in self-repression; and if he could do so he would merely be substituting meaningless inactivity for meaningless activity, with some lessening of distraction, perhaps, but no increase in real expressiveness. What he must learn to do is not to bottle up his energies but to direct them into useful channels; to select a few decisive, meaningful movements instead of many meaningless ones, and pour his energies into the selected ones. He must, of course, coöperate with the director in designing and timing those movements, to be sure that they do not create distractions or unbalance stage pictures; and he must not carry them to the point of overemphasis. He must try to learn, as every artist must, how to select those bold, telling strokes which convey the maximum suggestion of meaning with the minimum amount of detail. Reducing the number of strokes will accomplish little unless they are well chosen. Any child can draw a man by making a crude circle for the head, an ellipse for the body, and four lines for the arms and legs; but an accomplished cartoonist can draw a man with an equal number of strokes, and actually catch a likeness, an attitude, or a suggestion of vitality in action. In the same way an actor may put five minutes' worth of energy into three well-chosen movements or bodily actions and be more intelligible and less distracting than if he had made fifty unimportant movements in the same period.

The late Sir Henry Irving, in spite of his awkwardness, was a master at selecting the telling gesture. The same informant I have quoted before recalls a striking example. "When Irving was killed in *Becket*," he says, "he was struck down at the top of a flight of about three steps, in the transept of the cathedral. He rolled down the steps to the stage level, and lay there, with his right arm, from shoulder to elbow, on the floor, but his forearm standing vertical. This remained for a few seconds, and then the forearm fell; you could almost see the life going out of his body at that instant."

EXAGGERATION

A certain degree of exaggeration is a natural—almost an inevitable—accompaniment of such selection. Bodily action is only one of many elements to which the principle applies, and it is not necessary to repeat what has already been said on the subject. But the actor should not forget that the purpose of exaggeration in theatre arts is twofold. It is not merely to overcome the difficulties of space and distance, but also to accomplish

the purpose of selection itself in emphasizing the significant or essential as against the insignificant or subordinate. Psychologically, its effect on the audience is to signal the fact that the selection and emphasis are intentional on the artist's part, not accidental. The degree of exaggeration should be just enough to accomplish that purpose, and no more. The degree will vary with the physical conditions of the theatre, the nature and style of the play, and the importance (at the moment) of the actor's part. But too much is almost worse than too little, and inevitably suggests over-acting.

CODIFIED SYMBOLISM

The term "codified symbolism" is obviously tautological, since a symbol is not a symbol unless it has a certain code value in conveying meaning; but I use it to emphasize the fact that in pantomime, as already suggested, the codification of symbols has been pretty extensively developed. All communicative arts are codified, in the sense that communicative symbols must have approximately the same meaning for the sender and the receiver if they are to be understood. Codes and conventions change, of course, but are most effective communicatively when they do not change too rapidly.

A well-selected bodily action may have communicative value on the stage because it is instinctive and naturally indicative of a common meaning; or it may have value because it has been long accepted as part of a code habitually familiar to the audience. In the present age of experimentation (and even confusion) the communicative codes of the theatre, including that of bodily action, are less universal and stable than they used to be; yet it is still safe to say that those actions which conform to an established code are more readily understood than those which express too much individuality or originality in characterization.

However, there is a close interrelation between selection and codification. In selecting the most significant actions or gestures the actor is naturally influenced by his knowledge of existing codification, and chooses the ones which have the strongest symbolic value. Conversely, when he has reason to select an action not previously codified in order to achieve originality in characterization, he will seek to establish its symbolic value as quickly as possible, first by exaggeration and then by sufficient repetition to make the action part of the code, at least for that particular play.

Thus, if he wishes to suggest a puzzled state of mind he may select the well-codified symbol of scratching his head; if he wishes to suggest comic

desperation he may select the familiar device of gritting his teeth and seizing his hair with both hands; or if he wishes to suggest sudden determination he may select the standard combination of actions by simultaneously rising from a chair, pounding his fist on an adjoining table, and lifting his chin and flashing his eyes. But if he wishes, let us say, to be somewhat more original in portraying a character who is very often in a puzzled state of mind, and to do so without the perfectly clear but unoriginal scratching of the head, he may select an action somewhat less usual and more peculiar to the total characterization he has in mind—perhaps a pulling at the lobe of one ear, or a pressing of one thumbnail into the point of the chin with the mouth open, or a nodding of the head with a vacant smile while the eyes blink unintelligently. Having selected the most appropriate symbol, he first exaggerates just enough to call attention to it, and then repeats with sufficient frequency and uniformity to establish its code significance. Audiences are quick in grasping an actor's intent when he is trying to codify his symbols; in these restless days people seem eager to freshen all sorts of conventions, or adopt new ones—hence the tremendous popularity and rapid change of popular slang. They will not readily accept symbols that are ill-chosen or unintelligible, but they will quickly accept the codification of symbols that have an initial impact of appropriateness. And since the eye is more alert than the ear, and (in the theatre, at least) subject to fewer distractions, they will catch on even more readily to the codified symbolism of actions and gestures than to that of words, and with rather less awareness of a conscious intent.

The artist best qualified to create a new style is the one who has first mastered the old; and the actor best qualified to select his own bodily actions and to codify them is the one who has first studied the symbolism of bodily action according to older codes, not only by reading up on the history of pantomime and on the Delsarte and similar "systems," but by observing carefully the movements and gestures of older actors as he sees them on stage and screen.

In observing older actors he is likely to notice the fact that they often seem to have better control of their bodies than the youngsters. They may be slowed down by age, and some of their repose may be purely self-defensive, but on the whole they are likely to show more poise and balance in their movements, and more economy and precision of expression in their gestures. Some of this may be due simply to longer experience; but some of it is due to their having been more rigorously trained, when young, in the traditional rules of stage movement and business.

TRADITIONAL RULES IN MOVEMENT AND BUSINESS

The value of traditional rules in the arts is always in dispute, and anything traditional is under constant attack from the exponents of utter freedom—which, more often than not, means freedom from the bother of learning fundamentals based on previous human experience.

In *The Art of Play Production* I cited a few of the more significant rules which all actors used to be taught in their apprenticeship—fourteen of them, to be exact. They were as follows:

1. The actor should face the audience when speaking.
2. Humorous or telling lines should be spoken straight front.
3. All important scenes should be played down stage.
4. Movement should follow straight lines.
5. An entering character should come well on stage, and not linger in the entrance.
6. When two characters enter in conversation, the one speaking should come last.
7. An exit should always be made on a line.
8. When two characters in conversation are to sit on a sofa, the one who is to talk most, or whose words are most important, should sit at the up-stage end.
9. When a character stands at stage right or left, his weight should rest on his down-stage foot.
10. When a character at right starts to walk left, he should start by taking a half-step with the left foot, followed by a full step with the right foot (and the reverse for a character at left, starting right).
11. When a character facing left is to back away right, he should shift his weight to the left foot and take his first step with the right.
12. All turns should be executed toward the audience.
13. When a character is to kneel on one knee, it should be his down-stage knee.
14. When a man and woman embrace, the man's down-stage arm should be below the woman's, his up-stage arm above.

In citing them, I attempted to trace their origins in older stage techniques, to analyze their motives, and to evaluate their usefulness in the changing techniques of the modern theatre. I pointed out that most of them had good reasons behind them, but that the reasons might no longer apply, or might apply only under certain conditions. Some of my readers apparently grasped only the rules and not the explanations; they accused me of attempting to cramp the freedom of the modern actor with cut-and-

dried ritual. I shall not repeat the explanations here; the actor who is interested may read them in the other book. It is sufficient to say that the only value to be looked for in such rules is one that rests on a continuance of some rational principle not invalidated by changing conditions. No procedure can be considered sound merely because it is traditional; but the wise observer will understand that few things last long enough in this life to become traditional unless there is some reason for them in the first place. What we really want to know is whether, under changing conditions, the reason still applies.

The greatest value of these and other old-time procedures is not in their rigid application as rules of art, but in their disciplinary effect in training the actor to select his actions with appropriateness and without distraction. I have directed many hundreds of rehearsals, most of them with at least some inexperienced players, and I have hardly ever got through a rehearsal without being distressed or interrupted by quite unnecessarily clumsy, awkward, obtrusive, distracting, inappropriate movements that would never have been committed by old-school actors trained under traditional rules. Perhaps the old ways were "stagey"; but nothing in this world is (to my eye) more obtrusively stagey than the totally untrained actor who is not at home on the stage—who seems always to have his weight on the wrong foot when it is time to walk, trips over his own feet by starting with the wrong one, and calls painful attention to himself by making his turns away from the audience when any regular theatre-goer would naturally expect him to turn the other way.

Body Training for Acting

Most people who give any thought to acting at all recognize the fact that the actor needs a flexible, responsive, well-trained body if he is to have any freedom of expression on the pantomimic side. There is some difference of opinion as to the relative values of dancing, fencing, eurhythmics, athletics, and so on, for accomplishing the purpose; but there is general agreement that the conditions of modern life do not equip the average boy or girl for expressive bodily action on the stage without some kind of special instruction. Put a high-school or college youth accustomed to sweater, slacks, and sport shoes into satin knee-breeches, lace cuffs, and jabot, and he will hardly know how to walk or to sit down. Take a modern girl accustomed to slouching and shuffling about in rolled-up overalls and loose, wedge-soled sandals and ask her to walk with grace and elegance in a Victorian drawing-room play and the result is about what you would expect.

Body training for the actor may be addressed to either of two quite different objectives. It may be specific training, designed to give him definite skills for use in certain parts or types of parts—training in fencing, for example, or in boxing, or in dancing, or even in piano-playing, as activities that he may some time have to portray on the stage. On the other hand it may be body training in the larger and more general sense, to improve his muscular control and coördination, his rhythmic feeling, his poise, his grace of movement, his resourcefulness in gesture, his sense of balance, and his general flexibility and responsiveness. Certain activities, such as fencing or dancing, may be useful in respect to both objectives; but he should not forget that both objectives exist, and that his personal needs must be analyzed in respect to both.

TRAINING FOR SPECIFIC SKILLS

An actor can hardly have too many skills, for he never knows when one of them may be useful. A professional actor may very well win (or lose) an engagement according to his ability (or inability) to fence, to dance, to sing, or to play some musical instrument. Nobody can be skillful at everything, and lack of any particular skill need be no bar to a stage career, though it may disqualify an actor for some particular part. In the talent pools of New York and other large cities there is a good deal of specialization, and many an actor lands a part because he is listed as a juggler, an acrobat, a toe dancer, or a xylophone player—or, for that matter, because he has a glass eye, a wooden leg, or cauliflower ears. But he may wait years for the right part. The amateur, not dependent upon engagements for a living, can perhaps afford to have fewer skills; yet even he will do well to cultivate as many as possible if he wishes to be useful in a variety of parts. He might even capitalize a glass eye or a wooden leg, but I do not recommend his acquiring them for the purpose.

Among the skills properly classified as bodily action, dancing is one of the most generally useful to the all-round actor. Social dancing, including the older forms suitable to eighteenth- and nineteenth-century plays as well as current styles, is the type most likely to be expected of an actor not specifically chosen for his dancing ability in a specialized part. Most young people are familiar with the latest dances of their own set, but the more at home they are in the styles of today the more helpless they are when asked to do a Viennese waltz, a minuet, a schottische, or a two-step. For several hundred years, down to World War I, the social dances of most periods and most nations, despite great variation in pace and mood, had one element in common: people danced rhythmically, in time to the music. Shortly

after World War I, and possibly as a result of the chaos and confusion resulting from it, social dancing changed fundamentally. What at first passed for "syncopation" degenerated into mere formless dragging, and two generations of young people have been raised to a concept of dancing more social (and sexual) than rhythmic. Nine-tenths of the dancers one sees today in the hotels and restaurants clutch each other and sway languidly, timing their movements to their partners but not to the music, and dragging each other around with no regard whatever to the rhythm, even of the drums. The much-maligned "jitterbugs" were almost the only social dancers between the two wars who paid any attention to the beat of the music; happily, the recent revival of square-dancing in some regions seems to promise better things for the future. The young actor whose concept of dancing is a maudlin drag has much to learn if he is to take his part in a stage protrayal of a minuet or a lancers. It is not just that he does not know the steps, but that his whole experience has been negative.

If he has had some training in stage dancing he will be somewhat better equipped. But much of that is also specialized in current modes. Training in tap-dancing is good preparation for tap-dancing and not much else. Training in the modern American form of ballet will help him if he is to take part in "musicals" on the order of *Oklahoma!* or *Brigadoon*. Training in classic ballet will have little practical application, though it will do more for his habitual grace and body control than some other types; while training in what is called "the modern dance" will be helpful chiefly on the pantomimic side, and will do less to teach either grace or rhythm. In other words, most of the special forms will be useful as preparation for their own kind of thing, and their value will be measured by the probability of his having to use them.

Next to dancing, the most useful body training is doubtless fencing. Many of the older dramas involve swordplay of one sort or another, and an actor who has had no instruction in fencing feels very much at a loss when asked to play a part calling for such action. Unfortunately, most instruction in fencing available today is in terms of the romanticized Italian style, involving much lively footwork, but employing only light foils in a highly technical game of lunge and thrust. It is good exercise to develop grace and poise, and good preparation for parts in plays calling for that style, but historically and dramatically quite wrong for many period plays—particularly those belonging to the periods when men flailed each other with huge two-handed swords, or to periods (like the Elizabethan) when they used two swords, cutting and thrusting with a hefty double-edged sabre in one hand and parrying with a short sword or dagger

in the other. The actor who sets out to learn fencing as a stage skill should seek an instructor who knows the history of fencing and of its conventional-ization on the stage. The usual fencing-team coach will be of doubtful help. Dramatically, it is better to be technically imperfect in the right style than almost perfect in the wrong one. When a play calls for two-handed fencing, few people will know whether the actor is doing it with high skill or not, but they will grasp and enjoy the imaginative suggestion. If he substitutes conventional foil fencing, he loses the authentic flavor; and if he is less than an expert with the foils there are sure to be fencers in the audience who will spot his imperfections. But whatever the style called for, he is likely to rise to it more effectively if he has at least had a sword in his hand before.

A little experience in acrobatic tumbling will do the young actor no harm. Not that he is so likely to be assigned the part of an accomplished acrobat, but he may well have to take part in rough-and-tumble scenes that involve physical falls, and he will not only do them more easily and convincingly if he has been trained for it, but will be much less likely to break his neck.

No physical accomplishment is to be despised as part of an actor's training, since his profession comprehends the whole of life, but those men-tioned are the ones he can least afford to neglect entirely.

Body Training for General Responsiveness

Apart from special skills for use in specific parts, most actors need a good deal of body training just to make their bodies flexible and responsive, and to give them good coördination and control under the difficult con-ditions of stage work. I have mentioned some of the difficulties young actors have even in such simple matters as learning to walk with grace and dignity. Some of these may be due to current bad habits, others simply to lack of experience. Others, undoubtedly, are due to the nervous and emotional strains of acting itself; and the awkwardness of beginners in acting is not a passing manifestation of this decade or century but some-thing which has always plagued them and probably always will. As every director knows, it is one thing to suggest to an actor a piece of appropriate action or an expressive gesture, and quite another to get him to perform it without an appearance of pain or distress.

Many of the difficulties actors experience in bodily action and gesture are the result of acquired inhibitions. Children are generally much freer in bodily expression. Yet even children begin to acquire certain inhibitions at an early age, especially those related to embarrassment or self-conscious-

ness. You can see the process working when a child is play-acting in the nursery with much bodily expression and then suddenly discovers that a grown person is watching him. If he does not balk and refuse to go on at all, he becomes awkward and inhibited. The inhibitions of self-consciousness, plus those of social discipline, are cumulative over the years, and by the time the individual is old enough to be considering acting as a serious study he is likely to have lost a good deal of his natural freedom.

Body training for the actor must therefore be largely corrective, designed to free him physically from acquired inhibitions, overcome self-consciousness, and restore the natural coördinations of childhood. It is not so much a matter of developing abnormal or unusual bodily skills as of recapturing those that are his normal birthright.

For this kind of training also I recommend dancing as the best all-round exercise. But there are many kinds of dancing, and they are not all equally useful. Present-day social dancing is probably the least useful, and is actually detrimental to the rhythmic sense. Tap-dancing is good exercise, and effective in developing the sense of rhythm, but is rather too cramped and specialized to be very helpful in restoring general freedom of bodily action. Training in classic ballet is helpful if not carried to excess; it certainly encourages grace of movement and muscular coördination. But since to be effective for its own purposes it must be started early and continued over a long period, it often *is* carried to excess so far as the needs of an all-round actor are concerned; an actor who has had too much ballet training is apt to show it in all his movements, springing about the stage a little too lightly and striking graceful poses a little too readily. This is true in a lesser degree of training in modern ballet. The modern dance, being more directly pantomimic, is much more helpful in teaching the actor pantomimic gesture, including the process of simplification, exaggeration, and codification; but like modern social dancing it maintains a close association with blurred, amorphous rhythms, and it is my observation that actors with training in the modern dance often have a bad sense of timing in their stage movements.

The best kind of dancing for its indirect effect on the actor's poise, timing, and freedom of bodily action, is stage dancing in the greater variety of styles and rhythms current in the last quarter of the nineteenth century and the first quarter of the twentieth—supplemented, perhaps, by various styles of folk dancing or square dancing. Such dancing would involve so many different paces and kinds of movement that the actor would be in no danger of falling into any one mannerism; their only point of similarity would be that all would teach him poise, freedom, bodily

balance, and precision in timing. The experience might well include the easier types of soft-shoe dancing, buck-and-wing, line and figure dancing, waltzing in strict tempo, stage versions of the polka and schottische, perhaps some semi-acrobatic dancing, and so on. Paces should include slow and fast waltz time, two-step, one-step, cake-walk time, lancers, polka, Irish jig, Highland fling, and especially schottische time, one of the very best paces to teach a strong bodily sense of rhythm. There are dozens of other good ones, and variety is highly desirable. Modern rhythms need not be excluded, even the blurred ones; but the young actor cannot afford to let them enslave him.

A special pattern of rhythmic body training for the stage was highly popularized a few years ago under the name of "Dalcroze Eurhythmics" (after its originator), and is still taught in many schools of acting. It had undoubted merits, but its vogue seems rather on the decline, perhaps largely because the system was so highly specialized. Certainly it was most effective when combined with many other exercises.

Athletic activities in general, chosen with variety and moderation, are obviously helpful in developing the actor's body and strengthening his coördinations. Some of these, however, are also highly specialized, and if carried to the point necessary for individual prowess may give the actor more mannerisms than freedom. Everybody is familiar with the characteristic round-shouldered slouch of the football player, not always an asset on the stage. The track champion often shows a high-strung tension which is of doubtful value to the actor. The accomplished swimmer learns reversed breathing rhythms not helpful to voice control. The overtrained fencer may have some of the same mannerisms as the ballet dancer, suitable enough for some plays and parts, but not for all. Tennis is perhaps the best game to develop bodily agility and balance of the sort useful to the actor; but a well-designed system of setting-up exercises is even better—though not so pleasurable as a game.

A reasonable amount of military training (especially when combined with daily setting-up exercises) is decidedly helpful in building good carriage, poise, and sense of rhythm—all desirable qualities for the actor. When the returning G.I.'s of World War II went back to college in company with high-school graduates who had never had such training, their superiority in the qualities mentioned (and also for the most part in good manners) was plainly evident to their teachers. Opponents of military training profess to believe that it makes stiff, brainless automatons of young men; but after watching the veterans of two World Wars readjust themselves to civilian activities (including acting) I am convinced that

most Americans and all actors would be greatly benefited by some experience in it.

Doubtless there are many other forms of body training that would benefit the actor, however unrelated they may seem to his particular task. It is also possible for him to devise some special exercises more directly addressed to the training of his body in pantomimic action and meaningful gesture. They are likely to be most effective if designed or chosen by the individual to fit his own needs; but the following suggestions may give the student a hint of the possibilities; the list is not intended to be at all comprehensive, nor equally suitable for all actors, but rather to illustrate the kind of list he might make for his own use:

1. Practice walking as a child, a youth, a middle-aged person, an elderly person, and a senile invalid; as a happy person, a thoughtful person, an excited person, a grief-stricken person, an angry person, a stealthy person, an arrogant person; as a person in pain, or weary, sick, lame, partly paralyzed, intoxicated, drugged, or stunned by shock.

2. Practice sitting down and rising under similarly varied circumstances.

3. Practice walking with a heavy bundle balanced on the head.

4. Practice walking back and forth between stage right and stage left, stopping occasionally at one of those positions; try resting the weight now on the down-stage foot, now on the up-stage foot; see which makes for ease and grace in starting and in turning; keep face and body turned partly toward the audience most of the time. Don't look at your feet; look over the heads of the imaginary audience.

5. Practice entering the stage from right, left, and center; from an open archway; from an open door, closing it after you; from a closed door, opening it and closing it; from a door swung down stage and off; from one swung down stage and on, and so on. It is not necessary to practice with real doors; use the imagination.

6. Practice indicating in pantomime or sign language (without words or lip movements) such simple ideas as: "I am hungry," "I am tired," "What brings you here?" "What shall I do next?" "Who is that?" "I give up!" "How's that again?" "You louse!" "What's the use?" "Please don't hurt me!" and so on.

7. Practice walking in every available kind of footwear—high heels, low heels, shoes too big, shoes too small, heavy boots, light slippers, sandals, moccasins, and so on.

8. Practice walking, sitting down, and rising in every sort of garment—long trousers, knee breeches, plus-fours, shorts, slacks, overalls, long skirts, ankle-length skirts, short skirts, hoop skirts, hobble-skirts, kilts, dressing gowns, and so on. Practice with chairs or sofas of different heights. Practice with different impedimenta, such as canes, swords, crutches, handbags, knitting bags, heavy burdens, and so on.

9. Practice the gestures accompanying a long speech, or harangue, thinking but not uttering the words. Practice them as different characters might have made the speech—Washington, Lincoln, Theodore Roosevelt, Bryan, Coolidge, Hoover, Huey Long, Hitler, Mussolini, Henry A. Wallace, Colonel Blimp, or Senator Snort.

10. Practice exaggerating your own movements to the point of burlesque. Walk with exaggerated dignity, exaggerated bravado, exaggerated timidity, and so on. Try to cultivate freedom through exaggeration, with the tongue in the cheek. There is no better way to break down one's self-conscious inhibitions.

The cultivation of a reasonably responsive body and reasonable skill in expressive bodily action on the stage is no more an exact science or a prescribed ritual than the cultivation of a good voice and good diction. It is rather a matter of intelligence, common sense, and a great deal of application. Like everything else, it is much harder for some than for others. But in freeing the body, as in freeing the imagination, one must learn the trick of conquering inhibitions and "wearing the heart on the sleeve." It cannot be done secretively.

CHAPTER XVII

Performance

TO SOME actors public performance is just a continuation of rehearsals with a little added excitement and a feeling of satisfaction in the rewards of appreciation and applause. To others it is a terrifying ordeal, fraught with dangers of stage fright, of forgetting lines, of not doing as well as expected. To still others it is a welcome release from the boredom of rehearsals, the opportunity at last to show off ability by beginning to act. There are some actors who go all to pieces at the first performance, revert to faults the director thought he had ironed out weeks before, and develop new ones under the temptations created by audience response. There are others who never seem able to do their best—even with honest effort— until the audience is in.

It is well for the young actor to take stock of himself and consider whether he is inclined to run to extremes in any of these directions. If the first performance is just another rehearsal to him, either he is lacking in sensitivity or he has been remarkably successful in acting at rehearsals with full imaginative completeness. If he is unduly alarmed at the first performance it may be merely because he is a beginner experiencing stage fright for the first time—in which case it may comfort him to know that most of our great actors suffer the same discomfort on a first night, even after forty years of experience. Or it may be because he is thinking too much about himself and whether he will make a good impression, and too little about his imaginative characterization. Or—heaven forbid!—it may be because he has neglected his responsibilities, is not really sure of his lines, and has good reason to distrust himself. If he is relieved that the boredom is over, and delighted that he can now begin to act, he may well ask himself whether his attitude at rehearsals has been all it should be, and whether he is not putting a foolish trust in so-called inspiration, or relying too much on the audience to supply the imagination for him.

In general, the young actor who runs to none of these extremes but experiences a few symptoms of each has most reason to be encouraged. He is probably normal. The actor who is unmoved by the presence of the first audience and the one who is unreasonably alarmed by it are not in as

happy a situation, but there is no reason to think that either is incurable. The one who has been impatient of rehearsals and who is confident that he will be all right as soon as he "feels" the audience is the one who has most cause to worry—and is least likely to do so. He may well be the victim of too much shallowness of purpose, too much egotism, too much vanity, or too little imaginative sincerity in working up his part. His worst danger is that he may cut loose too violently when the audience is in, yield too easily to audience response, mistake every little success for a flash of genius, and begin "mugging" the audience at the expense of sincere characterization. Every experienced director knows that such an actor is the hardest to restrain, and the one most likely to become a self-exploiting virtuoso instead of a real artist.

The Approach to Performance

As the opening night draws near, there are some things an actor can do to ease the shock of transition from rehearsal to performance.

For one thing he can begin to rely less on the director and more on himself. A wise director will coöperate in this by finishing his detail work early, sparing the actors unnecessary interruptions in the last few rehearsals, and encouraging their sense of imaginative continuity by putting them largely "on their own." Actors of experience appreciate this opportunity. An actor need not feel that he is forbidden to consult with the director or seek help from him during the last rehearsals and first performances; but he should remember that directors are busy and harassed people at that stage of the proceedings, bothered by endless questions from carpenters, electricians, property men, costumers, business staff workers, press agents, reporters, photographers, and friends trying to wangle tickets or special favors, and that their answers to actors are likely to be more hurried and less helpful than they might have been earlier. It is just as important as ever that the actor should be part of the team and not a lone wolf; but he should realize that it is now time to accept his responsibilities and carry on without further coddling or nursing.

It seems childish to say that the actor should move heaven and earth to be sure of his lines before the opening performance, since he ought to have done that long before. But many an actor who should know better seems willing to take a chance on the fact that he has got through a rehearsal or two without prompts and to neglect his lines in the critical days and hours before the opening night. Many a time I have seen an actor who was letter perfect three weeks before the opening go off his lines badly at the first performance—or perhaps at the second or third.

This comes of ignoring two things: the disruptive effect of first-night excitement, and the simple fact that the human memory is really a progressive forgettory, a leaky sieve which loses part of its content every day unless more is put in than leaks out. The actor who stops studying as soon as he thinks he knows his lines, and relies on the last few rehearsals (often with two or three days' interval between) to keep him up in them, is inviting trouble. A "smart aleck" will scoff at the suggestion, but a smart actor will run over his lines, preferably with someone to read cues, at least once a day for the last week or two before the opening, no matter how well he thinks he knows them; and he will continue the practice after performances begin. It may seem an unnecessary waste of time, but there is nothing else so soothing to the nerves, or so effective in providing that little extra boost of confidence which makes for a firm, sure performance. Even the seasoned professional can blow up in his lines after two hundred consecutive performances; but he is far less likely to do so if he gives them a quick run-through every afternoon.

Another thing the actor can do as the opening night draws near (if the matter is in his hands at all) is to see that his costume is ready, and right, that his make-up problem is solved, that any hand props he may have to use are properly selected and properly placed on the stage or in the wings. He should not make a nuisance of himself by usurping responsibilities, countermanding the orders of the stage manager or arguing with costumers or property men. But there is a middle course between that and the feeble dependence of some actors on having everything done for them by somebody else, or handed to them at the proper instant by a mind reader. Any good property man, for example, is only too glad to have a clear understanding with the actor who is to use certain hand props as to where and how he wants them placed and just when he will need them.

In a well-equipped and well-organized theatre provision is made for emergency supplies such as first-aid bandages, antiseptics, cough drops, indigestion pills, and the like; also for scissors, pins, needles, spare buttons and other items often needed in a hurry. The wise actor will not trust to such provision, however, and will have his own emergency equipment, appropriate to his own costume, habits, and condition of health. Women, with their elaborately equipped handbags, are less apt to be caught off guard in such matters than men; but any actor will enjoy his first-night performance a great deal better if his kit includes his favorite gargle, a good antacid stomach settler, a soothing eyewash to take excess make-up out of his eyes, a strong antiseptic for cuts or scratches, some gauze and adhesive tape, a spare shirt and collar, spare buttons to match any he

might possibly lose, needles, thread, safety-pins, a nail file, a hand mirror, a spare belt, a spare tie, spare shoelaces and garters, an extra handkerchief or two, a hairbrush, a whisk broom, some cold cream and tissue for removing make-up (whether he does his own make-up or not), soap, towels, and anything else that might be urgently needed just before or after curtain time. Though no emergency may arise, the sense of security that results from such preparedness is highly conducive to an unworried and imaginative performance.

BACK-STAGE MORALE

Many great actors and directors have recognized the need for some technique to offset the demoralizing effect of back-stage confusion, especially in the first few performances. Salvini is said to have made a practice of dressing and making up in time to spend an hour pacing up and down before a performance in order to work into the character imaginatively. Stanislavsky not only did something similar himself, but discouraged his actors from small talk back stage and urged them to spend some time meditating in character in order to "get into the circle." Some directors will permit no conversation in the green room except about the play; others urge the actors to stay in their dressing rooms until called, either going over their parts or thinking themselves into character. Still others take the opposite view, and urge their players not to think of their parts at all until just before they enter, on the theory that they are less apt to be unduly tense that way.

The truth is that no fixed ritual in the matter is wise; there are too many variables. When the actors are well rehearsed and sure of their parts the tension of excitement and expectation may actually key them up and result in a very good first performance—in which case the greatest danger to their morale may be that of a reaction and letdown in the second or third. On the other hand, if they are shaky on their lines and the last few rehearsals have been ragged it is usually better for them to come early, keep calm, stay in their dressing rooms, and go over their parts. Much depends on the type and mood of the play, the methods of rehearsal, the arrangement of the theatre, the position of the green room (if any), the size and comfort of the dressing rooms, the type of setting, the amount of bustle and confusion back stage, the method used for calling the players for their entrances, and so on. For the individual actor much depends on the nature and length of his part, on whether he is on stage at the first curtain, on how and when he makes his first entrance, on whether he has to achieve a subtle mood immediately on entering, or merely an obvious one. But the

greatest variable of all is the individual temperament of the actor. Some actors can joke and gossip off stage and then jump instantly into a fully imaginative mood and walk on the stage completely in character; others must have time and freedom from distraction in order to work into the mood.

The back-stage morale of the actor is greatly enhanced when the organization is good. When he gets the impression that the stage manager knows his business, that the crew is efficient, that the lights will work smoothly and surely, the off-stage effects occur promptly on cue, and the curtain go up and come down on time, he feels a comforting sense of reassurance, and is much more likely to play with smoothness and confidence.

Perhaps the most important phase of back-stage organization in its direct effect on the actor is the call system, which may be anything from a hit-or-miss dependence on a thoughtful prompter to an elaborate setup of microphones and loud speakers. The traditional method is the direct one by which a "call-boy," employed for the purpose, summons the actor from his dressing room for each entrance, either on instructions from the prompter or on the basis of a special "call sheet"; if the call-boy himself is reliable this is still the best system, especially when double-checked by the prompter. In some modern theatres the prompter does the calling by means of push buttons, sounding electric buzzers in individual dressing rooms—a fine system if the prompter is careful to push the right button, and the actor happens to be in his dressing room at the time. In other modern theatres, chiefly non-commercial ones, loud speakers are placed in green room, lavatories, and dressing rooms, with microphones on the stage to pick up cues as spoken by the actors. When such a system is turned on continuously it defeats its own purpose after one or two performances, for the actors get weary of listening to it and learn to shut it out of consciousness; a better plan is to have the signal cut in by the prompter just for one or two lines at a time on marginal cues in the prompt book, so spaced as to give each actor one or two well-timed warning cues for each entrance.

But whatever the system used—or lack of system—the actor should teach himself to coöperate with it rather than to depend upon it. Calls are not intended to relieve him of responsibility, but merely to check on him and reduce the chance of his embarrassing others through forgetfulness and incompetence. It should be a matter of pride with him not to need them. The danger point is not usually the first performance, but the third or fourth. The anxiety of the first night keeps him exceptionally alert; but if he escapes disaster for two or three nights he jumps to the conclusion

that he knows the routine thoroughly now, and has no further need to worry. That is when he lets down, allows somebody or something back stage to distract him, and misses an entrance cue.

My own most embarrassing moment on any stage occurred in the fourth performance of a production of Shakespeare's *A Midsummer Night's Dream*. We were using blackout curtains between scenes, and had made an extra division just before the comic love scene between Titania and Bottom (with his ass's head). Playing Bottom, I had taken my place in the darkness, and as the lights came on I said my line and began my "woosel cock" song, expecting Titania to interrupt with her famous exclamation, "What angel wakes me from my flowery bed!" Peering through the ass's mouth, however, I was horrified to discover that no Titania was sleeping on the flowery bed. Titania, it developed, was out in the "prop" room playing poker with the stage crew, and had missed her call. I had to prolong my solo rather painfully while our alert Puck dashed off to summon the fairy queen, who finally spoke her line, not rising from the flowery bed but sprinting breathlessly on from the wings! In the first three performances she had been perfectly reliable; but last night's perfection is of no effect on tonight's audience in the theatre of living actors.

It is debatable whether actors with reasonably good imaginations need a great deal of magic hocus-pocus about working up and maintaining the mood and feeling of the character back stage, either before or during the performance; but the example just given—by no means an unusual one—illustrates a much more practical reason why the actor should keep his mind on his job every minute of the time till the final curtain is down. He should do so to guard against the ever-present hazard of distraction, which may cause him to miss a cue regardless of how well he knows his part or how many times he has played it. Unless some utterly foolproof call system exists to summon him for his next entrance—no matter where he is, or what he is doing, or how long his "wait"—he should allow nobody to tempt him into irrelevant conversation or any other seemingly harmless diversion. This is a real problem, and it has nothing to do with any mystic notion about "getting into the circle," or "being" the character spiritually or emotionally.

The temptation is strong among actors—even veterans—to make casual remarks to each other when waiting in the wings. As they listen to the lines being said on stage, noting slight changes in rhythm or inflection, and in audience response, as compared with those of previous performances, their very interest in their work heightens this temptation. But every actor should remember that the briefest and seemingly most harmless comment

to another actor may divert that actor's attention at the precise instant when his cue is spoken and cause him to miss his entrance or be late for it. A good rule is: Do not speak to another actor unless you know his next cue as well as your own, and know positively that there is a safe margin of time both for your comment and his answer. A still better rule is: Do not speak to another actor waiting for his cue, even if you are sure there is plenty of time.

The actor waiting for his entrance cue is subject to another temptation, quite likely to bring disaster to himself as well as to others. That is the temptation to think ahead and start mentally rehearsing the coming scene. It is one of the best methods known for missing the cue itself, and also for making the actor jittery and uncertain during the scene. He should listen for the cue, of course; and before that for a warning cue several lines ahead. He should be clear in his mind which scene is coming, what properties he is to carry on (if any), what the mood and tempo of his entrance are to be, and what his entrance line (if any) is to be. But he should vigorously resist all temptation to anticipate anything beyond that. An actor who knows his scene perfectly well, and has been through it successfully many times, can get himself into a frightful dither by running over lines as the moment nears and suddenly discovering that he cannot remember the fourth or fifth line. Actually he would remember it well enough in its proper rhythm and context; but failing to recall it *out* of context he grows panicky, and perhaps bungles the scene quite unnecessarily.

With all its hazards, however, life back stage is, and should be, fun. In advising concentration and alertness, and warning against distraction, I do not mean to suggest that actors should get no joy and companionship out of their work, or look upon it as consecrated drudgery. To those who act only for pay or for fame it may be largely that; but to most players, and certainly to most of those in amateur and community theatres, it is a joyous adventure in creative group art. The spirit of the hobby-rider, mentioned in the chapter on Rehearsal, should be carried over into performance. There is plenty of time for social contact and group conversation before and after a performance, between the acts, and (for some players) during long waits; and there is no need to impose rigid silences on everybody all the time. The point is simply that the true hobby-rider is not, and should not be, content with anything second-rate; and that first-rate performance can only be achieved when all those concerned are fully aware of the pitfalls and thoroughly determined not to get caught in them.

Going On

As the cue comes and the actor walks out of the darkness of the wings into the glare of the lights and the presence of the audience, he moves from the secret artificiality of scene braces, lighting cables, and stage hands into a new world of collective imagination, rather terrifying to the beginner, and always a bit exciting even to the veteran. To be sure, the actor does not experience the complete visual illusion which the audience is supposed to experience, and is never entirely able to escape the mechanical evidences of artifice. He can still see some of the scene braces, the backs of some flats, various hidden lights as well as the more obvious footlights and border lights, the red exit lights in the auditorium, perhaps some lobby lights, and the unfinished or unpainted backs of some stage properties; and if he allows himself to look he can often see other actors standing in the wings, stage hands moving about, and perhaps the prompter waiting ominously for him to forget his lines. But one of the first things he must learn is *not* to look at such things—rather to ignore them. In this he is helped by the brightness of the stage lights and the relative obscurity off stage.

There is a peculiar psychological transformation as one goes on stage, never quite at its maximum in rehearsal, but felt at its full value when the audience is in. It is hard to describe, and harder to analyze; but it is very ancient and significant in theatrical history. Having experienced it, one begins to understand the magic circle which primitive man drew on the ground to separate the mystic unreality of his ceremonials from the commonplace surroundings of the world outside. The world of illusion and the world of reality are never unrelated; yet they are never quite the same thing, and between them is a sharp line that somehow feels like a wide gulf. Outside, looking in, the actor in the wings is aware of the crude realities at his elbow, but thinks of the doings on stage as the illusion. As he walks into the scene, however, things seem to reverse themselves; the world of illusion becomes imaginatively real for him, and the back-stage mechanics of realism fade into the obscurity of half-forgotten unreality.

One need not regard this experience as something occult or supernatural, to be treated as sacred, and spoken of in awesome, reverential tones; but there can be no doubt of its importance as a manifestation of imagination at work. That it is a good thing for the theatre there can, likewise, be no doubt; if it were bad, the theatre would have perished long ago. But it does have certain dangers for the inexperienced or unstable actor. When

its impact is too sudden or unexpected, he may be flustered and disconcerted; he may lose composure or forget lines. When it proves too enticing, it may tempt him into "mugging," "gagging," or overacting of one sort or another. It is precisely because actual performance before an audience is inescapably different from rehearsal in its psychological relationships that I have urged throughout this book the importance of adequate rehearsal, and of whole-hearted acting at rehearsals. True, no rehearsal recognized as such, even with some invited guests, can bring quite the same sense of stepping into the magic circle of illusion as a full-fledged performance; but the closer the approximation achieved in rehearsal, the less the demoralization of the actor at the first performance, and the greater the chance that the first few performances will be smooth and sure. The release of the actor's sense of illusion as he steps on the stage is after all only a release of what has already been thoroughly prepared for; it cannot create for him something that is not there. It cannot tell him what the play is about if he has not read it; it cannot reveal the author's conception of the character if he has not studied it; it cannot teach him his lines or business if he does not know them. In other words, the artistic and inspirational stimulus in the presence of the audience is in direct proportion to the preparation that has been made for it in rehearsal.

Once the actor is on stage he is surrounded by certain dangers and temptations against which he ought to be warned. Yet he should also be warned against the mistake of letting his mind dwell on them too fearsomely, to the detriment of his imaginative freedom. Some of them can be wholly or partly conquered in rehearsal, but some lurk unsuspected in the presence of the audience.

To begin with a brutally practical matter, the nervous actor making his first entrance can very easily spoil it by tripping over the doorsill. Interior doorways in real houses do not, ordinarily, have sills, but doors in interior stage settings do; and even open doorways have pieces of strap iron across them to keep the flats from warping and make them easy to handle when being moved. Whether these obstructions are covered by rugs or exposed, actors who drag their feet and actresses trying to manage high heels often trip over them, sometimes after years of experience. Beginners are always warned against them, and usually learn to negotiate them quite well in the last few rehearsals. But "on the night," as the first entrance brings a sense of imaginative reality, the eager actor too often forgets the wretched things, and stumbles after all. A comedian may get a laugh at almost any other time by pretending to trip over something, but when he trips on his first entrance a theatre-wise audience correctly diagnoses it as clumsiness

on the actor's part rather than the character's, and does not consider it funny. In *The Cherry Orchard*, Tchekhov lets his comic character Epikhodov stumble on his first entrance and drop the nosegay he is carrying; audiences sternly refuse to laugh at that because it looks to them like accidental bungling rather than legitimate comedy. It is doubtful whether stumbling has ever been very good comedy anyhow since its first thousand years, but certainly the most inappropriate time for it—and the most likely—is on the nervous actor's first entrance.

A second practical hazard is that of unexpected change. Directors and technicians are inclined to be perfectionists, and after sending the actors home from the last dress rehearsal they may work all night changing a lighting effect here, the position of a rug there, the angle of a chair or a table or a divan somewhere else; or they may decide to have the actress who has been wearing a red dress change to a green one, or make up their minds that some piece of furniture is unsatisfactory after all and send out a hurry call for something entirely different. And in all likelihood they will forget to warn the actor, who will not know about it until he walks on the stage in the presence of the audience and is suddenly confronted with something strangely different. After six or eight performances most actors can take such changes in stride and not be bothered by them, especially if there have been several of them from night to night; but unforseen changes at the first performance are disconcerting to say the least. And that is precisely when they are most likely to happen, since the dress rehearsal so often reveals faults previously overlooked.

It is not a bad idea therefore, for the actor to look the set over before the act begins just to make sure that furniture and properties are in their familiar places. He should not get in the way of the crew when they are setting the stage, nor disobey any rules the director may have set up about loitering on the stage; but he can usually manage to find out about any important change if he tries. And if that is not possible, he should make his first entrance with a mental reservation to expect the unexpected and not be too much flustered by it.

A similar reservation should, in fact, be the actor's constant companion while on stage, for it is always the unexpected developments which make trouble in performance—unexpected sights or sounds, unexpected changes in the rhythms or inflections of other players, unexpected audience reactions, unexpected cuts and prompts, unexpected failure of lighting changes, off-stage effects, and so on. An actor who is letter perfect and quite comfortably sure of himself when things are going smoothly in their accustomed rhythm can go completely blank in his mind when another

actor forgets a line or gives a wrong cue. Since the possibilities are too numerous to be foreseen and prepared against in detail, his best defense is a kind of general resignation, a fatalistic awareness that anything can happen and probably will, and that there is no use being apprehensive about it. After all, acting is just a game, a sophisticated form of play, to be carried through with the hobbyist's determination to do his best, but with the thought that the audience is in the game, too, and not disposed to look upon a slip of tongue or memory as an unpardonable sin. People will readily forgive a slip from an amateur because he is an amateur; and they will forgive one from a professional in their pleasure at discovering that he is human and fallible just like anybody else. They will far more readily forgive an accidental slip which they attribute to nervousness than they will a piece of acting suggestive of poor preparation, bad taste, or egotistic self-exploitation. If the actor has done his best to prepare well and to play his part with imaginative sincerity, he may face the possibility of bungling a line, or giving a wrong cue, or having to take a prompt, with no fear that anybody in the American theatre will demand his bloody liquidation. He should by all means try hard to avoid such disasters, but for the fun of doing well rather than the fear of consequences.

In the chapter on Rehearsing mention was made of certain bad habits often built up in rehearsal and carried over into performance, including those of inadequate voice, of looking down too much, and of looking expectantly at the prompter when in difficulty.

If the opening performance is given to a full house, almost the first difference the actor notices as he goes on stage is a change in the acoustics. A full house absorbs the sound of the voices with much less reverberation than an empty or half-empty one—the contrast being more noticeable in some theatres than in others. This affects different actors in different ways. Some, missing the echo, fear that they are not talking loud enough, and begin to shout in an effort to get the echo back; but the majority seem to react in the opposite way. They sense the fact that it is easier to be heard in a full house, and so relax too much, speaking in tones that sound weak and let down. Since the acoustics really are better in a full house the reduced tones are often audible; but psychologically they are bad because they give the audience an impression of weak or timid playing; also they allow no margin of surplus volume to take care of the coughs and sneezes and other distractions which harass the listeners. It is wise, therefore, for the actor to expect some softening of the acoustics, and to be on guard against the temptation to reduce his voice level too much.

It sometimes takes two or three performances to restore the voices to the

proper level, even though that level may have been maintained in many rehearsals. After five or six performances it is likely to slump again whenever the actors become depressed or jittery by reason of an unresponsive audience, or a disconcerting error in lines, or bad news back stage. I have seen players take the edge off a comedy by speaking in weak, inelastic tones, because word had just spread back stage of the sudden death of a beloved colleague. No actor would do this if he knew it; but it is because the tendency creeps up on him subconsciously that it seems worth while to warn him against it.

The habit of looking down too much is common with beginners, and the problem of overcoming it is sometimes rather involved. Much depends upon the lighting arrangements in a particular scene, and on the design and proportions of the theatre itself. The common practice of conducting stage rehearsals under first-border lights only, with no foots, encourages the fault; and wise directors demand bright footlights at rehearsals to discourage it. The tendency of many scenic artists to light plays without footlights puts a still stronger incentive on the actor to look at the floor, especially when most of the light is coming in a blaze from the balcony rail at just the angle to annoy him if he looks slightly upward and speaks—as the saying goes—"to the wide wide world." The actor must make up his mind that he is going to have to face bright lights a good part of his life, and must learn to do so easily, without blinking or squinting, and without looking down to avoid them. He does not have to look squarely at any one light, and it would be very bad for his eyes indeed to look directly at a high-powered spot. The trick is to look past the lights into space, at just enough difference in angle to avoid focusing the glare on the retina. In most theatres he will normally look out above the footlights and below the balcony lights or beam lights. Occasionally, in a theatre with low balcony and relatively high stage, he may have to place the "wide wide world" above the balcony.

If he has been rehearsing with footlights and has got used to looking out over them at empty seats, he may suddenly feel self-conscious at the first performance in the realization that the seats are no longer empty, and may be tempted to look down even more, between his feet and the footlights. This is not so likely to be a problem when the lights are so arranged as to make the audience quite invisible; but when the actor can see faces beyond the footlights he is likely to do one of two things; look down (or up) too much in the effort to avoid seeing them, or accept them communicatively and start "mugging"—which is worse. One of the most important and practical disadvantages of the modern tendency to abolish footlights is

that it renders the audience more visible to the actors, and increases the difficulty of maintaining æsthetic distance for the actor who does not look down.

Covering Errors and Taking Prompts

It is the natural ambition of every actor to get through a production with no slips and no prompts. Unfortunately, some express their ambition largely in wishful thinking and do not work very hard to make it a reality. Others, having naturally good memories, experience comparatively little trouble from the start, and so tend to become overconfident. Others do work hard, and master their parts thoroughly, so that they are not likely to need prompts as long as things are going smoothly. But things do not always go smoothly, and a slip on one actor's part is likely to make another actor miss a cue, even if letter perfect himself. As I have more than once indicated in this book, neither professional experience nor a long run will make an actor or actress completely immune to lapses of memory; and disaster sometimes strikes without warning or apparent reason. One of the most famous Juliets of our time forgot her lines in the boudoir scene after several hundred performances; the unexpectedness of it so disconcerted the veteran actress playing the nurse that she forgot hers also, and both sat speechless while the prompter (who had grown careless after months of inactivity) was rushing to his desk and frantically trying to find the proper page. So, no matter how often we may say that the best way to take a prompt is not to need one, it is still true that the actor may have to take one, and should therefore know how to "cover" that or any other stage emergency with the least possible distraction to the audience.

A surprising number of slips, cuts, and stage waits which seem to the actors almost cataclysmic pass quite unnoticed by the audience, so long as the actors seem unruffled and do not betray their difficulties by such giveaway actions as tapping the forehead, looking appealingly or expectantly at the prompter, or saying, "Oh!—Yes!" when they hear the prompt. If the actors show confidence in themselves, the customers usually have confidence in them. I have seen a company confuse cues and play three or four pages of the second act in the middle of the first, and later play the same scene over again with a few improvised changes in the wording, with nobody in the audience aware of anything wrong beyond a little unexplained obscurity in the play. In the original production of *Papa Is All* I saw the actress playing Emma rush on and say, "I've brought you a letter!", and then hastily add, "I left it in the barn—I'll get it!" and dash off again, to return in about three seconds with the forgotten prop; and

as I glanced quickly about me I saw that hardly anybody in the audience had realized that the slip was not part of the play. Again and again I have heard actors call each other by the wrong character names (one of the commonest slips to which they are addicted) while not one person in fifty noticed the error—though nearly everybody does notice it if the actor realizes his own error and corrects himself. All this is not to suggest that mistakes are unimportant, or that the actor should not do everything in his power to avoid them. It is simply to point out that once a mistake is made it should be covered or ignored, and not emphasized by correction, unless the correction is absolutely vital to the continuing action of the play.

Errors of omission, cuts, slips, garbled lines, and so on, seldom do irreparable harm in themselves; they are momentary flaws, like flickers on a movie screen or ripples of interference on a television set, or misprints in a book. But a passing flaw can be turned into a serious piece of misinformation for the audience and confusion for the actors by too much eagerness in improvising or "faking" lines to cover a break. Some actors—especially those who have had an overdose of training in improvisation—are proud of their ability to "ad lib" in emergencies, and eager to indulge it at the slightest opportunity. When somebody forgets a line or fails to make an entrance promptly, they keep right on talking, maintaining the illusion and characterization, and covering the break so well that the audience is fooled completely. The great trouble is that in so doing they often ruin the play. I have seen an actor make the entire motivation of his part unintelligible by "ad libbing" in Act I a bit of information of which the character was not supposed to have knowledge until Act III—merely to cover a slow prompt. I have even known an actor to give an entire plot away prematurely by an improvised "cover line."

Actors are sensitive—as they should be—to the proper rhythm and flow of the action; and when it is interrupted by a wrong cue or a stage wait they become unduly alarmed and even panicky. A three-second wait for a prompt or an entrance seems like an eternity, and the temptation to fill in with improvisation is very strong—so strong that the actor often fails to wait for his prompt, starts improvising, and then cannot hear the prompt when it comes. I recall one amusing example when I was on stage with another actor who started garbling a line. He was close to the prompt box, and I heard the prompter give him the correct line almost instantly; but he was so busy trying to improvise himself out of difficulty that he could not hear the prompt, and kept on floundering through a tangle of words, getting more and more involved, and farther and farther from the text,

though still perfectly in character. Suddenly the prompter leaned toward him and said, firmly, "Shut up, damn ya, and I'll give ya the line!" It was inelegantly expressed, but excellent advice, applicable to many emergency situations.

Improvisation may be an excellent device in classroom work, as a means of developing the actor's imagination; but in actual performance it is a jewel-studded booby trap. In its power of maintaining illusion and keeping the actors in character, its momentary effect may be good. But the actor falling back on improvisation to cover his own or some other actor's forgetfulness must, of necessity, feel the illusion from the character's point of view—not the author's; and in doing so he is extremely apt to draw on his total knowledge of all items from all stages of the character's life and all acts of the play. He has no time to think out their plot implications and select what is harmless; and as a result he may save the illusion at the moment only to falsify the author's whole plan and purpose.

One hears a great deal of nonsense about quick thinking in emergencies, and this or that actor's cleverness in saving a situation by saying or doing just the right thing. In my observation, most cases of the kind result either from pure luck in blurting out the right thing (just as often it is the wrong thing), or from previous conditioning. It is like quick thinking in baseball, which is seldom really quick thinking at all, but quick *action*—based upon previous careful thought, and conditioned by patient daily drill in making limited choices and performing selective actions according to prescribed formulas. The actor who is most likely to do or say the right thing in an emergency is not the ready improviser, but the one who has anticipated that specific emergency and has a plan ready to meet it; or the one who has certain well-rehearsed formulas for meeting similar emergencies whenever they arise; or the one who has been through so many emergencies that he has been conditioned into doing the right thing almost by habit. The one who stops to think out a plan will probably end in panicky confusion and forget his next lines as well.

There are, of course, moments when improvisation may be helpful to cover a very long stage wait, provided the improvised matter is innocuous in itself, does not demand an answer from other players, and does not drown out the prompter. The most unassailable improvisation I ever heard came from an actor playing Snake in *The School for Scandal;* he forgot a line, said "Uh—I—uh—" and not hearing any prompt, went on with, "Oh, by the way—uh—well, no!—the less said about that the better!"— ending with a tone of finality that left the audience delightfully (and permanently) mystified, but gave the prompter two or three seconds in which

to shoot him his line before collapsing with suppressed laughter. That gem of vacuity could not be used very often, but the principle it illustrates has many applications. It was completely noncommittal, and it ended with a seemingly intentional pause which did not sound like a stage wait and did give time for the prompt.

Perhaps the most dangerous type of error in its potentialities for disrupting the performance as a whole is not that in which an actor forgets a line and gets stuck, but that in which he precipitately gives the wrong line—one that belongs in a later (and perhaps similar) scene, or one that has already been given in an earlier scene. In the latter case the actor whose cue is thus repeated may detect the error and refrain from giving his response a second time, and the prompter may cut in in time to prevent a replaying of the scene; but in the former case the actor addressed may easily be fooled by the wrong cue and give the line belonging to it, with the result that a page, or a scene, or a whole act may be cut, and the actors find themselves playing a later scene, while the prompter vainly tries to restore order. This kind of thing happens with distressing frequency in theatres where rehearsal time is inadequate, or where the players work from sides and learn their parts too literally by cue. A prompter finds it difficult to make himself heard when the actors go right on talking; but he should realize that an audible prompt is much better than a garbled play, and he should, if necessary, shout the correct line. When an actor jumps a page or more, it often cuts another actor's entrance; in that case the actor affected can sometimes rescue his comrades by going right on stage and interrupting with his proper entrance line; the first thing a good prompter does in such cases is to send the actor on for that purpose. Such an entrance may be a little irrelevant, but it seldom seems as strange to the audience as it does to the players, and it usually diverts audience attention long enough to enable the other actors to collect their wits.

Even in the best-regulated and most efficient theatres, all hands must be constantly alert to avoid these sudden and unexpected cuts and cutbacks. An actor on stage who gets what he recognizes as a wrong cue should not be trapped into giving the corresponding wrong line; he should give the correct line, even if the wrong cue makes it sound incoherent, for incoherence on one line is quickly passed over, but the garbling of whole scenes can wreck the play. Cuts are most likely to occur when two scenes have certain similarities in wording, or business, or grouping of characters.

The hazards of possible error in performance are so numerous and so infinitely varied that it would be impossible to discuss them all—or even to foresee them all. But the young actor trying to learn how to "cover"

effectively may find it helpful to ponder all, and adopt some, of the following condensed suggestions:

1. Remember that the play's the thing—not just one line, or one character.

2. Know your lines as well as it is possible to know them—by cue, by meaning, by chronological order, by mood, and by rhythm. Know the order so well that a wrong cue will not fool you, and you will know the right speech without the cue.

3. While on stage, listen to meanings and rhythms, not just to cues.

4. When an actor gives you the wrong cue, give him the right line anyhow, even if irrelevant. If you can modify it enough to conceal the irrelevancy without too much stumbling or delay, well and good—but be sure to give the next speaker his right cue.

5. When you hear other players going off their lines and giving each other wrong cues a moment before you are to speak, cut in with your own right speech at the first opportunity, making it a little louder than usual to tip off the others. Many an incipient chaos has been checked that way.

6. When you have forgotten a line without being aware of it, and suddenly hear your prompt, or realize that the stage wait is of your making, do not start violently and say your line hurriedly. Say it a little more slowly than usual, and with a little more volume, and perhaps a little more expression.

7. When you realize you have forgotten a line, do not turn and glance at the prompter, or tap your forehead, or assume a worried expression. Hold everything, and listen carefully for the prompt. If you do not hear it clearly enough to be sure of it, do not start sputtering or improvising; wait for the repeat. True, a second prompt is twice as embarrassing as the first, but a third is ten times as embarrassing; and if you drown out the second you will need the third.

8. If a prompt does not come instantly when you need it, do not be in a hurry to improvise; wait a little longer. Remember that it does not seem as long to the audience as it does to you, especially if you give no sign of panic.

9. If you *must* improvise, try business first, rather than lines. If standing, move deliberately (not suddenly) to another spot, look out a window or into a mirror, or pick up something from a table, or place a chair and sit down; if sitting, get up (not too hastily) and go for a match, or a cigarette, or to look out the window, or what not. But listen for the prompt, and do not make noises that may prevent you from hearing it. As soon as you get your prompt and have said your line, return to your routine position and business (being sure to replace any prop you have moved).

10. If the wait is too long to be covered by business, and you must improvise lines, keep them in character so far as tone and mood are concerned, but say nothing that bears on the plot—not, at least, unless you are perfectly clear about it and certain that it can do no mischief (if you were, you would probably know your proper line). Talk about the weather, or about the health of a fictitious person not mentioned in the play.

11. If the stage wait is caused by the failure of a character to enter, fill in with movement, business, or inconsequential patter, but do not try to go ahead with the play. Do *not* say, "What can be keeping So-and-So?" By the time you have said it the prompter will have said it more profanely back stage, and you will only tip off the audience. Remember, again, that the time is much shorter than it feels to you, and that somebody back stage is surely working to solve the problem. But make your actions bold and decisive, even if you do nothing more than grunt or sigh, flop in a chair, move a cushion, or straighten your tie. If you must improvise a line say it loudly and clearly; avoid the weak, timid tones that so often call attention to bad moments which would otherwise pass unnoticed.

12. When an off-stage effect like a doorbell or telephone bell fails to materialize on time, do not be in a hurry to say "I think I heard the doorbell," or "Was that the telephone?" Wait a few seconds, filling in, if necessary, with a bit of business, a yawn, or a bit of small talk, and the chances are the effect will come. A little delay does no great harm; but when an actor says, in empty silence, "Was that the telephone?" and an instant later the bell goes off like a fire alarm, illusion is shattered.

13. When a character fails to make a scheduled entrance, consider quickly whether it would be logical and feasible for you to go and call him, or to send somebody else. Do not do it unless you are sure. (The best way to meet this situation is, of course, to prepare for it in advance, by considering in rehearsal just what you would do in each case if an entering character failed to show up. That might seem like borrowing trouble; but the great thing about an emergency adequately prepared for is that it usually does not happen.)

14. Never under any circumstances allow yourself to think ahead beyond your next speech, or get to wondering whether you are going to miss a cue or bungle a line. That is the surest method known for inviting unnecessary trouble. The temptation is always greatest when you have just made one slip, or some other actor has, and your confidence has been momentarily shaken.

15. If you have two scenes in which you play from the same stage position, with similar groupings of characters, similar lighting, mood, or tempo, or similar cues, be especially alert to avoid confusing them or letting other actors confuse you. (Such scenes should be rehearsed with special care, and all points of similarity noted, so that effective mnemonic aids may be devised to forestall confusion. The problem is easily solved in advance by ingenuity and application— but *not* by mere lamentation over the similarities, or profane remarks about the author of the play.)

Naturally, nobody could be thinking of all these things all the time; if he were, he would have no time or energy left to act. Nor do these brief notes exhaust the possibilities. They are given merely to outline the problem of "covering," and no actor can master that problem in a few lessons

by learning rules. What it takes is a long period of gradual adjustment based on months and years of experience. The fifteen points here given may easily be built up to fifty—and all of them may be subject to exceptions. But perhaps they will help the actor to get started on a program of self-discipline.

ON-STAGE MORALE

At this point the reader may be thinking that I have made acting seem like a terrible ordeal—a state of torment in which the poor player frets his hour upon the stage in perpetual fear of impending disaster, concentrating all his faculties on the negative task of keeping out of trouble or squirming out of it after falling in. Let us remind ourselves that what is most complicated in detail is not necessarily most important. In all the arts, the negative considerations about what not to do, and what has gone wrong, and why, naturally lend themselves to more detailed analysis than the more general considerations of what to do, and what is going well. Indeed, it is only when something has gone wrong, or is in danger of going wrong, that we should indulge in detailed analysis at all. When things are going right it is better to trust ourselves, imaginatively and creatively, hoping that our own talents and good sense, together with what we have learned about fundamentals, will enable us to achieve something generally good.

Enough, then, of the dangers and hazards in performance, and the task of avoiding or covering errors. Let us think instead of the joy of performance; of the opportunity to do something positive, creative, artistic, and satisfying. How, let us ask, can the actor adjust his attitude while on stage to achieve a maximum of creative satisfaction for himself and of æsthetic pleasure for his audience?

To answer that question we need, not a detailed analysis, not another list of fifteen points, but a simple reminder of two or three fundamentals, discussed as generalities early in this book, and shown from time to time in many of their applications.

First of all, while on stage, the actor should strive to feel the dual nature of acting—not to think about it consciously, or analyze it, but to feel it in a general, all-over way; to feel his dual function, on two planes of existence, as artist and as instrument. This will include (as artist) the attitude of sharing appreciation of the play with the author and the audience, and (as instrument) the maintenance of æsthetic distance or detachment. The means by which these things may be done are enormously variable and the choice relatively immaterial; but the dual attitude is all in all.

Secondly, he should use his imagination for all it is worth—intensively

rather than extensively. That is, he should imagine the life of the character, and the action of the play, as vividly and whole-heartedly as possible, trying always to intensify the sincerity and richness of his concept, but always in keeping with the concept previously worked out in rehearsal and agreed upon as appropriate to the play; he should *not* allow his imagination to run wild in fresh fields, falsifying the author's concept and creating a new and unpredictable character at every performance. He should not be ashamed or afraid of feeling emotion, but should keep his intentions fixed on imagination, leaving emotion to take care of itself. And always he should strive to do his imagining in terms of the group, and as part of the group, rather than as a separate individual. When all the actors in a group succeed in doing this, the inner community of understanding built up among them does more for the imaginative truth and vitality of the performance than any actor could do by himself.

Finally, whatever the nature of the play—serious or frivolous, pleasing or painful—the actor should strive to act with vitality, enthusiasm, and enjoyment. Nothing is deadlier on the stage than indifference. Technical perfection is always desirable, but vitality is much more important. One can forgive a few imperfections in the actor who plays with conviction and imaginative enthusiasm; but there is not much to be said for the colorless actor, however smooth and efficient, who bores himself and his audience to the point of weariness.

There is perhaps a little danger that the actor who does have enthusiasm and vitality may expend too much of it too early in the play, and have too little left with which to build up the major climaxes later on. This is especially likely to happen if the director has made the common mistake of neglecting the last act in rehearsal in his eagerness to perfect the first ones. And of course there is always the danger that enthusiasm untempered by judgment may lead to overacting; but this is an obvious hazard, already given sufficient emphasis.

In general, good on-stage morale is a matter of good teamwork, good sportsmanship, and good creative imagination. But while we are still generalizing, let us again remind ourselves that good morale in performance is not to be expected unless there has been good morale at rehearsal—and plenty of rehearsal.

AUDIENCE PARTICIPATION

Doubtless the one thing which keeps the theatre of "round" actors vitally alive in the face of economically severe competition from the movies, the radio, and television, is the sense of audience participation.

Actor and audience join in a creative exercise of the imagination, and the rapport between them adds to the pleasure of both.

This is a stimulus, but also a temptation, to the actor. First of all it is a tremendous stimulus to his imagination. Many an actor who seems hopelessly dull and unimaginative in rehearsal suddenly wakes up to the meaning of his part under the impact of audience response. Inexperienced actors sometimes find this response at a first performance very unexpected, and seem almost flabbergasted to discover that their lines really have meaning, and that the play is moving or amusing. After several weeks of rehearsal in which the same lines have been repeated again and again without any audience response, and often with critical interruptions, it is easy for the players—even experienced ones—to have lost their freshness of interest, and to have fallen into the habit of repeating their words absent-mindedly, with little consciousness of their direct meaning, still less of their implications, and still less of their imaginative overtones. As a result, it may take them one or two performances to get readjusted to the full flow of meaning. Within certain limits the stimulus of audience response is highly beneficial in reawakening their imaginations and giving their acting truth and vitality.

Audience response is also a stimulus to the actor's pride in doing his work well. This, too, can be beneficial, but within even narrower limits. The hazard that goes with it is not difficult to discern. A reasonable desire to do one's best and a reasonable satisfaction in the sense of achievement when audience response indicates success are not inconsistent with sincere acting and sound art. But human nature being what it is, there is always some danger that the actor who has tasted the flattery of audience appreciation may have his ego inflated and be tempted into playing for applause rather than for imaginative truth. An actor who has begun to feel this intoxication soon finds out, unfortunately, that audience response is easy to get—provided you don't care how. It is always easier to get an audible response by "hamming" a scene than by playing it sincerely; easier to force a laugh or a tear by exaggerated buffoonery or sentimentality. It takes more skill and judgment to analyze a response than to get one; it is never easy to know whether a ready response is deep and genuine, or whether it is that quick, nervous reaction to the obvious which people give so easily and regret so sheepishly a little later. Response cannot be safely measured by volume of sound. There are always some nitwits in an audience who will laugh louder at the wrong things than the judicious will at what is really humorous; and there are always shallow sentimentalists who will sniffle loudest at the cheapest kind of tear-jerking. If

actors would keep this in mind they would not be so readily tempted into thinking that each audible response is a tribute to their own genius or skill, and into an ever-increasing competition with the other fellow to get more laughs or more applause. The danger is extremely insidious, and many an actor who has started with high ideals of artistic sincerity has allowed himself to slip so gradually into a habit of playing for applause that he has no suspicion of the extent to which he has cheapened himself.

The best defense against this sort of temptation is for the actor to keep telling himself that he is part of a team; that it includes the author and director as well as the other actors; that as a member of the team it is part of his job to make the play as enjoyable and satisfying to the audience as possible; that audience response, even to one of his own lines, is in no sense a personal tribute to him, but merely an evidence that the team as a whole is winning the game; that what he may be tempted to regard as applause for his acting may be approval of the line itself, or enjoyment of the characterization, or amusement at the situation, and may be quite as much a tribute to the author as to him. But the temptation to vanity is very strong in the life of an actor, and he needs a strong character himself to resist it.

There is another hazard in audience response especially troublesome to the beginner, and by no means confined to those of weak character. When, in the first or second performance, an actor discovers by the nature of the response that an audience attaches a meaning to his lines which he had not fully realized was there, he is likely to be grateful for the hint, and to seize upon it imaginatively as part of the common creative experience. When the meaning so discovered happens to be the right one, or one consistent with the larger meanings intended by the author, no harm is done. But audiences sometimes jump too readily at meaning not so intended, especially when not familiar with the play, and if this happens too often a pliable actor is easily misled into false interpretations. After all, the author has some right to decide what the play is about, and presumably he knows; while the audience cannot know until after it has seen the play. A wise actor, therefore, will not allow the impulses of an audience to dictate to him too completely. He will remember, too, that different audiences respond differently to the same play, and that while it is often possible to humor them by minor shifts in emphasis or tone, it is not fair to the author, nor to the integrity of the art, to allow each audience to rewrite the play to suit itself.

This danger is always greatest when a play is inappropriately chosen for the taste and temperament of the audience concerned. Audiences accus-

tomed to moronic farce are almost sure to laugh in the wrong places at a
high comedy. Audiences nourished on factual realism respond quite inaccurately, if at all, to poetic or abstract plays. Audiences used to one
kind of play may, when confronted by something different, respond only
to the novelty for novelty's sake, and persistently miss the point. Such
experiences are hard on the actor, especially in those extreme cases in
which he is asked to cast pearls before swine, or to serve swill to ladies and
gentlemen. He should welcome and enjoy every evidence of imaginative
audience participation so long as it is in key; but he should not permit
off-key responses to distort his imaginative concept, and he should not
depend upon audience response to supply him with the imaginative suggestions he has failed to supply for himself.

One thing that every actor must learn can be learned only in actual performance. That is how to adjust the action and tempo to meet unexpected
or varying audience response with as little damage as possible to the
continuity and to the poise of the actors. As we have seen, audiences do
vary greatly in their responses from night to night, even in the same community and social group. An actor may be caught off guard one night by
an unexpectedly hearty laugh on a certain line, and may have to interrupt
himself and repeat part of the next line after the laugh has died down. The
next night he may be more cautious and wait for the laugh, only to be
embarrassed by a dismal silence. These uncertainties are inevitable, and
the actor must learn to face them without being flustered. The only helpful
rule is the traditional one to "hold everything" whenever the audience
interrupts with laughter or applause, and not to go on until it begins to
die away; but only long experience will teach an actor to feel a response
coming (or not coming) the necessary fraction of a second ahead of time
to permit of his making the best allowance for it. It is most difficult to
gauge the less audible types of response—to know, for example, whether a
quiet scene is being played faster than the audience can take it, or not fast
enough to sustain interest and emotion. But actors do learn these things,
and seasoned players may do a scene in three minutes for one audience,
stretch it over four for another, and be right both times. Much of what
was said in an earlier chapter about timing and following through may be
applied to this problem.

Perhaps the most trying experience in performance is learning to face a
relatively unresponsive, or "cold," audience without being cast down and
disconcerted, and without letting it affect the quality of one's playing.
After all, the main difference between a warm and a cold audience (assuming that they are from the same social group) may be the fact that the

first includes two quick-witted hearty laughers on the sixth row, and the second does not. Any audience less audibly responsive than last night's audience seems to the nervous actor to be missing half the play, and he naturally feels exasperated and frustrated by it. But he must teach himself to realize that even the deadest audience includes some people capable of appreciating the play, and to make up his mind that he must not lessen their enjoyment by giving only a half-hearted performance himself. The less he plays for applause and the more he plays for his own imaginative satisfaction, the better his chance of resisting the effect of a cold audience and giving the quiet customers their money's worth.

The Curtain and the Call

As the moment for the final curtain approaches, many actors experience an increase of tension. If the effect is imaginative, and leads simply to a heightening of climax, it is much to be encouraged, and is likely to result in what the theatre calls "a good curtain." But the actor should not allow it to tempt him into rushing the conclusion with undue haste—a common fault in many arts—or into tipping off the audience prematurely as to the outcome.

In some plays, of course, the latter does no harm. When the ending is not intended to be mysterious or surprising but is rather the inevitable culmination of forces already understood by the audience, a growing certainty as to the outcome, pointed up by clearer, firmer playing, and even by a little increase in speed, may strengthen the final curtain. There are other plays, however, in which the effectiveness of the curtain depends upon the unexpectedness with which the ending comes about; and in such cases the actor must be careful not to anticipate, or to give the slightest hint of what he knows is about to happen. Not until the "tag" line is being actually spoken should there be any heightening of volume or emphasis which might serve as a tip-off.

However, the actor who delivers the tag line should make sure that it is heard. When it is timed to coincide with a descending curtain there is always the danger that a division of attention or a rustle of excitement as people see the curtain starting down may obscure the line; and of course there is the usual possibility of a competing cough or sneeze. It is wise, therefore, for the actor concerned to be very sure of his projection on that line, with a little extra clarity, a little extra volume, and a little extra care in facing front. The tag line of Lonsdale's *Aren't We All?* is the title of the play, the significance of which is not revealed until that moment. I have seen a performance of that play fall completely flat at the end be-

cause the actor speaking the tag line failed to give it sufficient force, clarity, and significance to carry through the breaking tension. Many other plays have surprising, amusing, pathetic, or powerful tag lines which add greatly to their total effectiveness; and the actor should take particular pains not to muff such a line. The danger of his doing so is greatly increased by the traditional stage superstition that a tag line must never be spoken in rehearsal. Violation of this rule, in the opinion of many old actors, is sure to bring disaster on the production. There is no use arguing with people who are superstitious; like those who cannot eat margerine unless it is dyed yellow, they are immune to logic. But the actor who has a tag line to speak, and who dare not risk the outraged screams of his comrades by speaking it in open rehearsal, should take pains to rehearse it extra well privately (when the jinx presumably does not apply), and to have a clear understanding with the prompter and curtain-puller as to the timing of line and curtain.

For other actors on stage at the final curtain the most important warning is just as homely and practical as that about not tripping over the doorsill at the first entrance. It is to restrain any impulse to look up at the curtain just at the critical instant, to see whether it is coming down on time; or to follow it with the eyes as it descends; or to show panic if it is a trifle late. It is wise for an actor to consider in advance just how he will behave if the curtain does happen to be a little late. He will follow through, of course, paying no attention to the curtain itself, but keeping his mind fixed on the last idea in the play. If he is sitting or standing still at the curtain line he should hold his position firmly until the curtain is down, no matter how long it seems; if he is in motion he should follow the motion through to its final objective. Actually the danger of serious delay is very slight. A final curtain is often a half-second late (which seems a long time to the actor), but it is rarely three seconds late, even in the worst-regulated theatres. The actor should not be too quick to break the picture, however, even when the curtain is all the way down, for some curtains have a way of bouncing a little before settling into place, and it is rather distressing to an audience to have the dramatic illusion of the final moment rudely shattered by a vision of running feet. It should, of course, be the stage manager's business to see that such things do not happen, but neither stage managers nor curtain-pullers are infallible, and the actor should play safe.

With the curtain down, it is all over but the curtain call (and of course the post-mortem discussion, which we shall not consider).

The curtain call is likewise the director's or stage manager's business; it is for one or the other to say, subject to theatre policy, whether there is

to be a curtain call at all, whether there is to be more than one, whether
the first is to be a tableau call repeating the stage picture as it was just
before the curtain, which actors are to take each call, whether they are to
remain in character, and how they are to be arranged. But the actor is
still responsible for the way he carries out his part of it.

Unfortunately many actors fail to realize the importance of a curtain
call, or the extent to which a player is judged by the final impression he
leaves with the audience.

In the commercial theatre, bitter experience has taught the theatre-goer
to expect very artificial curtain calls. He knows that the manager will try
to force as many calls as he can squeeze out of the audience, and he is
prepared to see the actors—especially the star—take them with a good
deal of vanity and some effort to monopolize the attention. He does not
like it, but accepts it rather cynically as an inescapable part of "show
business," and on the rare occasions when it does not happen he is duly
pleased and a bit surprised. In the non-commercial theatre he expects a
little more modesty, and is usually satisfied with one or two unpretentious
calls, taken by the whole cast. But if he has enjoyed the play a little more
than usual, he feels inclined to show it by a generous number of calls, and
likes the sensation that he is giving the players a little more applause than
they expected. He does not like to see them take it with painful ama-
teurishness, and cools off quickly if they seem startled or confused on a
first or second call, do not seem to know their places, how to stand, and
whether to bow or not. But he cools off even more quickly if he finds them
too well prepared, bowing and smirking effusively in imitation of second-
rate professionals. And he particularly dislikes the one actor in the group
who behaves as if the call were exclusively for him.

The wise actor, therefore, will steer a middle course in taking curtain
calls, adjusting his behavior to that of the group, and to prevailing local
custom. He will not be noticeably more backward, or more forward, than
the others. He will naturally look pleased if the audience has apparently
enjoyed the play, but he will not make the mistake of supposing that their
applause is mainly for his outstanding performance. He will be well aware
that the unguarded moment of the curtain call is the moment when an
actor with a prima-donna complex is most likely to give himself away,
even if he has restrained his attitude in performance.

I once knew a very able player who (pretending modesty) always asked
the director to put him at the end of the line in the curtain call rather
than at stage center. But as the curtain rose for the call he always contrived to be a half-second late in walking on, with the result that all eyes

shifted to him as the only figure in motion, and were focused on him at the precise moment that he made his modest, self-deprecatory, but perfectly timed bow. It worked quite well the first few times, but he soon had a reputation for it, and both audiences and directors got tired of having him around. I knew another and even more able player who managed to conceal his insufferable vanity from audiences in performance (though not from his comrades in rehearsal), but who gave himself away at the curtain call each night by bowing more violently than his fellows, smiling more broadly, beaming more happily at the players to his right and left, and kissing the hand of the leading lady more effusively than seemed necessary.

An actor need not be stupid, or awkward, or naïve about taking his call, but he can take it with dignity and quiet restraint. It will help him greatly if he remains imaginatively in character, and in key with the play—not to the extent of continuing the action or situation, but sufficiently to show a decent respect for the illusion just concluded, and an unwillingness to shatter it too cruelly.

In other words, as the final curtain descends, the actor should leave with his audience a conclusive impression of unimpaired good taste. If there is any better principle to guide him in his art, from the first rehearsal to the last curtain call, I do not know what it is.

Bibliography

AN EXHAUSTIVE bibliography on acting alone, ignoring other phases of theatre study, would fill a large volume and tax the resources of scholarship; and it would not remain exhaustive very long. The following lists are intended rather to be highly selective, including only those works which the author has some reason to think might be helpful to the serious student of acting in relation to the scope and limitations of this book.

An excellent bibliography on the art, theory, and technique of acting has been compiled by the Committee on Research of the AMERICAN EDUCATIONAL THEATRE ASSOCIATION, and is obtainable in pamphlet form from that organization (Office: University of Michigan). The student should also know Miss ROSAMOND GILDER's compilation on *Theatre Collections in Libraries and Universities* (pub. by Theatre Arts, 1936), a descriptive list of sources rather than of books. These two will open a wide field for him. In addition, he will find extensive bibliographies in many of the works listed below, some general and some covering special fields; the most helpful ones are indicated in the comments.

ORIGINS, HISTORY, AND ÆSTHETICS OF ACTING

CHENEY, SHELDON. *The Theatre: 3000 Years of Drama, Acting, and Stagecraft.* (Longmans, Green, 1935.)
  Emphasizes the physical theatre, but offers the actor a good historical picture of theatre as well as drama.
FREEDLEY, GEORGE, and REEVES, J. L. *A History of the Theatre.* (Crown Publishers, 1941.)
  One of the best one-volume histories, giving more attention to actors and acting than most. Copiously illustrated. Exceptionally extensive bibliography.
HAVEMEYER, L. *The Drama of Savage Peoples.* (Yale U. Press, 1916.)
  An anthropologist's contribution to the philosophy of acting.
RIDGEWAY, WILLIAM. *The Dramas and Dramatic Dances of Non-European Races.* (Cambridge U. Press, 1915.)
  Offers the kind of broadening most actors need badly.
ZUNG, CECILIA. *Secrets of the Chinese Drama.* (Shanghai, Kelly & Walsh, 1937.)
  A beautifully illustrated book, covering Chinese acting techniques as well as production methods.
BUTCHER, S. H. *Aristotle's Theory of Poetry and Fine Art.* (London, Macmillan, 1911.)
  The standard introduction in English to the father of æsthetics.
LANGFELD, HERBERT S. *The Æsthetic Attitude.* (Harcourt, Brace, 1920.)
  Has exerted a profound influence on the philosophy of acting.

SANTAYANA, GEORGE. *The Sense of Beauty.* (Scribner, 1896.)
A writer of first rank on a subject vital to all artists.

SULLY, JAMES. *An Essay on Laughter.* (Longmans, Green, 1902.)
A general discussion, still widely read.

BERGSON, HENRI. *Laughter: An Essay on the Meaning of the Comic.* (Macmillan, 1911.)
Another well-known attempt to explain humor.

MEREDITH, GEORGE. *An Essay on Comedy and the Comic Spirit.* (Scribner, 1918.)
Perhaps the most famous essay on this subject.

SMITH, WINIFRED. *The Commedia dell' Arte.* (Columbia U. Press, 1912.)
The best-known book on the comedy of improvisation.

HARBAGE, ALFRED G. *Shakespeare's Audiences.* (Columbia U. Press, 1941.)
Interesting discussion of actor-audience relationship.

HARBAGE, ALFRED G. *As They Liked It.* (Macmillan, 1947.)
A fascinating analysis of audience attitude, and of the relation between æsthetic and ethical motivations.

SPRAGUE, A. C. *Shakespeare and the Actors.* (Harvard Press, 1944.)
Much information about traditional stage business.

ODELL, G. C. D. *Shakespeare from Betterton to Irving.* (Scribner, 1920.)
Provides a good background for the Shakespearean actor.

DORAN, JOHN. *Annals of the English Stage, from Betterton to Kean.* (London, Nimmo, 1888, 3 vols.)
Old, but readable, especially on actors and audiences.

BAKER, H. B. *History of the London Stage and Its Famous Players.* (London, Routledge, 1904.)
Covers the period from 1576 to 1903.

RUSSELL, W. CLARK. *Representative Actors.* (London, Warne, n.d.)
An old book, but full of acting lore. Short biographies and intelligent criticisms of many British actors from Alleyne to Boucicault.

WAXMAN, S. M. *Antoine and the Théâtre Libre.* (Harvard Press, 1926.)
The best account of the free theatre movement, which profoundly altered modern acting techniques.

BROWN, THOMAS ALLSTON. *History of the American Stage.* (N. Y., c. 1870.)
Includes biographies of actors, 1733 to 1870. Not very accurate.

CRAIG, EDWARD GORDON. *On the Art of the Theatre.* (London, Browne, 1911. Rep. Dodd, Mead, 1925)
The book which stirred up modern controversy and experimentation in theatre arts. Contains his proposal of "übermarionettes."

BELASCO, DAVID. *The Theatre Through Its Stage Door.* (Harper, 1919.)
Defends the realistic concept of acting and staging.

MAMMEN, E. W. *The Old Stock Company School of Acting.* (Boston Public Library, 1945.)
A research study of the Boston Museum and other repertory theatres. Rich in footnotes, but not always accurate. Extensive and unusual bibliography.

FLANAGAN, HALLIE. *Arena.* (Duell, Sloan & Pierce, 1940.)

A history and defense of the late Federal Theatre, by its director. Sidelights on the economic and social position of the actor.

FLANAGAN, HALLIE. *Shifting Scenes of the European Theatre.* (Coward, McCann, 1928.)

Includes enthusiastic eulogy of the Soviet theatre and some account of the acting.

VAN GYSEGHAN, ANDRE. *Theatre in Soviet Russia.* (London, Faber, 1943.)

A glowing tribute to theatre as social and political propaganda, with a sneer at art, by a left-wing Britisher.

HOUGHTON, NORRIS. *Advance from Broadway.* (Harcourt, Brace, 1941.)

An interesting survey of the non-commercial theatre across the U. S., by a writer from Times Square.

REED, JOSEPH VERNER. *The Curtain Falls.* (Harcourt, Brace, 1935.)

A brutally frank account of "show business" lunacy, union ruthlessness, and artistic temperament, by a Broadway producer who had enough.

PLAY PRODUCTION

(Among the scores of books on production many are elementary, and many, including some of the best, are devoted largely to direction and stagecraft. I list here only a few of some possible special interest to the student of acting.)

ÇAPEK, KAREL. *How a Play Is Produced.* (London, Bles, 1928.)

Humorous, but how true! By a famous playwright, writing about professional actors and managers.

DOLMAN, JOHN, JR. *The Art of Play Production.* (Harper, Rev. Ed., 1946.)

Written from the director's viewpoint, but includes a chapter on theories of acting. Extensive bibliography.

OMMANEY, KATHARINE A. *The Stage and the School.* (Harper, 1932.)

One of the best for the actor at high school age. Has a very extensive bibliography.

HEFFNER, H. C., SELDEN, S., and SELLMAN, H. D. *Modern Theatre Practice.* (Crofts, 1946.)

One of the better practical handbooks on all phases of production. Very extensive bibliography.

BOSWORTH, HALLIAM. *Technique in Dramatic Art.* (Macmillan, 1934.)

Objective in treatment. A production book but more often used as a text in acting.

THEORY AND TECHNIQUE OF ACTING

ARCHER, WILLIAM. *Masks or Faces.* (London, Longmans, 1888.)

The most helpful book ever published on the art of acting, but out of print, and rather rare.

FITZGERALD, PERCY. *The Art of Acting.* (Macmillan, 1892.)

Brief but interesting lectures given at the Royal Institution and elsewhere.

DIDEROT, DENIS. *The Paradox of Acting (Le Paradoxe sur le Comédien).* (Trans. by W. H. Pollock.) (London, 1769.)

The famous controversial essay, revived by Coquelin in 1881.

COQUELIN, CONSTANT. *The Actor and His Art*. (Boston, Roberts, 1881.)
  The monograph which started a war of words.

SHAFTESBURY, EDMUND. *Lessons in Acting*. (c. 1885.)
  A very rare old book which includes a most remarkable collection of drawings to illustrate acting attitudes.

GARCIA, GUSTAV. *The Actor's Art*. (London, Simpkins, 1888.)
  One of the more comprehensive attempts to codify the whole technique of acting, including gesture.

AYRES, ALFRED. *Actors and Acting, Elocution and Elocutionists*. (Appleton, 1894.)
  An old book, but a meaty one, especially on the technique of speaking lines. Valuable information on actors' methods.

CALVERT, LOUIS. *Problems of the Actor*. (Holt, 1918.)
  A readable book, by a fine actor of the old school.

BENSON, SIR FRANK. *I Want to Go On the Stage*. (London, Benn, 1931.)
  A disillusioning handbook by an actor celebrated as a great teacher of actors.

LEES, C. LOWELL. *A Primer of Acting*. (Prentice-Hall, 1940.)
  One of the best primers. Includes copious exercises, and a lengthy bibliography especially complete in elementary books.

SELDEN, SAMUEL. *First Steps in Acting*. (Crofts, 1947.)
  A new type of primer, by a successful writer of short texts.

FRANKLIN, MIRIAM. *Rehearsal*. (Prentice-Hall, 1938.)
  A thorough lesson book for those who like the graded-exercise method in heavy doses.

COLVIN, E. B. *Face the Footlights*. (Whittlesey, 1940.)
  A practical "do" and "don't" book on acting, with many unusual wrinkles and an attempt to codify the simpler elements of pantomime in modern terms.

BOLESLAVSKY, RICHARD. *Acting: The First Six Lessons*. (Theatre Arts, 1937.)
  Stimulating chiefly to those who like a picturesque, figurative, mystical approach.

STANISLAVSKI, CONSTANTIN. *An Actor Prepares*. (Theatre Arts, 1936.)
  One of the most influential books, by a great actor, known also as a great teacher.

COLE, TOBY. *Acting*. (Lear, 1948.)
  A handbook designed to explain the Stanislavski method. Illustrated.

ALBRIGHT, H. D. *Working Up a Part*. (Houghton Mifflin, 1947.)
  One of the newest handbooks, well reviewed.

YOUNG, STARK. *Theatre Practice*. (Scribner, 1926.)
  Despite the title, this deals largely with theories of acting.

EUSTIS, MORTON. *Players at Work*. (Theatre Arts, 1937.)
  Reports of interviews with contemporary actors on their methods and theories of acting.

HUGHES, GLENN. *The Penthouse Theatre*. (French, 1942.)
  Largely the history of a theatre, but includes some account of the special problems and techniques of arena acting.

SHEA, GEORGE EDWARD. *Acting in Opera*. (Schirmer, 1915.)
  The most available book in this specialized field. A more up-to-date one is needed.

BODILY ACTION AND PANTOMIME

(In addition to the items by SHAFTESBURY, GARCIA, and COLVIN, above, the following books should be helpful to the student of gesture and bodily action.)

BROADBENT, R. J. *A History of Pantomine.* (Simpkins, Marshall, 1901.)
The best-known general history. Covers the Harlequinade and the English pantomime.

DELAUMOSNE, L'ABBÉ. *The Delsarte System.* (Albany, Werner, 1884.)
A complete explanation of the great man's ideas by one of his pupils.

ADAMS, FLORENCE A. *Gesture and Pantomimic Action.* (Albany, Werner, 1891.)
One of the more elaborate expositions of codified gesture, with many illustrations.

LUTZ, FLORENCE. *The Technique of Pantomime.* (Berkeley, Sather Gate, 1927.)
Alarmingly complete in its catalogue of moods and gestures.

HISTORICAL AND CRITICAL REMINISCENCES

(From a vast group of miscellaneous comments on actors and acting the following seem most likely to be worth browsing through.)

LEWES, GEORGE HENRY. *On Actors and the Art of Acting.* (Brentano, n.d.)
Contemporary criticism of great nineteenth-century actors and actresses by one of the most penetrating observers of the age.

FITZGERALD, PERCY. *The World Behind the Scenes.* (London, Chatto, 1881.)
Contains a lengthy and informative discussion of the methods of famous old actors.

RYAN, KATE. *Old Boston Museum Days.* (Little, Brown, 1915.)
Reminiscences of a great repertory theatre that had to call itself a "museum" to be respectable.

ROURKE, CONSTANCE. *Troupers of the Gold Coast, or the Rise of Lotta Crabtree.* (Harcourt, Brace, 1928.)
A picturesque account of acting in the gold-rush days.

WINTER, WILLIAM. *The Wallet of Time.* (Moffat, Yard, 1913.)
Reminiscences of actors and acting by the dean of American critics.

EATON, WALTER P. *Plays and Players.* (Stewart, Kidd, 1916.)
Reprints of dramatic criticisms and essays, including an especially good one on George Arliss.

TOWSE, J. RANKIN. *Sixty Years of the Theatre.* (Funk, Wagnalls, 1916.)
Stimulating discussions of actors and acting by a New York critic who held his post for 43 years. A veritable store-house of intelligent, analytical criticism, colored by a slight preference for the more violently emotional style of acting.

WOOLLCOTT, ALEXANDER. *Enchanted Aisles.* (Putnam, 1924.)
A popular collection of dramatic opinions and essays by the most readable of Broadway critics in his time.

WOOLLCOTT, ALEXANDER. *Mrs. Fiske: Her Views on the Stage.* (Century, 1917.)
Opinions of an actress who could think, reported by a man who could write.

ARTHUR, SIR GEORGE. *From Phelps to Gielgud.* (London, Chapman, 1936.)
Comments on actors and acting in many periods. Introduction by Mr. Gielgud.

GILDER, ROSAMOND. *John Gielgud's Hamlet.* (N. Y., Oxford, 1937.)
> An analysis of what some people considered the best modern interpretation of *Hamlet*.

GILDER, ROSAMOND. *Enter the Actress.* (Houghton Mifflin, 1931.)
> An account of the first women in the theatre, and their work.

SAYLER, OLIVER. *Inside the Moscow Art Theatre.* (Brentano, 1925.)
> An American observer describes the Stanislavsky method.

BIOGRAPHIES OF ACTORS AND ACTRESSES

(There are literally hundreds of these, since almost every actor who is too modest to write his autobiography has some friend or admirer eager to do it for him. Unfortunately, most of these books deal largely with the glamour of stage life or the personalities of the subject and his friends, and tell little or nothing about the artistic theories and methods by which he or she attained success. The following titles have been chosen because they represent at least minor departures from this rule. All are more or less interesting, but some are much more helpful than others.)

ANDERSON, MARY. *A Few Memories.* (Harper, 1896.)
> Written (she says) to warn and help young girls with stage ambitions.

ARLISS, GEORGE. *Up the Years from Bloomsbury.* (Blue Ribbon Books, 1927.)
> One of the most entertaining autobiographies, and not without some comment on acting problems and experiences.

BERNHARDT, SARAH. *The Art of the Theatre.* (London, Bles, 1924.)
> One of the greatest actresses of all time talks about her art—and other things.

GROSSMAN, EDWINA BOOTH. *Edwin Booth.* (Century, 1894.)
> His daughter's recollections, and many of his letters, with a few bits of acting lore sprinkled through them.

GOODALE, KATHARINE. *Behind the Scenes with Edwin Booth.* (Houghton Mifflin, 1931.)
> More widely read than the regular biographies.

COHAN, GEORGE M. *Twenty Years on Broadway.* (Harper, 1925.)
> Will teach much about theatre life but little about acting.

CORNELL, KATHARINE. *I Wanted to Be an Actress.* (Readers' League, 1941.)
> More contemporary and possibly a little more instructive than most of the auto-biographies.

STEBBINS, EMMA. *Charlotte Cushman.* (Houghton, Osgood, 1878.)
> The standard biography. A few hints on acting emerge from the floods of eulogy.

EDGETT, E. F. *Edward Loomis Davenport.* (Dunlap Society, 1901.)
> Sidelights on acting in the old days of repertory stock, at the Arch St. Theatre and elsewhere. The Davenports represent one of the oldest "royal families" of the theatre (from 1680).

DREW, MRS. JOHN. *Autobiographical Sketch.* (Scribner, 1899.)
> Includes some helpful reminiscences of old actors and acting, and of the Arch St. Theatre at several periods.

FORBES-ROBERTSON, SIR J. *Player Under Three Reigns.* (Little, Brown, 1925.)
  Autobiography of an intellectual Hamlet, with some advice to the players.

REES, JAMES. *The Life of Edwin Forrest.* (Phila., Peterson, 1874.)
  The standard biography, and meaty, but not always accurate. Contains more eulogy than criticism.

ALGER, WILLIAM R. *The Life of Edwin Forrest.* (Lippincott, 1877. Limited Ed., 100 copies.)
  A monumental two-volume work, now pretty rare. More analytical than Rees.

PARSONS, MRS. CLEMENT. *Garrick and His Circle.* (London, Methuen, 1906.)
  One of the best treatments of Garrick as an influence. Some side lights on his technique.

HEDGCOCK, F. A. *David Garrick and His French Friends.* (Duffield, c. 1912.)
  Contains some interesting comparisons of English and French acting and actors.

HOPPER, DEWOLF. *Once a Clown, Always a Clown.* (Little, Brown, 1927.)
  A breezy, informal collection of reminiscences, including a most illuminating one about Sarah Bernhardt.

PLAYFAIR, GILES. *[Edmund] Kean: Paradoxical Genius.* (Dutton, 1939.)
  A critical biography of one of the most famous of all actors.

CREAHAN, JOHN. *The Life of Laura Keene.* (Phila., Rogers, 1897.)
  Biography of the star at whose "benefit" Lincoln was shot. Reveals much more about her artistic principles and methods than most biographies of actors.

KOMISARJEVSKY, THEODORE. *Myself and the Theatre.* (Dutton, 1930.)
  Correctly titled, but full of interesting ideas and opinions on acting, presented with humor and clarity.

LE GALLIENNE, EVA. *At 33.* (Longmans, Green, 1934.)
  One of the most instructive of the more recent biographies, by one whom the critics have called a "cerebral" actress.

LOGAN, OLIVE. *Before the Footlights and Behind the Scenes.* (Parmalee, 1870.)
  A fat tome of old-time stage gossip, sentimental, but informative.

POLLOCK, SIR FREDERICK (Ed.). *Macready's Reminiscences.* (Macmillan, 1875.)
  An edited autobiography, containing much exposition of a very thoughtful actor's aims and methods, if you dig for it.

WILSTACH, PAUL, *Richard Mansfield.* (Scribner, 1908.)
  A thorough, if too eulogistic, account of the man and his methods.

MORSE, FRANK P. *Backstage with Henry Miller.* (Dutton, 1938.)
  Biography of an actor-manager whose experience bridged the gap between the old ways and the new.

MORRIS, CLARA. *Life on the Stage,* and *The Life of a Star.* (McClure, 1902 and 1906, 2 vols.)
  Remarkably interesting as human documents, and fairly rich in reflections of her own aims and methods in acting.

MORRIS, CLARA. *Stage Confidences.* (Lothrop, 1902.)
  Anecdotes and advice for stage-struck young ladies. Very readable.

MURDOCH, JAMES E. *The Stage.* (Phila., Stoddart, 1880.)
  Reminiscences of fifty years. Somewhat richer in humorous anecdote than in help-

ful instruction; yet it gives a vivid picture of actors and their ways in the heyday of the American theatre.

SALVINI, TOMMASO. *Autobiography*. (Century, 1893.)

Generally personal, but contains one helpful chapter on how he studied his art.

CAMPBELL, THOMAS. *The Life of Mrs. Siddons*. (Harper, 1834.)

A fascinating story of the actress who was hissed off the London stage but came back to become the most popular stage idol in English history.

SKINNER, OTIS. *Footlights and Spotlights*. (Bobbs-Merrill, 1924.)

Readable, gossipy, full of amazing tales of slipshod, devil-may-care professional theatre, along with serious discussions of the actor's art. The chapter on emotion in acting is possibly the most helpful.

SKINNER, CORNELIA OTIS. *Family Circle*. (Houghton, Mifflin, 1948.)

Contains interesting sidelights on the Skinners and on Madame Modjeska and her art.

STANISLAVSKY, CONSTANTIN. *My Life in Art*. (Little, Brown, 1924.)

Largely a history of the Moscow Art Theatre, but gives his theories of acting rather more clearly than his later book.

STODDART, JAMES H. *Recollections of a Player*. (Century, 1902.)

Contains much history of famous companies and players in the last quarter of the nineteenth century.

TYLER, GEORGE C. *Whatever Goes Up*. (Bobbs-Merrill, 1934.)

Reminiscences of a manager who cared enough about the old ways to promote a distinguished series of revivals. Ghost-written in breezy style by J. C. Furnas. Chapters about many famous actors and actresses.

WALLACK, LESTER. *Memories of Fifty Years*. (Scribner, 1889.)

More about actors than acting, by one of a famous family.

WARDE, FREDERICK. *Fifty Years of Make-Believe*. International Press Syndicate, 1920.)

Written for admirers rather than students, but covers a great deal of ground in theatre experience.

VOICE TRAINING AND PHONETICS

(These, of course, are controversial subjects, and there is no general agreement as to which are the best books. The following are among the most widely used, but the student would do well to compare several in each field, and not to believe everything he finds in print on either subject.)

BRIGANCE, W. N. *Your Everyday Speech*. (Whittlesey, 1939.)

A good, common-sense American approach to the general problem of speech training.

MCLEAN, MARGARET P. *Good American Speech*. (Dutton, Rev., 1939.)

An older work, cited for contrast, the standards being northeastern and cosmopolitan rather than midwestern, and savoring more of the stage than the street.

KANTNER, C., and WEST, R. *Phonetics*. (Harper, 1933, Rev. 1941.)

Perhaps the most popular American text on the subject.

THOMAS, C. K. *An Introduction to the Phonetics of American English.* (Ronald Press, 1935.)

A scholarly but liberal treatment, which does not agree on all points with the preceding one.

BENDER, J. F., and FIELDS, V. *Phonetic Readings in American English.* (Pitman, 1939.)

A practical exercise book for learning I.P.A., with transcriptions of many varieties of American speech. More accurate in vowel symbols than most books on the subject.

KENYON, J. S., and KNOTT, T. A. *A Pronouncing Dictionary of American English.* (Merriam, 1944.)

Deals only with pronunciation, using I.P.A. symbols, simplified to the point of some inaccuracy. American standards.

JONES, DANIEL. *An English Pronouncing Dictionary.* (Dutton, 7th Ed., 1946.)

Also confined to pronunciation, and the first English dictionary to use I.P.A. The London standard. No actor should be without it.

American College Dictionary. (Text Ed., Harper, 1948.)

A general dictionary of somewhat larger size than most student dictionaries. Uses compromise phonetic symbols for indicating pronunciations, and bases its standards much more on numerical prevalence and less on tradition than either of the pronouncing dictionaries mentioned above. Very well printed and bound, and popular with students for general use.

GREET, W. CABELL. *World Words.* (Columbia U. Press, 1948, Rev.)

A special pronouncing dictionary of place and proper names.

FOWLER, H. W. *Modern English Usage.* (Oxford, 1926.)

British in standards, but the most stimulating and helpful book available on the more vexing and difficult questions of usage. Gives reasons. Highly readable, even witty.

HERMAN, L. and M. S. *Manual of Foreign Dialects.* (Chicago, 1943.)

An original and enterprising attempt to present the phonetics of 31 dialects, using a system of notation which some readers find more startling and baffling than the I.P.A. Should be helpful to those who can master the code.

MURDOCH, JAMES E. *The Technique of the Speaking Voice.* (Stephens, 1915.)

An old text by an actor whose own voice was one of the most famous. Based on Rush's *Philosophy of the Human Voice*, it presents the older ideas as well as any.

ANDERSON, VIRGIL. *Training for the Speaking Voice.* (Oxford, 1942.)

One of the most widely used of recent texts.

LAWSON, F. D. *The Human Voice.* (Harper, 1944.)

A still more recent one.

STANLEY, DOUGLAS. *Your Voice.* (Pitman, 1945.)

A recent re-statement by the author of a famous but controversial system of voice training, primarily for singers, but not uninteresting to speakers and actors.

KARR, HARRISON M. *Your Speaking Voice.* (Glendale, Cal., Griffin-Patterson, Rev. 1946.)

A book in very modern style, with many illustrations and many quotations on vocal method by well-known speakers.

SCREEN, RADIO, AND TELEVISION

(There is a great volume of literature on these subjects, but surprisingly little of it bears helpfully on the technique of acting, especially in the last two fields. Most of the following books throw more light on the background of these arts than on their special problems in acting.)

MARSH, MAE. *Screen Acting.* (Stokes, 1921.)
> One of the few easily available books on this subject, by a star of the silent screen. Much about pantomimic action.

ALBERTSON, LILLIAN. *Motion Picture Acting.* (Funk, Wagnalls, 1948.)
> A new publication in this field, lavishly advertised.

WALLER, JUDITH. *Radio; The Fifth Estate.* (Houghton Mifflin, 1946.)
> A general survey of radio as it is. Extensive bibliography, but with little reference to acting problems.

ABBOT, WALDO. *Handbook of Broadcasting.* (McGraw-Hill, 1937.)
> Not new, but the best-known book of its kind. Contains 22 pages on radio dramatics, including a few on acting.

CREWS, ALBERT. *Radio Production Directing.* (Houghton Mifflin, 1944.)
> Written from the viewpoint of the director, but contains more information of possible use to the actor than any radio book so far.

WEAVER, LUTHER. *The Technique of Radio Writing.* (Prentice-Hall, 1948.)
> Includes some discussion of radio drama, which might be of interest to the actor; also presents the advertiser's viewpoint in a way to give the actor pause.

COTT, TED. *How to Audition for Radio.* (N. Y., Greenberg, 1946.)
> A recent handbook for radio speakers and actors.

ROSE, OSCAR. *Radio Broadcasting and Television.* (Wilson, 1947.)
> An annotated bibliography, containing many titles on other phases of these industries, but few on acting.

HUBBELL, RICHARD T. *Television Programming and Production.* (Murray Hill Books, 1945.)
> The most comprehensive book on television arts, with some material on acting techniques.

EDDY, CAPTAIN W. C. *Television; The Eyes of Tomorrow.* (Prentice-Hall, 1945.)
> A popular exposition of the mechanics and business of television, but includes a chapter on acting for that medium.

STAGE MAKE-UP

(There is no substitute for practical experience in this field, but the actor who would learn to do his own make-up, as every actor should, will find many books available on the subject. Among the most practical are some of the pamphlets put out by the manufacturers of materials. From the long list of published books I would suggest one of the following as likely to fit the actor's need.)

CHALMERS, HELENA. *The Art of Make-Up.* (Appleton, 1925.)
> An older elementary handbook, still popular.

CORSON, RICHARD. *Stage Make-Up.* (Crofts, 1942.)

Much more thorough and comprehensive, and more up to date, but still limited to the more common techniques.

STRENKOVSKY, SERGE. *The Art of Make-Up.* (Dutton, 1937.)

Still more elaborate. Covers some of the more difficult techniques in plastic make-up so popular with those who like to do things the hard way.

MISCELLANEOUS REFERENCE WORKS

SOBEL, BERNARD. *Theatre Handbook and Digest of Plays.* (Crown, 1940.)

An extremely useful book in dictionary form, containing information about actors, plays, theatre history, theatre techniques, etc. Not exhaustive (it is only one volume), and not 100 percent accurate, but well worth owning. Lengthy bibliography.

The Encyclopædia Britannica.

The later editions of this world-famous reference work include excellent articles by modern theatre leaders on many phases of theatre technique, including acting.

ALLEN, JAMES TURNEY. *Stage Antiquities of the Greeks and Romans.* (Longmans, Green, 1927.)

This little factual work contains most of what is really known about the ancient theatre. Good bibliography.

NEILSON, W. A., and THORNDIKE, A. H. *The Facts About Shakespeare.*

Another tiny volume that contains practically all that is really known about Shakespeare, leaving out the guesswork. Good bibliography.

FURNESS, H. H. and others. *The Variorum Shakespeare.* (Lippincott)

A tremendous, multi-volume work, still not quite finished, with which the student actor who hopes to act Shakespeare should get acquainted; a mine of comparative comment on the texts and their interpretation.

PERIODICALS

(Many important articles on acting, as on other phases of theatre art, are to be found in the periodicals, including the files of those no longer published. Among the latter, mention should be made of the American *Theatre Magazine*, the English *Theatre Magazine*, the *Theatre Guild Magazine*, the *Drama*, the German *Das Theater*, and many others. The student should know how to use the *Reader's Guide to Periodical Literature*, an annual index; also the *Dramatic Index*, a specialized supplement since 1909. Listed below are a few of the more recent periodicals likely to be useful.)

Theatre Arts (formerly *The Theatre Arts Monthly*). (New York.)

From 1916 to 1948 a serious, tasteful periodical for artists in the theatre, including actors, and the one indispensable publication in its field. In February, 1948, it was sold to the owners of the defunct *Stage*, and became a glamour magazine of "show business"—useful, perhaps, in its own field, but quite foreign to its long and honorable tradition

National Theatre Conference Bulletin. (Cleveland, N.T.C.)

A quarterly bulletin full of stimulating material for workers in the non-commercial theatre, including actors.

The Theatre Annual. (N. Y., The Theatre Library Association)

An annual publication, since 1942, of scholarly studies on the theatre, including some on acting.

The Quarterly Journal of Speech. (Organ of the Speech Association of America, formerly the National Association of Teachers of Speech, with offices at the University of Missouri.)

Published since 1915, it contains most of the important articles on educational dramatics, including many on acting and the teaching of acting; also critical reviews of old and new books in the field, and of hundreds of articles in popular and professional journals.

Variety. (New York.)

The weekly newspaper of "show business" in all its forms.

PERIODICAL ARTICLES, MONOGRAPHS, ESSAYS, AND EXCERPTS

(Many of the most valuable items in this classification will be found in the *Publications of the Dramatic Museum* of Columbia University. These have appeared at various dates in groups of small volumes, each containing several items. These include many reprints of famous speeches or essays on theatre, especially on acting, some of them long out of print or extremely difficult to find in any other edition. A few of the most important titles are mentioned below, together with a selected list of short items on acting from many other sources.)

Columbia University: *Publications of the Dramatic Museum.* Selected Titles:

Boucicault, Dion. "The Art of Acting." (Introduction by Otis Skinner.)
Boucicault, Dion. "Coquelin—Irving."
Coquelin, Constant. "Actors and Acting."
Coquelin, Constant. "Art and the Actor."
Coquelin, Constant. "A Reply to Mr. Henry Irving."
Coquelin, Constant. "A Reply to Mr. Dion Boucicault."
Gillette, William. "The Illusion of the First Time." (Introduction by George Arliss.)
Jenkins, H. C. F. "Mrs. Siddons as Lady Macbeth and as Queen Katherine."
Arnold, Matthew. "Letters of an Old Playgoer."
Irving, Henry. "M. Coquelin on Actors and Acting."
Kemble, Frances Ann. "On the Stage." (Introduction by George Arliss.)
Talma, Francois. "Reflexions on the Actor's Art."

Abbott, Hazel. "The Soviet Theatre—Acting and Staging." (*Quarterly Journal of Speech*, Oct., 1937.)

Adams, W. Bridges. "Shakespearean Tradition in the Theatre." (*Quarterly Journal of Speech*, Nov., 1930.)

Barshay, Bernard. "Gordon Craig's Theories of Acting." (*Theatre Annual*, 1947.)

Bishop, Truman. "Broadway in the Parlor." (the Penthouse Theatre) (*The Coast*, Oct., 1940.)

Corbin, John. "Hamlet Without the Play." (the Barrymore *Hamlet*) (*New York Times*, Nov. 26, 1922

Craig, Gordon. "Henry Irving." (*Theatre Arts*, Jan., 1938.)

Daykarkhanova, Tamara. "The Face of the Actor." (Art of make-up) (*Theatre Arts*, May, 1931.)

Dean, Frederic. "Grand Procession of Hamlets." (*N. Y. Times Mag.*, Dec. 17, 1922.)

Dolman, John, Jr. "A Laugh Analysis of *The School for Scandal*." (*Quarterly Journal of Speech*, Nov., 1930.)

Dolman, John, Jr. "From the [radio] Listener's Point of View." (*Quarterly Journal of Speech*, April, 1934.)

Dolman, John, Jr. "Hamlet with Thrills." (the Bel Geddes *Hamlet*) (*Emerson Quarterly*, Jan., 1932.)

Dolman, John, Jr. "Jim Dandy, Pioneer." (*Quarterly Journal of Speech*, Feb., 1944.)

Downer, Alan. "The Diary of Benjamin Webster." (English actor, great-grandfather of Margaret Webster) (*Theatre Annual*, 1945.)

Downer, Alan. "Macready's Production of Macbeth." (*Quarterly Journal of Speech*, April, 1947.)

Eaton, W. P. "Talma." (*Theatre Arts*, July, 1926.)

Eisenstein, Sergei. "Enchanter from the Pear Tree Garden." (Mei Lan-Fang.) (*Theatre Arts*, Oct., 1935.)

Eustis, Morton. "Acting as a Business." (*Theatre Arts*, May, 1934.)

Eustis, Morton. "Theatre with a Union Label." (*Theatre Arts*, Oct., 1932.)

Fiske, Harrison Grey. "The Inside of the Bag of Tricks." (*Saturday Evening Post*, Oct. 20, 1923.)

Gemmill, Paul F. "Equity: The Actors' Trade Union." (*Billboard*, Aug. 13, 1927.)

Gielgud, John. "An Actor Prepares." (*Theatre Arts*, Jan., 1937.)

Gilder, Rosamond. "Farewell to *Theatre Arts*." (by its ex-editor) (*National Theatre Conference Bulletin*, April, 1948.) (See also "Posthumous Praise" of *Theatre Arts* by many authors in the same issue.)

Gilder, Rosamond. "Hamlets." (A critical comparison) (*Theatre Arts*, Dec., 1936.)

Gilder Rosamond. "Mrs. John Drew." (*Theatre Arts*, May, 1943.)

Green, Harriet. "Gilmor Brown's Playbox." (*Theatre Arts*, July, 1935.)

Gresham, William L. "Mama and Papa." (interviews with Mady Christians and Leo G. Carroll) (*Theatre Arts*, April, 1945.)

Hardwicke, Sir Cedric. "The Moribund Craft of Acting." (*Theatre Arts*, Feb., 1939.)

Houghton, Norris. "Laurette Taylor." (*Theatre Arts*, Dec., 1945.)

Irving, Henry. "Address at Harvard, March 30, 1885." (*The Critic*, April 4, 1885.)

Lomas, C. W. "The Psychology of Stage Fright." (*Quarterly Journal of Speech*, Feb., 1937.)

Lunt, Alfred. "Why Make Up?" (*Theatre Guild Mag.*, Nov., 1928.)

Mansfield, Richard. "Concerning Acting." (*No. Am. Review*, Sept., 1894.)

Marshall, Herbert. "The Oldest Actor in the World." (*Theatre Arts*, Oct., 1947.)

Martin, John. "How Meyerhold Trains His Actors." (*Theatre Guild Mag.*, Nov., 1930.)

Matthews, Brander. "The Old Stock Companies." (*Century*, Jan., 1921.)

Mitchell, Lee. "Some Principles of Stage Fencing." (*Quarterly Journal of Speech*, Dec., 1942.)

Motyleff, Ilia. "One World in Acting." (*Quarterly Journal of Speech*, April, 1946.)

Nathan, George Jean, and Cohan, George M. "The Mechanics of Emotion." (*McClure's*, Nov., 1913.)

Powell, Vio Mae. "Dramatic Ritual as Observed in the Sun Dance." (*Quarterly Journal of Speech*, April, 1947.)

Quinn, Seabury. "Macready's Farewell to New York." (the Astor Place riots.) (*Theatre Arts*, Oct., 1947.)

Rich, Marian. "Natural Speech." (*Theatre Arts*, July, 1945.)

Selden, Samuel. "Surface and Under Imagery in Acting." (*Theatre Annual*, 1944.)

Serlin, Oscar. "Every Day Is Christmas." (Theatre vs. Show Business.) (*Theatre Arts*, Jan., 1945.)

Seymour, William. "Disciplining the Player." (*Theatre*, Aug., 1919.)

Skinner, Otis. "After Booth." (*Theatre Arts*, July, 1926.)

Sprague, A. C. "Edwin Booth's Iago." (*Theatre Annual*, 1947.)

Stevens, Virginia. "Gielgud Rehearses Medea." (*Theatre Arts*, Nov., 1947.)

Stokes, Leslie. "The B.B.C. Third Program Presents . . ." (*Theatre Arts*, Feb., 1947.)

Stokes, Sewell. "The Oliviers." (*Theatre Arts*, Dec., 1945.)

Thorndike, Dame Sybil. "I Look at the Audience." (*Theatre Arts*, Jan., 1932.)

Tyson, Raymond. "Acting for Radio." (*Quarterly Journal of Speech*, Dec., 1939.)

Voscovec, George. "Comedy Written and Comedy Improvised." (*National Theatre Conference Bulletin*, Nov., 1943.)

Warren, William (and others). "Success on the Stage." (*No. Am. Review*, Dec., 1882.)

Wolf, Abraham. "Wells of Mankind's Eternal Laughter." (*N. Y. Times Mag.*, April 15, 1931.)

Wolfe, Thomas. "Portrait of a Player." (Richard Mansfield.) (*Theatre Annual*, 1947.)

Woollcott, Alexander. "Emotion in Acting." (*N. Y. Times*, April 2, 1922.)

Wyse, Aileen. " 'Mrs. Hillcrest' and the Press Agent." (*The Drama*, Jan., 1922.)

Glossary of Stage Terms

(No attempt is here made to cover all the rapidly changing technical terms of interest chiefly to back-stage workers; the following list includes only those established terms which the actor is most apt to hear, and ignorance of which is most likely to cause him embarrassment.)

ACT DROP. The working curtain which is closed between acts. May refer to a lighter temporary curtain behind the permanent one.

AND CAKES. Actor's slang for a contract clause by which the manager agrees to pay the actor's board.

APRON. The forestage. That part of the stage extending beyond the curtain-line. Applied chiefly to the reduced forestage of the nineteenth century, not the deep one of the eighteenth.

ARENA PRODUCTION. Production in a central acting space with the audience sitting all around it.

ASBESTOS. The fireproofed safety curtain, whether made of asbestos or some other material.

ASIDE (*noun*). A line or speech delivered by the actor away from other characters, and more or less communicatively to the audience.

BACK CLOTH. Same as BACK DROP.

BACK DROP. A drop used as the most remote background of a set.

BACK STAGE. Properly the portion of the theatre back of the proscenium but outside the stage itself. Loosely used by some to include all offstage areas behind the scenes.

BACKING. A flat, hinged flat, or drop used as background for a door or window in the set.

BALLOON (*verb*). To blow up in one's lines; actor's slang.

BARNSTORMING. Playing successively in many small towns, usually in one-night stands, often in improvised theatres.

BATTEN. Any strip of wood or metal used to stiffen a piece of scenery; especially a pipe or length of wood suspended on the lines for hanging drops.

BIT. A very small part, but usually with some lines, as distinguished from a walk-on.

BLACKOUT. A sudden, complete extinguishing of lights; sometimes used instead of a curtain to divide scenes.

BOARDS, THE. An old name for the stage in general.

BORDER. Properly a shallow drop suspended from the lines as part of the overhead masking in open settings. Less correctly, a nickname for a strip of border lights.

BORDER LIGHTS. Lights hung between the borders to light the set from above.

BOX SET (or SETTING). A closed set consisting of wall flats and a ceiling piece.

BUILD IT (*verb*). To build up the tension, tempo, or climax of a scene.

BUNCH LIGHT. An open box reflector containing a "bunch" of small lamps; now largely replaced by high-wattage olivettes.

BUSINESS. *See* STAGE BUSINESS.

BUSKIN (*figurative*). A symbol for tragedy.

BUSKIN, SOCK, COTHURNUS. Do not believe the popular definitions of these terms; *see* Allen's *Stage Antiquities*.

CABLE. The insulated cord feeding current to lighting units, and skillfully placed for the actor to trip over.

CALL BOARD. The back-stage bulletin board, on which casting and rehearsal calls and other items are posted.

CALL-BOY. A boy or man (nowadays it may be a girl) whose duty is to call the actors for their entrances.

CARRIAGE TRADE. Aristocratic patronage at the box office.

CLAPTRAP. A cheap device to trap or catch applause.

CLEARERS. *See* PROPERTY MAN.

CLOSET DRAMA. A play written to be read rather than acted—or one more suited to that purpose, whatever the author may think.

CLOWN. A rough, uncouth, comic character—historically quite different from a fool or jester, and from a Harlequin, Pierrot, or Pantaloon.

COLUMBINE. The chief female character in historic pantomime.

COMMEDIA DELL' ARTE. The Italian comedy of improvisation, especially in the sixteenth century.

COTHURNUS (KOTHORNOS). *See* BUSKIN.

COUNTER-WEIGHT. A sandbag or other weight rigged to balance the weight of a piece of flied scenery for easier lifting. May crack the skull of an actor standing in the wrong place.

CUT DROP. A drop with part of its area cut away, as in the case of a woodland set.

CUT-OUT. A ground-row with a cut profile.

CYC, SIKE, or SYKE. Abbreviation or nickname for cyclorama. The first spelling is the usual one.

CYCLORAMA. A curved back drop or cylindrical wall partly encircling the stage.

DIMMER. A rheostat, autotransformer or other device for reducing electric current, especially to dim the lights gradually.

DIRECTOR. The artist in charge of a production. In the commercial theatre his responsibility usually ends when performances begin.

DOCK. Storage space for scenery.

DOG TOWN. Any town commonly used by N. Y. managers to try a show out before the N. Y. opening—"to try it on the dog."

DOME. *See* SKY DOME.

DOWN STAGE. Toward the audience.

DRAPES. Hanging units of cloth or other non-rigid material.

DROP. Any full length curtain hung on the lines, either for background or to divide scenes.

ECCENTRIC COMEDIAN. The old stock company name for a funny man as distinguished from a comedy lead.

EXTRA. The modern term for a supernumerary.

FAKE (*verb*). To cover by improvising lines (or business).

FLAT. A unit of scenery stiffened by some sort of framework to keep the surface flat.

FLIES. The space above the stage; not the borders hung in the flies.

FLOODLIGHT. A lighting unit which spreads the light, usually without a lens.

FLY (*verb, trans.*). To haul something up into the flies. The past tense and past participle are "flied." ("Flown" is nonsense, a nicety often heard from those distrusting their grammar or their theatre history. "Flied" means "put in the flies"—not "given a ride on a kite." It is no more ungrammatical than "floored" or "cornered" or "housed" or "treed.")

FLY GALLERY. The overhead platform from which the fly lines are operated (omitted in some modern theatres).

FLYMAN. A stage hand assigned to operate the lines.

FLOATS. The British term for foots, or footlights.

FOOTLIGHTS. Strip lights or boxed lights set in the floor at the front of the stage.

FOOTS. Nickname for footlights.

FORESTAGE. The stage in front of the proscenium; very large in eighteenth century theatres.

FRONT (or OUT FRONT). The front of the house; everything outside the proscenium except the apron or forestage (if any).

GAG. A humorous or picturesque interpolation, not in the text of the play.

GALLERY. The second, upper, or rear balcony. Traditionally, also, the more emotionally demonstrative crowd apt to be sitting there.

GELATINE FRAME. A frame of metal or wood to hold gelatines or other color mediums, and often stacked where actors can knock it over with a clatter.

GELATINES. Sheets of colored gelatine (or plastic) used to give color in lighting units.

GRID. Nickname for the gridiron.

GRIDIRON. The framework above the stage (whether of wood or metal) which holds the pulleys carrying the lines.

GRIP. A stage hand assigned to moving scenery on the stage level, as distinct from a flyman.

GROUNDLINGS. The poorer patrons, who, in Shakespeare's time, stood on the ground in the pit instead of sitting in the top gallery.

GROUND-ROW. A low piece of scenery set in front of a sky drop to give depth to a distant view.

HAM. Slang for a poor actor, especially one who overacts. Said to have originated in the fact that most actors itch to play Hamlet and many do—even in other plays.

HAND PROPS. Small items of stage property carried on by the actors instead of being placed on the stage.

HARLEQUIN. A stock character in historical pantomime, especially in the type called "Harlequinade."

HOUSE. The auditorium; also, figuratively, the people in it.

HOUSE LIGHTS. The auditorium lights.

INGENUE. The female juvenile lead, usually cast for sweet ingenuous parts as contrasted with the soubrette.

JACK-KNIFE STAGE. An arrangement of two wagon stages, pivoted at opposite sides to swing alternately into acting position.

JOG. A narrow flat used to make a slight offset in a wall.

JUDICIOUS, THE. Hamlet's term for the more intelligent members of the audience (*Hamlet's Advice to the Players*).

JUVENILE. The young actor (or less frequently, actress) playing characters up to the age of 25 or thereabouts; not necessarily a child.

LASH (*verb*). To fasten flats together with lash lines.

LASH CLEATS. The metal spurs on the backs of flats over which the lash line is caught to draw the flats together.

LASH LINE. A piece of sash cord hung at one edge of a flat to permit lashing it to the next one.

LEFT. *See* STAGE LEFT.

LEFT CENTER. The area roughly halfway between stage center and extreme stage left.

LEG DROP. A drop cut out at the center so that it functions as a border and two wing drops (the "legs").

LEGIT. The old-time trouper's slang for the "legitimate" drama, as distinguished from musical and variety shows.

LIMELIGHT. The center of emphasis, the term deriving from old-type spotlights in which a heated cylinder of calcium or limestone provided a strong white light.

LINES. The ropes used to suspend scenery in the flies.

LONG LINE. The line in each set of lines running over the pulley farthest from the pin rail.

MARIONETTES. Doll actors; specifically the type operated by strings, from above, as distinguished from puppets. The terms are often confused.

MASK (*noun*). A more or less rigid covering for the actor's face to disguise him without cosmetic make-up.

MASK (*verb*). To trim the setting in such a way as to hide all off-stage areas not meant to be seen.

MASQUE or MASCARA. A make-up preparation for darkening or lightening the hair, especially the eye-lashes.

MOVEMENT. *See* STAGE MOVEMENT.

MUGGING. Looking communicatively at the audience, especially with too much facial expression.

OFF STAGE. Outside the acting area or visible area of the stage.

OLIVETTE. A flood-light mounted on a standard.

ONE. *See* SCENE IN ONE.

PANTALOON. A stock character in historic pantomime. Same as *Pantalone*.

PAPER (*verb*). To fill the house by issuing many free passes.

PIERROT. A stock character in historic pantomime.

PIN RAIL. The rail to which the fly lines are belayed, whether located on a fly gallery or elsewhere.

"PLACES!" The stage-manager's call to the players to warn them that the act is about to begin.

PLASTIC (*noun*). A synthetic material.

PLASTIC (*adjective*). Three-dimensional; having a feeling of depth as well as height and width.

PRACTICAL. An adjective applied to any piece of stage property that actually works, or can be used.

PRODUCER. In the U. S., usually the owner or chief owner of a production. In England, usually the director.

PROPERTIES. All items of visible stage equipment not part of the scenery and not electrical.

PROPERTY MAN. Foreman of property men, usually called "clearers."

PROPS. Nickname for properties; also for the property man.

PROSCENIUM. The wall which divides the stage from the house.

PROSCENIUM ARCH (or FRAME). The opening in the proscenium through which the audience sees the play.

PUPPETS. Doll actors; specifically, those operated from below as in the traditional Punch and Judy shows.

REGISSEUR. The Continental European term for the master director.

REPERTORY. The practice of keeping several plays alive and playing them in frequent but often irregular rotation.

REVOLVING STAGE. A circular turntable stage. Inaccurately applied to other types of swinging or pivoted stages.

RHYTHM. Properly, a more-or-less regular recurrence of emphasis in any medium. Sometimes loosely used to cover style, mood, etc.

RIGHT. *See* STAGE RIGHT.

RIGHT CENTER. The area roughly halfway between stage center and extreme stage right.

SCENE. 1. A setting. 2. A locality suggested by the setting. 3. A piece of

action taking place with continuity and without change of locality. 4. A piece of action having some unity of thought and mood. 5. (In European drama) A conversation unbroken by exits or entrances and ending when either occurs.

SCENE IN ONE. A scene played shallow, usually before a drop; traditional term going back to the days of wing settings operating in grooves, numbered 1, 2, 3, etc.

SCENE IN TWO. A slightly deeper scene equivalent to the depth of two sets of grooves in the old days.

SHIFT (verb). To change settings.

SHORT LINE. The line in each set attached to the scenery on the side nearest the pin rail.

SILL IRON. The metal strip across a door opening for actors to trip over.

SKY DOME. A cyclorama which includes spherical curvature above to take the lights and create the illusion of space; usually of plaster or other heavy, rigid construction.

SOCK. *See* BUSKIN.

SOLILOQUY. A passage spoken by the actor when alone or apart. It may be communicative, like an aside, or purely meditative.

SOUBRETTE. A young actress usually cast for pert vivacious parts.

SPOT. Nickname for spotlight.

SPOTLIGHT. A lighting unit with lens and reflector to concentrate the light.

STAGE BRACE. A length of wood or metal, usually extendable, for bracing flats from behind and tripping actors.

STAGE BUSINESS. Any bodily action performed as part of the play, especially one involving an individual actor rather than the group. An older term than Stage Movement, and more inclusive.

STAGE CARPENTER. Head foreman of stage hands and foreman of grips and flymen.

STAGE ELECTRICIAN. Foreman of the electrical crew.

STAGE LEFT. The part of the stage to the actor's left as he faces the audience (British terminology often reverses this).

STAGE MANAGER. The back-stage executive, responsible for running the production under the director's instructions, and after the director is through.

STAGE MOVEMENT. The planned movement of actors about the stage, especially in relation to the grouping. Often combined with, or a part of, stage business.

STAGE PROPS. Items of property placed on the stage before an act (even though handled later by the actors).

STAGE RIGHT. The actor's right as he faces the audience (American usage).

STAGE SCREW. A hand screw for fastening the stage brace to the floor.

STOCK. In the old days, a resident repertory company. Later, a second rate company producing plays hurriedly for a local audience, usually with a

weekly change of bill. Now usually a summer company, playing at a resort, with a student group to help pay the bills.

"STRIKE!" The stage-manager's call to the crew to begin changing a set, and a warning to the actors to get out of the way immediately.

SUPERNUMERARY. An extra player, beyond the number regularly employed, brought in to play a walk-on part.

TAG LINE. The final speech of a scene, or more especially of the whole play.

TEASER. The permanent first border, serving with the tormentors as an adjustable false proscenium frame.

THEATRE. The ancient name for a place to see shows, coming down to us from the Greek *theatron* through the Latin and French. A word full of tradition and flavor in its English form. The spelling "theater" is an atrocity, foisted upon the American masses by journalists and printers, and detested by theatre-lovers generally.

TORMENTOR ENTRANCE. The down-stage entrance, right or left, immediately adjacent to the tormentor. Historically, the entrance may have been so called before the flat.

TORMENTORS. The permanent flats or drapes just behind the proscenium, serving with the teaser as a false proscenium.

TRAP. A trap-door in the stage floor.

UNSKILLFUL, THE. Hamlet's term for the less intelligent members of the audience (*Advice to the Players*).

UP STAGE. Toward the rear of the playing space, away from the audience.

UP-STAGE (*verb, trans.*). To put another actor at a disadvantage by keeping up stage, forcing him to talk away from the audience, with his back to it.

UP STAGE (*predicate adjective*). Addicted to the practice of "up-staging" others —literally or figuratively.

WAGON STAGE. Any rolling or sliding platform on which scenery is pre-set to be moved quickly into place.

WALK-ON. A part without lines such as might be played by an extra or supernumerary.

WING FLATS. The flats masking the wings. Historically, the wings probably got their names from the flats, not the reverse, but to old actors "the wings" meant the space, not the scenery.

WINGS. The off-stage spaces right and left of the acting area. Inaccurately, the flats or drapes masking the wings.

WOODWING. A wing flat (usually with a hinged flap) painted as part of a woodland setting.

X-RAY BORDER. The first row of border lights, just behind the proscenium; usually made up of varied types of spots and floods.

Index